W9-CAZ-431

BACKPACKER

THE NATIONAL PARKS COAST TO COAST

100 BEST HIKES

Editor's Note

Most multiday hikes within the National Parks System require a permit. We have provided contact information for the parks; inquire with the backcountry office to obtain all necessary permits.

FALCONGUIDES®

An imprint of Rowman & Littlefield
Falcon and FalconGuides are registered trademarks and Make Adventure Your Story is a trademark of Rowman & Littlefield.
Backpacker is a registered trademark of Cruz Bay Publishing, Inc.

Distributed by NATIONAL BOOK NETWORK

Author: Ted Alvarez
Editor: Dave Costello
Copyeditor: Aleta Burchyski
Designer: Nancy Freeborn
Maps: Brandon and Molly Keinath © Rowman & Littlefield

British Library Cataloguing-in-Publication Information available

ISBN 978-1-4930-1965-6
ISBN 978-1-4930-2693-7

The paper used in this publication meets the minimum requirements of American National Standard for Information Sciences—Permanence of Paper for Printed Library Materials, ANSI/NISO Z39.48-1992.

Photo: Dovapi / Thinkstock

BACKPACKER®

THE NATIONAL PARKS COAST TO COAST

100 BEST HIKES

FALCON GUIDES®

GUILFORD, CONNECTICUT
HELENA, MONTANA

CONTENTS

Photo: George Burba / Thinkstock

Olympic
North Cascades
WA
Mount Rainier
Glacier
MT
Theodore Roosevelt
ND
Crater Lake
OR
Redwood
ID
Yellowstone
Grand Teton
WY
Wind Cave
Badlands
SD
Lassen Volcanic
Rocky Mountain
NE
Yosemite
NV
Great Basin
UT
Kings Canyon
Pinnacles
Arches
Capitol Reef
Black Canyon of the Gunnison
Bryce Canyon
Zion
Canyonlands
CO
Sequoia
Death Valley
CA
Great Sand Dunes
Mesa Verde
Grand Canyon
Channel Islands
Joshua Tree
Petrified Forest
AZ
NM
Saguaro
Guadalupe Mountains
Carlsbad Caverns
TX
Big Bend
Kobuk Valley
Gates of the Arctic
AK
Wrangell-St.Elias
Denali
Lake Clark
Katmai
Kenai Fjords
Glacier Bay
Haleakala
Hawaii Volcanoes
HI

National Parks of the United States of America

Delicate Arch, Arches National Park, Utah
Photo: gcgebel / Thinkstock

INTRODUCTION

BY TED ALVAREZ

My history with the national parks predates my memory. In a favorite family photo, I'm standing in front of a lake—more of a pond, really—on the eaves of Rocky Mountain National Park, brandishing a stick with a row of gleaming rainbow trout hanging from it. Dressed in camo colors and sporting a buzz cut still mashed into bedhead shapes, I'm beaming. If I stare hard enough, I can follow a breadcrumb trail of dim memories to my time in the park as an 8-year-old. I remember learning the word *ptarmigan* and being confused by the *p* when my uncle spelled it; a hike around a crystal lake remains out of focus, but I can clearly see my Velcro shoes toeing a thick ponderosa root that braces the muddy trail edge. It was my first experience with the high-altitude tundra, an alien landscape I would swoon over in a few decades' time. But mostly I just remember a bunch of big rocks.

My real formative experience would come 13 years later, in Glacier National Park. I saw the Crown of the Continent for the first time around 4:45 a.m., bleary-eyed and half delirious from an ill-considered all-night drive from Wyoming's Bighorn Mountains. My East Coast college roommate Ken and I were dumb enough to hike in jeans but smart enough to understand that this could be the best day of our postgraduate road trip. I remember scary bear alerts posted on soggy yellow paper at the entrance station, dark violet clouds obscuring all but black Lake McDonald. After two hours without being able to make out much more than ominous foliage and slick pavement, we popped up through the fog into the sun and I experienced Glacier as many have: shark-fin peaks crowding the windshield, the Weeping Wall pouring diamonds into the road. I saw my first real live glacier, groaning and creeping inexorably forward even though I couldn't see its progress. Finally, the pièce de résistance came on our drive out: A cinnamon-brown bear rising from a river, shaking itself dry, and giving us a look from the opposite bank before slipping into a wall of willow. I couldn't tell what kind of bear. I wanted to know. I was done.

Sure as a boulder rolling downhill, that single day in the national parks spun me into a career chasing the wild. As such, I've been fortunate enough to visit mountain ranges, forests, and coasts around the world. But I keep returning to our national parks—the fantastical red-rock desert scapes, alien rainforests, and wide array of toothy peaks still make me feel like there's no place like home.

Photo: SteveMcsweeny / Thinkstock

Hopi Point, Grand Canyon National Park, Arizona

One of my greatest privileges has been seeing our parks expand the horizon for so many others. I've seen vanloads of bickering families go quiet when Yosemite Valley's granite temples pop impossibly out of hiding from behind scrub oak hills, and I've seen kids identify crinoid fossils in the Grand Canyon before the guiding ranger can even ask the question. I've seen soaked couples beaming over coffee after tent failures on the Olympic coast. To me, these small moments of transformation mirror the big-picture grandeur embodied by our nation's grandest places. They are evidence of a connecting thread between the Shoshone who first wondered at the seething, colorful portal to evil spirits in Yellowstone's Norris Geyser Basin and the throngs doing the same thing hundreds of years later. How many times has this happened in the past century?

In 1983, the revered Wallace Stegner said, "National parks are the best idea we ever had. Absolutely American, absolutely democratic, they reflect us at our best rather than our worst." For a century, the National Park Service has preserved this continent's wildest places and finest natural cathedrals—and the parks have preserved our wildest, finest selves. Not everyone sees the world's largest tree in Sequoia and decides to become a ranger or a botanist. But in trying to wrap your arms (or just your eyes!) around it—for an hour, a day, a weekend—we cultivate our greatest American qualities, which serve us in so many other ways: wonder, adventure, freedom, stewardship, and the desire to share those with everyone else who values them.

Photo: iStockPhoto.com / ventdusud

There is no better place to forge a relationship than in national parks—with family, with friends, with yourself. And there's no better way to do it than stepping onto a trail. You don't have to go far. In my experience, the first whiffs of wilderness come just a few feet beyond the trailhead. Along with my colleagues at *BACKPACKER*, I've assembled what I think are the 100 best places to do that, from day hikes to weeklong wilderness adventures, from easy strolls to hair-raising climbs. The parks are for everyone, and accordingly there's an adventure here for everyone.

Of course, selecting the 100 best hikes in places as astonishingly diverse and mind-meltingly beautiful as our national parks is pretty ridiculous. My hope is that you'll try a few of these and be so inspired you'll make your own definitive list. What are you waiting for? Go.

THE NEXT 100 YEARS

Most people wouldn't dream of tossing their trash on the ground at one of our prized national parks. But piling up all those empty chip bags and soda cans in the parks' parking-lot bins is only a little better than littering: Rangers in the country's most remote, pristine places still have to deal with disposing loads of trash. When we throw something away, what we're essentially saying is, "It's your problem now!"

In 2013, the 7 million visitors to Yosemite, Grand Teton, and Denali National Parks collectively left behind more than 16.6 million pounds of waste for the National Park Service staff to deal with. Of that, 9.7 million pounds—including Christmas lights, mattresses, and lots and lots of random discards—went to landfills.

Now the National Park Service, in cooperation with Subaru (operating the first zero-landfill automotive plant in the country since 2004), is asking a provocative question: Can we make garbage a thing of the past in our national parks? Since 2015, they're teaming up on pilot projects in Yosemite, Grand Teton, and Denali to try to divert all waste headed to the landfill. They'll be working throughout the three parks and their gateway communities to study how stuff comes in and becomes trash and to figure out how to encourage visitors to leave less—or better yet, no—garbage behind.

Learn more about the effort to make these parks zero-landfill at Subaru.com/environment.

YOU CAN HELP

On your next park vacation, use these tips to reduce the trash you personally create.

PLAN AHEAD Eliminate garbage before you even get to the park: Buy food in bulk and pack it in reusable containers. Bring reusable plates and utensils and avoid the disposable stuff when eating out. Remove packaging from new gear before leaving home.

USE A REFILLABLE WATER BOTTLE Disposable plastic water bottles are the scourge of the parks. But of course, you need to stay hydrated—especially on hot summer hikes. Solution: Bring refillable water bottles.

Photo: Aidan Lynn-Klimenko and Madison Perrins

Hadlock Falls, Acadia National Park, Maine
Photo: Marc Muench / Tandem Stock

ACADIA
NATIONAL PARK

Cadillac Mountain, Acadia National Park, Maine

ACADIA NATIONAL PARK
CADILLAC MOUNTAIN VIA DORR MOUNTAIN

Summit three Acadia peaks on an 8.8-mile loop, traversing the rugged topography of Mount Desert Island and passing overlooks of neighboring bays and island clusters along Maine's coastline.

At 1,530 feet, Cadillac Mountain is Acadia National Park's highest point and the tallest peak on the eastern seaboard. But because of the peak's height, position, and longitude, Mount Desert Island's flat summit is also among the first places in the country to see the sun rise. Even when not gilt with the nation's first light, it's a fine showcase for the deep green forests, glassy ponds, pink granite ramps, and wide ocean views that define the first national park in the eastern United States.

Yes, there's a road to the summit—but let the pikers drive to the top. This 8.8-mile loop avoids the RV crowds and lets you summit three peaks over 1,000 feet. From the Sieur de Monts Spring Nature Center, head southwest on a trail that switchbacks up the wooded lower slopes of Dorr Mountain. Along the way, you'll catch intermittent views of the Porcupine Islands and Frenchman Bay. Midway up the mountain, the trail traverses south before steepening to crest Dorr's summit (1,270 feet). From here, hikers will drop down into a rocky gully on the west face before clambering up through the large granite boulders littering the ascent on the east ridge of Cadillac Mountain. At the top, expansive views of the Atlantic stretch off to the south; constellations of islands stretch to the horizons. Stop for lunch or explore the multiple side trails spidering off Cadillac's summit.

To continue the loop to 1,248-foot Pemetic Mountain, follow a wide gravel road 100 feet from the visitor center down the west face of Cadillac Mountain. Go right at a three-way junction to descend to Bubble Pond, where still waters reflect rounded peaks ringing the placid pool. Nearby, fast-flowing Bubble Brook is a great spot to tank up. Next, follow signs on the bike path for Pemetic Mountain; a gradual climb through forest canopy eventually widens to the open, rock-slab summit. After descending this third peak, the trail climbs to the top of one more ridge before descending along Canon Brook and heading north past the Tarn and back to the Sieur de Monts Spring Nature Center where you began.

BONUS FOR EARLY RISERS: Start well before dawn and you'll beat the crowds and catch a spectacular summit sunrise.

Photo: iStockPhoto.com / jrphoto6

Text: Trung Q. Le and Michael Lanza

DISTANCE: 8.8 miles

TIME REQUIRED: 1 day

DIFFICULTY: Intermediate

CONTACT: Acadia National Park, (207) 288-3338; nps.gov/acad

THE PAYOFF: Three broad summits high above an island-speckled sea.

TRAILHEAD GPS: 44.3622512817383, -68.2080230712891

FINDING THE TRAILHEAD: From Cottage Street and Main Street in Bar Harbor, head south on Main Street/US 3/Acadia Byway. In 2.3 miles, turn right onto Acadia Byway. In 0.1 mile, turn left into the Sieur de Monts Spring Nature Center.

WAYPOINTS & DIRECTIONS

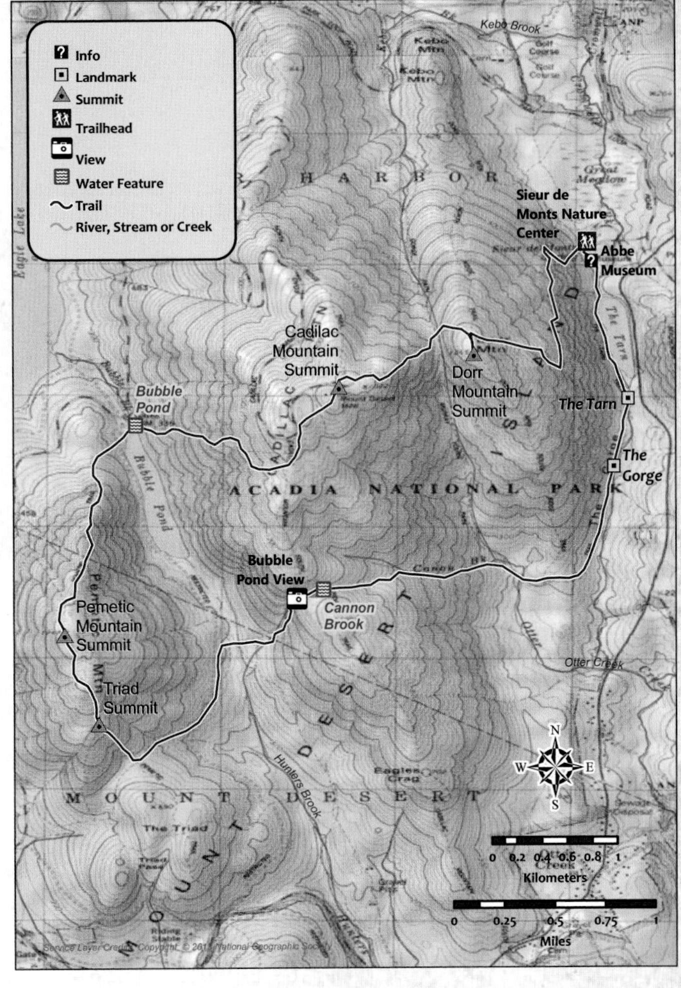

GPS: 44.362251, -68.208023 The loop starts behind the Sieur de Monts Spring Nature Center. Head southwest on the trail that switchbacks up the wooded slopes of Dorr Mountain.

GPS: 44.354568, -68.216143 Dorr Mountain summit.

GPS: 44.352306, -68.225807 Cadillac Mountain summit.

GPS: 44.349751, -68.240402 Continue left on the trail around Bubble Pond (the Bubble Pond parking area is to the right). Bubble Brook is a good source of treatable water for drinking if needed.

GPS: 44.335384, -68.245528 Pemetic Mountain summit.

GPS: 44.329239, -68.243134 Stay left at the Y junction, heading southeast. The Triad Trail on the right leads to the summit of the Triad.

GPS: 44.337818, -68.228844 Look northwest for a bird's-eye view of Bubble Pond.

GPS: 44.338428, -68.226936 Canon Brook.

GPS: 44.346851, -68.206146 The Gorge.

GPS: 44.351471, -68.205101 Continue straight at three-way junction, heading back toward Sieur de Monts Spring Nature Center. To the left, the Ladder Trail ascends Dorr Mountain. To the right is a small parking area. Ahead, the trail travels alongside the western banks of the Tarn.

GPS: 44.362059, -68.207802 Sieur de Monts Spring Nature Center.

GPS: 44.360893, -68.207717 Abbe Museum.

A dizzying view from the Precipice Trail in Acadia

ACADIA NATIONAL PARK
PRECIPICE TRAIL

Ladders and iron rungs help you take a heart-pounding climbing route up Champlain Mountain to deep blue views of the Atlantic coast.

Why simply hike a mountain when you can climb it? With ladders, iron rungs, and slender rock ridges to help you hoist yourself up 1,000 hair-raising feet, this route is more like a jungle gym than a trail. Luckily you don't need special gear to scale Champlain Mountain on the Precipice Trail, but a strong grip and nerves of steel won't hurt. Bonus: A spiking heart rate and big dose of adrenaline come free with the terrain.

The crucible comes early: A giant boulder bolted with iron rungs blocks the path. If you get the willies just thinking about climbing it, turn back. From here, an iron railing guides you across granite ledges and outcroppings. A wooden bridge spans an airy gap, and steps lead to the beginning of the proper climb. Scramble diagonally up a cliff band to reach a set of ladders and rungs that aid you where the rock goes vertical. Below you, rolling forest washes out to the sea's edge, but keep your eyes on the iron bars that trace faults and shelves in the cliff's face. A final set of ladders and rungs leads to an airy cat-walk that swings out into space; face down this challenge and the last stretch is a simple uphill hike across the granite summit block. For the effort, you'll earn big views over an

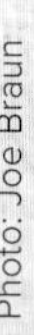
Photo: Joe Braun

Atlantic coastline scattered with chunky granite islands and riddled with veiny inlets. Let your nerves cool on a hike back that connects the easy-breezy forest hike of Champlian North Ridge Trail to the roller-coaster granite steps of the Orange and Black Trail, which closes the loop.

DISTANCE: 2.6 miles

TIME REQUIRED: 1 day

DIFFICULTY: Intermediate

CONTACT: Acadia National Park, (207) 288-3338; nps.gov/acad

THE PAYOFF: Summit views on a ladder-assisted, white-knuckle climb.

TRAILHEAD GPS: 44.349479, -68.188075

FINDING THE TRAILHEAD: From the Sieur de Monts entrance, follow the one-way Park Loop Road two miles, until you see the sign for the Precipice Trail parking lot.

WAYPOINTS & DIRECTIONS

GPS: 44.349540, -68.188126 Head west from the trailhead.

GPS: 44.349202, -68.189263 Boulder Block. Turn left ahead at the junction, continuing southwest on the Precipice Trail.

GPS: 44.350614, -68.190529 Cross the wooden bridge.

GPS: 44.350936, -68.194005 From the Champlain Mountain Summit, look out over the Atlantic Ocean to the east.

GPS: 44.357840, -68.191731 Veer right at the junction with the Orange and Black Trail, returning to the Precipice trailhead.

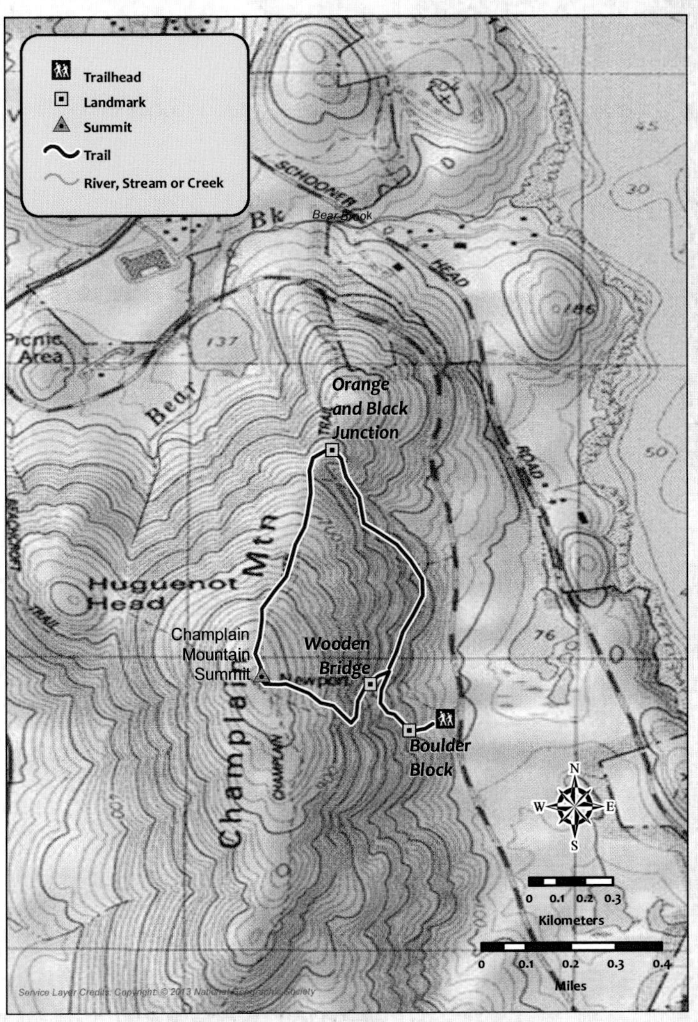

Dramatic rock formations along the Park Avenue Trail in Arches National Park, Utah
Photo: Jonathan Gewirtz / Tandem Stock

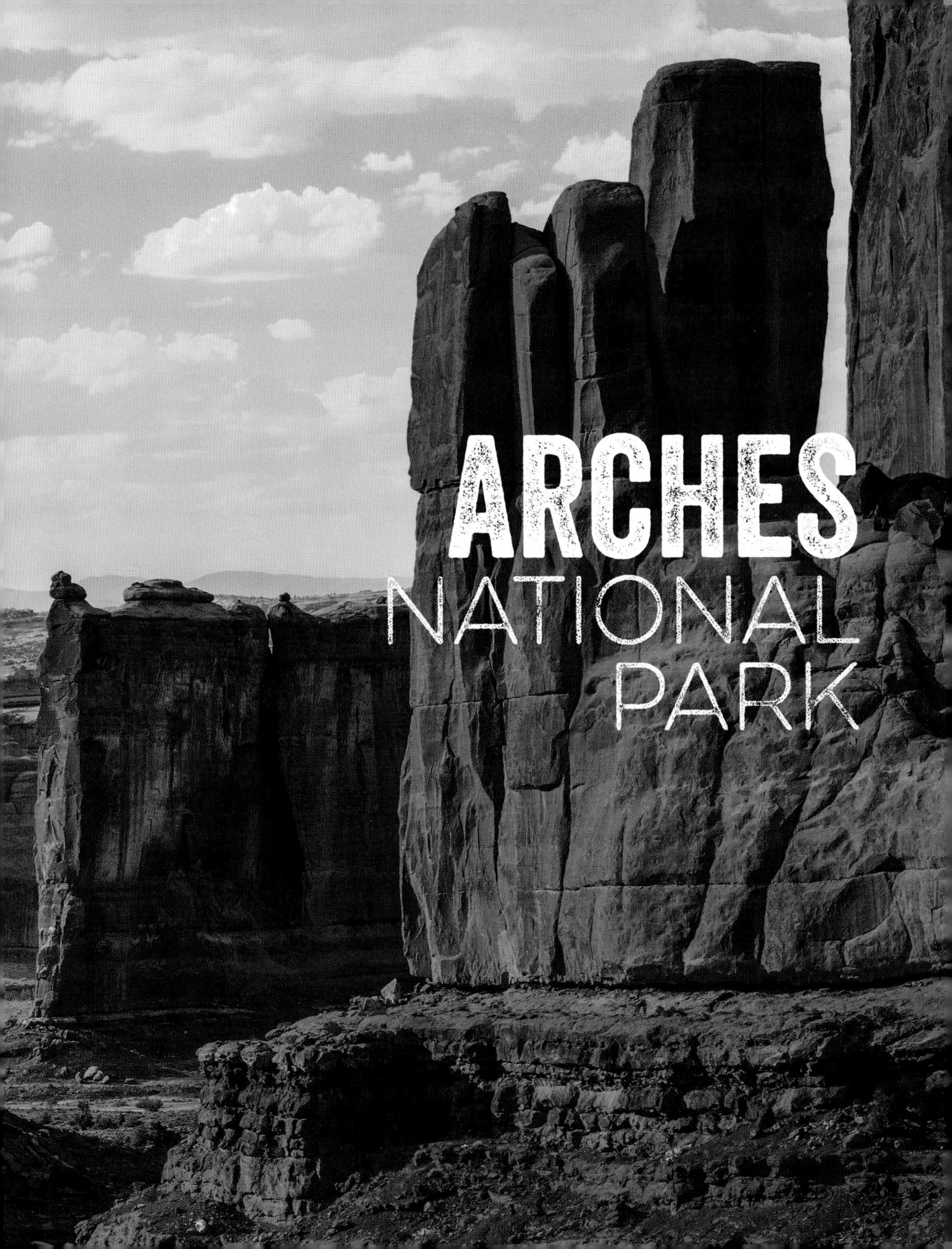
ARCHES
NATIONAL
PARK

Partition Arch on the Devils Garden Trail in Arches

ARCHES NATIONAL PARK

DEVILS GARDEN

Hike into a red-rock paradise full of wind-and-water sculptures that seem to defy gravity.

To see the widest variety of ways in which wind and water can morph a crack in sandstone into a physics-confounding arch, hit the Devils Garden Trail. No fewer than eight arches pock this exhilarating scramble. Head northwest on the gravel trail past yucca and cacti into a sandy sea of crimson rock. Turn right onto a spur past Tunnel Arch (which looks like a sandstone Arc de Triomphe) to Pine Tree Arch, aptly named for the skirt of pinions at its base. Backtrack and turn right to continue on the main path. Veer left at the Y to visit the most famous arch on this rout: Landscape, a thin ribbon of rock that stretches the length of a football field.

Shortly after, hike past the blocky remains of the Wall Arch, which collapsed in 2008. Turn left past honeycombed fins to reach Navajo Arch, a massive slab of brick-red rock with a small peephole. Head south to reach Partition Arch, and walk to the far side for a vibrant vista of wacky red rock formations spanning the park. Return to Navajo Arch and turn left to peer at the short stack of egg-shaped windows known as Double O Arch. Then veer right at the Y onto Primitive Trail, but first look left to spy the enormous black-varnished obelisk Dark Angel in the distance.

Follow cairns over line-seared sandstone slabs and down moderate slopes to drop into a sandy wash, which you'll follow left. After a short while, turn right to exit the drainage and scan the right-hand side for Black Arch and a surrounding garden of sandstone fins. Complete the loop by returning to the Y just before Landscape Arch. Gulp water and return to your car.

Photo: iStockPhoto.com / alacatr

DISTANCE: 7.2 miles

TIME REQUIRED: 1 day

DIFFICULTY: Intermediate

CONTACT: Arches National Park, (435) 719-2299; nps.gov/arch

THE PAYOFF: You'll see eight amazing arches on this route.

TRAILHEAD GPS: 38.782742, -109.595275

FINDING THE TRAILHEAD: From Moab, go about 5 miles north on US 191 and turn right onto Arches Entrance Road. Follow signs 18 miles to Devils Garden trailhead.

WAYPOINTS & DIRECTIONS

GPS: 38.782742, -109.595275 Trailhead.

GPS: 38.784916, -109.596734 Turn right onto a spur past Tunnel Arch to Pine Tree Arch, with a skirt of piñon pines on its base.

GPS: 38.787676, -109.598708 Pine Tree Arch. Retrace your steps and turn right to continue north on the main path.

GPS: 38.791123, -109.606290 Landscape Arch.

GPS: 38.792459, -109.607742 Wall Arch.

GPS: 38.794220, -109.610298 Turn left past honeycombed fins to Navajo Arch, a massive rock arc with a small peephole.

GPS: 38.791355, -109.609159 Navajo Arch. Head south to reach Partition Arch.

GPS: 38.791707, -109.608450 Partition Arch.

GPS: 38.799246, -109.621045 Double O Arch. Peer at the short stack of its egg-shaped windows. Then veer right at the Y intersection onto Primitive Trail, but not before identifying the enormous, black-varnished obelisk Dark Angel in the distance to the left.

GPS: 38.801407, -109.627526 Dark Angel. To see Dark Angel more closely, veer left at the Y intersection with the Primitive Trail, and then retrace those steps to return to the main trail.

GPS: 38.800136, -109.620144 Devils Garden view.

GPS: 38.799902, -109.621582 Primitive Trail.

GPS: 38.802212, -109.609802 Black Arch view.

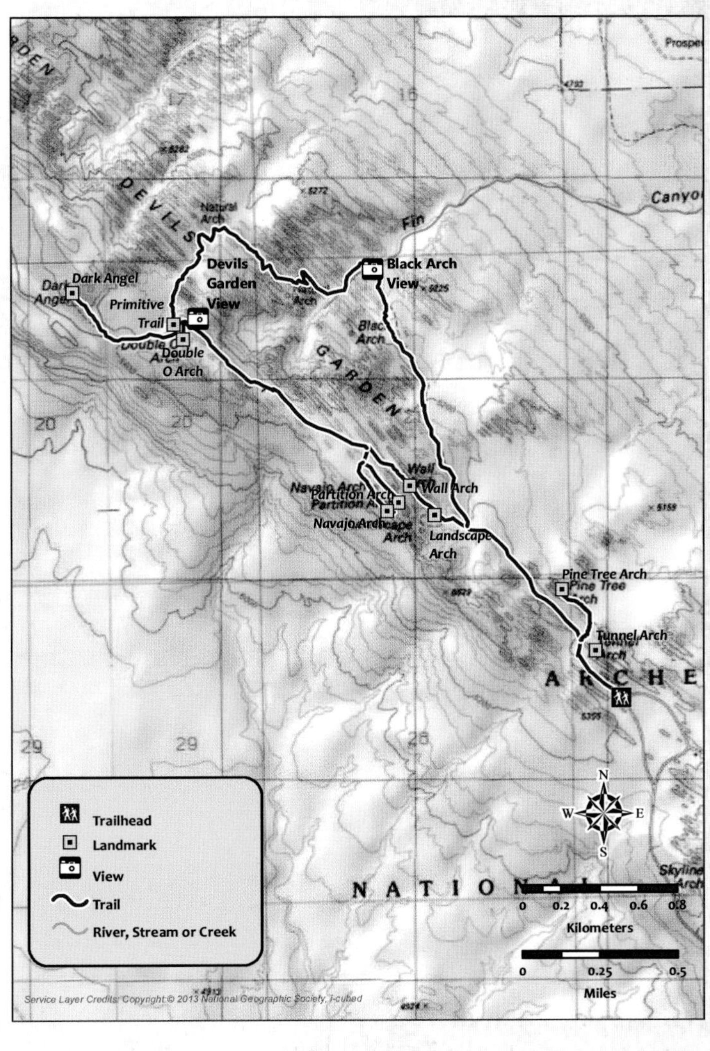

RANGER PROFILE

GLENN REYNOLDS

The Storyteller
Arches National Park, Utah

"The first time I ever had an in-depth interaction with an NPS ranger was with Glenn, and he lived up to everything I thought a ranger would be."

—Jerami Martin, *Backpacker* reader

There are speakers and presenters who breeze through their material by rote. Then there are storytellers, the type who read their audiences and calibrate their material on the fly. By the time they finish, they don't need applause. They already know: You were listening. Glenn Reynolds, an interpretive ranger, weaves tales of ancient people together with the landscape to deepen the Arches experience. "My motivation is for the moment of silence that can form from reflection or introspection about how what I've said relates to who they are," Reynolds says.

FAVORITE SPOT: Tower Arch

Get the geologic drama without the crowds on the 3.4-mile out-and-back to this distinctive arch on the park's remote northwest side. Hoof it up a mesa with views over the knobby Klondike Bluffs, then descend through the pink-sand desert to the 92-foot-long arch crowned with a thick stone spire.

TRAILHEAD: Tower Arch

Delicate Arch, Arches National Park, Utah

ARCHES NATIONAL PARK
DELICATE ARCH

Climb a massive slickrock ribbon and stand beneath one of the park's most iconic landmarks on this 3.1-mile out-and-back.

Of the 2,000-plus sandstone hoops that adorn this park, Delicate Arch is the most famous, and it remains remarkably unchanged by wind, water, or controversial climbing attempts. (For now.) It's easy to see why the postcard-perfect arch graces stamps, quarters, and license plates: Twin sandstone pillars join 65 feet in the air, looming like a chaps-wearing cowboy cut off at the waist. The inner span frames the undulating red expanse of Utah's desert and the snowy mountains beyond like no other rock formation in the Southwest.

Though perennially popular, add this classic 3.1-miler to your list of must-do hikes in Arches National Park. From the large parking area, follow the well-maintained Delicate Arch Trail to the northeast, passing a spur trail to the Wolfe Ranch Cabin on the left. Desert scrub, stunted piñon, and ruddy rock formations flank the trail as you gently climb above Winter Camp Wash. After 0.8 mile, the route ascends a massive slickrock outcropping

Photo: iStockPhoto.com / jropelato1

dotted with cairns. Don't forget to turn around every once in awhile for striking views to the southwest of ruddy cliffs and mountains. At the top of the slickrock ramp, head north for a slight descent into a sandy wash dotted with piñon, juniper, and sandstone rock formations. At mile 1.4, traverse a narrow slickrock catwalk cut into the walls of the cliff. Sandstone rock formations tower above the wash on the left-hand side of the trail. Delicate Arch comes into view 0.1 mile later—drop your packs and savor incredible views of this natural sandstone arch, which rises in front of the Cache Valley and the La Sal Mountains. Follow the same route back to the trailhead.

PRO TIP: To share the arch with a handful of strangers instead of a few hundred, target a snow-free weekend November through February.

RANGER PROFILE

MICHAEL MATTHES

The Role Model
Arches National Park, Utah

"He is quiet and creative. He will take the time to have a genuine conversation about the park with you."
—Victoria Allen, *Backpacker* reader

Growing up as a city kid in St. Louis, Michael Matthes didn't visit his first national park until he was 23. A day trip to Arches turned into two, then three. Thirteen years later, he works as an interpretive ranger in the park that captured his imagination. His goal: Get visitors to look past their screens and connect to the park. There's no end to that kind of work and no rulebook, but there are highlights. "One visitor was probably 7 or 8 years old," he says. "At the end of the activity book, I like to ask my junior rangers one question: What can you do to help the park? He looked up at me and said, 'I can be just like you.'"

FAVORITE SPOT: Park Avenue

The ratio of desert majesty to effort doesn't get any better than this quiet 2-mile out-and-back through a canyon lined with Arches' most iconic rock sculptures. "My season always begins with the song of the canyon wren while hiking Park Avenue," Matthes says.

TRAILHEAD: Park Avenue or Courthouse Towers Viewpoint

DISTANCE: 3.1 miles

TIME REQUIRED: 2–5 hours

DIFFICULTY: Easy

CONTACT: Arches National Park, (435) 719-2299; nps.gov/arch/

THE PAYOFF: Basking under the most iconic rock in the Southwest.

TRAILHEAD GPS: 38.7356489, -109.5204735

FINDING THE TRAILHEAD: From the entrance of Arches National Park, head north on the park's main road. In 11.6 miles, turn right at the signed three-way junction. Go 1.2 miles to the Delicate Arch parking area on the left.

WAYPOINTS & DIRECTIONS

GPS: 38.735649, -109.520473
Trailhead.

GPS: 38.736401, -109.519203
Steel Footbridge over Salt Wash.

GPS: 38.738201, -109.513901
Winter Camp Wash.

GPS: 38.740231, -109.512100
The massive slickrock outcropping comes into view.

GPS: 38.740479, -109.509804
Climb the slickrock ribbon and turn around for views to the southwest.

GPS: 38.741816, -109.505217
Take in the hardy piñon and juniper trees.

GPS: 38.744185, -109.502084
Slickrock Catwalk.

GPS: 38.743950, -109.499348
Delicate Arch.

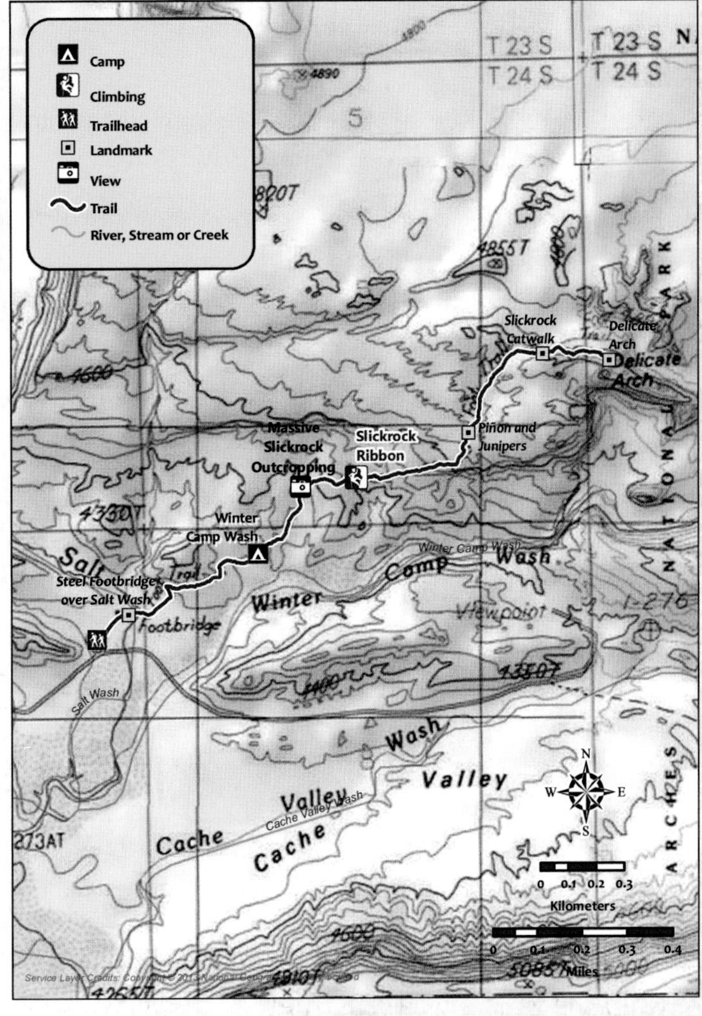

The "badlands" of Badlands National Park, South Dakota
Photo: iStockPhoto.com / fotoguy22

BADLANDS
NATIONAL
PARK

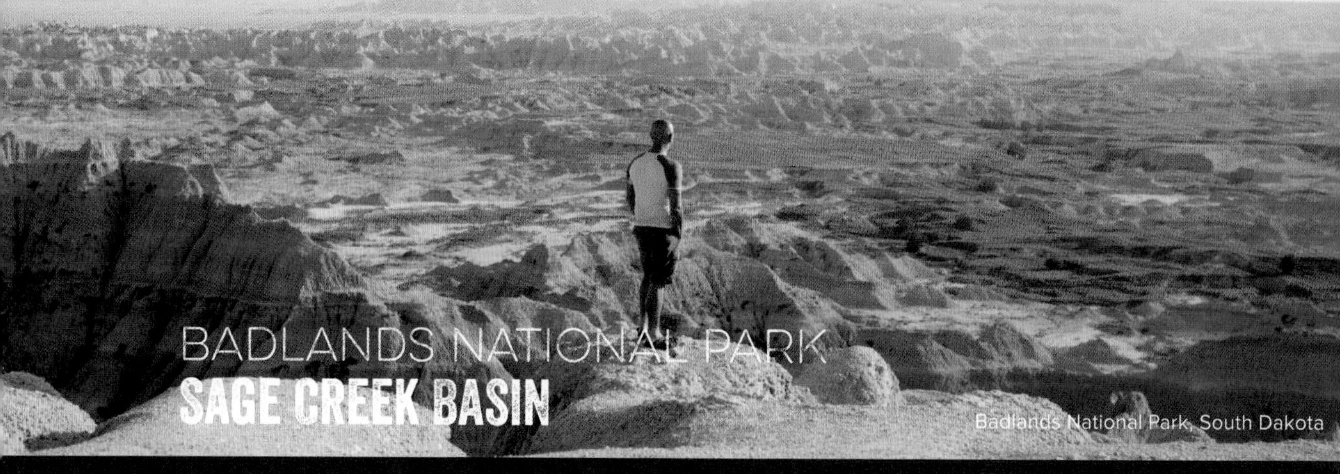

BADLANDS NATIONAL PARK
SAGE CREEK BASIN

Badlands National Park, South Dakota

This backcountry route weaves through pinnacled formations, serpentine washes, and expansive grasslands in Badlands National Park's Sage Creek Wilderness Area.

Pioneers crossing America's sea of grass must have felt despair when they encountered the waterless, impassable collection of crumbling spires and buttes that the Lakota people and fur traders alike named the Badlands. The Old West lives on: Intrepid backpackers can experience a whiff of that fear when they experience the intimidating solitude and otherworldly, rugged terrain in Badlands National Park's remote Sage Creek Wilderness Area. Home to herds of roaming bison and pronghorn antelope—and surrounded by pinnacled rock formations, endless prairie, and labyrinthine washes—the trailless expanse in the park's North Unit is the setting for this 3-day, 22-mile loop.

From the backcountry trailhead at the Conata Picnic Area, 12 miles south of Wall, meander southwest through knee-high grass, skirting the base of the Badlands formations and the occasional pronghorn boneyard (watch out for rattlers). After 2 miles, pass through a gated barbed-wire fence and veer northwest toward Deer Haven, a juniper-covered oasis perched in the striking rock spires ahead. Nearly a mile later, climb crumbly mounds that slope up to the lush confines of Deer Haven. At the oasis, find a flat spot to pitch your

Photo: Aidan Klimenko

tent and spend the night in an amphitheater of towering pinnacles. The Badlands' impressive geology is about 80 million years in the making, with wind and water carving successive layers of sedimentary deposits—shale remnants of an inland sea, Black Hills river mud, and Rocky Mountain volcanic ash—into the multicolored strata adventurers see today.

On day two, weave through juniper stands and ascend 0.3 mile to a narrow ridgetop—and the route's high point. Descend the backside of the ridge into a steep-banked wash pockmarked with mud puddles and pancake-shaped bison prints. Keep an eye out for these massive animals as you round the numerous bends in the wash; about 800 live in the park. Although bison appear mild-mannered, they're unpredictable and can charge you at speeds of up to 30 miles per hour. Adjust your route to avoid coming face-to-face with wandering herds.

Follow countless snaking bends northwest to a T junction at mile 4.1 and turn left. At mile 6, bear left where a dry creek bed enters on the right; leave the wash 0.6 mile later.

The next 3.5 miles traverses the Sage Creek Basin, a vast grassland veined with more high-walled washes. Scan the periphery for buffalo before rolling in and out of the sandy gullies. Stop for lunch at a grassy-banked pond 8.2 miles into the loop (the route's only water source). Two miles later, leave Sage Creek Basin and hike west over mounded formations into Tyree Basin; spend your second night here.

On the last day, navigate south-southeast through a maze of washes en route to Sage Creek Pass, a large gap in the Badlands formations. At mile 15.5, angle east past a private ranch; trace the fenceline for a mile before ducking under a north-south fence that blocks the route. Just past the fence, squeeze through a gap in the formations and descend to the Conata Basin for the 3-mile stretch back to the first gate. From here, retrace your steps to the Conata Picnic Area.

CAUTION: There is no potable water in the Badlands backcountry. Hikers must pack in all of their water. Carry at least a gallon per person per day. Badlands National Park has no formal backcountry permit or reservation system. Hikers are advised to visit the Ben Reifel Visitor Center for planning assistance, safety tips, directions, and regulations.

DISTANCE: 22 miles
TIME REQUIRED: 3 days
DIFFICULTY: Intermediate
CONTACT: Badlands National Park, (605) 433-5361; nps.gov/badl

THE PAYOFF: Explore off-trail in a wilderness with more bison than boot prints.
TRAILHEAD GPS: 43.83472, -102.201573
FINDING THE TRAILHEAD: From Wall, drive south on SD 240. In 11.1 miles, turn right onto Conata Basin Road. In 0.6 mile, turn right into the parking area for Conata Picnic Area.

Text: Kim Phillips

WAYPOINTS & DIRECTIONS

GPS: 43.834720, -102.201573 Head west and then south from the trailhead.

GPS: 43.840478, -102.234875 Drop your pack and take a break. This overlook showcases views of Deer Haven and the Conata Basin. In 150 feet, crest a grassy ledge and head north.

GPS: 43.841399, -102.234178 Deer Haven Pinnacles. This group of striking pinnacles tower above the juniper-dotted oasis. Spend the night at this grassy perch and savor the five-star views. The next day, navigate northeast through the junipers. Pick the best route up the formations to reach the ridgetop (and the route's high point).

GPS: 43.842946, -102.230680 Descend the backside of the ridge and drop into a sandy wash. Pass intermittent mud puddles and patches of dried, cracked mud. As you follow the serpentine wash to the northwest, you'll pass bison footprints and scat. Keep an eye out for these massive animals as you round the numerous bends in the wash.

GPS: 43.847686, -102.237319 Turn left at the T junction. Continue following the wash.

GPS: 43.861933, -102.284142 This grassy-banked pond is the only water source on this trail.

GPS: 43.863861, -102.329717 Set up camp near the base of the formations in Tyree Basin.

GPS: 43.820989, -102.276122 Duck under the fence that runs north-south and blocks the route. Next, descend the formations on a steep slope that drops down to the Conata Basin.

GPS: 43.831717, -102.242106 Duck under the fence and head east 0.8 mile to close the loop of the hike; pass through the fence, then retrace your route back to the Conata Picnic Area.

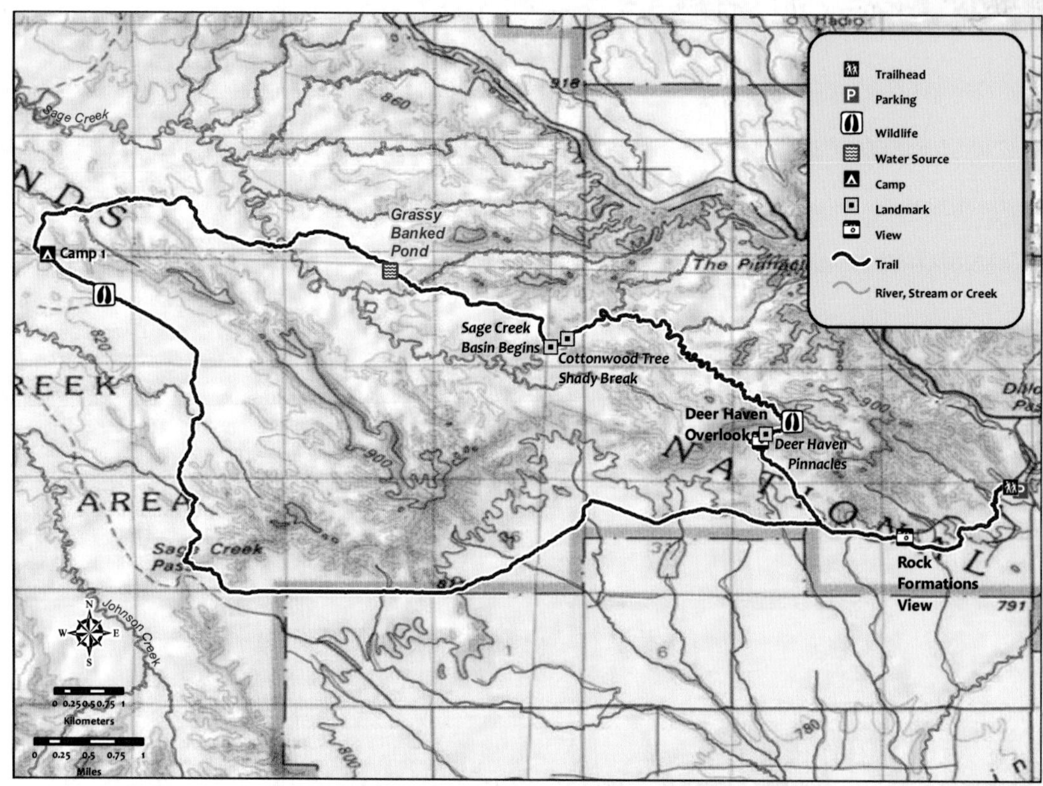

HOW TO PHOTOGRAPH PERFECT SUNSETS

Master exposing these high-contrast scenes to capture the outdoors at its best.

GET READY Figure out when and where the sun will set. Best bet: The Photographer's Ephemeris app will tell you the exact angle for any spot and date. The iOS version includes an option to forecast whether the clouds will light up (this usually happens after the sun is down). Low-tech option: Find west with a compass, and look for high clouds with a clear horizon. Start getting in position to shoot an hour before sunset.

GET SET Compose a wide shot to include points of interest such as flowers, a tent, or a lake, but avoid framing any of them (or the sun itself) smack in the center. If conditions are right for colorful clouds, fill two-thirds of your frame with sky. Otherwise, compose with more land.

SHOOT Use a tripod, since light will be low. Expose for the brightest part of the scene. (On smartphones, tap the sky.) It's OK that the land will seem really dark. Keep shooting; the colors will evolve up to 45 minutes after the sun is down. Later, use the shadows slider in photo-editing software to lighten the dark sections until the images look like what you remember. App to try: Adobe Photoshop Express (free for Android, iOS, and Windows).

DON'T FORGET SUNRISE The technical details and end result are very similar, except the best colors are often just *before* the sun rises.

KEY SKILL: HDR High dynamic range (HDR) imaging combines multiple shots with different exposures into one image to help capture scenes with a big spread between dark and light spots, a common challenge with sunset scenes. Using a tripod, take three to seven images at varying exposures, capturing color in the brightest areas and full detail in the darkest. In a photo-editing program like Adobe Lightroom, find an HDR option from the drop-down menus, then fine-tune. Avoid adding halos where dark and light meet, so much brightness to the shadows that it looks like full daylight, or ghost effects where something moves between images. Shortcut: Use an HDR smartphone app or built-in camera function like the iPhone's.

PRACTICE Improve your skills by shooting at least one sunset per week, even at home.

Text: Genny Fullerton

Sweeping views of the Chihuahuan Desert from the top of Emory Peak in Big Bend National Park, Texas
Photo: Andrew R. Slaton / Tandem Stock

BIG BEND NATIONAL PARK

Chisos Basin, Big Bend National Park, Texas

BIG BEND NATIONAL PARK
SOUTH RIM TRAIL

Explore one of the Lower 48's last remaining wild corners on this loop from the High Chisos Mountains to the South Rim escarpment.

From the tops of its highest peaks to the river bottom of the Rio Grande tracing the international border with Mexico, Big Bend National Park's 6,000 feet of elevation encompass extremes in temperature, topography, and wildlife. June brings broiling heat to the Chihuahuan Desert at Big Bend, but the 7,400-foot Chisos Mountains in the park's center are a welcome escape. From high in these "ghost" peaks, you'll get hundred-mile views into Mexico, huge rock towers, unique vegetation such as Texas madrone and piñon pine, and abundant wildlife like javelina, mountain lions, and Mexican black bears. Make a weekend of it on this difficult 13.9-mile loop from the Chisos Basin, a natural rock bowl at 5,400 feet, to the sheer ridge along the South Rim. Begin climbing on the steep Laguna Meadows Trail, then stay left at the junction to reach the Southwest Rim Trail. Follow the path 1.7 miles along the ridge's contour, where the vistas—peaks, mesas, and arroyos—are as big as the 2,000-foot drop to the desert floor. Spend the night at one of the rim's backcountry campsites—Southwest 1 through 4 are closest to the edge, but the Northeast sites are most secluded. Descend on the rocky, wooded Boot Canyon Trail, catching a glimpse of the boot-shaped pinnacle formation as you go. Time on your hands? Hike the 1-mile spur to Emory Peak, the Chisos Mountains' highest at 7,832 feet. Take the Pinnacles Trail back down to close the loop.

Photo: iStockPhoto.com / yenwen

Text: Melissa Gaskill

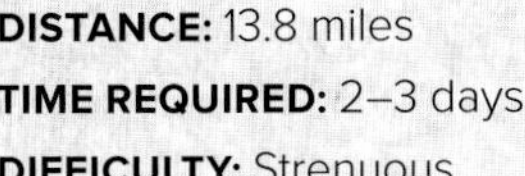

DISTANCE: 13.8 miles

TIME REQUIRED: 2–3 days

DIFFICULTY: Strenuous

CONTACT: Big Bend National Park, (432) 477-2251; nps.gov/bibe

THE PAYOFF: Stay cool on a high-elevation hike with long-distance desert views.

TRAILHEAD GPS: 29.27008, -103.301373

FINDING THE TRAILHEAD: From Alpine, go 99 miles south on TX 118. Turn right on Basin Road and go 6.4 miles to the Chisos Basin trailhead, next to the ranger station.

WAYPOINTS & DIRECTIONS

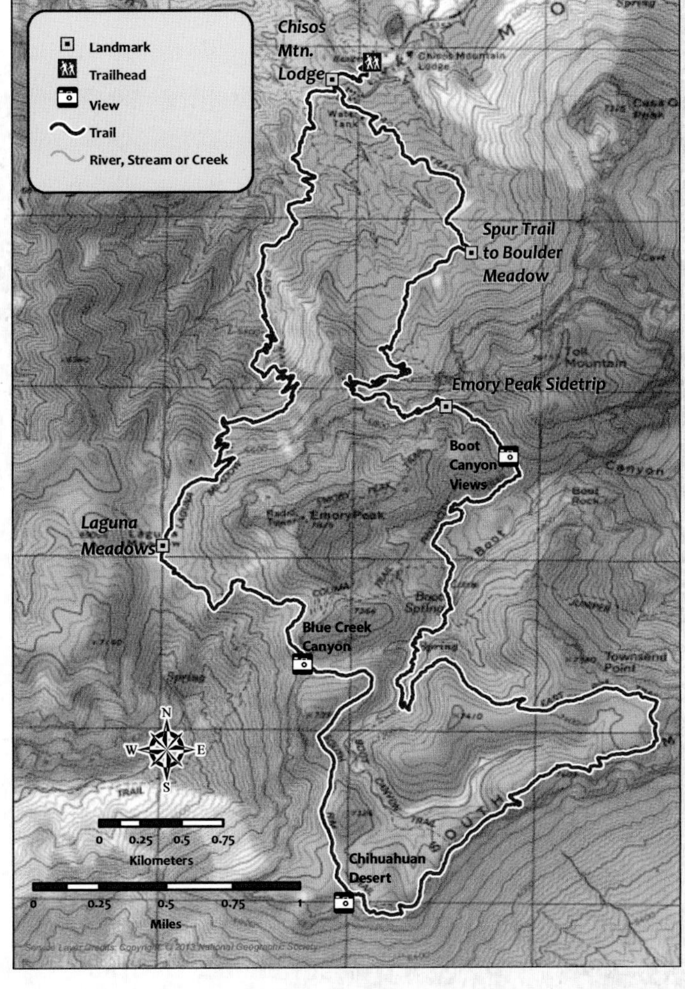

GPS: 29.270080, -103.301373 Trailhead.

GPS: 29.269196, -103.303579 Hike south behind Chisos Mountain Lodge, then bear right onto Laguna Meadows Trail.

GPS: 29.266773, -103.304628 Continue right at the T.

GPS: 29.244643, -103.312792 Laguna Meadows. Primitive campsites to the west (permit required).

GPS: 29.241231, -103.309915 Hike through old forest of juniper, madrone, and Arizona cypress. Take the left fork at the Y with Blue Creek Canyon Trail.

GPS: 29.241469, -103.305169 Stay right at intersection with Colima Trail.

GPS: 29.225795, -103.303009 Sweeping views of Chihuahuan Desert and Mexico from the South Rim.

GPS: 29.228517, -103.297060 Stay right at the intersection with Boot Canyon Trail.

GPS: 29.236078, -103.299897 Turn right onto Boot Canyon Trail.

GPS: 29.249266, -103.293866 Great views down Boot Canyon behind you.

GPS: 29.251909, -103.297331 ***Side Trip:*** Put your gear in a bear box; climb 0.8 miles southwest up 7,825-foot Emory Peak. Serious switchbacks descend ahead.

GPS: 29.260003, -103.295921 Spur trail descends to Boulder Meadow, a primitive campsite.

GPS: 29.265629, -103.299769 Continue downhill to the parking area, where Mexican jays jump branch to branch under dappled shade.

The Black Canyon of the Gunnison in Colorado
Photo: iStockPhoto.com / dschnarrs

BLACK CANYON OF THE GUNNISON NATIONAL PARK

BLACK CANYON OF THE GUNNISON NATIONAL PARK

NORTH VISTA TRAIL TO S.O.B. DRAW

Descend into one of the country's deepest gorges.

Think you've seen deep, sheer, and narrow? Not until you go rim to river in this mind-bendingly steep gash. The 48-mile-long canyon swoops to a depth of 2,722 feet and stretches just 40 feet across at its narrowest point. Light barely enters this snaking, achingly deep Colorado canyon, and the almost perpetually dark, cracked gneiss and schist walls give this park its name. Hike the 7-mile North Vista Trail: This out-and-back path that skirts the north rim before ending atop 8,563-foot Green Mountain. Pass through piñon and juniper to grandiose views of the river, including a stop after 1.2 miles to catch cross-canyon vistas at the appropriately named Exclamation Point. Ready to go deep? Then descend the S.O.B. Trail on ropes and chains to the inner canyon.

Venturing down is more controlled fall than hike, but you'll get in-your-face views of Colorado's tallest cliff, gold-medal trout fishing, and a bottom-up perspective that few ever see. From the North Rim trailhead, skirt the chasm's edge for 0.3 mile before the descent begins in earnest. There's no marked trail, so pick your way through the hippo-size boulders, avoiding both hidden cliffs and the route's legendary, eight-foot-tall poison ivy. (Long sleeves and pants are recommended.) You'll finally exhale when you hit bottom—1.8 miles and 1,800 vertical feet later. Press another 0.8 mile downstream to the wider, wilder second beach. Rest up: Tomorrow, your way out is straight back up.

Photo: Lisa Lynch / NPS Photo

Text: Elisabeth Kwak-Hefferan

DISTANCE: 12.2 miles

TIME REQUIRED: 1–2 days

DIFFICULTY: Strenuous

CONTACT: Black Canyon of the Gunnison National Park, (970) 641-2337; nps.gov/blca

THE PAYOFF: A wild river, gold-medal trout, insanely deep and dark canyon walls.

TRAILHEAD GPS: 38.586753, -107.705390

FINDING THE TRAILHEAD: From Grand Junction, take US 50 south for 29 miles to CO 92; go east 30 miles to Crawford. Continue on Dogwood Avenue, 3850 Drive, and Black Canyon Road (closed in winter) 13 miles to the North Rim Campground.

WAYPOINTS & DIRECTIONS

GPS: 38.586753, -107.705390 Trailhead. Go northwest on North Vista Trail.

GPS: 38.589067, -107.721419 Turn left at the spur for Exclamation Point Overlook.

GPS: 38.587324, -107.720518 Exclamation Point Overlook. Retrace the route back to the North Vista Trail and turn left.

GPS: 38.595172, -107.735410 Take in the views of Green Mountain Summit before retracing the route to the trailhead.

GPS: 38.585277, -107.715797 The S.O.B. Draw Riverside Campsites must be accessed from the S.O.B. Trail, a descent involving ropes and chains that starts at the North Rim Campsite.

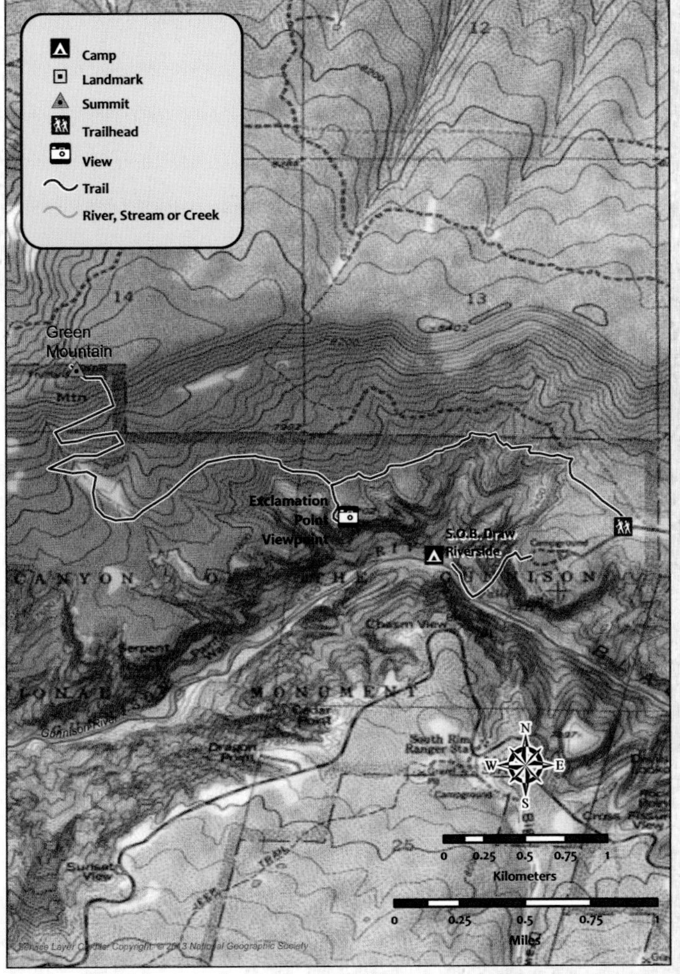

A thunderstorm approaches Bryce Canyon National Park, Utah
Photo: iStockPhoto.com / zodebala

BRYCE CANYON NATIONAL PARK

Sunrise over the hoodoos of Bryce Canyon

BRYCE CANYON NATIONAL PARK
FAIRYLAND LOOP

This 8-mile trail is arguably the most scenic day hike in Bryce Canyon and is less busy than other single-day loops.

The eroded pink pillars of Bryce Canyon create mazes stretching to the park's pine-forested rim. But route finding is simple on this scenery-rich stroll through the pink cliffs and hoodoos (otherworldly freestanding pinnacles also called "fairy chimneys") of Bryce Canyon's distinctive Claron Formation. The clear, well-graded track is ideal for fit hikers who have issues like weak ankles or knee injuries that might make the rougher treks nearby too difficult.

Begin this 8-mile, counterclockwise loop at the much quieter Fairyland Point rather than overwhelmed Sunrise Point. Hike south on the Rim Trail to Sunrise Point, and take advantage of the near-continual overlooks of the odd-shaped rock formations of Fairyland below. You'll be down there on the second half of this loop.

Nearing Sunrise Point, turn left onto the well-signed Fairyland Loop and descend past increasingly spectacular walls of pinkish siltstone and small arches that frame the views of cirques farther south. Within 1.5 miles you'll encounter a junction with the Tower Bridge spur trail. It's a quick out-and-back to this marvel of red rock, named because its boxy shape and rocky span resemble the Tower Bridge in London. Then backtrack to the main loop.

You'll begin a series of rising traverses that proceed counterclockwise around Boat Mesa, the impressive backdrop for much of the hike. En route you'll find a wealth of trail-side hoodoos. These make excellent foregrounds for scenic photos of the background mesa and rims.

Some of the best places to linger are near the eastern (far) end of Boat Mesa. Several gravelly ridges allow you to walk away from the main trail to secluded sites that offer more rewarding rest breaks.

Photo: iStockPhoto.com / MJFelt

Text: Steve Howe

From the eastern end of the loop, just follow the gradual climb back up to the rim near Fairyland Point. The route's best scenery is generally in the first half, and last quarter mile, of the loop. If needed, hop on the free shuttle bus back to your car.

Take all the water you'll need, and plenty of sunscreen and snacks.

DISTANCE: 8 miles

TIME REQUIRED: 4–6 hours

DIFFICULTY: Intermediate

CONTACT: Bryce Canyon National Park, (435) 834-5322; nps.gov/brca

THE PAYOFF: Top-notch, accessible views of the park's signature hoodoos and formations.

TRAILHEAD GPS: 37.649231, -112.147293

FINDING THE TRAILHEAD: From Panguitch, head south for 7 miles on US 89 to UT 12. Turn left and go 13.5 miles to Bryce Canyon National Park Rd. Turn right and drive 3.5 miles to park headquarters. Take the free park shuttle from here to Fairyland Point.

WAYPOINTS & DIRECTIONS

GPS: 37.649231, -112.147293 Trailhead. From Fairyland Point, head south on the Rim Trail to begin this loop.

GPS: 37.631958, -112.162632 Turn left and drop into Fairyland; a right turn leads up to Sunrise Point, another trailhead.

GPS: 37.634685, -112.148076 You'll see seasonal waterflow here in the springtime and after rains.

GPS: 37.633355, -112.145873 The spur trail to the right leads to Tower Bridge, a unique span of eroded red rock.

GPS: 37.631937, -112.144629 View of Tower Bridge; return to main loop.

GPS: 37.635501, -112.143485 Trail begins to traverse ridges of Boat Mesa.

GPS: 37.637050, -112.132447 Swing north to close the loop at Fairyland Point.

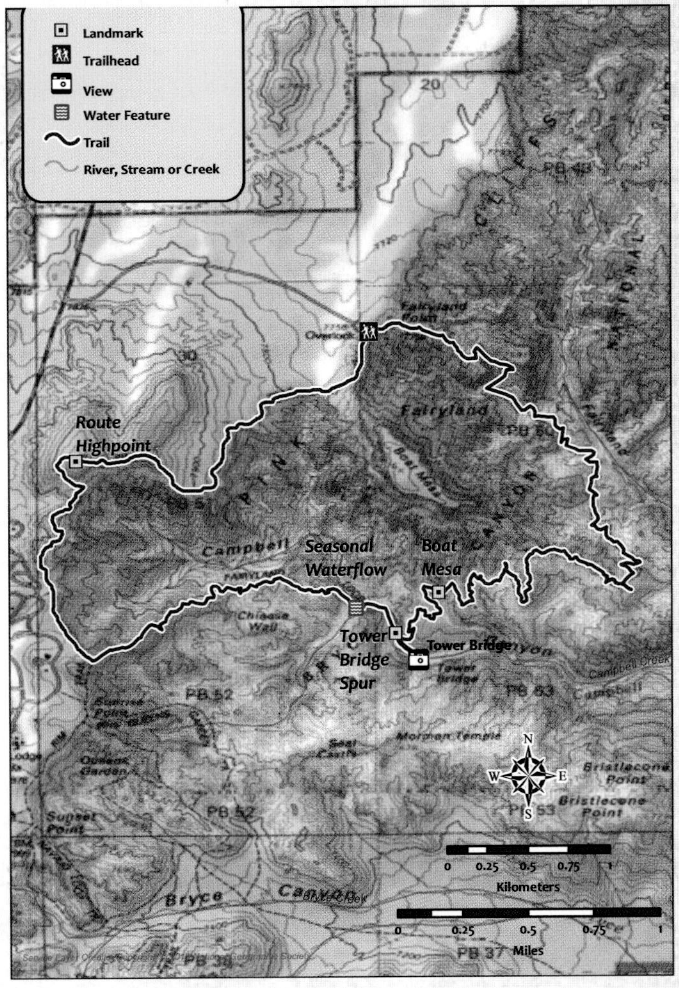

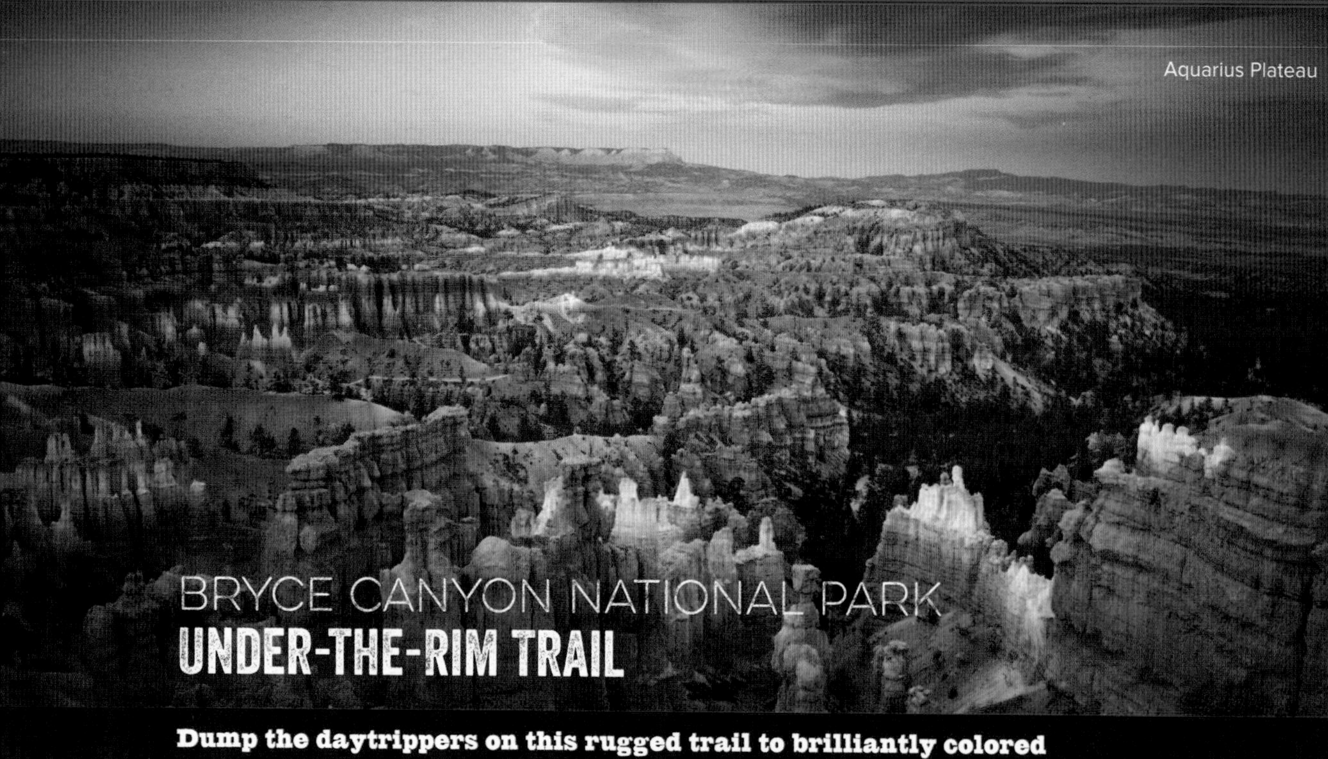

BRYCE CANYON NATIONAL PARK

UNDER-THE-RIM TRAIL

Dump the daytrippers on this rugged trail to brilliantly colored backcountry cliffs and hoodoos.

This three-day, 22.1-mile trek drops 1,000 feet from Bryce's overlooks into spire-filled basins, then arrows south away from the crowded day-hike loops to 9,115-foot Rainbow Point, the park's highest spot. From Bryce Point trailhead, keep right, following signs for the Under-the-Rim Trail. You'll hike southeast across a timbered bench, then drop steeply to the Hat Shop, a series of improbable white boulders perched cap-like atop dirt pedestals at mile 1.9. Pass through the first campsite at Yellow Creek's right fork and curve north along Yellow Creek, one of two reliable water sources on the trek. You'll reach Yellow Creek Campsite at mile four, a great camp for night one. It's creekside; top up water here before taking off, because the trail is bone dry for the next 12 miles.

From the campsite, the path climbs south, then veers west on a traverse to Pasture Wash, then up and over a series of steep passes to the Sheep Creek Campsite and the Right Fork of Swamp Canyon Campsite. Keep trekking 1.7 miles up Swamp Canyon, wrapping around Swamp Canyon Butte onto a tilted plateau where you'll pass a junction with 0.9-mile Whiteman Connecting Trail. At mile 14, you'll come to a sandy ridgeline that's an excellent lunch spot with reliable breezes and long views. Pass ponderosa stands and the Natural Bridge Campsite (take a side hike west about 0.5 mile to see the bridge) before taking another twisty climb to a junction with Agua Canyon Connecting Trail. Ahead, spot the intricate traverses you'll follow around the headwaters of Willis and Black Birch Creeks over the next 2.4 miles to Iron Spring Campsite. Iron Spring is the last reliable water source. The next morning, drop down to Black Birch Creek before a 1,200-foot, 2.9-mile climb to the end at Rainbow Point.

Photo: NPS Photo

Text: Steve Howe

DISTANCE: 22.1 miles

TIME REQUIRED: 3 days

DIFFICULTY: Strenuous

CONTACT: Bryce Canyon National Park, (435) 834-5322; nps.gov/brca

THE PAYOFF: Wild solitude and challenge amidst the park's most dramatic scenery.

TRAILHEAD GPS: 37.603362, -112.156041

FINDING THE TRAILHEAD: Bryce lies on UT 12 between Panguitch (25 miles west) and Escalante (50 miles east). From either direction, turn south on UT 63 and drive 3.8 miles to the park. It's 18 miles to Rainbow Point. Leave a car or bike here as a shuttle (pack U locks), then park at Bryce Point.

WAYPOINTS & DIRECTIONS

GPS: 37.603362, -112.156041 Trailhead sign.

GPS: 37.590868, -112.143738 Great views of Hat Shop, a series of improbable white boulders.

GPS: 37.587706, -112.147662 Nice campsite on the Right Fork of Yellow Creek; reliable water.

GPS: 37.585583, -112.163455 Nice side strolls north and northwest to Yellow Spring and dramatic cliffs beneath Paria View.

GPS: 37.577856, -112.186634 Needle-floored Ponderosa Glades in Pasture Wash.

GPS: 37.578828, -112.201777 Sheep Creek Campsite.

GPS: 37.576811, -112.212761 Right Fork Swamp Canyon Campsite.

GPS: 37.561144, -112.230067 Whiteman Connecting Trail. It's 0.9 mile to rim and road if hikers need to bail out.

GPS: 37.526676, -112.241170 Natural Bridge Campsite. Good walking through ponderosa groves in the area.

GPS: 37.491788, -112.244137 Iron Spring is a good water spot, though the water is often algae filled. Try prefiltering it through a standard conical coffee filter.

GPS: 37.475281, -112.240224 Rainbow Point, the trip's endpoint.

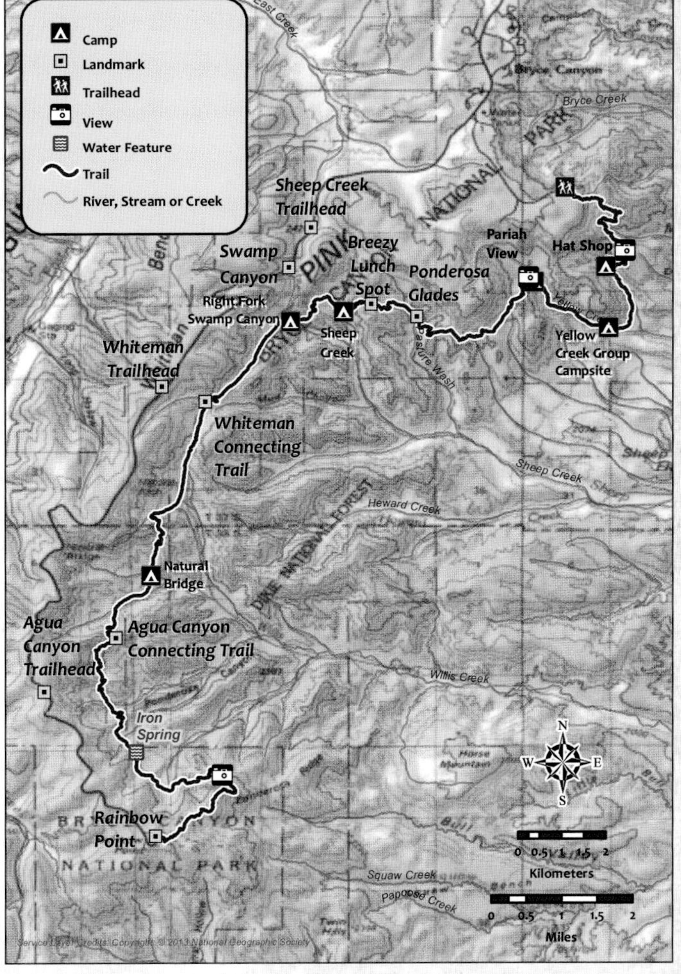

Sunrise in the Needles District of Canyonlands National Park, Utah
Photo: Neal Herbert / NPS Photo

CANYONLANDS
NATIONAL PARK

The Green River in Canyonlands

CANYONLANDS NATIONAL PARK
GOLDEN STAIRS TO SWEET ALICE LOOP

Outrageous spires and hidden springs highlight this 3-day loop through the park's challenging Maze District.

Canyonlands' endless labyrinths of shiprock mesas, soaring red walls, and melted-hell sandstone formations inspire rapturous responses—none more eloquent than that of the park's foremost poet hermit, *Desert Solitaire* author Ed Abbey. Every spring, thousands of hikers and 4WD campers head into the Maze, drawn by Abbey's paeans to its remoteness and beauty. But most ignore the spectacular Fins country in the district's southern end, with its imposing towers of banded sandstone. This 30.7-mile tour connects three lightly visited slickrock canyons in that area via sketchy trails, easy scrambles, and a fast return trek on a dirt road. Several reliable water sources make extended stays feasible, and you can tailor your challenge level by wandering to the many isolated ledges and spur canyons. The only hitch? A high-clearance 4WD vehicle is required to reach the Golden Stairs trailhead.

Your hike starts spectacularly as you cross the narrow stone ramp of China Neck, with dizzying views off either elbow, then wind 2 miles down the rugged Golden Stairs Trail to the Standing Rock jeep road. A short road mile leads to an unmarked parking area beneath twin red-rock pinnacles known as the Mother and Child. From here, a faint trail threads down into Range Canyon past a hidden Anasazi ruin and a historic cowboy water source called Lou's Spring; then an established trail takes you through the tight hallway of the Chute before arrowing across open basins toward the distant Doll House.

The big attraction, however, is a side trip into the forks of Sand Tank Canyon, both walled in by corkscrewing sandstone pinnacles banded in pink, orange, and white. Don't hurry through this country; surprises and secluded nooks are everywhere. You can follow established trail east all the way to the Doll House, but a more interesting exit climbs from the upper reaches of Sweet Alice Canyon to deposit you on Standing Rock Road near its namesake formation. From there, it's a fast 9-mile road walk back to the foot of the Golden Stairs Trail. You can complete this last section with a mountain bike or 4WD shuttle, but Standing Rock Road is long and tortuous, even for the toughest vehicles.

Photo: iStockPhoto.com / fotozotti

Text: Steve Howe

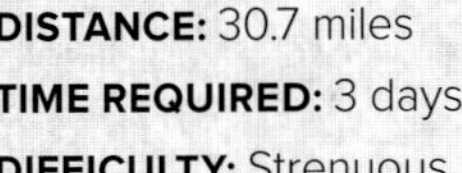

DISTANCE: 30.7 miles

TIME REQUIRED: 3 days

DIFFICULTY: Strenuous

CONTACT: Canyonlands National Park, (435) 719-2100; nps.gov/cany

THE PAYOFF: Secluded canyons in Ed Abbey's favorite playground.

TRAILHEAD GPS: 38.143867, -110.08313

FINDING THE TRAILHEAD: From the Maze District turnoff, just south of Goblin Valley junction on UT 24, go 46 dirt-road miles east to the Hans Flat Ranger Station (open 9 a.m. to 4:30 p.m.) and pick up your permit. Continue south for 14 high-clearance miles to the four-wheel-drive Flint Trail, then descend 4 miles to the Golden Stairs trailhead.

WAYPOINTS & DIRECTIONS

GPS: 38.143867, -110.083130 Golden Stairs Trailhead. Hike east up the China Neck.

GPS: 38.143799, -110.077187 Take in the sweeping vistas at the plateau rim.

GPS: 38.135715, -110.078903 At the road intersection turn left.

GPS: 38.139568, -110.070686 Here is the unsigned Range Canyon trailhead: A small rectangle of rock sits just beneath twin pinnacles, the Mother and Child. Start counter-clockwise loop.

GPS: 38.134418, -110.062614 Range Canyon. Turn left here for short out-and-back trip to Lou's Spring.

GPS: 38.135700, -110.061134 Lou's Spring, a developed cowboy spring with reliable water and a catchment tank.

GPS: 38.132717, -110.060349 Trail leaves wash.

GPS: 38.133350, -110.019981 Turn left into Sand Tank Canyon.

GPS: 38.136333, -110.021080 Take another left into the side canyon of Sand Tank Creek.

GPS: 38.139050, -110.024918 Slab climb detours around impassable dry fall.

GPS: 38.138351, -110.025764 Excellent campsite.

GPS: 38.142834, -110.033134 Small arch and pothole at upper reach of canyon fork, possible water source in wetter seasons; return to the main part of Sand Tank Canyon and hike north.

GPS: 38.146198, -110.017464 Superb views of fins and good campsites.

GPS: 38.161865, -110.007263 Possible water from spring and pool hidden inside small rock arch.

GPS: 38.165066, -110.012184 The terminus of Sand Tank Canyon, no exit. Backtrack to the Sand Tank Canyon turnoff and take a left.

GPS: 38.131966, -110.017136 Well-cairned trail leaves Sand Tank Canyon to the east.

GPS: 38.138882, -110.007484 Very subtle trail leaves wash. Follow scant cairns to east-northeast.

GPS: 38.154316, -109.990700 Standing Rock pinnacle becomes visible ahead. You'll meet the Standing Rock road just east of it.

GPS: 38.169483, -109.988747 Follow canyon all the way until it dead ends in cliffs and three distinct forks. Follow the rightmost (east) fork. Several slickrock potholes at junction may hold water.

GPS: 38.168335, -109.987297 Canyon Rim. Find faint trails across slickrock to the east.

GPS: 38.168098, -109.986351 Scramble up 20-foot cliff to the next level of rim. Turn north and avoid cryptogamic soils by hugging rim.

GPS: 38.175968, -109.988297 Trail intersects Standing Rock Road—Standing Rock pinnacle sits some 300 yards to the east. From here, pick up second car or mountain bike, or hike the road 9 miles back to the trailhead.

(*Map on next page*)

CANYONLANDS NATIONAL PARK

GOLDEN STAIRS TO SWEET ALICE LOOP

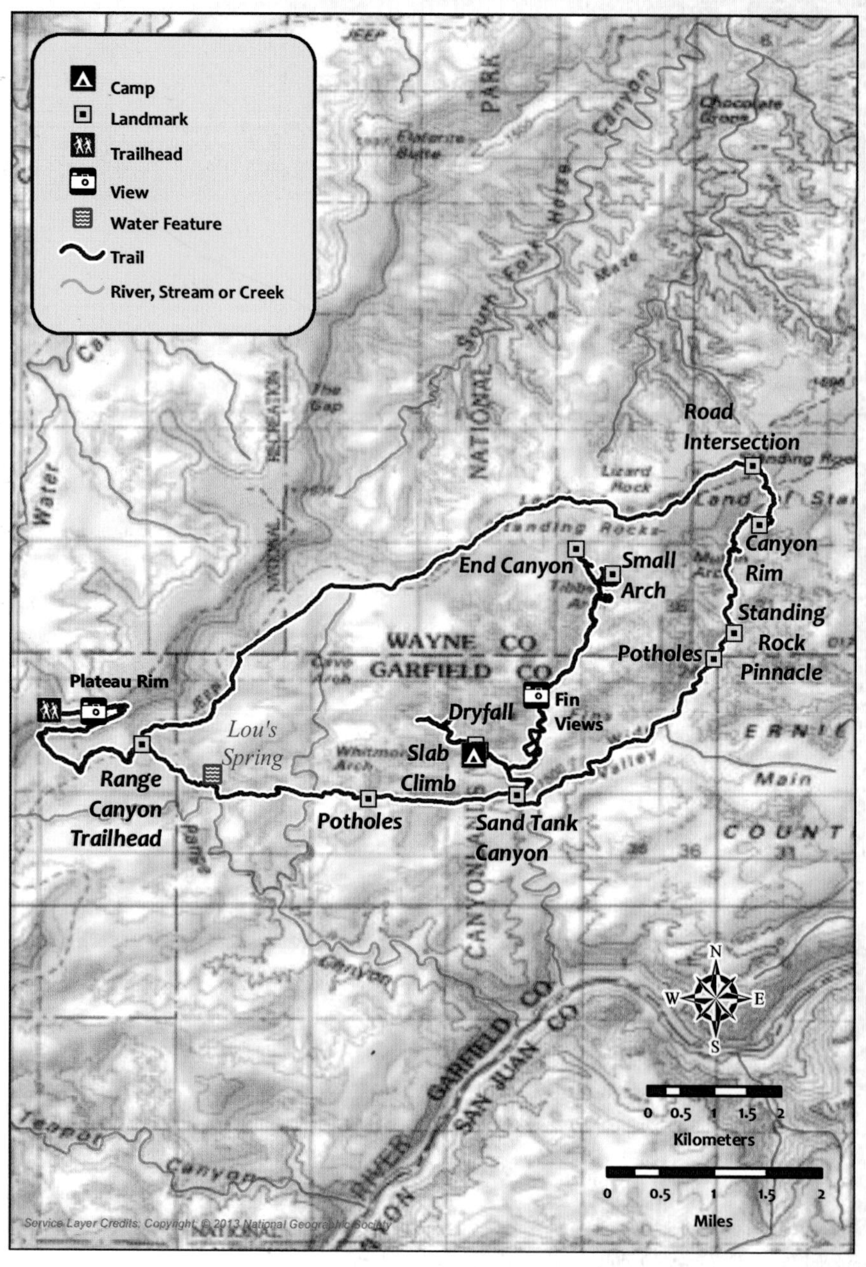

Hydration packs allow easy access to water

STAY HYDRATED

Like wine to the gods, water is the nectar of athletes. "Losing just 1 percent of weight from water loss can impair performance," says Colleen Cooke, a sports nutritionist at the Boulder Center for Sports Medicine. Countless hikers and mountaineers have turned to her for advice on nutrition. Their number-one question: How do I stay hydrated? Here's what she recommends.

DRINK EARLY. While you sleep, you lose as much as 1.5 pounds of fluid through sweat and respiration. Before breaking camp, replenish with 16 to 24 ounces of water, a sports drink, or noncaffeinated tea.

SIP OFTEN. According to Cooke, some hikers walk for three hours, sip a few ounces on a rest break, and pay for it at the end of the day. Instead, drink 4 to 6 ounces of liquid every 20 minutes; it'll help you feel strong, even on the last hill. Hydration bladders encourage drinking more than water bottles.

ADD ELECTROLYTES. "Sweat is made up of sodium and potassium, which need to be replaced," says Cooke. If they're not, you'll likely feel sluggish. Sip a sports drink (powdered versions work well in the field) or munch on salty snacks.

EAT CARBS. "Every gram of carbohydrate you eat pulls three grams of water into your digestive system, which helps keep you hydrated," explains Cooke. Cooke recommends a carb-protein-fat ratio of 60-20-20 for backpackers on multiday trips.

WATCH FOR SYMPTOMS. Headaches, dizziness, and difficulty concentrating can signal dehydration. The fix: Rest, eat, and drink. Anxiety, a weak or rapid pulse, and clammy or hot and dry skin point to serious dehydration. Set up camp: A long rest, a good meal, and lots of water are your best bets for feeling stronger in the morning.

Doll House area of the Maze District

CANYONLANDS NATIONAL PARK

SYNCLINE LOOP

Mystical pinnacles highlight a rare introductory route to Canyonlands' Maze District.

The jigsaw-puzzle cliffs of Canyonlands National Park's Island in the Sky district plunge so steeply to the meandering river thousands of feet below, hiking there feels like walking off the edge of the earth. Get a taste of the experience on this loop on the Syncline Trail, linking the scrubby washes that surround Upheaval Dome. The literal centerpiece of this loop is an anomaly in an already otherworldly landscape. Two theories attempt to explain the deformed rock in the 3-mile-wide Upheaval Dome area, but whether it's a meteorite or a long-dissolved salt formation, you'll catch a spectacular panoramic view of the jumbled geology near the trailhead.

From the parking area, the route turns left and follows the Syncline Loop Trail clockwise through piñon and juniper woodland along the south side of the formation. You'll switchback from the mesa top, descending into a giant sandstone maw with views of the Green River.

At the bottom of the sandy crater, skirt the dome, following the valley floor until you climb back up through a lush riparian zone on the north side to join Syncline Canyon Trail at mile 3.5. The first mellow mile of climbing is followed by a steep scramble back toward the Island in the Sky. You can trace the route in either direction, but hiking clockwise saves the jungle-gym scrambling section for the ascent. A difficult climb and navigational challenges (read: scattered cairns) are almost guaranteed on this hike and extreme desert temperatures are always possible. If you question your route-finding skills, fitness, or level of preparedness, consider the short-and-sweet Overlook Trail as an alternative.

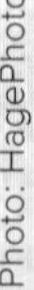
Photo: HagePhoto

Text: Steve Howe and Chuck Graham

DISTANCE: 7.6 miles

TIME REQUIRED: 1 day

DIFFICULTY: Moderate

CONTACT: Canyonlands National Park, (435) 719-2100; nps.gov/cany

THE PAYOFF: Plunge off Canyonlands' Island in the Sky to the river below.

TRAILHEAD GPS: 38.426298, -109.926184

FINDING THE TRAILHEAD: From Island in the Sky Visitor Center, continue 6 miles south, then turn right (west) on Upheaval Dome Road. Go 4.8 miles to the trailhead.

WAYPOINTS & DIRECTIONS

GPS: 38.426298, -109.926184 Hike west from the trailhead. Most of the traffic at this well-developed trailhead is for the short Overlook Trail.

GPS: 38.426847, -109.926002 Turn left and follow the rocky Syncline Loop Trail through piñon and juniper woodland along the ridge.

GPS: 38.427950, -109.939606 The mesa top ends, and you'll begin a steep series of downhill switchbacks into the valley below.

GPS: 38.431261, -109.947503 At this rock notch, stop to catch your breath—and downvalley views of the Green River.

GPS: 38.431606, -109.949423 Begin following a sandy basin at the bottom of the crater, surrounded by 1,000-foot high walls.

GPS: 38.444615, -109.956536 Join the Upheaval Canyon Trail and turn right (northeast). See the high walls and shiprocks of Upheaval Canyon to the northwest.

GPS: 38.444441, -109.953164 Reach a junction with the Syncline Valley and begin climbing up.

GPS: 38.444607, -109.952641 This view of Upheaval Canyon rewards those who travel this rugged desert loop.

GPS: 38.449317, -109.949333 There are several flowing, freshwater pools about halfway through Syncline Valley and uphill from the route's only campsite after the Upheaval Canyon junction.

GPS: 38.452083, -109.945183 One of several freshwater springs in the canyon.

GPS: 38.452007, -109.945483 Begin a fun scramble through giant boulders.

GPS: 38.452973, -109.944785 Here, crawl through a rock tunnel in a scattered boulder field. After this point, you'll begin another sharp ascent into the valley.

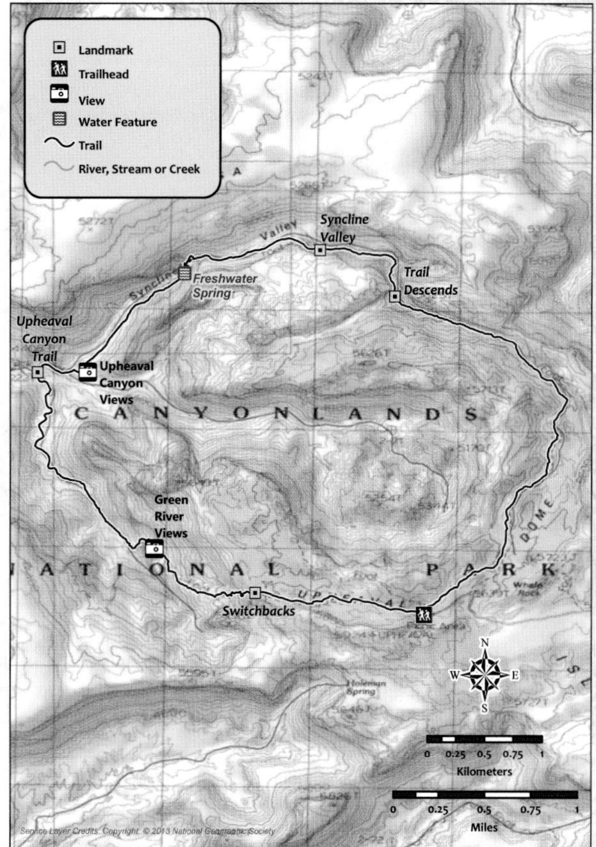

GPS: 38.453850, -109.934467 A fairly reliable stream flows through the Syncline Valley, and near its beginning you'll encounter a lush, garden-like riparian area—a good spot for a break.

GPS: 38.450367, -109.928533 Here, the trail ascends a steep ramp and passes below a pour-off (a chute linking two wash areas) on a cliff band. Although the entire park is prone to flash flooding, be especially wary in this area during inclement weather.

GPS: 38.448648, -109.924436 Continue through mellow piñon and juniper forest covering the mesa to reach your trailhead.

Druid Arch

CANYONLANDS NATIONAL PARK

CHESLER PARK TO SALT CREEK CANYON

Hit up the park's highlights—slickrock scrambles, mesa-top views, and hoodoo-dotted canyons—on this unreal weeklong trek.

The Needles District, in the park's southeastern reaches, is a slickrock playground of labyrinthine canyons, hoodoo gardens, giant arches, expansive meadows, and prehistoric ruins. See the best of it on a 49.3-mile point-to-point that rollercoasters from canyon bottoms to butte tops with hundred-mile views. From the Elephant Hill trailhead, hike south to the adjacent mesa top, climbing steadily past aromatic sagebrush and canyons capped with mushroom-like spires. As you gain elevation, turn around for a pace-halting scene: The snowcapped La Sal Mountains rise to 12,000 feet behind distant mesas and gorges, while pink-and-white-striped rock towers line the foreground.

At mile 1.3, bear right before passing through two less-than-10-foot-wide gaps in the slickrock and descending to Elephant Canyon. Ditch your pack in the wash for a 3.6- mile side trip to Chesler Park, a sweeping meadow enclosed by spires. First, climb southwest up a side canyon and traverse a sandstone ledge above the canyon floor. Next, turn left at mile 2.4, and crest a pass bordered by toothy formations. Soon after, the route enters Chesler's 960-acre expanse stippled with bunchgrass and rimmed by 800-foot-tall, multi-colored spires. On windy days, you can hear the breeze whistle as it whips around the formations. Return to Elephant Canyon, then head south 0.6 mile to your first camp perched on a slickrock bench.

Photo: iStockPhoto.com / lightphoto

Text: MacKenzie Ryan

The next day, go south 0.2 mile to where the canyon forks. Leave your pack, grab day-hiking supplies, then bear right for a 4.5-mile round-trip to 85-foot-high Druid Arch, reminiscent of Stonehenge; backtrack to your pack. Now head southeast up the east fork of Elephant Canyon, and climb a metal ladder into neighboring Squaw Canyon (mile 11.7). Traverse northeast along the exposed northern rim of the canyon for a mile, then turn left for a grin-inducing obstacle course: Jump over a three-foot-wide gap, tightrope walk across logs lining the bottom of a five-foot-wide rock tunnel, then climb up a pourover to a red-rock pass. Drop into Big Spring Canyon and follow it northeast 1.4 miles to your second camp (mile 14.4).

Day three's hike tracks northeast to Squaw Flat trailhead after less than two miles (take a 0.5-mile detour to fill water in a nearby campground), then wind south into Squaw Canyon through a wide, hoodoo-rimmed meadow. At mile 18.4, veer left for a slickrock scramble to a 5,480-foot pass; carefully descend a steep pourover with loose rocks into Lost Canyon. Follow the snaking, cottonwood-lined wash northeast for 2.5 miles past pools with bullfrogs and salamanders, and turn right at the junction. Sleep at a campsite 100 yards away.

On the fourth day, tackle a dizzying traverse that runs east on ledges roughly 200 feet above lower Lost and Squaw Canyons; climb down a ladder through a claustrophobic, 3-foot-wide slot; then descend stone steps into lower Salt Creek Canyon. In late summer, you may spot black bears snacking on the fruit of prickly pear cactus. Sleep at Angel Arch Camp, shaded by two large cottonwoods.

Start your 9.1-mile fifth day with a four-mile out-and-back to Angel Arch, named for the winged figure that seems to be leaning back on the 135-foot-tall arch. Next, hike south through grassy clearings with wild rose bushes to Upper Jump, a 15-foot waterfall pouring down tiered ledges. Overnight where the canyon broadens (mile 39.9).

Slow your pace on the sixth day to savor a 5.3-mile stretch of relics left by ancestral Puebloans in 1200 A.D. You'll pass a round stone-and-mortar granary, pictographs (one resembles four figures playing musical instruments), and cliff dwellings. Camp at mile 45.2.

On the last day (4.1 miles), follow the overgrown creekbed south. The lush riparian scenery transitions back to parched desert as the trail gains 1,000 feet in two miles to the rim of Salt Creek Mesa and your shuttle car.

DISTANCE: 49.3 miles

TIME REQUIRED: 5–7 days

DIFFICULTY: Strenuous

CONTACT: Canyonlands National Park, (435) 719-2100; nps.gov/cany

THE PAYOFF: The best week in Canyonlands.

TRAILHEAD GPS: 38.141810, -109.827187

FINDING THE TRAILHEAD: From Moab, drive south on US 191 for 40 miles and turn right on UT 211 W. In roughly 20 miles, turn left onto Beef Basin Road/CR 107. Continue 17.2 miles to parking at the Cathedral Butte/ Upper Salt Creek trailhead. Park a car, and backtrack to UT 211 and turn left. In 17 miles, turn left on the unnamed road. In 0.3 mile, turn right at the Elephant Hill sign. Go 3 miles to parking. Or, try a commercial shuttle like Coyote Shuttle (coyoteshuttle.com).

WAYPOINTS & DIRECTIONS

GPS: 38.141810, -109.827187 From the Elephant Hill trailhead, hike south to the adjacent mesa top, climbing steadily past aromatic sagebrush and canyons with capped, mushroom-like spires.

GPS: 38.125848, -109.832473 Bear right, following the sign to Chesler Park and Druid Arch. Pass through a less-than-10-foot-wide gap in the slickrock, then enter a sage field surrounded by a semicircular sandstone cliff.

GPS: 38.125293, -109.837365 Walk through another slickrock gap and descend into Elephant Canyon.

GPS: 38.123552, -109.839982 ***Side Trip:*** Cross sandy wash. Ditch your pack in the wash for a 3.6-mile excursion to Chesler Park.

GPS: 38.120863, -109.847874 Trail goes left along mouth of a canyon rimmed with hoodoos. Go left at the Y junction.

GPS: 38.118106, -109.849845 Bear left and hike south into Chesler Park.

GPS: 38.106468, -109.849514 Stop and take in this 960-acre expanse stippled with bunchgrass and rimmed by 800-foot-tall multicolored spires. Return to Elephant Canyon and your pack; turn right and head south into Elephant Canyon for 0.6 miles to your first camp.

GPS: 38.116404, -109.838065 Spend the first night at EC2, on the right. The next day, go south 0.2 mile to where the canyon forks.

GPS: 38.114689, -109.835925 ***Side Trip:*** Leave your pack, grab day-hiking supplies, then bear right for a 4.5-mile round-trip to 85-foot-high Druid Arch.

GPS: 38.089029, -109.831155 Stop at the foot of 85-foot-high Druid Arch, reminiscent of Stonehenge. Backtrack to your pack.

GPS: 38.114633, -109.835789 Grab your pack and head southeast up the east fork of Elephant Canyon.

GPS: 38.104947, -109.826331 Climb a metal ladder into neighboring Squaw Canyon and traverse northeast along the exposed northern rim of the canyon for a mile.

GPS: 38.109464, -109.816332 Follow cairns as they wind along the canyon rim. Turn left for a grin-inducing obstacle course: Jump over a three-foot-wide gap, tightrope-walk across logs lining the bottom of a five-foot-wide rock tunnel, then climb up a pourover to a red-rock pass.

GPS: 38.109317, -109.817817 Top of the pass. Next, drop into Big Spring Canyon and follow it northeast 1.4 miles to your second camp at BS2.

GPS: 38.126546, -109.812246 Camp at BS2. To start day three, hike northeast less than 2 miles to Squaw Flat trailhead.

GPS: 38.140366, -109.808176 Bear right at the Y junction.

GPS: 38.142998, -109.803763 Squaw Flat trailhead. Take a 0.5-mile detour to fill water in Campground B, then wind south into Squaw Canyon through a wide, hoodoo-rimmed meadow.

GPS: 38.132714, -109.794905 Go left at Y junction. Follow the sandy trail south into Squaw Canyon through a wide, hoodoo-rimmed meadow.

GPS: 38.107193, -109.802944 Carefully descend a steep pourover with loose rocks into Lost Canyon.

GPS: 38.121759, -109.777768 Turn left toward Peekabo Spring.

GPS: 38.121019, -109.776890 Sleep at LC1. On the fourth day, you'll tackle a dizzying traverse that runs east on ledges roughly 200 feet above lower Lost and Squaw Canyons; climb down a ladder through a claustrophobic, three-foot-wide slot; then descend stone steps into lower Salt Creek Canyon.

GPS: 38.120366, -109.776479 Top of boulder climb.

GPS: 38.117283, -109.770302 Views north of Wooden Shoe Arch.

GPS: 38.114534, -109.754949 Walk through a roughly 15-foot gap, located next to some ancient rock art.

GPS: 38.075315, -109.765407 Look over your left shoulder to see a crescent arch.

GPS: 38.069770, -109.767712 Sleep at Angel Arch Camp, shaded by two large cottonwoods. Start the 9.1-mile day five with a 4-mile out-and-back to Angel Arch. Continue south to the junction.

GPS: 38.068290, -109.768341 ***Side Trip:*** Turn left for a detour to Angel Arch.

GPS: 38.051799, -109.756514 Angel Arch. Stare up at this striking arch.

GPS: 38.068290, -109.768341 Backtrack to the junction and turn left; hike south through grassy clearings with wild rose bushes.

GPS: 38.056632, -109.769574 Pass through a clearing with breathtaking views of spires.

GPS: 38.043179, -109.764705 Turn left to see the Upper Jump, a 15-foot waterfall pouring down tiered ledges.

GPS: 38.039709, -109.763806 Spend the night at SC3 where the canyon broadens (mile 39.9). On the sixth day, slow your pace to savor a 5.3-mile stretch of relics left by Ancestral Puebloans in 1200 A.D. You'll pass a round stone-and-mortar granary, pictographs, and cliff dwellings.

GPS: 38.034861, -109.751901 Downclimb through narrows.

GPS: 38.034483, -109.749412 Look left to see another dwelling. Pass the All American Man pictograph.

GPS: 38.014123, -109.744290 After the stream crossing, look left across the meadow for views of a dwelling.

GPS: 38.010573, -109.742642 Skinny arch.

GPS: 37.986173, -109.743161 Turn left to camp at SC1 or SC2. On the last day (4.1 miles), follow the overgrown creekbed south.

GPS: 37.961208, -109.729688 Bear left on Salt Creek Trail. Ahead: The lush riparian scenery transitions back to parched desert as the trail gains 1,000 feet in two miles to the rim of Salt Creek Mesa and your shuttle car.

GPS: 37.949307, -109.706083 Pick up your shuttle and return to the trailhead.

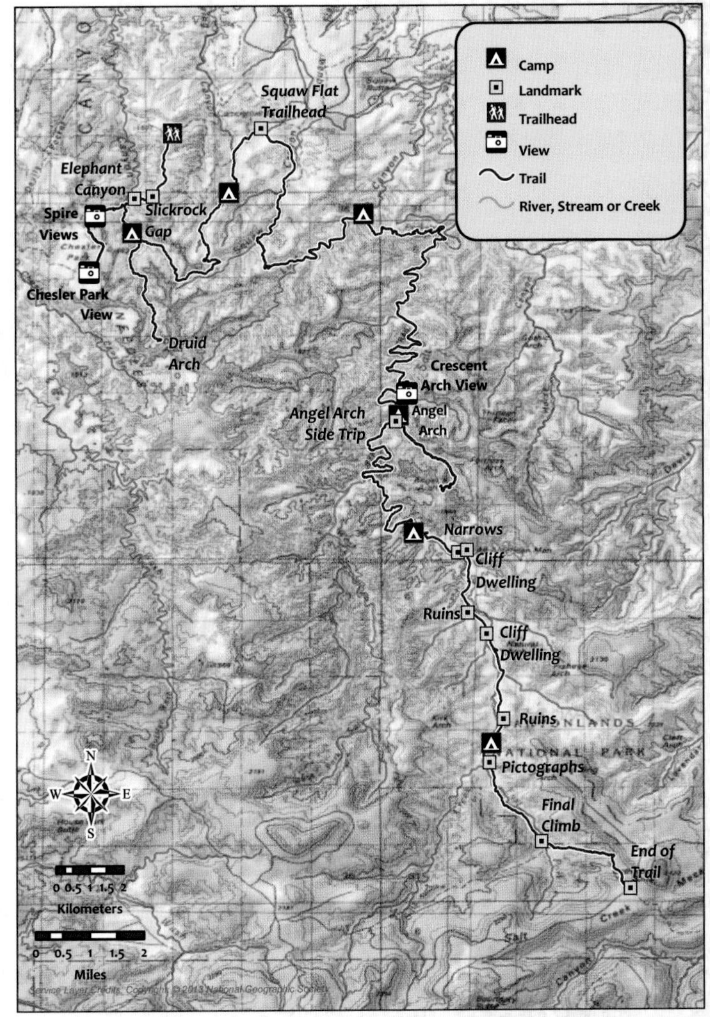

IT'S NEVER TOO LATE TO START BACKPACKING

Roxanne Fleming, 60, of Washington, D.C., took her first hike at age 57, and in the three years since, has already visited Everest Base Camp, summited the Grand Teton, and hiked in Patagonia's Torres Del Paine. Here's her best advice for late bloomers.

START SLOWLY. "At the beginning, I just walked outdoors. Next I found a wide path near my house and did small hikes nearby."

SET A GOAL. "Once I realized how much I loved doing this, I figured out somewhere I really wanted to go. For me it was Everest Base Camp. If you don't know your spot, go through an atlas or a book on hiking to pick whatever you like. Then figure out how to get there. I joined two local hiking clubs to help me train."

GET THE GEAR. "Comfortable shoes make all the difference. I'm astounded by how many people get blisters or have issues with their feet. Try your shoes on, and buy from somewhere you can take them back if it turns out they're not working for you. I also really like having a hydration system. I don't want to have to take the time to open a water bottle and drink it; I'm just concentrating on getting myself to my destination."

FIND A BUDDY. "I had a friend with me at the beginning; conversation helps make it more enjoyable. Then I relied a lot on guides from the local clubs as I learned the ropes. Hiking on your own comes later."

MAKE NEW FRIENDS. "My husband and kids are supportive, but this is my thing. It's been a nice way to kind of reinvent myself. I have had a few friends say, 'Eww, how can you do it?' 'How can you go without taking a shower?' Forget the whole poop situation, we won't even get into that. But listening to my own heart and soul, I know this is something I want to do. I like my identity as a backpacker. I had never been an outdoors kind of gal before. I'm not sure we ever know for sure why we do anything. All I know is it's working right now."

Photo: iStockPhoto.com / amriphoto

Text: Rachel Zurer

The Hoh River Trail, Olympic National Park, Washington
Photo: Dave Costello

Temple of the Sun (foreground) and Temple of the Moon (background) in Capitol Reef National Park, Utah
Photo: Ian Shive / Tandem Stock

CAPITOL REEF
NATIONAL PARK

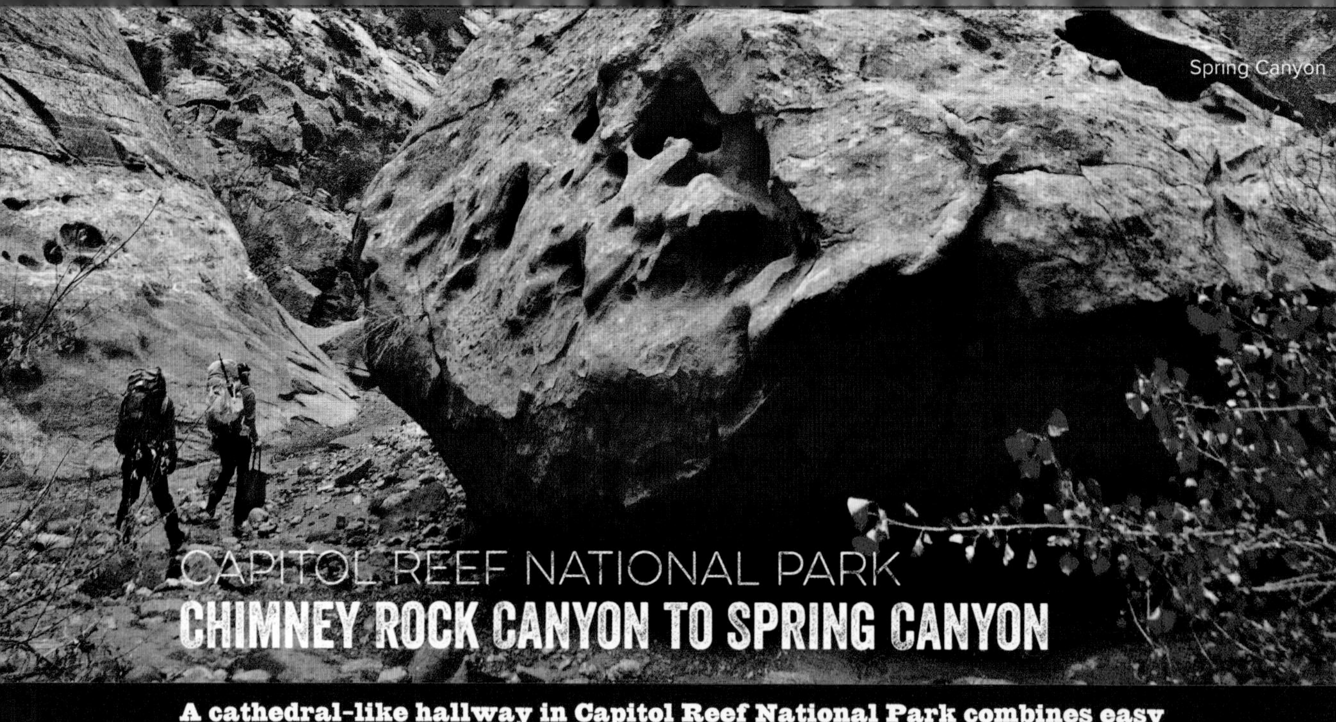

CAPITOL REEF NATIONAL PARK

CHIMNEY ROCK CANYON TO SPRING CANYON

A cathedral-like hallway in Capitol Reef National Park combines easy canyon hiking and foolproof route-finding with life-list sights.

In a state littered with canyon parks, Capitol Reef is the hidden gem. Its isolated location in south-central Utah keeps summer throngs away. They're missing out. The 100-mile-long centerpiece canyon of the upthrust Waterpocket Fold hides golden sandstone domes, skyscraping canyons, and dark narrows that rank among the best (and most secret) in the Southwest. You don't need to tackle Capitol Reef's hardest terrain to see some of its best scenery. This 10-mile, cathedral-like hallway combines easy canyon hiking and foolproof route-finding (there's only one way to go) with life-list sights, like lush cottonwoods backdropped by massive sandstone amphitheaters. From the Chimney Rock trailhead, good trail leads into the deep cleft of Chimney Rock Canyon.

At mile 2.9, intersect Spring Canyon and hang a right, leaving the maintained path behind. In 1 mile, the wash drops through a slot canyon. Explore it until an abrupt, sketchy downclimb; detour around on a trail along the left (north) rim of the narrows. The wash-bottom route continues past overhanging cliffs to a spring with good water at mile 6.5.

Continue beneath towering cottonwoods until you ford the Fremont River (usually knee to thigh deep) and pop out on UT 24. Leave a shuttle car here, or you can hitch or bike the seven-mile return west to the trailhead. (But cyclists must finish with a steep, 3-mile hill climb).

You need carrying capacity for 2 gallons of water per person in warm weather and a filter to treat sometimes-murky water. There are potholes along the way that are typically reliable, but sources can come and go.

Photo: Kim Phillips

Text: Steve Howe

DISTANCE: 10 miles

TIME REQUIRED: 1–2 days

DIFFICULTY: Intermediate

CONTACT: Capitol Reef National Park, (435) 425-4111; nps.gov/care

THE PAYOFF: Brave the soaring canyons and lush cottonwood groves of the waterpocket fold.

TRAILHEAD GPS: 38.315662, -111.304016

FINDING THE TRAILHEAD: From the park visitor center, drive west on UT 24 for 3 miles to Chimney Rock trailhead. Shuttle/end: From the park visitor center, drive 3.9 miles east on UT 24.

WAYPOINTS & DIRECTIONS

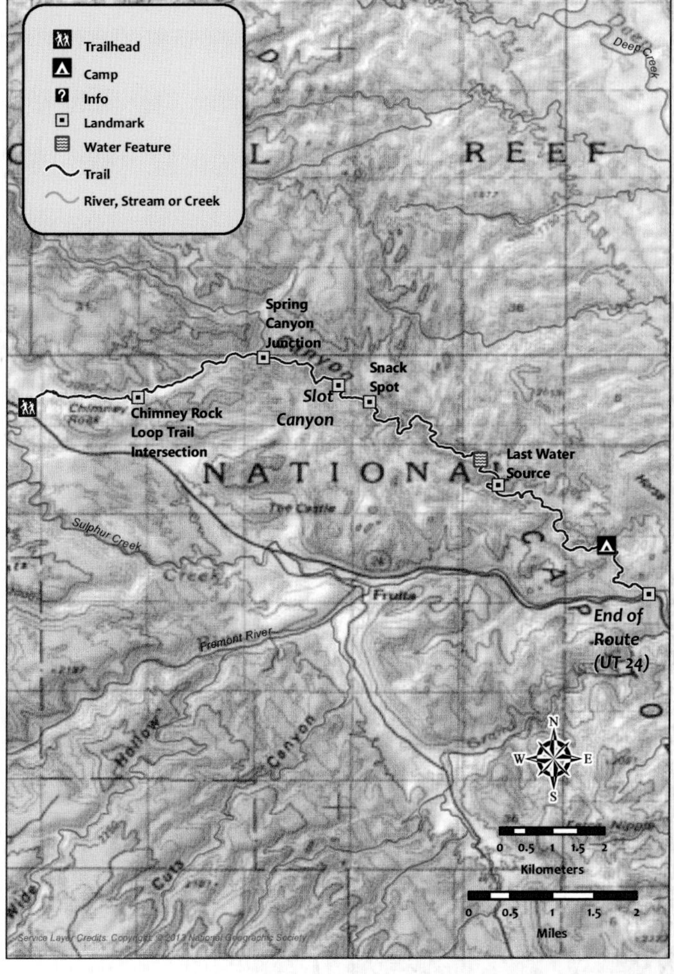

GPS: 38.315662, -111.304016 Hike northeast from Spring Canyon trailhead.

GPS: 38.317578, -111.298270 Continue straight at signed three-way intersection with Chimney Rock Loop Trail. Head east toward Spring Canyon.

GPS: 38.317377, -111.284908 Turn left at signed intersection with Chimney Rock Loop Trail.

GPS: 38.323979, -111.263415 Turn right/east/downstream at this signed junction with Spring Canyon.

GPS: 38.319375, -111.250505 Slot canyon on the right. Stay high on slickrock.

GPS: 38.319168, -111.250413 Narrows. The route traverses left of the narrows on a slickrock bench. You can descend the narrows, but this usually requires two steep down-climbs and skanky pool swims. Hike 5 minutes to see first drop.

GPS: 38.317192, -111.247169 Narrows end as steep-traverse trail descends back to wash.

GPS: 38.307960, -111.226836 Springs emerge from a boulder pile and run 0.25 mile downcanyon. Water quality gets better downstream.

GPS: 38.302956, -111.222897 Make sure your water reserves are full. From this point onward, there are no more water sources in this canyon.

GPS: 38.292914, -111.204238 Campsite #1, found at a sandy wash below sandstone cliffs.

GPS: 38.285374, -111.197379 Ford Fremont River; usually knee-to-thigh deep, but conditions always change. Bushwhack to UT 24. Tip: Scout water levels while dropping off your shuttle to avoid surprises.

GPS: 38.284996, -111.197081 End of route; pick up your shuttle.

CAPITOL REEF NATIONAL PARK

CAPITOL GORGE TO PLEASANT CREEK

Spend the night at a five-star campsite tucked in the broad slickrock bowls between Capitol Gorge and Pleasant Creek on this 7.7 miler in Capitol Reef National Park.

Hiking the red rocks of Capitol Reef

Forget the national parks system. Heck, forget the United States. Some of the *world's* best campsites sit in the broad slickrock bowls between Capitol Gorge and Pleasant Creek. Exploring this country requires route-finding southward from the eastern park boundary in lower Capitol Gorge, up along anonymous piñon-juniper ridgelines, and past superb viewpoints of the Waterpocket Fold's amazing geology.

There's no trail, but it's a relatively short distance with few hazards. (Expect some moderate scrambling and route-finding, and uncertain water sources. If you encounter any technical terrain, you're off-route.) After just 2 miles, break out onto naked slickrock, where you can wander almost at will, searching for flat tent sites, small ponderosa groves, and clear-water potholes. It's easy to follow the stony saddles southward. Most high points offer superb vistas along the Reef, or southeast toward the distant Henry Mountains. Unburden yourself from the trail mentality and let yourself explore. But make sure to take extra food: You won't want to leave.

Photo: Kim Phillips

Text: Steve Howe

DISTANCE: 7.7 miles

TIME REQUIRED: 2 days

DIFFICULTY: Intermediate

CONTACT: Capitol Reef National Park, (435) 425-4111; nps.gov/care

THE PAYOFF: The best sunrise camp in canyon country.

TRAILHEAD GPS: 38.233393, -111.124113

FINDING THE TRAILHEAD: From the park visitor center, drive 9 miles east on UT 24, then turn south on Notom Road. Continue 0.5 mile, then turn right. In 0.3 mile, bear left and go 0.25 mile to the trailhead on the right (west) side of road. Shuttle/end: From the park visitor center, drive 9 miles east on UT 24, then turn south on Notom Road. Continue 6.2 miles (road becomes dirt). Turn east at 5560 South/ Pleasant Creek Diversion Road. Go 1.6 miles and park at a turnoff overlooking Pleasant Creek.

WAYPOINTS & DIRECTIONS

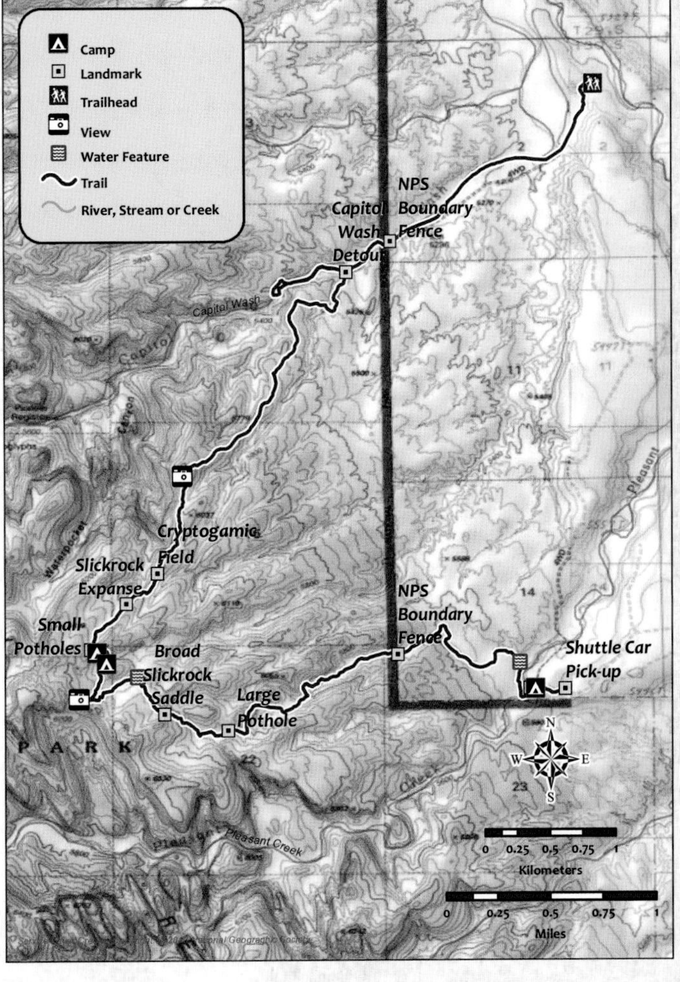

GPS: 38.233400, -111.124110 Trailhead.

GPS: 38.223065, -111.138100 Duck under NPS boundary fence.

GPS: 38.221042, -111.141147 *Side Trip:* Drop packs, then bear right (west) for a 0.8-mile out-and-back up Capitol Wash. On return, turn south, following the wash.

GPS: 38.219139, -111.144438 Follow the ridge to the southwest.

GPS: 38.201253, -111.154026 Watch your step as you navigate through the field of cryptobiotic soil.

GPS: 38.196020, -111.158160 Campsite #5. This slickrock amphitheater makes a stunning campsite overlooking the Henry Mountains.

GPS: 38.194419, -111.155382 Potholes, potential water, and ponderosas.

GPS: 38.190495, -111.151159 Descend slickrock bowls. Stay left, then right, to avoid rollover cliff bands.

GPS: 38.195838, -111.137660 NPS boundary fence. This tall fence doesn't touch the ground.

GPS: 38.195291, -111.129209 Pleasant Creek crossing. Jump across banks.

GPS: 38.193609, -111.128522 Cross Pleasant Creek.

GPS: 38.193551, -111.128143 Road and campsites sit above the bend in Pleasant Creek.

GPS: 38.193571, -111.126088 End of route. Pick up your shuttle car.

The Big Room at Carlsbad Caverns National Park, New Mexico
Photo: Ben Herndon / Tandem Stock

CARLSBAD CAVERNS NATIONAL PARK

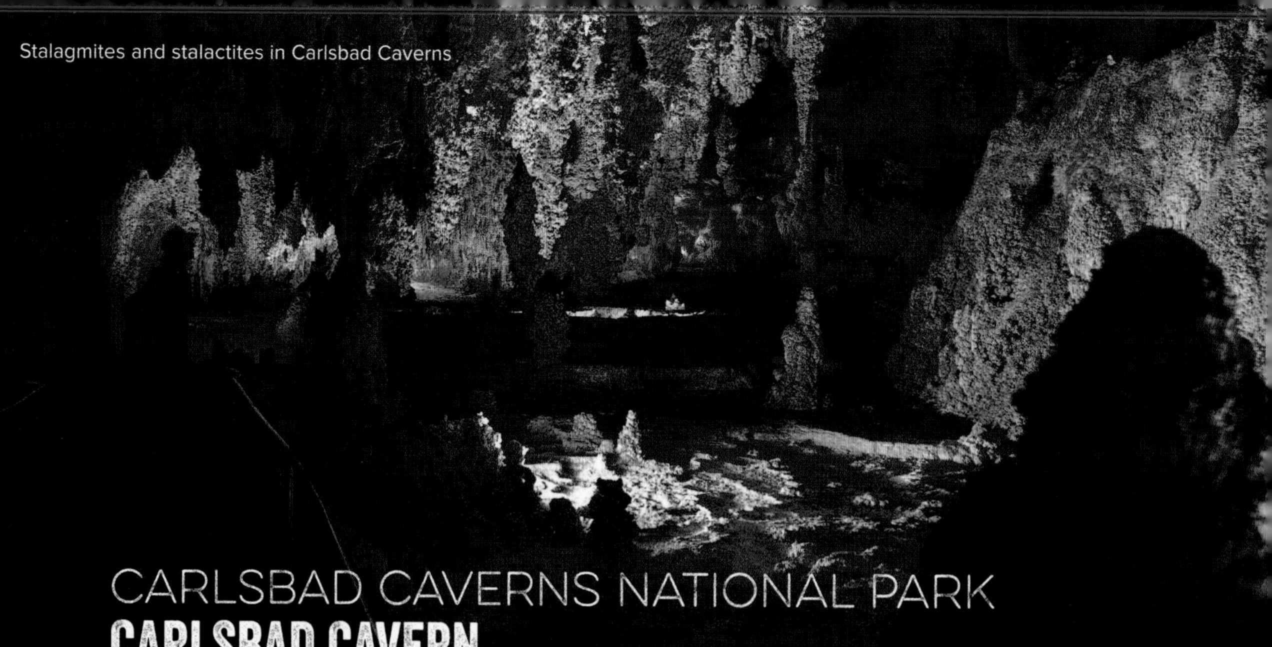
Stalagmites and stalactites in Carlsbad Caverns

CARLSBAD CAVERNS NATIONAL PARK
CARLSBAD CAVERN

Drop 750 feet underground through the bat-cave entrance of Carlsbad Cavern to see hundreds of impressive displays—stalactite-dripping nooks and crannies, massive domes, gypsum deposits, and fanciful rock formations.

The 119 known caves of Carlsbad Caverns are relics of an ancient sea—coral reefs and marine life predating the dinosaurs were transformed after death into limestone and carved by sulfuric acid. Though there are above-ground trails and other caving opportunities in Carlsbad Caverns National Park, the park's main attraction is a 2.5-mile self-guided tour through its namesake cave. From the visitors center, a wide paved path heads downhill toward the gaping natural entrance. Stop briefly for a ranger-led safety talk (and to hand over your tickets) before dropping into an amphitheater and into the mouth of the cave. The smooth trail switchbacks steeply, winding toward the literal twilight zone, the spot where natural light is no longer visible. Within the first mile, the trail drops almost 750 feet toward a 200,000-ton rock that fell to the cave floor near the entrance to a natural limestone chamber called the Big Room. At 8.2 acres, this is the largest single cave space by volume in North America.

The hike's second half is mostly flat and loops past some of the cavern's most impressive features: The Hall of Giants, a grouping of massive, totem-pole-like pillars; the Rock of Ages, which looms like a three-story tall caterpillar; and countless others. Bring a powerful flashlight or headlamp (and extra batteries) to help illuminate the features. Bring a warm layer, too: The cave's temperature stays at 56 degrees no matter how high the above-ground temperature soars.

Photo: iStockPhoto.com / David Parsons

Text: Kristy Holland

DISTANCE: 2.5 miles

TIME REQUIRED: 1 day

DIFFICULTY: Easy

CONTACT: Carlsbad Caverns National Park, (575) 785-2232; nps.gov/cave

THE PAYOFF: A mindblowing self-guided tour through America's preeminent cave.

TRAILHEAD GPS: 32.175358, -104.444146

FINDING THE TRAILHEAD: From Carlsbad, drive 20 miles south on US 180 and turn right onto Carlsbad Cavern Highway. Drive 7.3 miles to the visitor center and park headquarters.

WAYPOINTS & DIRECTIONS

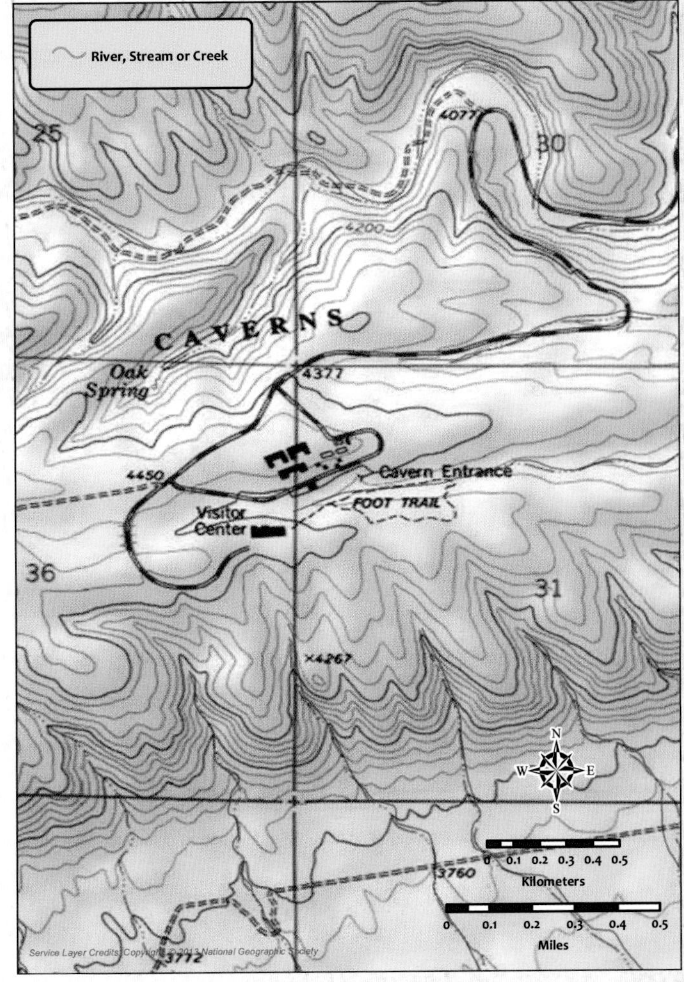

GPS: 32.175358, -104.444146 This hike begins at the ticket counter in the park's main visitor center.

GPS: 32.176593, -104.441853 Stop for the ranger-led safety talk before dipping into the canyon. This is also the last available restroom for more than 1 mile.

GPS: 32.176943, -104.440989 Skirt the amphitheater before dropping into the cave's natural entrance. The next 2.3 miles drop over 750 feet into the cavern.

GPS: 32.175458, -104.443671 An elevator shuttles hikers back and forth between the cavern and the surface. If you have knee or other medical problems that make the downhill hike unrealistic, you can still take the elevator to the Great Room for the flat, 1.2-mile loop. All hikers must take the elevator back to the surface.

GPS: 32.177084, -104.441091 Look into the mouth of the cave from the base of the amphitheater.

GPS: 32.176979, -104.440978 There are handrails along both sides of the trail starting here.

GPS: 32.176984, -104.440978 You'll smell evidence of the cave's Brazilian free-tailed bat colony here near the cave entrance.

GPS: 32.176979, -104.440984 One of dozens (maybe hundreds) of the route's notable stalagmites, this one is named Witch's Finger.

GPS: 32.176988, -104.440984 A map and directional signage greet hikers at the entrance to the Great Room. Continue straight to loop through the remaining 1.2 miles of the self-guided tour.

GPS: 32.176975, -104.440957 Enter the impressive Great Room.

GPS: 32.176975, -104.440957 This massive formation of gypsum is streaked with water-worn channels.

GPS: 32.176975, -104.440957 Toward the end of the loop, the formations get daintier and more delicate in the Chinese Theater. The walls close in for a close view.

GPS: 32.176975, -104.440962 The impressive Rock of Ages.

Inspiration point on Anacapa Island in Channel Islands National Park, California

CHANNEL ISLANDS
NATIONAL PARK

CHANNEL ISLANDS NATIONAL PARK

WATER CANYON TO EAST POINT

Venture off SoCal's coast for long beaches, hidden canyons, and abundant sea life.

Like a California Galápagos, the five islands of Channel Islands National Park both host endemic species and preserve California's coast as it was eons ago—all within spitting distance of Los Angeles. On day one, take a ferry to Water Canyon Campground, your base camp near the island's central hub.Spend three nights here for the grand tour of the island's northern shoreline, from East Point's beaches to Lobo Canyon's sandstone bluffs.

On day two, rise at dawn for the 13.5-mile out-and-back to East Point; the early start ensures a return before afternoon winds. Head east on Coastal Road, and in 1.3 miles, a 10-foot-high canopy of supersize, bonsai-like trees marks your entrance to the Torrey pine forest, one of two such groves in the world. (The other is in San Diego.) Head south on the Torrey Pines Trail, ascending sandy switchbacks to an old ranching doubletrack with views north to Skunk Point's white sands. Turn southeast, hike along a freshwater marsh, and join Coastal Road in 0.5 mile.

Pass several small beaches (which are closed March 1 to September 15 for snowy plover nesting) en route to East Point. Elephant seals and sea lions sun themselves here. Spot dolphins and whales between here and Santa Cruz Island to the east. Return by the same route—or continue to the southern shore if you want to beach camp.

On day three, begin the 14.3-mile round-trip to Lobo Canyon by heading west on the Cherry Canyon Trail for 1.9 miles above the crescent-moon-shaped Bechers Bay to Soledad Road. Continue east to Coastal Road, hike north for 0.3 mile, then turn west onto Smith Highway. In 3.1 miles, descend into Lobo Canyon. Knobby sandstone formations protrude above 100-to-300-foot-high walls with pygmy mammoth fossils embedded in them. Keep an eye out for tiny Pacific tree frogs, a keystone species that anchors the ecosystem by providing a critical food source.

Lobo Canyon broadens where the creek spills into a secluded cove. Descend to the small beach, which thumps with surf. Hike 0.6 mile west along the shoreline and return along Cow Canyon's eastern rim.

Photo: Chuck Graham

Text: Chuck Graham

DISTANCE: 13.5 miles

TIME REQUIRED: 3 days

DIFFICULTY: Intermediate

CONTACT: Channel Islands National Park, (805) 658-5730; nps.gov/chis

THE PAYOFF: Days of thumping surf, rare birds, seals, and empty beaches.

TRAILHEAD GPS: 33.993182, -120.044172

FINDING THE TRAILHEAD: From Ventura Harbor on Spinnaker Drive, catch the Island Packers boat to Santa Rosa Island. (805) 642-1393; islandpackers.com

WAYPOINTS & DIRECTIONS

GPS: 33.993182, -120.044172 From the campground at Water Canyon, take the old cattle road to the right and south toward the Torrey pine forest.

GPS: 33.993105, -120.041022 Descend into Water Canyon and cross over the creek, ascending on the other side.

GPS: 33.992406, -120.040693 Turn left at the gate and the Y fork.

GPS: 33.985464, -120.026420 After 1.3 miles, you'll reach the Torrey Pines trailhead. Turn right and ascend up switchbacks through the forest.

GPS: 33.982182, -120.025615 At trail fork, take singletrack a very short distance to an old cattle road and go left.

GPS: 33.980022, -120.013496 Arrive at T junction and go right on a ranch road to head south.

GPS: 33.976921, -120.007556 At the Old Ranch Pasture sign, go straight and continue south.

GPS: 33.992018, -120.053366 Head west on Cherry Canyon Trail for 1.9 miles to Soledad Road.

GPS: 34.000675, -120.059150 Continue to Coastal Road, then hike north for 0.3 mile.

GPS: 34.007173, -120.051187 Turn left (west) onto Smith Highway.

GPS: 34.004242, -120.089702 Descend into the gorge.

GPS: 34.002715, -120.089202 Trail swings to the right. Look for volcanic rock formations and views into the windswept gorge.

GPS: 34.003130, -120.091103 Follow the Lobo Canyon Trail. The picnic area is dominated by poisonous datura plants, sacred to Chumash Indians. Oaks line southern views during the descent into the canyon. *(continued)*

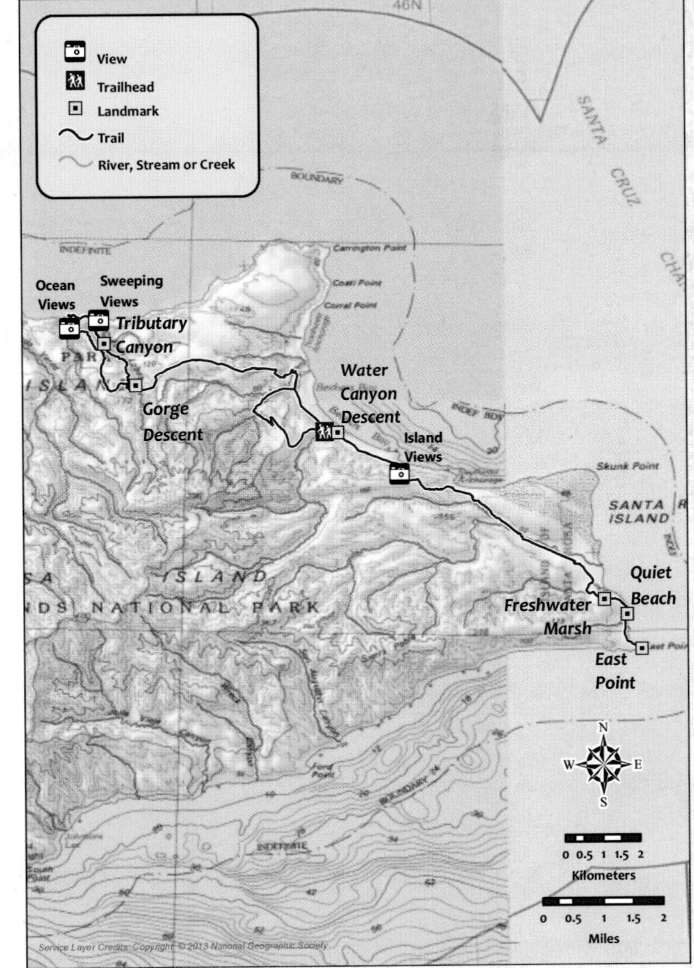

GPS: 34.013989, -120.097044 Here, the trail intersects with tributary canyon. ***Side Trip:*** Veer right into the canyon to explore the area a bit more.

GPS: 34.014679, -120.094606 Within Lobo Canyon are a few small side canyons. Lobo dead-ends in a cave surrounded by huge volcanic boulders sprouting plants. Backtrack to previous waypoint and turn right.

GPS: 34.019284, -120.098336 Continue straight. Optional: Turn right to reach the shoreline, a prime lunch spot with sweeping views.

GPS: 34.020498, -120.105483 Turn left and head south.

GPS: 34.017462, -120.105175 Hike south up a natural rock stairway. When you reach the top, look back at the ocean for prime views.

GPS: 34.016507, -120.100996 Trail intersects with doubletrack. Turn right (south), keeping Lobo Canyon slightly to your left. Continue back to the Lobo Canyon turnoff to close the loop; retrace your route to the trailhead.

RANGER PROFILE

MERRILL McCAULEY

The Helper

Channel Islands National Park, California

"My kid can't wait to go back out there all the time to see 'Merrill bear.'"
–Hillary Young, *Backpacker* reader

Want to know where the fish are? Curious what kind of flower that is? Strike up a conversation with a ranger like Merrill McCauley and you'll probably get more than you asked for. "Everyone is on vacation doing backcountry trips, and they're really making lasting memories," says McCauley, a protection (law enforcement) ranger. "So when you're able to teach them about the wildlife we have here and you're really friendly, and they say, 'Would you like to set up your tent next to mine and have dinner and have a chat?'—you're kind of a lasting memory for their visit to the park."

FAVORITE SPOT: Scorpion Anchorage

If emerald green water, frolicking seals, and yawning sea caves sound like a day well spent, jump in a kayak and paddle the shore between Scorpion Rock and Cavern Point (about a 2-mile trip). "The best time to go is early in the morning when the winds are calm," McCauley says. "You can also snorkel through a glorious kelp forest. They call it the Galápagos of North America."

CAMPING: Scorpion Ranch Campground ($15 per night)

INFO: nps.gov/chis

HIKE SMARTER
5 WAYS TO CLIMB HIGHER

Learn how to acclimate to higher elevation, descend safely, use crampons, self-belay, and layer smart.

1. ACCLIMATE WISELY Traveling from low to high elevation? Build in an extra day or two and allow your body to adjust, moderate your effort the first couple days, and try to avoid driving directly to trailheads above 10,000 feet (instead plan a day hike at a lower elevation). Stay hydrated (air is dry up high); avoid alcohol. Hike high, sleep low. Camp each day below the highest elevation you've reached. Avoid ascending more than 2,000 feet total per day. If symptoms of altitude sickness develop (persistent headache, loss of appetite, fatigue, loss of coordination), stop ascending. Go down if they don't improve within 24 hours.

2. DESCEND SAFELY Made it to the top? Congratulations. Now don't ruin your trip on the way down. Keep your knees slightly bent as your transfer weight to the downhill leg, absorbing impact with your muscles instead of your joints. Align your foot, knee, and hip on big downward steps. This helps prevent rolling an ankle and takes some strain off your muscles. Use your trekking poles like crutches when stepping off huge ledges. Plant them in front of you, on either side of where you want to land, and lower yourself in a controlled way using the poles for support. Glissading? Remove your crampons. If you tumble with spikes on, they can cut you, and catching a point can spin you out of control.

3 USE CRAMPONS CORRECTLY These spikes are your ticket to safely traversing steep snow and ice. But there's a learning curve: Flex your ankle with each step, so your foot is flat against the slope, bringing all points in contact with the ground. Don't move one foot until the other one (and your ice ax) are secure.

4. LEARN TO SELF-BELAY Walking unroped on steep snow? Use your ice ax to prevent a slide. With feet secure, plant the spike and shaft (adze forward) at least 6 inches deep. Keep your uphill hand on the ax head as you step. Repeat. If you slip, keep one hand on the ax head and grab the shaft with the other. Your weight should pull against the buried shaft.

5. LAYER SMART On alpine starts, it's tempting to bundle up against the chill. Start cold; you'll warm up fast going uphill and won't overheat.

Photo: Kim Phillips

A boardwalk in Congaree National Park, South Carolina
Photo: Paul Marcellini / Tandem Stock

CONGAREE
NATIONAL
PARK

CONGAREE NATIONAL PARK

KINGSNAKE TRAIL

Explore the country's last old-growth, lowland forest on an easy weekend in Congaree's flat, wildlife-packed terrain.

Congaree's diverse biosphere is the result of year-round overflowing of the Wateree and Congaree Rivers, which carry nutrients through the park's floodplain. Those nutrients provide a foundation for an astonishing display of muck-loving wildlife—including alligators, which hunt in black pools flanked by mossy cedar knees.

See them on a 10.1-mile overnighter that launches from the South Cedar Creek Canoe Launch, 6 miles east of the visitor center. Follow the Cedar Creek Trail across a wooden bridge over ink-black water. At 1.4 miles, turn right onto the Kingsnake Trail. Look for white-tailed deer and wild hogs flashing through the underbrush (and bobcats, opossums, coyotes, and raccoons at night). Passing 140-foot-tall cherry-bark oak trees, cross a bridge over murky waters to a large tupelo-cypress slough (think: Yoda's swamp on Dagobah in Star Wars). Trace the mud banks of Cedar Creek and turn right onto the Oakridge Trail at 3.6 miles. Cross the still creek on a footbridge and take an immediate right onto the yellow-blazed Weston Lake Loop Trail. At 4.5 miles, look left through a rare break in the canopy to see 0.2-mile-long Weston Lake, where kingfishers and herons hunt 49 fish species and 19 amphibian species amid boot-swallowing mud. No swimming: The lake is home to alligators, venomous snakes, and snapping turtles. Turn left onto a low boardwalk at 4.7 miles, and go 0.2 mile before turning left onto the wide Sims Trail. Hike 0.6 mile through young sassafras and beech forest bordered by cardinal flowers, Virginia dayflowers, and blue lobelia (blooms begin in June). Cross the bridge over Cedar Creek and make camp on a flat, open patch. (Fires are permitted).

The next day, return to the trail and turn right onto the Weston Lake Loop Trail. Walk 1.1 miles along the creek and look for river otters slipping from bankside dens into the dark water. Cross a bridge at 6.6 miles and turn right onto the Oakridge Trail, and then quickly turn left onto the Kingsnake Trail. Retrace your steps 3.6 miles under swaying drapes of Spanish moss to the trailhead.

Photo: iStockPhoto.com / JamesKarner

Text: Peter Rives

DISTANCE: 10.1 miles

TIME REQUIRED: 2 days

DIFFICULTY: Intermediate

CONTACT: Congaree National Park, (803) 776-4396; nps.gov/cong

THE PAYOFF: Reptile, otter, beaver, and bird sightings galore.

TRAILHEAD GPS: 33.819933, -80.787667

FINDING THE TRAILHEAD: From Columbia, take SC 48/Bluff Road east for 19 miles. Turn right onto South Cedar Creek Road and follow it 2 miles to the trailhead.

WAYPOINTS & DIRECTIONS

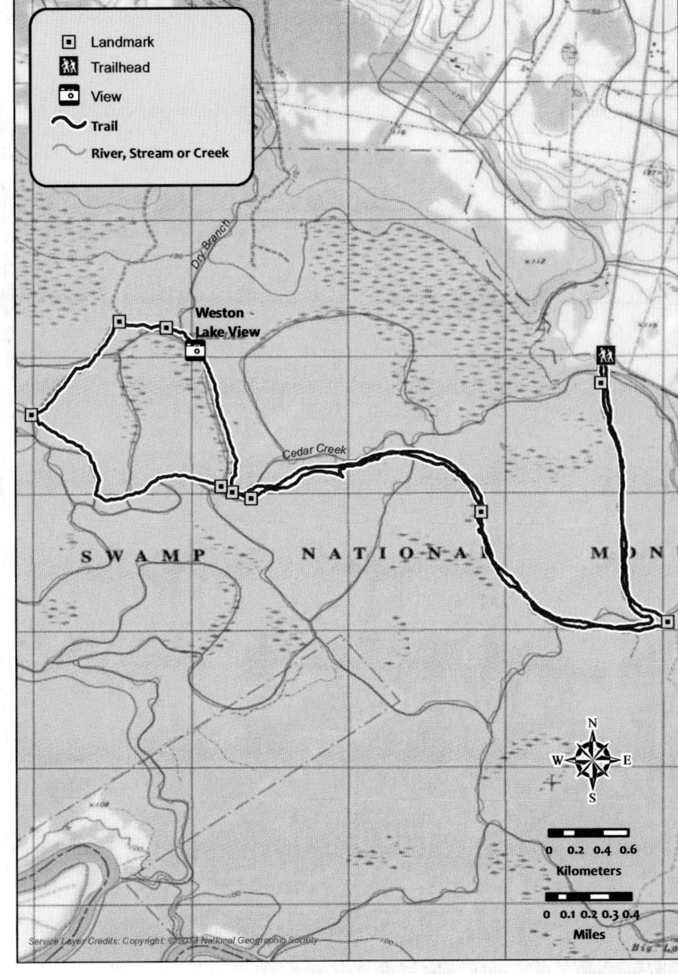

GPS: 33.819933, -80.787667 Set out on a 10.1-mile overnighter from the South Cedar Creek Canoe Launch, 6 miles east of the visitor center.

GPS: 33.818150, -80.788017 Follow the Cedar Creek Trail across a wooden bridge over ink-black water. Beneath a dense canopy, notice slimy cypress knees punctuating mirrored pools.

GPS: 33.802383, -80.783467 At 1.4 miles, turn right onto the Kingsnake Trail.

GPS: 33.809676, -80.796247 Passing 140-foot-tall cherrybark oak trees, cross a bridge over murky waters to a large tupelo-cypress slough

GPS: 33.810650, -80.812117 Trace the mud banks of Cedar Creek and turn right onto the Oakridge Trail at 3.6 miles.

GPS: 33.811050, -80.813417 Cross the still creek on a footbridge and take an immediate right onto the yellow-blazed Weston Lake Loop Trail.

GPS: 33.820391, -80.815902 At 4.5 miles, look left through a rare break in the canopy to see tiny Weston Lake, where kingfishers and herons hunt fish and amphibians amid boot-swallowing mud.

GPS: 33.821900, -80.817917 Turn left onto a low boardwalk at 4.7 miles.

GPS: 33.822333, -80.821083 Go 0.2 mile before turning left onto the wide Sims Trail.

GPS: 33.811441, -80.814185 Camp here for the night. The next day, return to the trail and turn right onto the Weston Lake Loop Trail. Cross a bridge at 6.6 miles and turn right onto the Oakridge Trail, and then quickly turn left onto the Kingsnake Trail.

Wizard Island, Crater Lake National Park, Oregon
Photo: iStockPhoto.com / bpperry

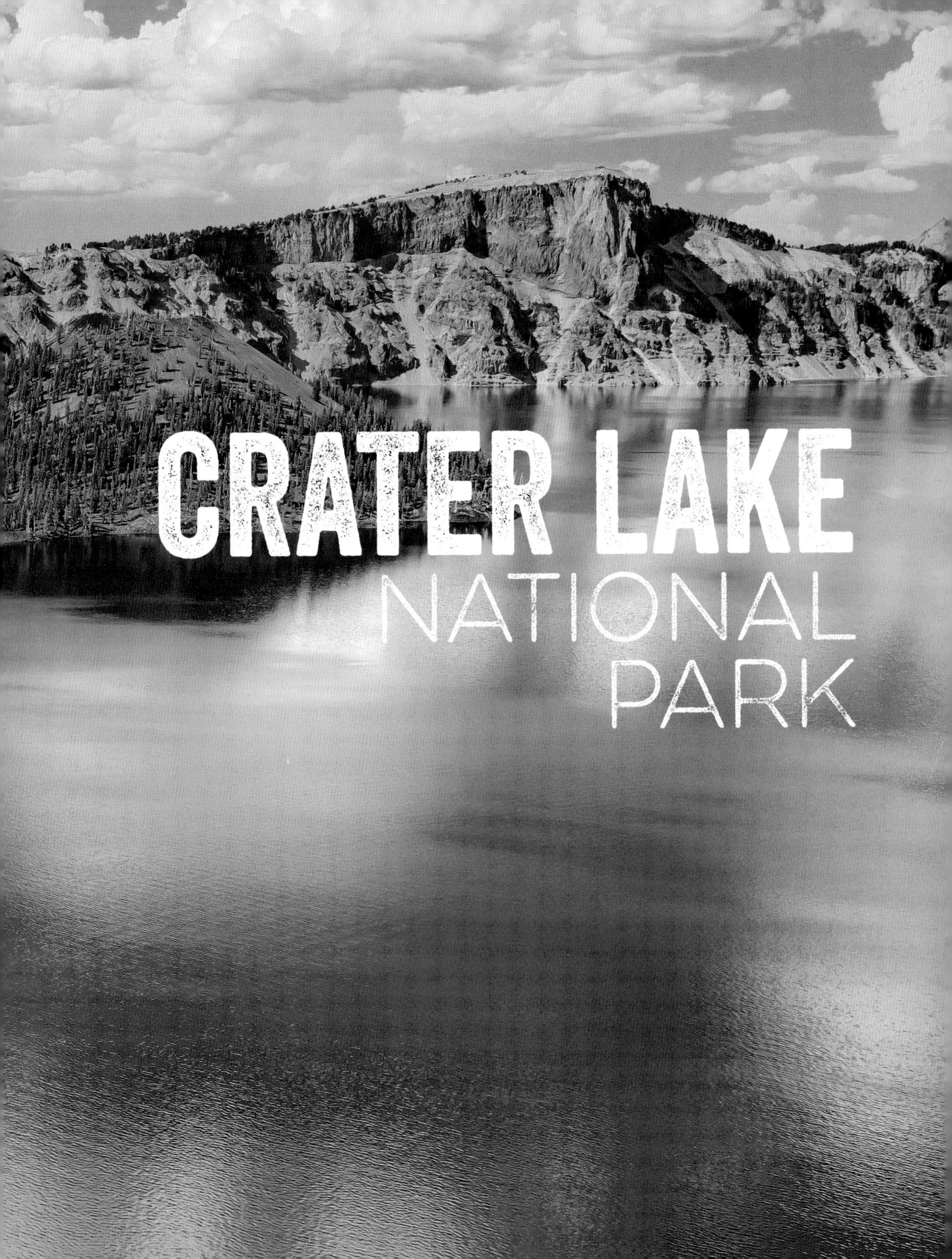
CRATER LAKE
NATIONAL
PARK

Mount Scott

Photo: iStockPhoto.com / Samson1976

CRATER LAKE NATIONAL PARK

MOUNT SCOTT

Travel into the fiery past of Mount Mazama on this 5.2-mile out-and-back to the park's highest peak, where sprawling views of the deepest lake in the United States await.

At 8,929 feet, Mount Scott is Crater Lake's highest point—and perhaps the best place to see the collapsed volcano of Mount Mazama cupping one of the clearest lakes in the world like a mirror to the sky. From the trailhead parking lot, begin hiking on well-marked trail that begins with heavy log signage. The first 0.25 mile winds up broken pumice with broad views of Mount Scott's north face. About 1 mile down the trail, breaks in the hemlocks and whitebark pines offer views of Mounts McLoughlin and (on the clearest days) Shasta, 160 miles to the south. Continue past mixed pumice and forest before beginning to switchback up the peak's north face; here, Mount Thielsen, an old volcanic neck, dominates the north horizon. You'll hit the saddle to see western vistas of Crater Lake and Wizard Island, the exposed, spiky relic of Mount Mazama's mighty lava flows.

The final summit ridge slopes upward for a gentle 0.2 mile to a fire lookout overlooking the Klamath Lake basin (Oregon's largest freshwater lake) and the surrounding high Cascade Mountains. Atop, you'll see Crater Lake, a solitary blue caldera formed 7,700 years ago by an eruption 42 times stronger than that of Mount St. Helens in 1980. Brave the wind and admire Crater Lake at a lunch spot beyond the fire lookout before turning back to retrace your steps.

Text: Melissa Stolazs

DISTANCE: 5.2 miles

TIME REQUIRED: 1 day

DIFFICULTY: Intermediate

CONTACT: Crater Lake National Park, (541) 594-3000; nps.gov/crla

THE PAYOFF: Big views of Crater Lake on the park's highest peak.

TRAILHEAD GPS: 42.929440, -122.029297

FINDING THE TRAILHEAD: From Eugene, take I-5 south to Roseburg; turn east onto OR 138, and follow 165 miles to the park's north entrance. Go left at Rim Drive to head east around the lake. After 9 miles, park at the Mount Scott trailhead.

WAYPOINTS & DIRECTIONS

GPS: 42.929119, -122.030701
From parking lot, begin hiking on well-marked trail.

GPS: 42.929440, -122.029297
Pass large log sign marking the trail.

GPS: 42.919609, -122.028900
Break for views of Mounts McLoughlin and Shasta to the south.

GPS: 42.917519, -122.017303 Begin substantial switchbacks as the trail climbs.

GPS: 42.919819, -122.020302 Stop here for majestic views of Crater Lake

GPS: 42.920311, -122.018600 Switchbacks continue as Mount Thielsen, an old volcanic neck, dominates the northern horizon.

GPS: 42.921650, -122.016899 Hit saddle; look to the west for vistas of Crater Lake and Wizard Island.

GPS: 42.922920, -122.016296 Arrive at craggy summit of Mount Scott (8,929 feet); continue past fire-lookout tower for lunch spots; retrace your path to the car.

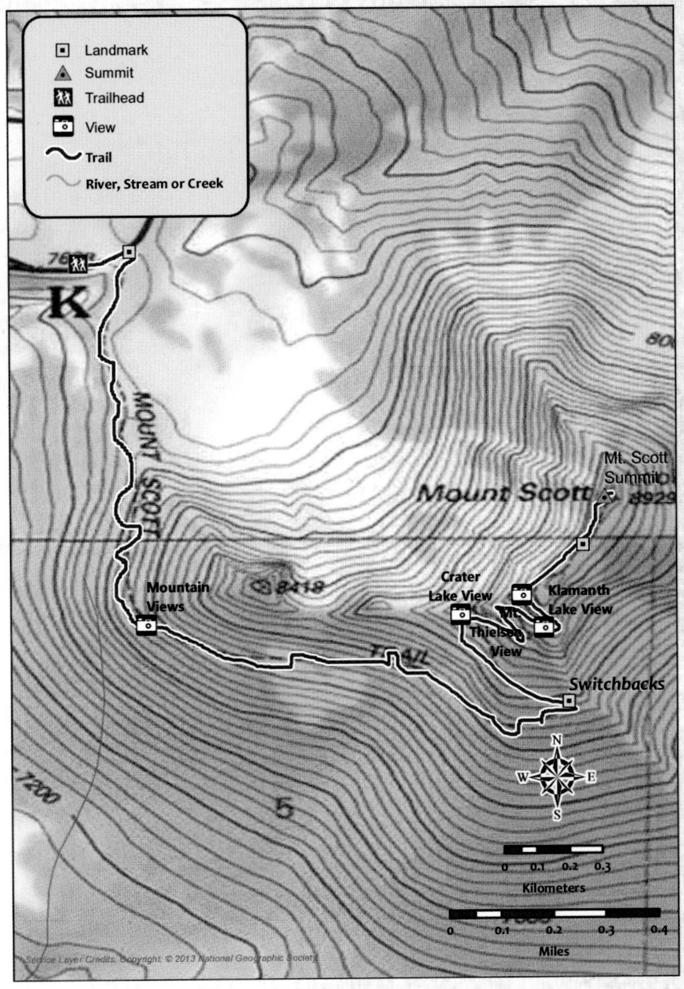

CRATER LAKE NATIONAL PARK
WINTER CIRCUMNAVIGATION

Circle Crater Lake in serenity and grandeur on snowshoes or skis.

Don't let winter in Crater Lake scare you off. Sure, the 183,224-acre national park receives 44 feet of snow annually. But all that powder—along with a sturdy pair of snowshoes or skis and some avalanche awareness—is your backstage pass to a Southern Cascades that few hikers ever see. The fourth season at Crater Lake redefines solitude, and locals say the area's trophy trip, a 33-mile circumnavigation of the lake, is the best multiday loop in the Pacific Northwest.

Crank it out clockwise. You'll cross open meadows teeming with pine martens, wind through hemlock forests draped in ice, and see the lake from every possible angle. (Keep a safe distance from overhanging snow cornices, draping the caldera's rim like frosting on a surrealist cake.) You can complete it in three moderately strenuous days, but pack an extra day's food and fuel, just in case. Leave your car at Rim Village, your last chance to down a hot bowl of soup and use a sheltered loo. Then follow the gently graded Hemlock Trail west until it hooks up with an unplowed section of Rim Road. Continue west for 3.8 miles to Watchman Overlook, the turnaround point for day-trippers. Looking south across the crater and the startlingly blue lake, you'll see the white pyramids of Mount McLoughlin, Union Peak, and, on the clearest days, California's 14,162-foot Mount Shasta.

The last time the 1,943-foot-deep lake froze completely over was in 1949. It stores a large amount of summer's heat, while windy surface conditions and relatively mild air temperatures keep the surface from icing. From Watchman, turn north and head down a

Photo: iStockPhoto.com / Somchaij

Text: Nancy Prichard Bouchard

DISTANCE: 33 miles

TIME REQUIRED: 3–4 days

DIFFICULTY: Expert

CONTACT: Crater Lake National Park, (541) 594-3000; nps.gov/crla

THE PAYOFF: Solitude, Crater Lake's impossible blue against a field of endless white, and the Southern Cascades' trophy trip.

TRAILHEAD GPS: 42.911131, -122.146950

FINDING THE TRAILHEAD: From Medford, take OR 62 north and west 65 miles to the park's south entrance at Munson Valley Road.

WAYPOINTS & DIRECTIONS

GPS: 42.913849, -122.151231 Follow Hemlock Trail west from Rim Village until it meets up with an unplowed portion of Rim Road.

GPS: 42.945837, -122.169600 Stop to take in the views of Wizard Island, which is actually a small volcano that formed within the caldera left behind by Mount Mazama.

GPS: 42.951051, -122.173204 Stay alert and watch your footing, as this section can be prone to avalanches.

GPS: 42.979535, -122.073641 Cleetwood Cove camping.

GPS: 42.914666, -122.070079 Take the left fork toward Kerr Notch to camp. Continue south and east to Sun Notch, before closing the loop in Rim Village.

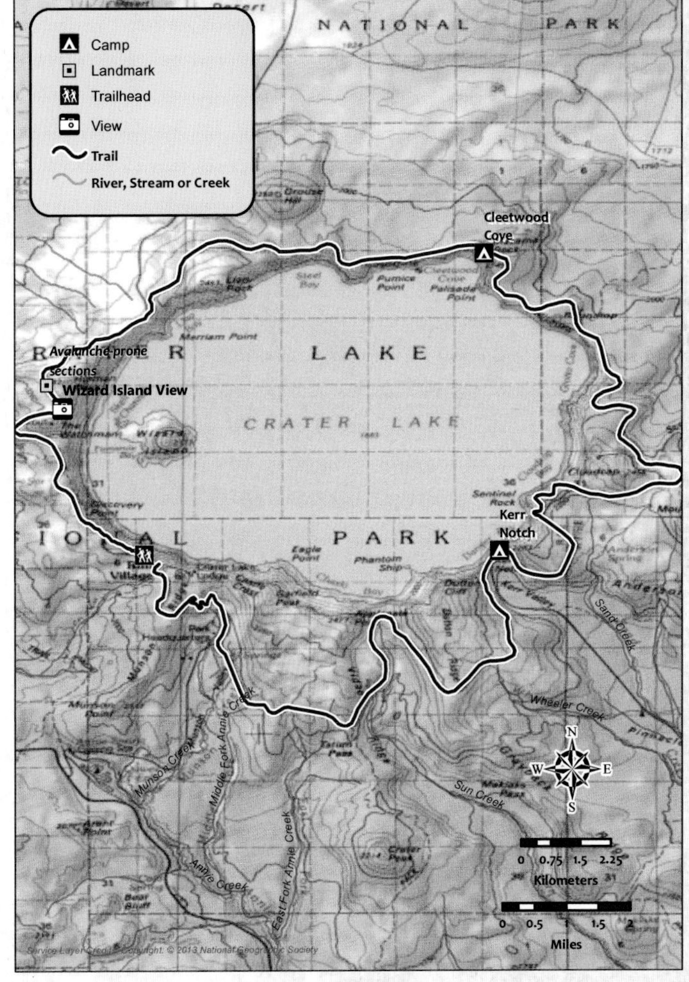

moderate slope to Wizard Island Viewpoint for a vantage as airy as any spied by a quidditch player. (Check out the 800-foot cinder cone rising from the west side of the lake.) As you continue on to North Junction, you'll pass through the first of a few avalanche-prone sections. Exercise caution and come prepared with beacons, probes, and shovels. An avy report and detailed maps of any bypasses come with your backcountry permit.

Camping choices are endless, but for the best wind protection, pick Cleetwood Cove, 10.7 miles from Rim Village.

After breakfast, head south out of Cleetwood. Fresh snowfall is common, making the surrounding pines look candy-coated. As you gain elevation, the park's high point, 8,900-foot Mount Scott comes into view. The trail zigzags along the rim, then skirts Scott's base. At 21 miles, the road splits. Take the left fork toward Kerr Notch, and plan to camp there. You'll have upper-deck views of Phantom Rock, a tiny island bathed in alpenglow. Mellower route-finding and terrain make day three a cruise. As you near Sun Notch, a popular day trip east of Rim Village, ski and snowshoe tracks signal your re-entry to civilization. After passing ice-encrusted Vidae Cliff and the turn-off to Crater Peak, you'll enjoy a 1.5-mile downhill before the last big climb back to Rim Village and another steaming bowl of soup.

Setting up a tent in cold weather
Photo: Ben Fullerton

COLD-WEATHER CAMPING

SLEEP BETTER THAN A HIBERNATING BEAR

Polar explorer Eric Larsen shares 12 secrets for keeping your core (and your gear) warm in the coldest weather.

FLATTEN YOUR SLEEPING SURFACE. As soon as you climb into your tent, use your knees to smooth out the area under your pad. "Don't wait until later to do this," Larsen says. "Once the snow melts and refreezes, it's hard to manipulate. I also create a shallow trough for myself, so I don't roll around."

BRING A CLOSED-CELL FOAM SLEEPING PAD. Even a warm bag is a cold bag without a good, insulated pad underneath it. Most air mattresses only insulate down to about 30 degrees. If you want yours for comfort, lay down a foam pad first.

PUT YOUR PARTNER'S PAD CLOSE TO YOURS. Less cold air will rise through the tent floor. Better yet, connect them with a coupling strap. Place stuffsacks and extra gear around the tent's inside perimeter to further insulate.

STASH YOUR BOOT LINERS IN YOUR BAG. Nothing hurts more than trying to ram your feet into frozen boots in the morning. Also stow electronics, batteries, fuel canisters, and anything else you don't want to freeze. (Buy a sleeping bag with a little extra length for this purpose.)

DON'T BURROW DEEP. "Moisture from your breath will get trapped in the bag," Larsen says. "Instead, cinch the draft collar and close the hood down around your mouth and nose, so you have a blowhole to breathe through."

MUNCH A MIDNIGHT SNACK. "If I wake up cold in the middle of the night, I wolf down Strawberry Clif Shot Bloks to fuel my engine," Larsen says. Other calorie-dense foods like chocolate, cheese, and nuts work well, too.

PREVENT SPILLS. Put a straw near your water bottle for no-mess drinking in the middle of the night.

PREPARE FOR MORNING FROST. On freezing nights, water vapor often condenses on the tent's inner walls, your sleeping bag, and packs, even with the door cracked. Once the ice melts, it will sop your gear. Control frost by keeping your gear covered or inside garbage bags, and by sweeping (with a tent brush) ice crystals into collectable piles before they melt.

DON'T HOLD IT. If nature calls in the middle of the night, don't procrastinate. It makes you colder in the long run, because your body has to burn calories to keep urine warm. Guys should consider using a designated pee bottle (mark it with tape or some other feature).

BUNDLE UP YOUR WATER BOTTLES. Wrap in insulated extra clothing or dedicated insulators.

HEAT UP YOUR BAG. Put a hot-water bottle in your sleeping bag at night and it'll radiate heat like a sauna stone.

Text: Kristin Hostetter

The Mesquite Sand Dunes in Death Valley National Park, Calif., Nevada
Photo: Beverly Houwing / Tandem Stock

DEATH VALLEY
NATIONAL PARK

Badwater Basin

DEATH VALLEY NATIONAL PARK

BADWATER BASIN TO GOLD VALLEY

This cross-country canyon trek in the Lower 48's largest national park goes from the lowest spot in North America to high peaks.

Hottest, lowest, driest: As befits the name, Death Valley is a land of frightening superlatives. Hike from the lowest spot on the continent to what is surely one of its least crowded on this 17-mile out-and-back. You'll trek from Badwater Basin, at 248 feet below sea level, through Sheep Canyon's towering walls to a high saddle with views of the Panamint Mountains.

From a pullout off CA 178, 29.3 miles south of CA 190, hike east over an alluvial fan (a triangle-shaped deposit of sand and rock left behind by seasonal water flows), gaining 400 feet in 1.1 miles to the mouth of the canyon. Craggy walls colored a hundred hues of brown, red, and pink shoot 600 to 1,200 feet above the canyon floor. Pass under them as you climb 1,000 feet to a fork. Bear right and continue another 1.3 miles–tacking on another 800 feet of elevation gain–to another fork. Stay left this time, veering west for the next mile. Then bear right at the most prominent fork in the canyon.

In the next 1.3 miles, the route climbs over three 30-foot waterfalls that are usually dry. Not comfortable with Class 3 scrambling (i.e., hands sometimes needed)? With some scouting, you can find user trails to the left of each waterfall. Soon, the canyon narrows to car width, then opens up to reveal Sheep Saddle, your next objective, 1 mile east. Approach the saddle by climbing big slabs of granite near its base, then scrambling over loose, steep talus, gaining 1,000 feet.

From the top of the 4,758-foot saddle, descend one mile southeast to an old prospecting road and follow it south 0.5 mile into Gold Valley, a secluded oasis of yucca and

Photo: iStockPhoto.com / Juli Scalzi

Text: MacKenzie Ryan and Roger Homrich

pickleweed surrounded by a horseshoe of rugged mountains. Wind can whip here, so camp on the lee side of one of the many sand mounds and boulders. Retrace your route back to Badwater Basin in the morning. Caution: Don't be tempted to create a loop via Willow Creek Canyon; it's impassable without climbing gear.

DISTANCE: 17 miles

TIME REQUIRED: 2 days

DIFFICULTY: Expert

CONTACT: Death Valley National Park, (760) 786-3200; nps.gov/deva

THE PAYOFF: Visit the lowest spot in North America.

TRAILHEAD GPS: 36.092387, -116.737330

FINDING THE TRAILHEAD: From Pahrump, Nevada, take NV 372 for 7.8 miles to the California border and CA 178. Go 19.2 miles to CA 127/CA 178. Turn right and go 1.7 miles to CA 178 (Badwater Road), then drive 41.2 miles to the pullout.

WAYPOINTS & DIRECTIONS

GPS: 36.092387, -116.737330
Head east from trailhead.

GPS: 36.084242, -116.723051 Enter the mouth of Sheep Canyon.

GPS: 36.082930, -116.702352 Dogleg south with the canyon.

GPS: 36.076947, -116.689581 Follow the S curve of the canyon as it winds northeast.

GPS: 36.080388, -116.674475 Go right at fork in canyon. From here, climb to Sheep Pass on loose talus and navigate around a series of 30-foot dry waterfalls.

GPS: 36.072731, -116.641357 Continue southeast.

GPS: 36.063405, -116.632381 Join Old Prospect Road, heading south.

GPS: 36.055729, -116.634060 Enter Gold Valley. At this point, turn around and retrace steps back through Sheep Canyon. (***Caution:*** Don't be tempted to create a loop via Willow Creek Canyon; it's impassable without climbing gear.)

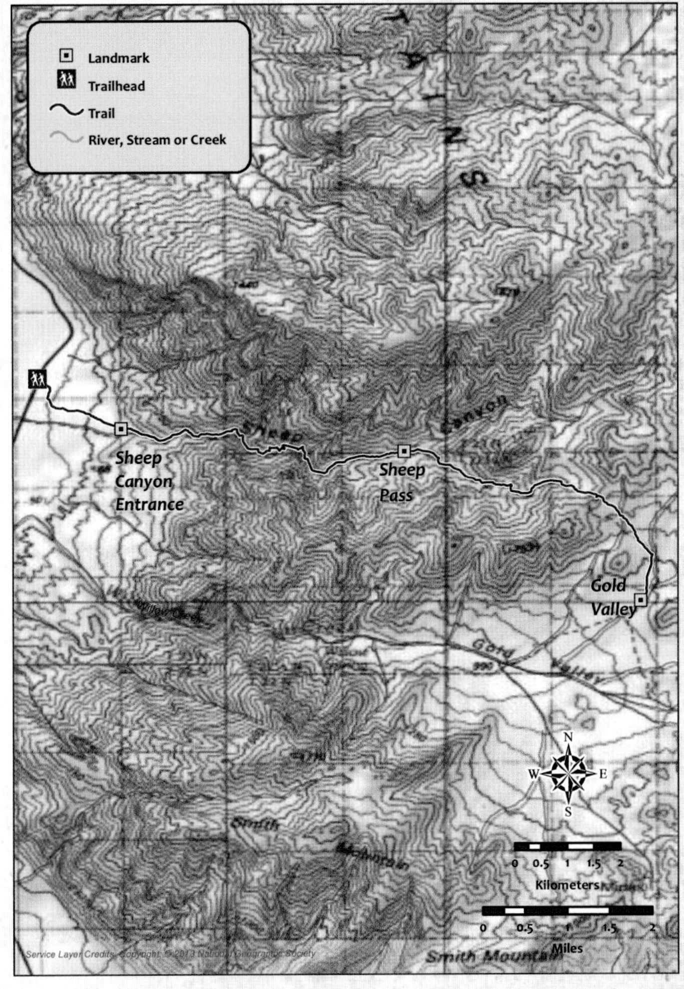

DEATH VALLEY NATIONAL PARK
EUREKA DUNES TO LAST CHANCE MOUNTAIN

This weekend getaway travels from Eureka Dunes, the highest dunes in California, to Last Chance Mountain, an 8,500-foot peak in Death Valley.

The Last Chance Mountains stretch north to south from the Nevada border into Death Valley National Park, bisecting Eureka Valley to the west and Death Valley to the east. The range's snowcapped, 7,000-foot mountains contrast remarkably against the sand, salt flats, and rugged canyons that surround them.

Get to this secluded range on a challenging weekend backpacking trip through one of California's emptiest quadrants. Hike north from S. Eureka Road for a moderate climb into the Last Chance Range. Make sure to turn around for views of the 700-foot Eureka Dunes, the highest dunes in California and some of the tallest in the United States. At mile 1.7, the route passes another viewpoint that showcases the dunes and the snowy Inyo Range. One mile later, the terrain flattens briefly between two 4,000-foot foothills, then continues north, following the canyon's wash. Keep left at the two forks in the canyon. After 6 miles, turn left onto Big Pine Road and follow it to Crater Mine. Just past the mine, hikers can set up camp off the dirt road on a flat area near the pass. Pick a spot with protection—this area can get very cold and windy.

The next day, follow the dirt road until it dead ends into the mountains. From here, you'll scramble up a steep, dirt slope to the first saddle in Last Chance Range. From the saddle, follow the ridgeline over 4 unnamed peaks to Last Chance Mountain. Route-finding will be necessary for this stretch to Last Chance Mountain—there is no trail and the terrain is extremely rugged. From the top of 8,456-foot Last Chance Mountain, savor views into the Last Chance Range, then turn around and follow the same route back to Eureka Dunes.

Maps and compass skills—in addition to a high level of fitness—are required for this route. You'll also want route-finding skills and the ability to haul in all your water. They don't call it Death Valley for nothing.

Photo: iStockPhoto.com / mandj98

Text: Roger Homrich

DISTANCE: 28.7 miles

TIME REQUIRED: 3 days

DIFFICULTY: Expert

CONTACT: Death Valley National Park, (760) 786-3200; nps.gov/deva

THE PAYOFF: California's highest dunes, extreme desert terrain.

TRAILHEAD GPS: 37.114918, -117.664433

FINDING THE TRAILHEAD: From Main Street and Line Street in Bishop, head south on N. Main Street/ US 395/US 6. In 14.6 miles, turn left at CA 168. In 2.3 miles, bear right onto Death Valley Road/Waucoba Road. In 36.4 miles, turn right onto S. Eureka Road. Go 10.7 miles to the start of this hike.

WAYPOINTS & DIRECTIONS

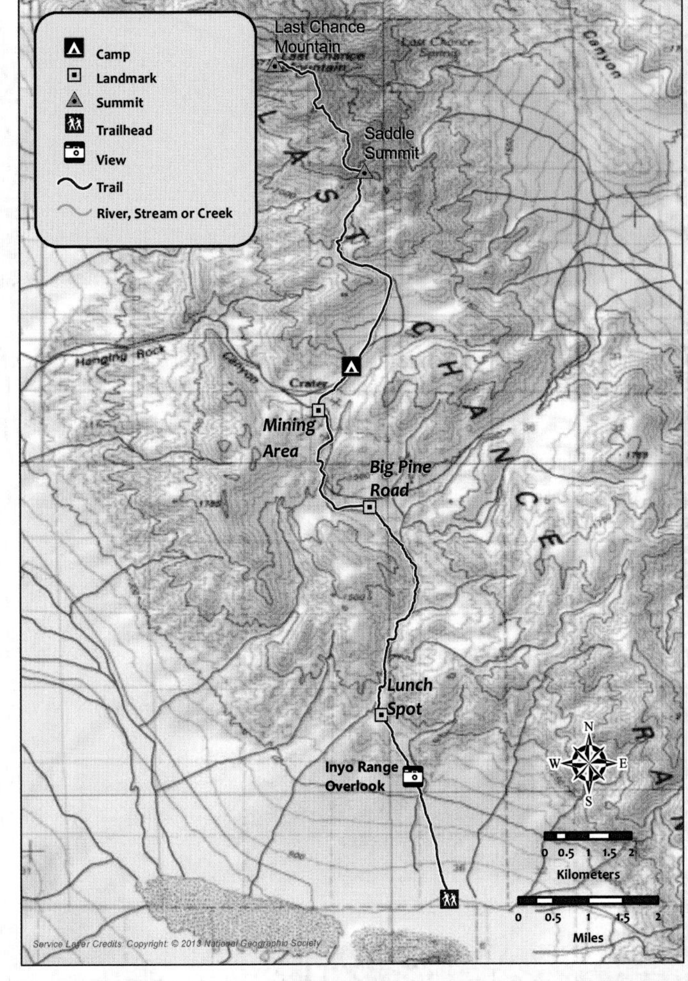

GPS: 37.114918, -117.664432 Hike north from S. Eureka Road. Make sure to turn around for views of the 700-foot Eureka Dunes

GPS: 37.139167, -117.671676 Take a moment to stop and look around at this overlook, which showcases the dunes below and the snowy Inyo Range. Continue north-northwest through the narrow valley between the foothills.

GPS: 37.151463, -117.678254 After climbing another 400 feet, rest at this flat, open area between two 4,000-foot foothills. Continue north through the canyon, following the wash. The canyon walls are a few hundred feet higher than the wash.

GPS: 37.172103, -117.671943 Bear left at an intersection between two canyon washes. Continue 0.75 mile over gravel, passing beautifully colored canyon walls before reaching another fork in the canyon.

GPS: 37.185765, -117.674844 Bear left at the second fork in the canyon. Once the canyon opens, continue northwest to Big Pine Road.

GPS: 37.192522, -117.680448 Follow Big Pine Road to the left and continue westward to Crater Mine.

GPS: 37.211720, -117.690921 After bearing left onto Big Pine Road, turn right and continue north past the mining area.

GPS: 37.220213, -117.684174 Camp off the dirt road on a flat area near the pass. Pick a spot with protection, because this area can get very cold and windy. From camp, follow the dirt road until it dead ends into the mountains. A mine shaft is at the end of the road. Route-finding will be necessary for the remaining stretch to Last Chance Mountain, there is no trail and the terrain is extremely rugged. *(continued)*

GPS: 37.258959, -117.681407 Scramble up a steep dirt slope to the first saddle in Last Chance Range. From the saddle, hike the ridgeline over four unnamed peaks to Last Chance Mountain. Head northwest to the first peak (7,853 feet). Go north-northwest to the second peak (7,978 feet). Continue northwest to the third peak (8,250 feet). Then head due north and turn east, skirting the ridgeline around the fourth peak (8,211 feet). Hike north then northwest along the ridge to the summit of Last Chance Mountain (8,456 feet).

GPS: 37.280141, -117.699808 Summit of Last Chance Mountain (8,456 feet). Savor views from the trip's high point, then turn around and follow the same route back to Eureka Dunes.

RANGER PROFILE

LAURA LYNN DELROSS

The Eye Opener

Death Valley National Park, California and Nevada

"Laura taught me that if you truly want to do something, just do it and don't look back."

—Bobby Kerr, *Backpacker* reader

Death Valley has beauty in all directions, but Laura Lynn DelRoss's favorite place to look is up. When visitors stargaze in Death Valley, she says, they always have the same reaction: "Oh no, there's a big cloud in the sky. We can't see the stars." When DelRoss, an interpretive ranger, tells them that the "cloud" is the Milky Way, the ensuing silence is her favorite sound in the park. "I've fallen in love with the ability to inspire people with their natural surroundings," she says.

FAVORITE SPOT: Mosaic Canyon

Look closely at the polished, serpentine stone curves near the entrance of this desert slot canyon. The rock contains intricate patterns of multicolored mineral fragments that juxtapose 450-million-year-old and 50-million-year-old rock. DelRoss calls the resulting Mosaic Breccia "lovely chaos." The 4-mile (round-trip) hike to a dry waterfall and back also serves up rosy-brown stone walls, winding narrows, and fun, easy canyoneering moves.

TRAILHEAD: Mosaic Canyon

INFO: nps .gov/deva

A dried up riverbed

STAND THE HEAT

Go ahead and brave sizzling temperatures, but be respectful of the dangers. Expedition-veteran Mark Jenkins shares his hard-won lessons.

1. Have a backup plan for when the waterhole you are absolutely sure has water is actually dry.

2. Bring hard candy to suck on while hiking.

3. Cotton retains moisture better than synthetics, and thus keeps you cooler (though it can limit range of motion).

4. Wear a full-brimmed hat and extra-dark sunglasses at all times. Even with the hat, you can get burned by light reflected off the ground. Use sunscreen on any exposed flesh, like your face and the backs of your hands, and reapply frequently.

5. Don't hike during the middle of the day, when temperatures reach their peak. Crawl as far back beneath a boulder or inside a cave as you can. Read a book, take a nap. Bring dark sunglasses.

6. Rely on yourself, not your guides or companions, to ensure you will have water.

7. Don't wear shorts or short sleeves. When the ambient temperature is above your body temp, more layers actually keep your body cooler. That's why you see Bedouins and other desert dwellers wrapped up.

8. Take off your boots and socks at every stop. This will keep your feet from baking and blistering. Change salty, sweaty socks frequently. (*continued*)

9. Know with certainty—absolute certainty—where your next source of water is and how long it will take to get there in severe conditions.

10. In desperation, peeing your pants is an effective method for cooling off.

11. Use a bladder with a mouthpiece rather than a bottle. You'll always drink more. Always bring a backup water bag.

12. If you're working hard in extreme heat, drink 5 quarts of water a day. Add a pinch of electrolyte mix to each quart (go easy on sweeteners; too much sugar in the heat will make you sick).

13. Plan your route to take advantage of terrain—shelves, ridges, ledges—and the arc of the sun, so you can hike in the shade as much as possible.

14. You need a pack with very good suspension to carry 20 to 30 pounds of water plus gear.

15. Hike at night. LED headlamps last for dozens of hours. (Avoid doing this in places with dangerous wildlife.)

16. Excessive heat, like excessive altitude, kills your appetite. Force yourself to eat.

17. In open country, hike from shade to shade; a half-hour moving, a half-hour resting beneath a cactus, a bush, a boulder.

18. Don't wear gaiters, they make feet sweat too much.

19. Know the symptoms of heat exhaustion and heatstroke. Heat exhaustion you can recover from; heatstroke, in a wilderness desert, could quickly be fatal. Check yourself and others at every rest stop for signs and symptoms.

Signs and Symptoms of Heat Exhaustion

Go on high alert if you see these symptoms in yourself or others. Early treatment can prevent heatstroke, which can be fatal.

- Headache
- Dizziness and lightheadedness
- Weakness

Photo: iStockPhoto.com / HABesen

- Nausea and vomiting
- Pale skin
- Profuse sweating
- Dark urine
- Increased heart rate

Signs and Symptoms of Heatstroke

This occurs when your body is no longer able to regulate its temperature. Heatstroke can cause shock, brain damage, organ failure, and death.

- Fever (temperature above 104 degrees)
- Irrational behavior
- Extreme confusion
- Hot, red skin
- Rapid, shallow breathing
- Rapid, weak pulse
- Seizures
- Unconsciousness

Treatment for Heat Exhaustion and Heat Stroke

1. With both heat exhaustion and heatstroke, your goal is to cool the victim as quickly as possible. Remove any non-cotton clothing and have the victim lie down in the coolest place available.

2. Apply cool water or wet cloths to the victim's skin. Fan the victim, and place cold compresses or ice on the neck, groin, and armpits.

3. If the victim is alert and not vomiting, give a sports drink or salted water (1 teaspoon per quart). The victim can drink about a cup every 15 minutes.

4. Seek medical attention immediately if you suspect heatstroke. Note: Victims can relapse after appearing to recover.

Denali as seen from Reflection Pond in Denali National Park, Alaska
Photo: Tim Rains / NPS Photo

DENALI NATIONAL PARK & PRESERVE

A tributary of the Toklat

DENALI NATIONAL PARK AND PRESERVE
TOKLAT VALLEY

Hike with grizzlies in this remote northern corner of Alaska's greatest park.

No matter what metric you use—size, challenge, scenic grandeur, wildlife, solitude—Denali is the park by which you'll measure all others. "Discovered" by Americans Harry Karstens and Charles Sheldon in 1906, the 6-million-acre wilderness is as raw today as it ever was, with 250 grizzlies, 100 wolves, and a caribou herd of 1,800. Backpacking here is just like the park: big and wild. Your way in is on a school bus retrofitted for hikers, but unlike your third-grade driver, the cheerful chauffeurs here will drop you anywhere along the 90-mile road. From there, it's wide-open tundra hiking, miles of braided rivers, and giant glaciers pouring off Mount McKinley. And the certain knowledge that no other place will ever make you feel so small.

The Toklat River is a virtual expressway for the park's legendary big game. In this wide-open, trailless drainage, we've watched wolves hunt snowshoe hares, dodged caribou running up river bars, and stood our ground while grizzlies bluff-charged camp. And oh, the views: When it's clear, you can't get a better look at McKinley without a bush plane or climbing guide.

Your trip starts with a ride to Ice Cream Gulch at mile 51 on the park road. Hop off the bus and bid goodbye to the tourists headed toward Wonder Lake. You're going south for 6 miles, along the east branch of the rushing Toklat River, where the Toklat wolf pack hunts

Photo: Ian Shive / Tandem Stock

Willie Karidis and Bill Velasquez

DISTANCE: 24 miles

TIME REQUIRED: 7 days

DIFFICULTY: Expert

CONTACT: Denali National Park and Preserve, (907) 683-2294; nps.gov/dena

THE PAYOFF: Track big game and get on predator patrol in the Toklat Valley.

TRAILHEAD GPS: 63.511798, -149.973276

FINDING THE TRAILHEAD: From the Denali Visitor Center, go to the park's Backcountry Information Center to obtain permits and a bear canister if needed, then purchase bus tickets at the Wilderness Access Center. Park at the Riley Creek Campground overflow parking area; take the park bus to mile 51 and get off.

WHERE ARE THE WAYPOINTS?

Denali National Park's backcountry is among the wildest places in North America, and that's exactly how the park wants to keep it: no signs, no trails, no campsites, no nothing. To help in the effort, we are not providing GPS coordinates for Denali hikes, as waypoints can lead to the establishment of social trails. Come prepared with good navigation skills, and use these maps as a planning guide. And remember, the park does not issue reservations, so be ready to hike in whatever units you get.

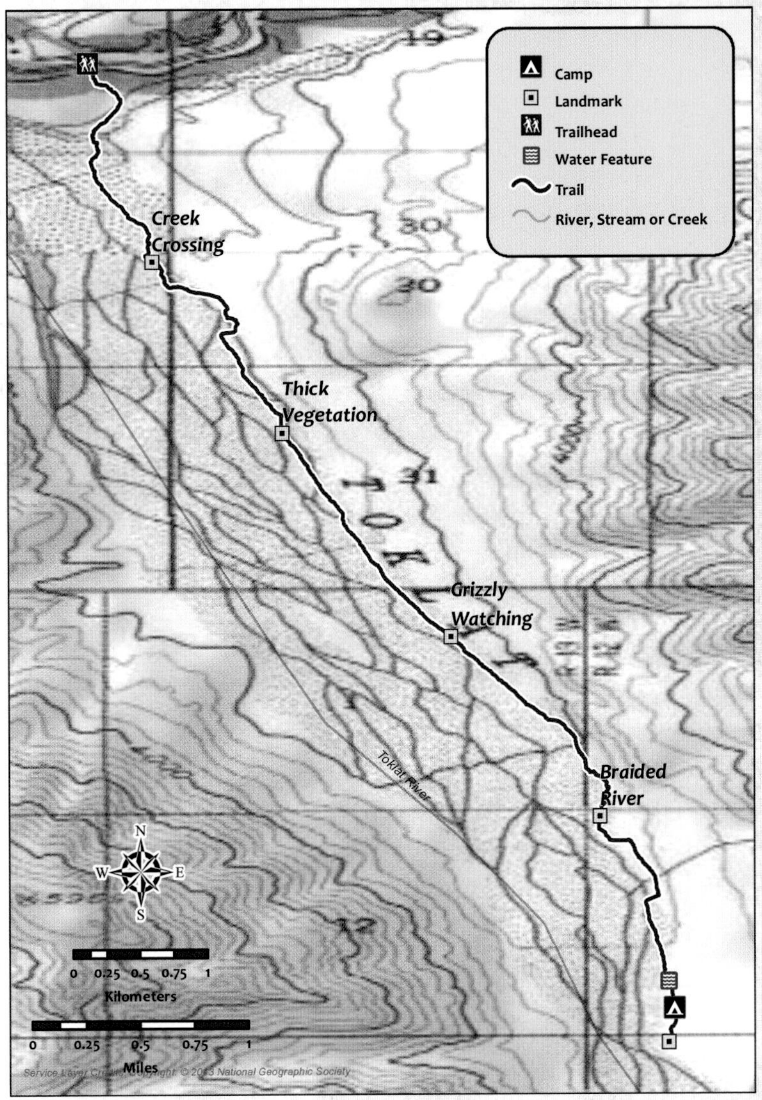

and howls from the ridgelines of their ancestral home. You'll know you've hit your first campsite when seemingly out of nowhere, a 400-foot waterfall explodes out of the glacier-carved mountains. Throw your tent down anywhere with good visibility (so you can see bears approaching), walk your food canister at least 100 yards from camp, and consider the thrilling and disconcerting fact that for the next five days, you're no longer at the top of the food chain.

The mistake that every Denali rookie makes? Overestimating travel speed. Squishy tundra and bushwhacking make for slow going, but the solution is easy: Allow an hour per mile, adjust your goals accordingly, and build in down days for exploring. Establish base camp on day two, then follow the river south for 2 miles to the toe of an unnamed glacier that pours off the northern spine of the Alaska Range in alternating strips of ice and moraine. One-tenth of Denali is covered in glaciers; spend a few hours exploring the clear blue crevasses and strange, worm-like insects called springtails that thrive on the porous ice. Back at camp, pad around the tundra looking for a kettle pond—shallow pools left in the wake of receding glaciers—to soak in under the midnight sun.

Break camp early the next morning and cross the Toklat (facing upstream and side-stepping, but never looking directly at the dizzying current). Follow the west bank north for 4 miles to an unnamed pass just south of Divide Mountain. Climb the 4,000-foot pass, which opens onto a panorama of white-capped mountains and is a great place to shoot sunrise and sunset pics of alpenglow on the distant peaks. Descend to the west branch of the Toklat and turn south, hugging the east bank for another 0.5 mile until you come to the first side canyon to your left. Set up camp and digest dinner with a 1.25-mile walk to the back of the steep-walled canyon, where a lush green bowl attracts Dall sheep ewes and their cotton white lambs.

On day four, pack your gear, but leave it in camp while you hike three miles south up the Toklat's meandering west branch, glassing the ridgelines for wolves hunting caribou and sheep. Backtrack to your gear, and hike north two miles to the Toklat bridge at the park road. Cross the bridge and hug the northeast bank for 1.5 miles north to the second of two rock-filled draws. Turn east, following the draw to a grassy divide. Set up camp in the forget-me-nots, and scramble to views of the East Fork Valley, multicolored Mount Sheldon, and, on a clear evening, the behemoth of all North American mountains, 20,320-foot Mount McKinley. Trace an unnamed ridge east, then south up Polychrome Mountain. Make camp in a grassy divide below the summit and scout a line up 4,961-foot Cabin Peak, the next day's climb.

The hike to Cabin's summit transitions from fragile mountain heather to jagged rock. Watch for moose down low, marmots sunning themselves up high, and arctic ground squirrels scurrying away at the top. The views from the summit include the lush Wyoming Hills and the pastel Polychrome Mountain. Return to camp. The next morning, hike back to the road, flag down the bus, and head out.

Note: There is no established trail system in Denali's backcountry. Map and compass skills are required

Hiking through dwarf fireweed

DENALI NATIONAL PARK AND PRESERVE

MOUNT EIELSON LOOP

Circle Mount Eielson, dash across scenic creek crossings, and ogle jaw-dropping views of the Alaska Range.

Located at the foot of the Alaska Range in Denali National Park and Preserve, this 14.6-mile route circles 5,802-foot Mount Eielson and offers incredible views of glacier-capped mountains—and on clear days, Mount Denali. Pick up your backcountry permit and a bus pass, then park your car at the Riley Creek Campground overflow lot. Take the Camper Bus to a pull-out on Grassy Pass, located 2.2 miles west of Eielson Visitor Center.

From Grassy Pass, pick up the social trail that cuts across the lush hillside and leads to a rock-strewn chute (make noise: black and grizzly bears live in the park). Descend this steep gully, then hike south-southwest across an expansive gravel bar, crossing the braided channels of the Thorofare River (vibrant wildflowers cover the ground). Near mile 2, continue past the Glacier Creek drainage and ascend a small ridge with big views of Mounts Mather, Deception, and Brooks. Next, bushwhack southeast back to the Glacier

Photo: Kim Phillips

Text: Kim Phillips

Creek drainage and follow the creek south to the Intermittent Creek drainage (mile 5.1). From here, it's a 1.5-mile climb to a sweet campsite perched above the valley.

On day two, continue the climb up the Intermittent Creek drainage to a broad saddle located between Intermittent Creek and Wolverine Creek. Drop your pack for a short, 0.6-mile side trip to a nearby ridgetop (clear days reveal Mount Denali to the southwest). Soak up the spectacular views, then backtrack to the saddle and follow animal trails that lead to the headwaters of Contact Creek. Descend this mile-long drainage to the Thorofare River gravel bar, and head north for the return trip to Eielson Visitor Center.

The next 4-mile stretch feature numerous stream crossings. Use caution when picking your route through the countless channels (the water temperature is roughly 36 degrees F). At mile 13.6, bear ri ght into the Gorge Creek drainage and head northeast for 0.3 mile to a small cairn marking an overgrown trail to the visitor center. Yell "Hey, bear" as you climb through the tall bushes flanking both sides of the path. The route ends at Eielson Visitor Center; catch a shuttle bus back to the Riley Creek parking area.

Note: There is no established trail system in Denali's backcountry. Map and compass skills are required.

DISTANCE: 14.6 miles

TIME REQUIRED: 2–4 days

DIFFICULTY: Strenuous

CONTACT: Denali National Park and Preserve, (907) 683-2294; nps.gov/dena

THE PAYOFF: Alaska Range views, ample opportunities to spot bears, caribou, moose, and wolves.

TRAILHEAD GPS: 63.426235, -150.374439

FINDING THE TRAILHEAD: Go to the park's Backcountry Information Center to obtain permits and a bear canister if needed, then purchase bus tickets at the Wilderness Access Center. Park at the Riley Creek Campground overflow parking area; take the Camper Bus to Grassy Pass, a pull-out located 2.2 miles west of the Eielson visitor center.

WHERE ARE THE WAYPOINTS?

Denali National Park's backcountry is among the wildest places in North America, and that's exactly how the park wants to keep it: no signs, no trails, no campsites, no nothing. To help in the effort, we are not providing GPS coordinates for Denali hikes, as waypoints can lead to the establishment of social trails. Come prepared with good navigation skills, and use these maps as a planning guide. And remember, the park does not issue reservations, so be ready to hike in whatever units you get.

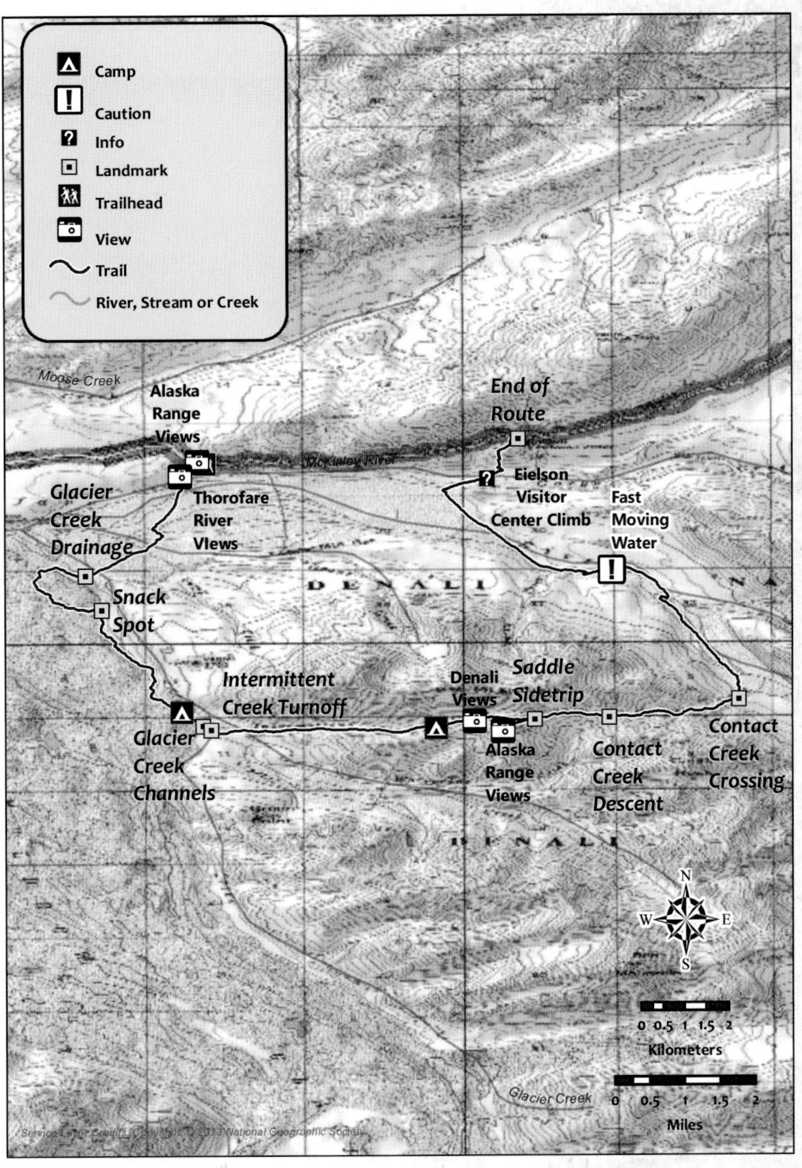

Dall sheep

DENALI NATIONAL PARK AND PRESERVE

SAVAGE RIVER LOOP

On a tight travel schedule or not ready to go off trail? Sample Denali on a rugged 3.8-mile loop to a rocky playground of Dall sheep and panoramas of North America's tallest peak.

Denali is a park of extremes—the highest peaks, the biggest, baddest wildlife, endless tundra. But nearly anyone can get a taste of it on the easy Savage River Loop. (The first 0.5 mile is even wheelchair accessible.) From the parking lot, head north on the main trail. After about 0.2 mile, turn right onto unmaintained trail. Begin a steady climb and look for grouse rustling the surrounding brush. Hike past jagged rocks as views of the braided Savage River Valley and (on sunny days) Mount Denali emerge. Traverse granite rock outcroppings, but keep a watchful eye (and ear) for rockslides. Once you arrive at a saddle, break for a snack to watch arctic ground squirrels scurry across trail. Extra caution: Bears seek shelter here on windy days, so make noise well before your arrival and carry bear spray.

Next, 0.5 mile later, listen for marmots whistling across a postcard-pretty valley with views of big peaks. Veer right at a junction just beyond to continue loop. Descend the ridge through low brush, following the trail to river. Turn left to hike alongside the roaring, chocolate-milk Savage River. Cross a bridge and continue up the hillside on rough trail. Just beyond the bridge, look for bright white Dall sheep grazing on the hillsides. Pass a riverside picnic area, a popular hangout for willow ptarmigan; continue on the maintained trail to parking lot.

Photo: iStockPhoto.com / RichardSeeley

DISTANCE: 3.8 miles

TIME REQUIRED: 1 day

DIFFICULTY: Easy

CONTACT: Denali National Park and Preserve, (907) 683-2294; nps.gov/dena

THE PAYOFF: Denali views and Dall sheep on a low-commitment trail.

TRAILHEAD GPS: 63.739162, -149.291138

FINDING THE TRAILHEAD: From Fairbanks, take AK 3 south for 124.6 miles to the park entrance, on the right. Follow signs to Savage River. Pass the visitor center, stay right at the roundabout, and go 14.7 miles to the parking lot on the right.

WAYPOINTS & DIRECTIONS

GPS coordinates are included for this Denali hike because it's on a trail.

GPS: 63.739162, -149.291138 From parking lot, head north on main trail.

GPS: 63.740803, -149.290985 Turn right onto unmaintained trail; begin steady climb, looking for grouse in surrounding brush.

GPS: 63.740196, -149.288162 Hike past jagged rocks as views of Savage River Valley and Mount McKinley emerge.

GPS: 63.743305, -149.268005 Hit saddle. Watch arctic ground squirrels scurry across the trail. Caution: Bears seek shelter here on windy days.

GPS: 63.739887, -149.277802 Listen for marmots whistling across a valley with postcard views; veer right at junction to continue loop.

GPS: 63.742294, -149.289841 Descend ridge through low brush, follow trail to river.

GPS: 63.751404, -149.291489 Turn left to hike alongside the Savage River.

GPS: 63.749260, -149.293869 Cross bridge, continue up hillside on rough trail.

GPS: 63.742676, -149.292770 Pass riverside picnic area, a popular hangout for willow ptarmigan; continue on maintained trail to parking lot.

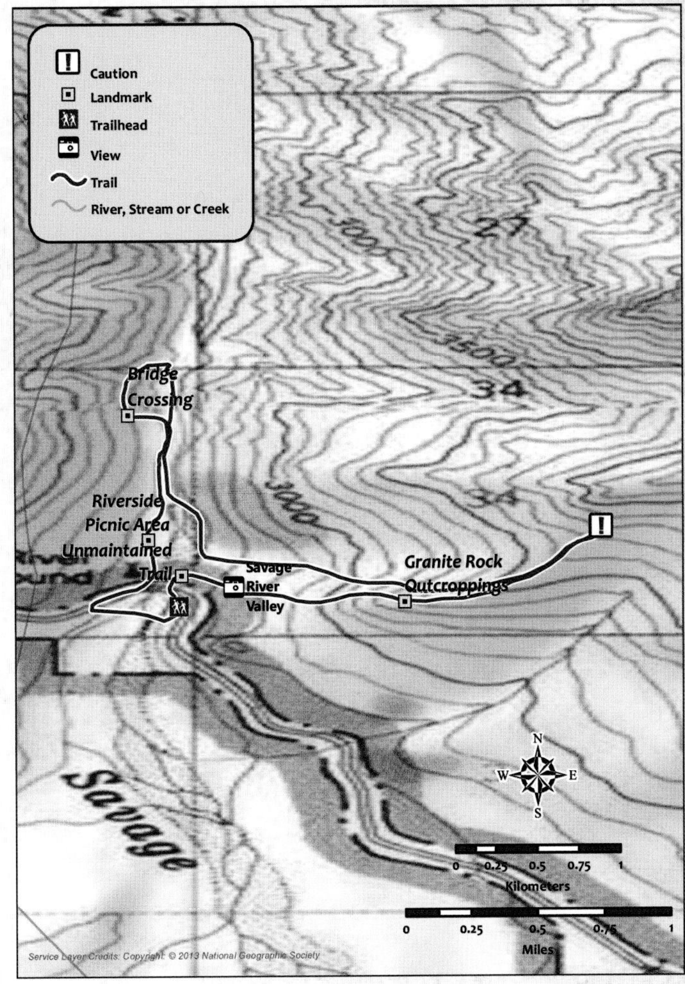

Sun filters through the pines at Long Pine Key Pond in Everglades National Park, Florida
Photo: Jonathan Gewirtz / Tandem Stock

EVERGLADES
NATIONAL PARK

EVERGLADES NATIONAL PARK

TEN THOUSAND ISLANDS LOOP

Kayak to pocket beaches and Gulf islands at Florida's southern tip.

The islands along Everglades National Park's northwest corner extend into the Gulf of Mexico. And while the park is famous for mangrove-choked swamp, the feel here is decidedly oceanic, with liquid horizons, crushed-shell beaches, big tides, and excellent fishing for sea trout, tarpon, jack, and snook. There are long crossings of bays and channels exposed to wind and waves, but most of the route is sheltered. Mazelike channels and endless green shorelines make navigation challenging, but shallow gaps through peninsulas and between islets let you avoid powerboat traffic.

Share the wild coast with shorebirds and marine life on this 49-mile, three-day loop. Park at the Gulf Coast Visitor Center, pick up permits, and file a trip plan. (You should have intermediate paddling and navigation skills.) Launch from the boat ramp and head southeast along the shore on a 3-mile paddle to the town of Chokoloskee. Continue southeast for 3.5 miles to Wilderness Waterway marker 127, then turn gulfward to pick your way through the mangrove maze of Rabbit Key Pass. Go past the white-sand paradise of Turtle Key before the 2.3-mile crossing to Rabbit Key. Lunch on shell-covered shores before heading southeast for the 3.7-mile crossing to Pavilion Key's long, sweeping beach.

Make camp on the island's northeastern side. The next day, head southeast between two mangrove-covered islands, then it's an 8.2-mile open-ocean crossing to Mormon Key. Follow the shoreline to the mouth of the Chatham River, then snake up sandbar-lined waterways to the upland campsite at Watson Place. (Tip: Gather wood for a fire to ward off bugs.) Continue 0.6 mile up the river on day three and veer left at the major fork. Continue until the water opens into Last Huston Bay and the Wilderness Waterway. Paddle northwest, reaching Sunday Bay in 3.2 miles, then turn north to the Sunday Bay Chickee, an elevated tent platform (with an outhouse!).

On the final day, head east-northeast to the Wilderness Waterway marker 125. Paddle across Cross Bay, Shoal Mud Bay, and Hurdles Creek, then head west to the Turner River and Chokoloskee. Take the canal for a lazy 2-mile cruise toward Everglades City, then turn under the causeway bridge to reach the ranger station.

Photo: Mac Stone / Tandem Stock

Text: Casey Lyons and Steve Howe

DISTANCE: 49 miles

TIME REQUIRED: 3 days

DIFFICULTY: Strenuous

CONTACT: Everglades National Park, (239) 695-3311; nps.gov/ever

THE PAYOFF: Dolphins, ospreys, and beaches highlight this 3-day coastal meander.

TRAILHEAD GPS: 25.845455, -81.387266

FINDING THE TRAILHEAD: From Naples, take US 41 south for 32 miles. Turn right on Collier Avenue and go 4 miles to a left on Copeland Avenue. After 0.6 mile, turn right at Oyster Bar Lane to reach the Gulf Coast visitor center.

WAYPOINTS & DIRECTIONS

GPS: 25.845762, -81.387090 Launch from the boat ramp and head southeast along the shoreline on a 3-mile paddle to Chokoloskee. Continue southeast to Wilderness Waterway marker 127.

GPS: 25.785010, -81.338573 At Wilderness Waterway marker 127, turn southwest to weave through Rabbit Key Pass.

GPS: 25.767175, -81.379638 Pass the mini paradise of Turtle Key and head south for the 1.2-mile crossing to Rabbit Key.

GPS: 25.751478, -81.378168 Rabbit Key's sandy area is on the northeast side of the island. Continue south for 3.5 miles to Pavilion Key.

GPS: 25.708585, -81.350929 Camp on Pavilion Key's long, sweeping beach, then head southeast for 4.4 miles to Mormon Key.

GPS: 25.671618, -81.289831 Land at the southern tip of Mormon Key, then paddle northeast to the island-dotted mouth of the Chatham River.

GPS: 25.695726, -81.272341 Head east-northeast around islands and over sandbars on the way to Watson Place.

GPS: 25.709073, -81.245666 Dock your kayak and camp in the high ground of Watson Place. Continue upstream, and head left at the fork.

GPS: 25.748794, -81.252712 Join the Wilderness Waterway in Last Huston Bay and continue north-northwest to Sunday Bay and then on to Sunday Bay Chickee. (*continued*)

GPS: 25.800535, -81.276629 Camp at this floating platform, then curve around the shoreline, heading west to Wilderness Waterway marker 125.

GPS: 25.802093, -81.293756 At marker 125, continue west-northwest through Cross Bay, Shoal Mud Bay, and Hurdles Creek.

GPS: 25.831261, -81.335821 Turn west-southwest to join the Turner River, which leads back to Chokoloskee.

GPS: 25.821449, -81.359081 Enter the causeway canal to the northeast of Chokoloskee and paddle west-northwest for 3 miles to the causeway bridge.

GPS: 25.839295, -81.381483 Turn west under the causeway bridge, being mindful of currents. Then follow the shoreline to the ranger station.

GPS: 25.845723, -81.386975 Pull out at the National Park Service dock.

RANGER PROFILE

SABRINA DIAZ

The Innovator

Everglades National Park, Florida

"She helped foster a new love and appreciation toward wilderness that will be with me for the rest of my life." —Sandeep Varry, *Backpacker* reader

To celebrate the 50th anniversary of the Wilderness Act, Sabrina Diaz, a supervisory ranger of interpretation, wanted to introduce a new generation to the Everglades. With a little luck, she would turn them into champions for the park. Thus was born the Everglades Wilderness Writing Expedition, which introduced ten young writers to the backcountry, served them weekend hikes, and culminated in a four-day trip. "One of the most important things about my job and the job of any park ranger across the country is to grow stewards," Diaz says. "Our job is to give people the information that they need to fall in love with a place and eventually become the voice of our parks and our natural areas."

FAVORITE SPOT: Snake Bight

This 3.2-miler to a tucked-away bay is ground zero for birders: During high tide in winter, hundreds of flamingos, roseate spoonbills, and pelicans gather near the boardwalk at the trail's end. "If you time it just right, you can witness thousands of birds," Diaz says. "It's just incredible."

TRAILHEAD: Snake Bight

INFO: nps.gov/ever

EVERGLADES NATIONAL PARK

NORTH NEST KEY

Enjoy Caribbean-quality water and beach camping on an open-sea weekend adventure.

This 18-mile out-and-back takes you through the sparkling seas and numerous islands of Florida Bay to an idyllic island just off the southern tip of the state. Spend one night or five—North Nest Key has siesta-inducing campsites and a fine swimming beach. (Note: Landing is prohibited on islands that lack designated sites.) The most interesting (and sheltered) route passes through Dusenbury Creek, Tarpon Basin, and Little Buttonwood Sound, all backyard waters to Key Largo. The route is exposed to wind, so a sea kayak is best.

As you enter Dusenbury Creek, watch for manatees feeding near navigation marker 41. At marker 42, bear right and paddle away from the busy Inland Waterway through a gorgeous, secluded mangrove tunnel. This deposits you in Tarpon Basin near marker 48. Cut west across Tarpon Basin and enter Little Buttonwood Sound at marker 52. From there, follow the sound's wind-sheltered southwest shore, then head out to open water via the sound's westernmost gap for a 4.5-mile crossing west-northwest to North Nest Key and the campsite dock on its western shore. North Nest and a handful of other camps in Florida Bay are the only Everglades backcountry sites that can be reserved by phone up to 24 hours in advance.

Photo: Mac Stone / Tandem Stock

Text: Steve Howe

DISTANCE: 18 miles

TIME REQUIRED: 1–5 days

DIFFICULTY: Intermediate

CONTACT: Everglades National Park, (239) 695-3311; nps.gov/ever

THE PAYOFF: Stay awhile at your own private beach

TRAILHEAD GPS: 25.144879, -80.397382

FINDING THE TRAILHEAD: Florida Bay Outfitters graciously provides free parking and launching for paddlers (a South Florida rarity) near milepost 104 on FL 1.

WAYPOINTS & DIRECTIONS

GPS: 25.144879, -80.397382 Paddle west from the Florida Bay Outfitters dock.

GPS: 25.143371, -80.423870 Turn southwest into mangrove tunnel near marker 42.

GPS: 25.129403, -80.455774 Last wind-sheltered point before open ocean.

GPS: 25.149570, -80.514618 Dock marks campsite on the west shore of North Nest Key. Return back to Florida Bay Outfitters' dock by the same route.

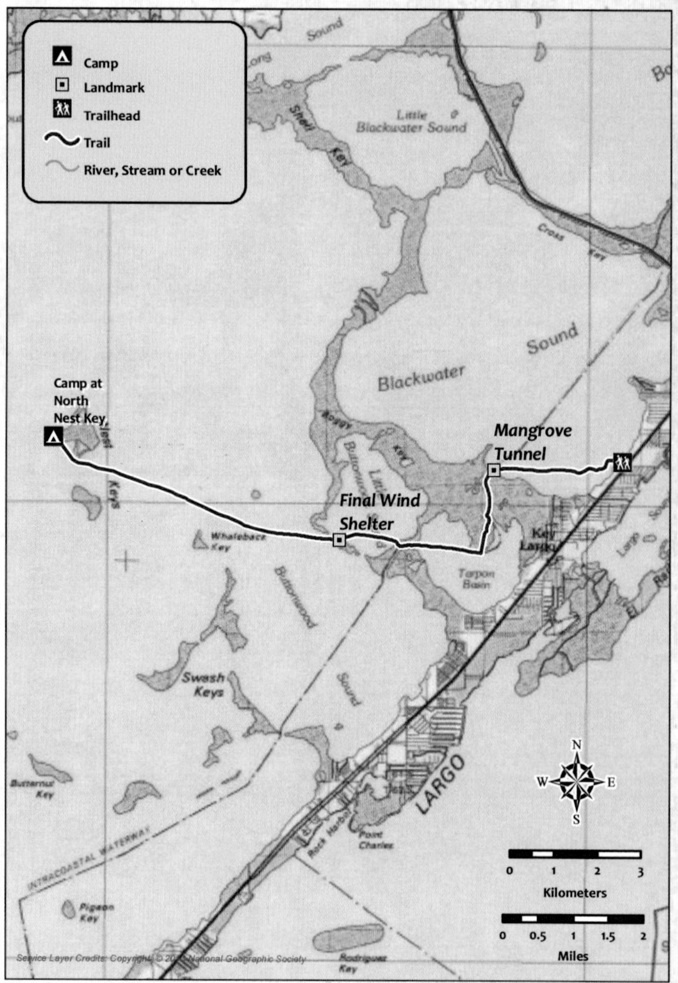

An anhinga spreads its wings

EVERGLADES NATIONAL PARK
COASTAL PRAIRIE TRAIL

You don't need a canoe to reach some of the Everglades' best beachfront campsites—or to see a blazing sunset and flocks of cormorants.

Ever backpacked on a river? Hike the Coastal Prairie Trail in southernmost Everglades National Park and you will. This is the place that pioneering conservationist and author Marjory Stoneman Douglas dubbed the River of Grass, since the massive ecosystem literally rests atop a torrent of water flowing imperceptibly from Lake Okeechobee in the center of the state to the Gulf of Mexico. The path is dry and your boots won't get wet—unless an alligator runs you off the trail. But surrounding you are swamps, sloughs, estuaries, and sawgrass prairie, all reminders that you're in a world of water.

The trailhead for the 15-mile round-trip Coastal Prairie Trail starts inauspiciously enough at Flamingo visitor center, a bustling tourist enclave 38 miles inside the park. Grin and bear it, because a short walk leaves the hubbub behind. The trail follows an old makeshift road once used by fishermen and workers picking wild cotton. Like them, you'll penetrate shady buttonwood groves, skirt mangrove-fringed lakes, and roll through wide, grassy plains. You're apt to see herons, hawks, bald eagles, egrets, pelicans, cormorants, ibis, osprey, roseate spoonbills, and lots of alligators.

In due time you'll earn your reward for the effort: Clubhouse Beach, a wild spit of sand about as far south as you can get and still be in Florida. Although the swift of foot can make the 15-mile trip in one day, that doesn't allow time to watch the sun set across the water, or listen to the waves gently lapping at the beach, or enjoy the breeze that sways the coconut palms (remnants of a failed plantation). Close your eyes and you'll think you're in Tahiti.

Text: Lynn Sedon

After setting up camp, you can explore to your heart's content—there are no formal trails, but the canals and mangroves will let you know when to turn around—or take a refreshing swim in Florida Bay. At night, without Miami's glare to light up the sky, the stars put on quite a show. And while the mating calls of the gators may not exactly lull you to sleep, they do make for unique bedtime listening.

DISTANCE: 15 miles
TIME REQUIRED: 1–3 days
DIFFICULTY: Intermediate
CONTACT: Everglades National Park, (239) 695-3311; nps.gov/ever

THE PAYOFF: Bird-watching, beaches, jungle.
TRAILHEAD GPS: 25.136971, -80.951858
FINDING THE TRAILHEAD: From Homestead, take State Highway 9336 for 48.6 miles to the Flamingo visitor center.

WAYPOINTS & DIRECTIONS

GPS: 25.136971, -80.951858 Coastal Prairie Trailhead begins at the end of Loop C for the Flamingo campground.

GPS: 25.138952, -80.973487 The trail follows an old makeshift road once used by fishermen and workers picking wild cotton.

GPS: 25.142099, -80.997305 Pass shady buttonwood groves, skirt mangrove-fringed lakes, and roll through wide, grassy plains.

GPS: 25.132192, -81.038804 Look for alligators, herons, and birds of prey in mangroves and estuaries.

GPS: 25.128618, -81.043396 Clubhouse Beach features swaying palms from an abandoned plantation. Set up camp (permits required) and explore mangrove swamps and sandy beaches to your heart's content.

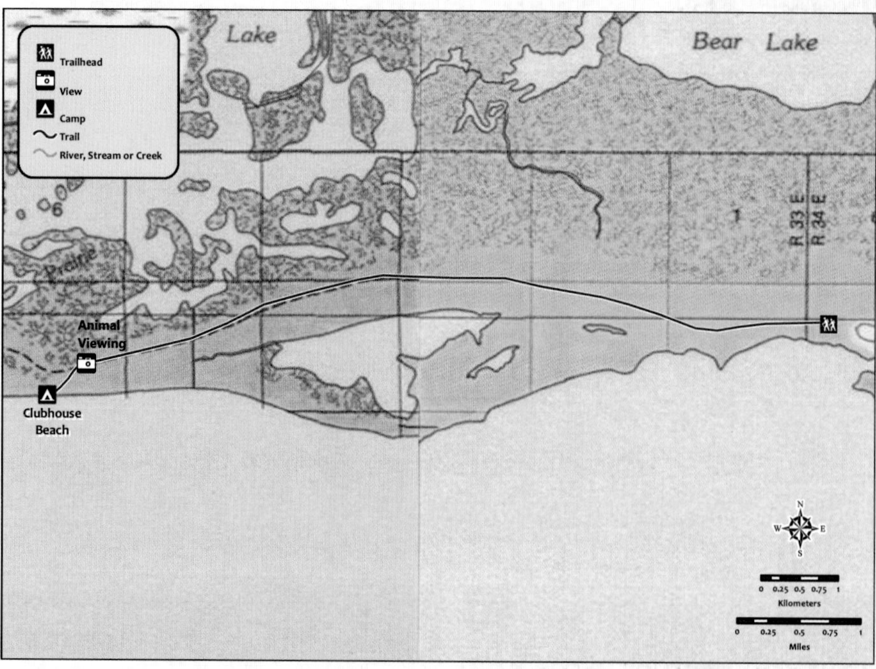

HIKE SMARTER

4 WAYS TO CAMP IN COMFORT

Learn how to set up bear bags and a cozy camp, protect yourself from wind, and eat right.

1. Pitch the perfect camp. Choose a site 200 feet from lakes and streams. Camp at established sites and on durable surfaces whenever possible. Hang your bear bag or stash your canister at least 200 feet downwind from camp. (See number 3 for bear bag tips.) In grizzly country, cook 200 feet or more downwind from your tent. In calm conditions, orient your tent door to the east for early sun. Look up to make sure no dead trees or branches threaten to fall on your site (especially in beetle-damaged forests in the West). Find a flat rock, preferably with a windbreak, for your kitchen.

2. Beat the wind. Spend extra time searching out a sheltered site, like in a low-lying forest. Above treeline, seek protection on the lee side of a rock outcropping or ridgeline. Orient your tent so the smallest side is facing the wind. If it's not raining, wait until the winds die down (often at sunset) to pitch your tent. You'll reduce the risk of damage from a big gust. Guy out your tent securely. Here's how: Tie small overhand loops at each end of a nylon cord (4 to 8 feet). Pull one end through a guy loop, then pass the other end through the loop in the cord to fasten it. Anchor the other end tautly to a stake.

3. Hang a bear bag. Select a pair of branches 20 feet apart and at least 15 feet off the ground. Attach one end of a 100-foot utility cord (3 millimeter) to a fist-size rock that's heavy enough to drag the line through dense boughs. Tie the other end to a tree trunk or any nearby sturdy anchor. Throw the rock over both branches in succession. Tie a knotted loop (bight) in the cord midway between the branches. Attach the food bag (the stuff sack for a tent works fine) to the loop using a simple overhand or slip knot, or a carabiner. Pull on the unsecured end of the cord to lift the bag high enough up to be out of a bear's reach from the ground (at least 10 feet) or in either tree (4 feet). Tie off.

4. Easy ways to improve the menu: Pack a few fresh, lightweight add-ins to boost the taste of any dehydrated meal. Ideas: cilantro, jalapeno, parsley, basil. Serve an appetizer. Soup is a no-brainer in cool weather. Upgrade any lunch wrap with an avocado; pack it in your pot to prevent squishing. Add butter. Use extra water in dehydrated meals, there's nothing worse than not-quite-rehydrated stroganoff. Flame control: If you must cook in your vestibule during a storm, prime a liquid-fuel stove outside and then pull it under cover.

Photo: Ben Fullerton

Johns Hopkins Glacier in Glacier Bay National Park, Alaska
Credit: NPS Photo

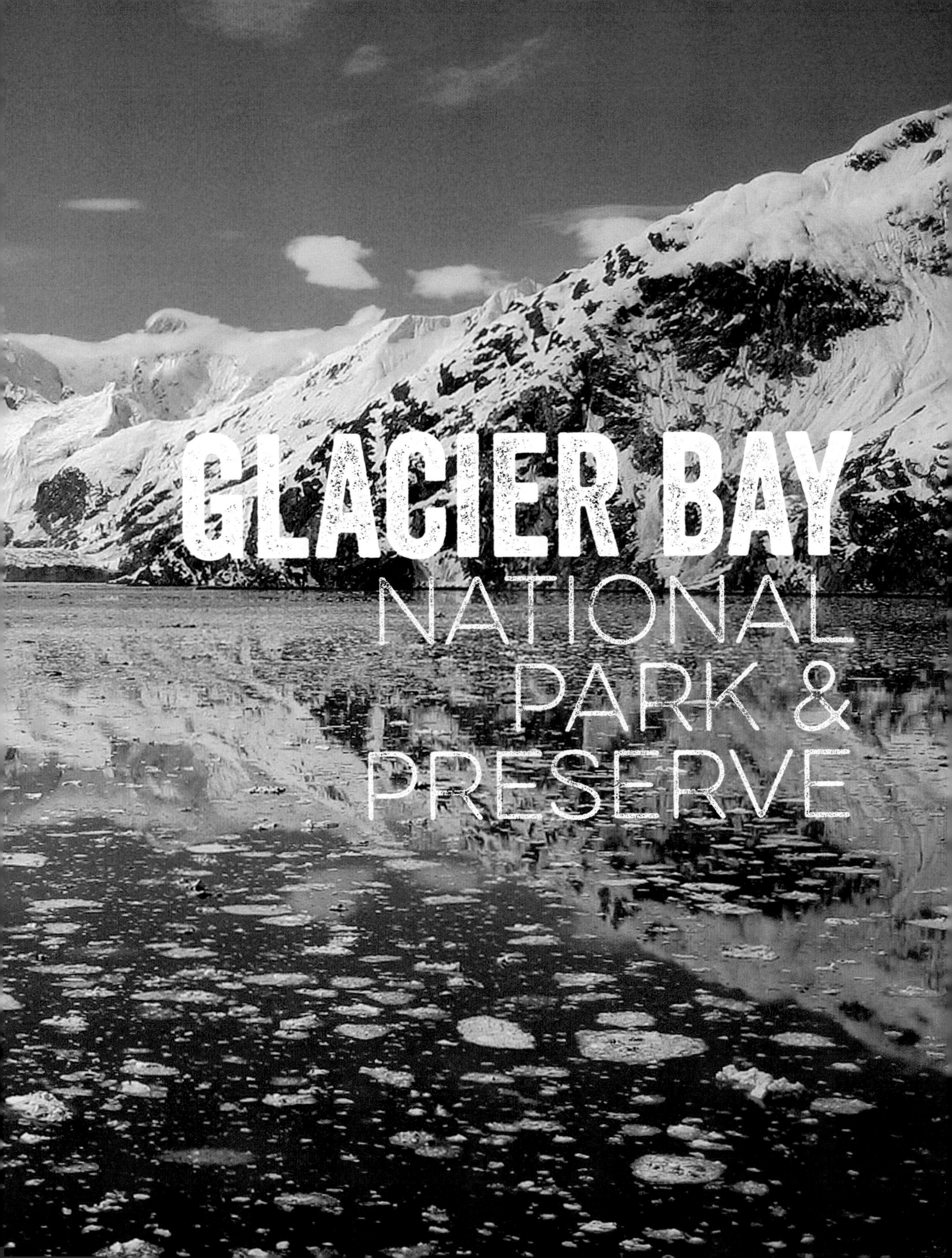
GLACIER BAY
NATIONAL
PARK &
PRESERVE

GLACIER BAY NATIONAL PARK & PRESERVE
MUIR INLET

Explore the inner reaches of the Muir Inlet on this 5-day paddle.

Paddle your kayak along Glacier Bay's dynamic shores and you'll literally see land being created before your eyes. As receding glaciers send sapphire-blue icebergs thundering into the bay, they expose new sections of rocky shoreline. And as the weight of the ice lifts, the land ringing the bay actually rises—up to an inch per year. McBride Bay, at this trip's northernmost point, is just 50 years old. Witness it all—and much more—on this 5-day, 45-mile journey.

In the spring, humpback whales breach the icy waters along with orcas and gray whales. Grizzlies, moose, and wolves patrol the forested shores year-round. Caution: As you paddle Muir Inlet, remain alert. Rolling icebergs and calving glaciers can create waves large enough to flip kayaks and dislodge careless tie-downs. Be cautious around icebergs, and view glaciers from at least 0.25 nautical mile away. Be sure to beach your craft well above the waterline; in late spring (when whales fill the inlet, but before the mosquitoes arrive), the tidal exchange reaches 20 feet.

Photo: Randall Tate / Tandem Stock

Text: Laura Fay

DISTANCE: 45 miles

TIME REQUIRED: 5 days

DIFFICULTY: Intermediate

CONTACT: Glacier Bay National Park and Preserve, (907) 697-2627;nps.gov/glba

THE PAYOFF: Spectacular seaside glaciers and wildlife—whales, seals, sea otters.

TRAILHEAD GPS: 58.784796, -136.050053

FINDING THE TRAILHEAD: Ride the Fairweather Express to the Mount Wright drop-off point to begin the paddling trip.

WAYPOINTS & DIRECTIONS

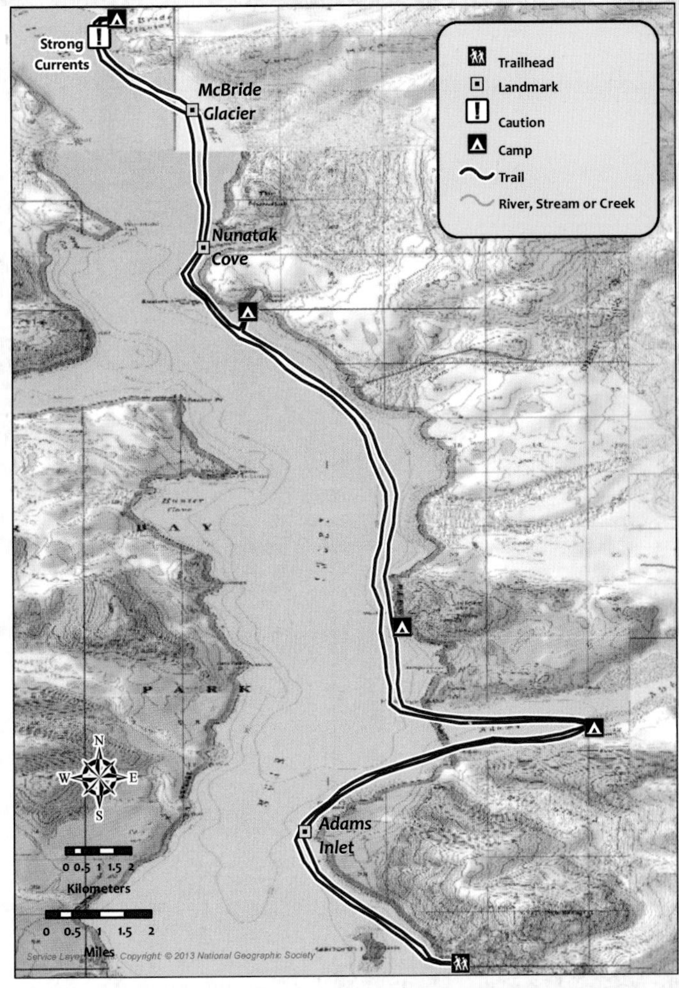

GPS: 58.784796, -136.050053 Launch your kayak and head northwest.

GPS: 58.794225, -136.067820 Stay close to the shoreline as you travel northwest toward Muir and Adams Inlets.

GPS: 58.819875, -136.092453 Round Muir Point and bear right (northeast) into Adams Inlet. Stay close to the shore as you paddle into Adams Inlet.

GPS: 58.846726, -136.012802 Hug the south shore and begin to look for potential campsites. Spend the night in Adams Inlet. Day two: Paddle west to the mouth of Adams Inlet, then head north toward Maquinna Cove.

GPS: 58.852654, -136.065502 After rounding Point George, paddle north into Muir Inlet. Stay close to the eastern shoreline, even as the route bends to the northwest.

GPS: 58.956737, -136.107559 Sheltered home of an 800-year-old Tlingit tribal village. Camp on the shore of this south-facing cove. Day three: Paddle northwest, keeping Sealers Island to your left.

GPS: 58.973817, -136.119747 Glide past Nunatak Cove, the small inlet on the right.

GPS: 59.010075, -136.122665 Paddle northwest past the point ahead. You'll pass the McBride Glacier ahead.

GPS: 59.029382, -136.148329 Do not paddle into McBride Inlet: its bottleneck shape means strong currents and violent tides. Continue heading north toward the shore; look east into the inlet for views of McBride Glacier.

GPS: 59.034190, -136.143265 After passing the mouth of McBride Inlet, find a suitable area to set up camp. Day four: Turn around and paddle south, retracing your route.

GPS: 58.873424, -136.065674 Hug the eastern bank to reach this beach campsite with unobstructed views of the lower bay's forested coast. Final day: Meet the ferry 10.3 miles south at the Mount Wright pickup.

Grinnell Peak is reflected in the still waters of Swiftcurrent Lake in Glacier National Park, Montana
Credit: Tim Rains / NPS Photo

GLACIER NATIONAL PARK

Kintla Lake

GLACIER NATIONAL PARK
BOWMAN LAKE TO KINTLA LAKE

Five mountain lakes, two mountain passes, and countless glacier-carved peaks highlight this epic shuttle hike in the Crown of the Continent.

There are no disappointing trails in Glacier. But to see the place at the apex of its glory—snow-scrubbed peaks, precipitous cliffs, meadows flush with Skittles-colored blooms and gigantic waterfalls—head to the park's remote northwestern corner. The first day, follow the flat shoreline of Bowman Lake; day two, climb 2,200 feet to touch the Continental Divide before it skirts the vertical headwall of Hole in the Wall, a 1,200-foot hanging glacier valley. You'll wind up in the snowfield-speckled high country and the cherry on top of the trip: the alpine zone connecting 6,255-foot Brown Pass and 7,478-foot Boulder Pass.

Boulder Pass is the route's high point at mile 17—camp in the boulder-strewn valley there, or press on to Brown Pass, a 2-mile-long gap dotted with tiny, bright blue pools and eastern views of Thunderbird Mountain, Mount Chapman, and back down to Hole in the Wall. Descend a headwall on a scenic, switchbacking trail—look for the Agassiz Glacier—toward Upper Kintla Lake. The westbound stretch of trail comes within 1.5 miles of the Canadian border and connects Upper Kintla and Kintla lakes as it skirts several burn areas below the Boundary Mountains and Starvation Ridge. Reaching Kintla Lake, however, isn't the end of the journey: it's 20 road miles between the trail's end and Bowman Lake, so plan ahead and arrange a shuttle either within your own group or with a local before your trip. (Commercial outfitters aren't permitted to travel to Kintla, so plan to be creative about your ride.)

Photo: iStockPhoto.com / Wirepec

Text: Elisabeth Kwak-Hefferan and Charlie Williams

DISTANCE: 38.8 miles

TIME REQUIRED: 4–5 days

DIFFICULTY: Intermediate

CONTACT: Glacier National Park, (406) 888-7800; nps.gov/glac

THE PAYOFF: Unreal wildflowers, glaciers, bears, and more in Glacier's remote northwest quadrant.

TRAILHEAD GPS: 48.888586, -114.200907

FINDING THE TRAILHEAD: From West Glacier, take Going to the Sun Road north and turn left on Camas Road. Drive 11.7 miles and turn right on N Fork Road. Go 13.3 miles north and turn right onto Polebridge. In 1 mile, turn right on Glacier Drive and proceed 1 mile to Bowman Lake Road. The trailhead is in 5.5 miles.

WAYPOINTS & DIRECTIONS

GPS: 48.828643, -114.201819 Parking for the Bowman Trailhead is along the main campground road next to the self-registration bulletin board. Follow the trail through lodgepole pines toward the lake, turn left on the road, and then bear right onto the trail. You'll pass the ranger cabin and a sign announcing the Upper Bowman Campground.

GPS: 48.837379, -114.195499 Stay to the right at this junction with the Numa Ridge Trail. The thick montane forest on the lake's north side is dominated by Douglas fir, but the brushy trail can be slick with black mud.

GPS: 48.904223, -114.121284 Nearing the north end of Bowman Lake is the campground spur trail. The two southernmost sites have the best views and a cooking-area fire pit, but the others are very secluded. Watch for eagle activity in the area. *(continued)*

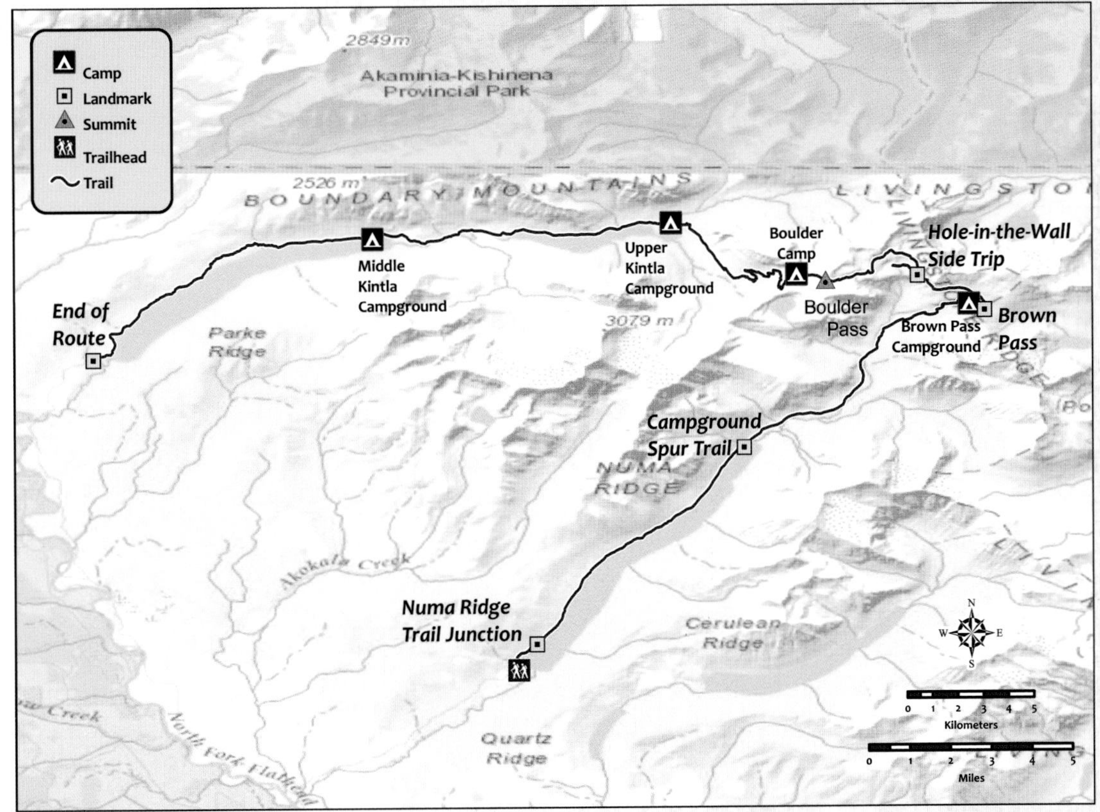

GPS: 48.911895, -114.109325 Cross a stream. Though low and easy to cross in late summer, spring runoff can make this (and the crossings of Pocket Creek, 3 miles ahead) much more difficult.

GPS: 48.934031, -114.078898 The trail crosses three Pocket Creek branches just north of their convergence with Bowman Creek. The first and last are less significant than the middle one where there is a bridge under construction. From this point, the climb intensifies toward Brown Pass.

GPS: 48.952776, -114.041090 The Brown Pass Campground is another option for nights one or two.

GPS: 48.957623, -114.053707 As the trail swings north, it cuts into the side of the cliffs of the Helena Formation. Although wide and safe, this short stretch of trail may challenge hikers fearful of heights. Up ahead, you'll pass over the lip of Hole-in-the-Wall before the trail splits.

GPS: 48.962638, -114.059286 Bear left at Y junction for a 1-mile round-trip to Hole-in-the-Wall's popular campground. (***Side Trip*:** Hiking to the base of the glacial cirque is a worthwhile detour for lunch or camping.) From Hole-in-the-Wall, return to this point and turn left, heading north.

GPS: 48.961117, -114.091902 You'll hike along the upper rim of the cirque, along the wall of a hanging valley, across a cairn-marked talus slope, and over several ledges en route to Boulder Pass. This 7,470-foot pass is the route's high point and the trip's halfway point.

GPS: 48.963130, -114.102315 A 0.1-mile spur trail leads north to the tent pads and food preparation area of Boulder Camp. From here, it's a thimbleweed-flanked, switchbacking, 3,250-foot descent toward Upper Kintla Lake.

GPS: 48.980837, -114.147177 Cross Kintla Creek on a bridge; ribbons and cairns mark the main trail. A sign up ahead marks the right-hand spur trail to Upper Kintla Campground.

GPS: 48.980709, -114.153566 There are four tent pads and a food-prep and fire area near the campground, and a hitching post for stock animals nearby. A gravel beach on the lakeshore is also nearby—a good place to dry gear.

GPS: 48.975960, -114.253008 The old Kintla patrol cabin precedes the middle Kintla Campground. There are six tent pads, a food prep area, a fire area, and a hitching post. On the gravel beach and in the lake are remnants of the early-20th-century Butte Well.

GPS: 48.937879, -114.345982 The trail splits less than half a mile from the route's end. Bear right to bypass the drive-in camping area and continue to the parking lot.

LOCATION: 48.935179, -114.352700 It's about 19 miles by road between Kintla Lake and Bowman Trailhead. Shuttle logistics can be difficult, but consider leaving a car or bicycle here, or hiring a ride in Polebridge or another nearby town before your trip.

Photo: iStockPhoto.com / monkeyflasher

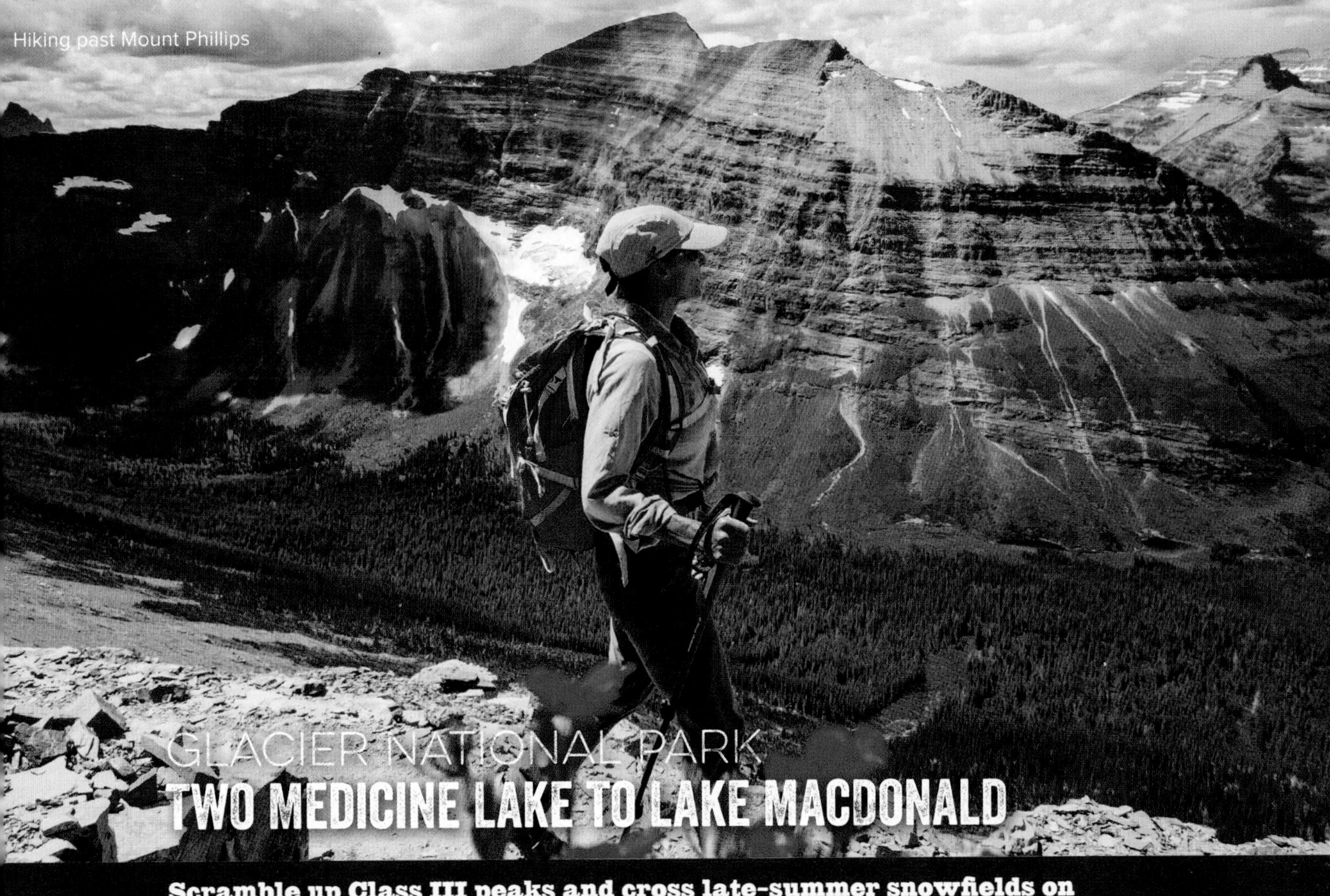
Hiking past Mount Phillips

GLACIER NATIONAL PARK

TWO MEDICINE LAKE TO LAKE MACDONALD

Scramble up Class III peaks and cross late-summer snowfields on this tough but straightforward trip through Montana's big-mountain country.

Glacier visitors face a can't-lose choice: Hike the quiet, spectacular southern half or its busier but marginally more dramatic northern environs. This 62-mile route opts for the the former, tracing ridgetops that the Blackfoot Indians revered as the backbone of the world, along Dawson, Triple Divide, and Gunsight Passes to Sperry Glacier and Lake MacDonald. The route passes thundering waterfalls, glaciers, and the shores of some of the park's largest lakes. But you'd best arrive in shape for big-mileage days.

From tranquil Two Medicine Campground, stroll to the outlet bridge of Two Medicine Lake. Hike west on the Dawson Pass Trail to Dawson Pass (mile 6.2), then north along high ridgelines, where you'll find smooth trail above yawning Nyack Creek and views west to the gigantic banded limestone pyramids of Mount Stimson and Pinchot Peak. Round the shattered horn of Flinsch Peak, and continue across a narrow spur of Mount Morgan. (Caution: The track crosses gullies that can retain hard ice well into summer.) From there, it's an easy mile over 7,874-foot Cutbank Pass, then 7,664-foot Pitamakin Pass. Your day ends at Morning Star Lake, which sits between 2,000-foot cliffs and a broad, spruce-filled basin at mile 13.6.

Photo: Andrew Peacock / Tandem Stock

Text: Steve Howe

Day two's 13-plus miles lead deep into grizzly country. From Morning Star Lake, continue north on the Cutbank Pass Trail under the lopsided pyramid of 8,315-foot Medicine Grizzly Peak to an intersection with the Triple Divide Pass Trail. Turn left and climb up the open, U-shaped valley of Atlantic Creek to Triple Divide Pass, a broad saddle beneath sweeping sedimentary cliffs. Watch for bighorn sheep as you drop through a dense thicket of fern and beargrass to camp at Red Eagle Lake (mile 27.4). Three miles beyond Red Eagle, the forested trail spits you onto the shore of St. Mary Lake. Turn west and pass beneath small trailside cataracts pouring off Red Eagle Mountain, great for soaking swollen feet. Beyond the lake, cross the St. Mary River (with two campsites available at Reynolds Creek, mile 42.6).

In the morning, hammer 2.7 miles up steep trail cut through cliff outcroppings to Gunsight Pass. The route ahead goes through an area with high user demand and only two small campsites. If you've scored a camping permit, drop to nearby Lake Ellen Wilson; alternatively, continue over Lincoln Pass and into Glacier Basin and base camp next to Sprague Creek.

On day five, tackle the 2.5-mile, 1,600-foot climb past Akaiyan Falls and Feather Woman Lake, and up the stone stairs of Comeau Pass to the Sperry Glacier Overlook, with its stunning rock and ice panorama. Have some mountaineering experience? Increase the challenge on day six with an attempt on the craggy, exposed, Class II–III East Ridge of 9,072-foot Edwards Mountain, which begins just west of Gem Lake at Comeau Pass.

Your final day includes a 6.7-mile plunge down to Lake MacDonald. From here, walk west along the road to Sprague Creek Campground. A free hiker shuttle operates along Going-to-the-Sun Road, but you'll need a commercial shuttle to Two Medicine Campground (try Glacier Park, Inc.; glacierparkinc.com).

DISTANCE: 62 miles

TIME REQUIRED: 5–7 days

DIFFICULTY: Strenuous

CONTACT: Glacier National Park, (406) 888-7800; nps.gov/glac

THE PAYOFF: Thread high peaks on this challenging thru-hike from Two Medicine Lake to Lake MacDonald.

TRAILHEAD GPS: 48.484571, -113.369079

FINDING THE TRAILHEAD: Take Highway 89 north from Browning and follow signs for Two Medicine entrance, about 13 miles from East Glacier.

WAYPOINTS & DIRECTIONS

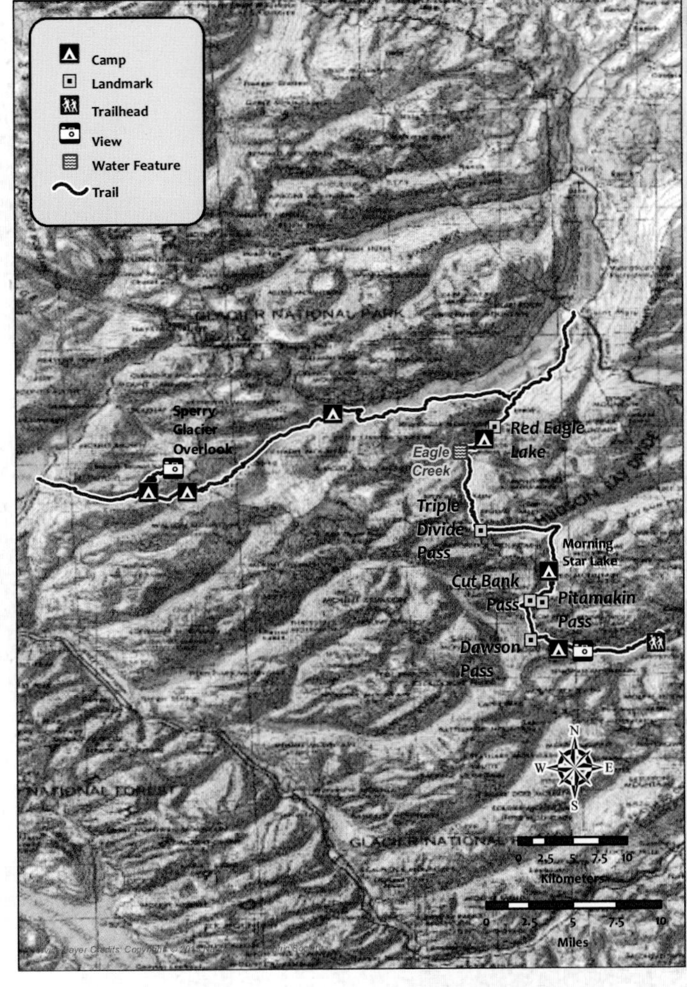

GPS: 48.484571, -113.369079 Begin at trailhead from Two Medicine campground.

GPS: 48.489705, -113.368692 Hike west on Dawson Pass Trail.

GPS: 48.477843, -113.419461 Take right fork to continue on Dawson Pass Trail.

GPS: 48.479778, -113.448815 Take left spur off of Dawson Pass Trail to reach the campsite at No Name Lake.

GPS: 48.481115, -113.445854 Coming from campsite, turn left on Dawson Pass trail to continue through Bighorn Basin.

GPS: 48.487230, -113.471947 Upon reaching the top of Dawson Pass, turn right to head north toward Mount Morgan.

GPS: 48.518345, -113.472417 Cut Bank Pass is located to the north. Follow the trail east toward Pitamakin Pass.

GPS: 48.517201, -113.462291 Turn left before reaching the high point of Pitamakin Pass to descend the pass and round the western side of Pitamakin Lake.

GPS: 48.541160, -113.456798 Find Camp 1 on the shores of Morning Star Lake.

GPS: 48.575897, -113.447914 Turn left at the T, onto Triple Divide Trail.

GPS: 48.573427, -113.459544 Take the right fork to continue on Triple Divide Trail.

GPS: 48.574179, -113.513532 Triple Divide Pass. Continue to follow the Triple Divide Trail north, eventually following the west shore of Hudson Creek.

GPS: 48.635816, -113.530290 Ford Eagle Creek.

GPS: 48.645840, -113.510120 The second camp is on the south shore of Red Eagle Lake.

GPS: 48.656075, -113.501601 Red Eagle Lake. To make a shorter trip, continue north on the Red Eagle Trail, staying right at the junction with the Saint Mary Trail and follow it into town. To continue with the hike, take a left at the junction, and follow the Saint Mary Trail west along the southern shore of Saint Mary Lake.

GPS: 48.666931, -113.634939 The third camp is downstream of Deadwood Falls. Exiting camp, stay left to follow Gunsight Pass Trail to the southwest.

GPS: 48.605787, -113.753815 Find a potential fourth campsite nestled along the north shore of Lake Ellen Wilson, below Gunsight Mountain.

GPS: 48.605674, -113.785315 This is another potential site for the fourth night of camping. From here, to get to the glacier overlook, take a right at the T on the south side of Glacier Basin and follow the trail past Akaiyan Falls and Akaiyan Lake to the observation point.

GPS: 48.624484, -113.764973 Take in the splendor of Sperry Glacier from this overlook. From here, retrace your steps to the T, and take a right to get on the Gunsight Pass Trail heading west. Continue following west to Lake McDonald, the trail terminus.

Brown bear

STAY SAFE IN BEAR COUNTRY

With a little prep, bears don't have to be the stuff of wilderness nightmares.

Prevent an Encounter

- **Don't hike alone.** Bears are less likely to attack groups than individuals.
- **Make noise. For real.** Bells are a nice thought, but loud conversation or singing will better alert bears to your presence. Given the opportunity, most bears will avoid a human encounter.
- **Carry bear spray.** Keep it handy, and know how to use it. Wait until a charging bear is within 60 feet, then sweep the spray to create a cloud at ground level. (Check out the primer at backpacker.com/view/videos/survival-videos/how-to-use-bear-spray/.)
- **Be scent smart.** Store food in bear canisters or hang it properly. Avoid fragrance-heavy shampoos and hygiene products; they smell just like food. Never, ever preemptively fire pepper spray around your tent; it's like marinating your campsite.
- **Stay vigilant.** Paying attention to terrain features can give you an advantage; if you come to a section of trail with recent evidence of bears (such as scat or overturned stumps), make extra noise. Give bears a chance to hear you and flee before their protective instincts kick in.

If Attacked by a Grizzly

- **Play dead.** Lie face down with your pack on, spread your legs (so it can't roll you), and protect your neck and head with your hands.
- **Climb a tree.** Grizzlies are poor climbers, but they can ascend trees if the limbs are arranged like ladder rungs. Make sure you can climb higher than 15 feet on slender branches.
- **Fight.** If a grizzly starts to attempt to eat you, or if you're attacked by a black bear, you have to fight. Go for the nose, eyes, and ears. Give it your all.

Photo: iStockPhoto.com / xijian

Grinnell Lake

GLACIER NATIONAL PARK
GRINNELL AND HIGHLINE LOOP LINK

Explore the most rugged, scenic, and wildlife-rich mountains in the Lower 48 on an epic day hike.

On this 14.2-mile epic, you'll climb past lakes, waterfalls, and the park's biggest glacier to the Garden Wall, then descend through the best wildlife habitat in Glacier. You'll need an ice ax, helmet, and possibly crampons, since you connect the Grinnell Glacier and Highline Trails via a snow gully. The best time is June, when solid snow fills the gully. Going this direction lets you see cornice conditions before committing.

From Many Glacier picnic area, hike 5.5 miles to Upper Grinnell Lake and its namesake glacier. Round the lake's northern end and climb the snow gully to the saddle atop the Garden Wall. There you'll hit the Grinnell Glacier Overlook Trail and descend steeply 0.8 mile to the Highline Trail. Turn southeast and traverse 7 relatively flat miles through excellent bighorn and mountain-goat habitat to the parking lot at Logan Pass. You'll want two cars and an early start for dropping off the shuttle.

NOTE: If crossing snow gives you the willies or conditions aren't favorable, you can hike an easier route in the same area (though without up-close glacier views) by connecting the Highline Trail, Swiftcurrent Pass, and the Many Glacier Valley for a 14.7-mile shuttle trek.

Photo: iStockPhoto.com / leezsnow

DISTANCE: 14.2 miles

TIME REQUIRED: 1 day

DIFFICULTY: Expert

CONTACT: Glacier National Park, (406) 888-7800; nps.gov/glac

THE PAYOFF: Glacier's best day hike.

TRAILHEAD GPS: 48.797629, -113.678523

FINDING THE TRAILHEAD: The Apgar West Entrance is off US 2, 160 miles north from Missoula.

WAYPOINTS & DIRECTIONS

GPS: 48.695465, -113.717594 Park a shuttle at the Logan Pass Visitors Center.

GPS: 48.797027, -113.668198 Start hike from the Grinnell Glacier trailhead, located in the picnic area in Swiftcurrent.

GPS: 48.761847, -113.739223 Don helmet, ice axe, and crampons and ascend a steep snowfield to pop over the Continental Divide and access the Glacier Overlook.

GPS: 48.762073, -113.743687 Look southeast from the overlook for a view of Grinnell Glacier and upper Grinnell Lake. Hang right to continue heading northeast to pick up the Highline Trail and take a sharp left onto the Highline Trail. The Continental Divide's Garden Wall will be on your left as you head southeast.

GPS: 48.734399, -113.725748 Look for Logan Pass to the south as Mount Gould looms to the northeast.

GPS: 48.710617, -113.715534 A series of waterfalls and cataracts tumbles down the face of the Continental Divide.

GPS: 48.695465, -113.717594 The hike ends at the Visitors Center at Logan Pass. Catch a Glacier bus back to Swiftcurrent, or find your shuttle.

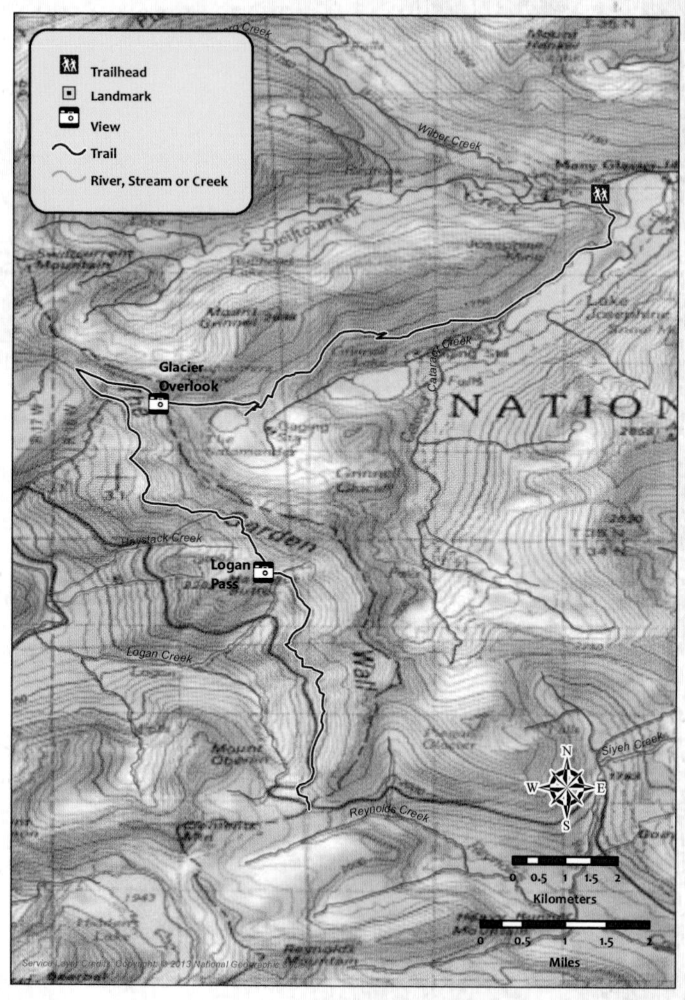

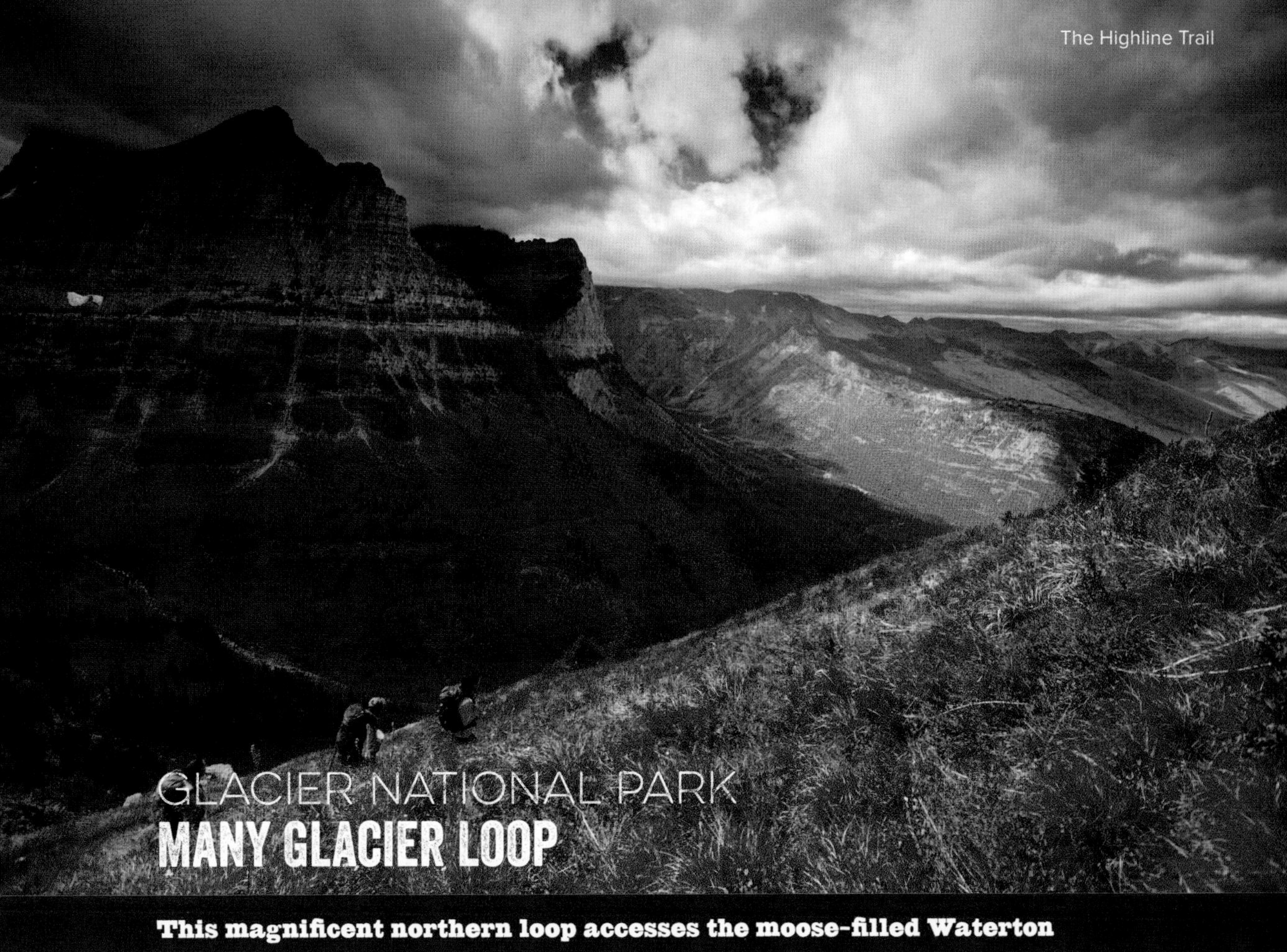

GLACIER NATIONAL PARK

MANY GLACIER LOOP

This magnificent northern loop accesses the moose-filled Waterton Valley backcountry and finishes with a grand finale along the Highline Trail, a mere topographical line below the Continental Divide.

Rule number one when planning a hike through this iconic park: Let your ambition match the scenery. This giant route fits the bill, as it tours through some of Glacier's highest trails only to drop through basins teeming with (sometimes dangerous) wildlife. Start from Many Glacier's Ptarmigan Tunnel trailhead and ascend past waterfalls to the tunnel at 7,248 feet. Descend to Elizabeth Lake, and at mile 11.2 pass 50-foot Dawn Mist Falls. Continue to the wire-assisted crossing of Cosley Lake's outlet and camp at the lake.

The next day's 14.5-mile section passes Glenns Lake and enters a glacial runout en route to 6,908-foot Stoney Indian Pass at mile 23.1. Descend 600 feet in 0.8 mile to Stoney Indian Lake (with camping), then reach a T junction at mile 26.3. Turn right toward Kootenai Lake, and camp along this grouping of reedy ponds with resident moose.

Head south to pick up the Highline Trail. Snake across mountainsides and under pine canopy to Fifty Mountain Pass at mile 35.7. Camp 1.3 miles later at the Fifty Mountain site.

Photo: Ben Herndon / Tandem Stock

Text: Casey Lyons

The next day starts with 0.3 mile across tundra and climbs to 7,422 feet, just below the Continental Divide. Stay high, enjoying big views of the Livingston Range as you contour past Cattle Queen Creek and over Ahern Pass. Take a break at the historic Granite Park Chalet at mile 48.6. Continue up to 7,161-foot Swiftcurrent Pass. Descend through bighorn habitat, and bottom out at Swiftcurrent Creek. Then it's 3.9 lakeside miles back to Many Glacier.

DISTANCE: 55 miles

TIME REQUIRED: 5 days

DIFFICULTY: Strenuous

CONTACT: Glacier National Park, (406) 888-7800; nps.gov/glac

THE PAYOFF: Get up close with the park's remaining glaciers.

TRAILHEAD GPS: 48.797629, -113.678523

FINDING THE TRAILHEAD: The Apgar West Entrance is off US 2, 160 miles from Missoula.

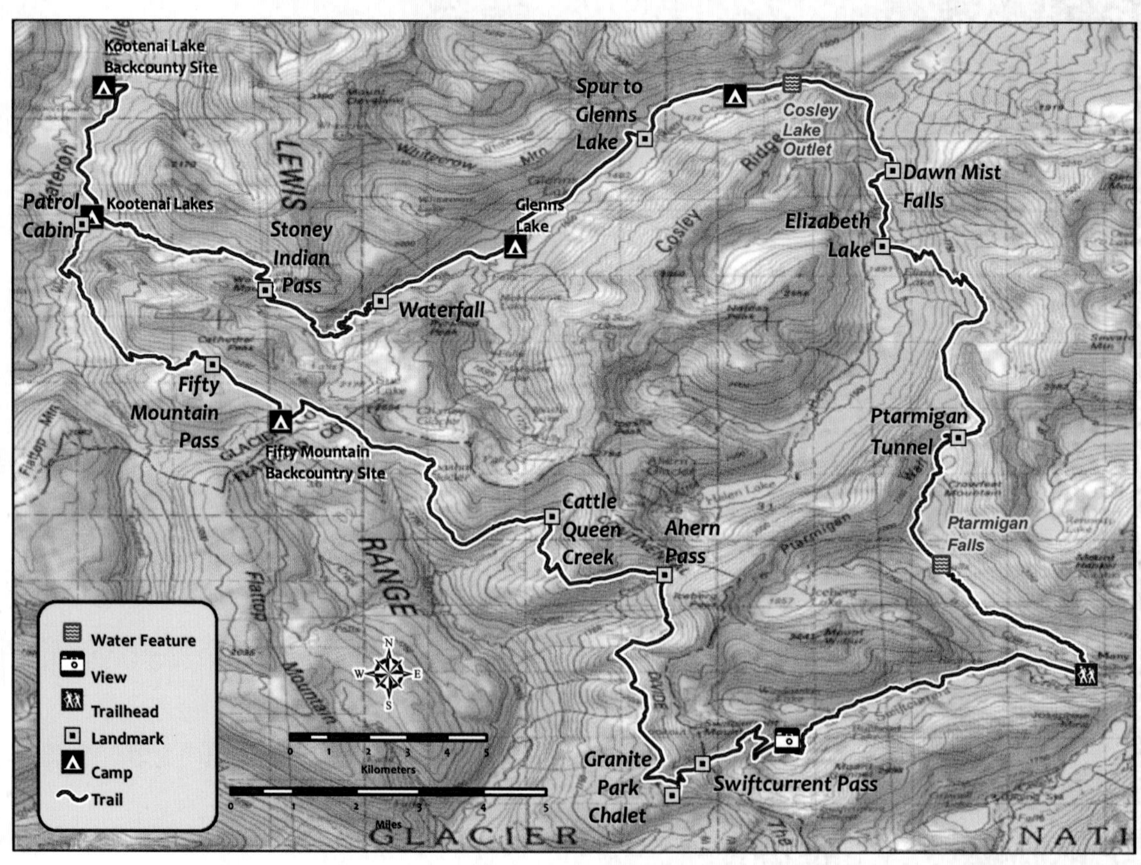

WAYPOINTS & DIRECTIONS

GPS: 48.797629, -113.678523 Trailhead. Bear right at the fork to begin a counterclockwise loop.

GPS: 48.822371, -113.713156 Stay right on the Ptarmigan Trail. Iceberg Lake Trail goes to the left.

GPS: 48.849651, -113.707760 Ptarmigan Tunnel.

GPS: 48.881740, -113.703709 Continue straight; the Red Pass Trail/Continental Divide Trail enters from the left.

GPS: 48.908319, -113.722778 Trail curves around 40-foot gusher Dawn Mist Falls, then descends to the pool below it.

GPS: 48.916139, -113.727272 Continue straight at the junction with the Belly River Trail.

GPS: 48.927350, -113.745456 Ford Cosley Lake's outlet (thigh-deep in September). In higher current (late spring and post-storm), use the guide wire for stability.

GPS: 48.927649, -113.746496 Go left at the junction. This area has high shrubs; stay on the alert for bears.

GPS: 48.926356, -113.759547 Turn left for a winding path to the Cosley Lake Campground.

GPS: 48.924991, -113.757177 Lakeside campsite at Cosley Lake. A nice communal kitchen area includes bear-bag lines. Obtain water from the lake itself.

GPS: 48.917841, -113.776920 Cross Kaina Creek on a log bridge.

GPS: 48.915114, -113.778448 Go left for camping at Glenns Lake. The loop continues to the right.

GPS: 48.888104, -113.814811 Bear right toward Indian Pass. In the next miles, you'll ascend above the Mokowanis River, with a series of waterfalls cascading over bedrock.

GPS: 48.881593, -113.865056 Stoney Indian Pass. Look southwest for the Shepard Glacier, and east to the summit of Stoney Indian.

GPS: 48.897611, -113.904851 Turn right at the T and hike to Kootenai Lakes campsites.

GPS: 48.926298, -113.896849 Go left at the spur trail to Kootenai Lakes.

GPS: 48.926045, -113.902241 Kootenai Lakes backcountry site. Moose frequent this area. All of these campsites are rutted by rain and roots, but the first one (immediately to the left as you get to the lake) is best.

GPS: 48.885179, -113.911525 Bear left onto the Highline Trail.

GPS: 48.865301, -113.877258 Fifty Mountain Pass. On clear days, you can see what the name suggests.

GPS: 48.852626, -113.861629 Fifty Mountain backcountry site. All sites are level, but slightly slanted.

GPS: 48.832200, -113.799478 Cattle Queen Creek.

GPS: 48.773301, -113.770907 Go right at the junction to visit the Granite Park Chalet, a Swiss-style lodge perched on a beautiful site, looking out to the Garden Wall.

GPS: 48.777961, -113.765337 Swiftcurrent Pass. It's all downhill from here.

GPS: 48.782952, -113.746265 Beautiful vista over Bullhead Lake toward Many Glacier.

GPS: 48.781056, -113.742771 The descent ends at a gravel bar on the Swiftcurrent River. Continue east on the Swiftcurrent Pass Trail to the trailhead marker.

Dawson Pass

GLACIER NATIONAL PARK

FIVE PASS AND RED EAGLE LOOP

Follow a historic abandoned trail across the true crown of the continent.

Glacier's steep ridges tend to rule out loops across the Continental Divide, particularly in the southern section of the park. But this 6-day, 54-mile counterclockwise route from Two Medicine is a thrilling exception. It breaches four magnificent trailed passes—Pitamakan, Triple Divide, Cut Bank, and Dawson—and features a stout cross-country traverse of Red Eagle Pass with its miles of spectacular tundra beneath a cirque of towering peaks. Prior to World War II, Red Eagle was one of Glacier's most popular destinations, but the war led to trail-maintenance cutbacks that have allowed the area to revegetate. Following the now-intermittent game trail is a significant challenge and this hike's crux.

The climb from Red Eagle Lake to its namesake pass requires bushwhacking, route-finding, several knee-deep stream crossings, and steep climbing on a goat path, but the vast alpine plateau near the pass yields fine camping. The real work comes as you descend to Nyack Creek: After navigating down to timberline, you must negotiate steep slopes covered with slide alder and deadfall for 3 hours. Then, more reward: excellent hiking along turquoise Nyack Creek, meadow-tenting at the base of Cut Bank Pass, and sublime vistas between Cut Bank and Dawson Passes. A word of caution: This route offers some of the finest high-country hiking in Glacier, but the Red Eagle crossing requires back-country expertise, strong legs, and good weather.

Photo: Andrew Peacock/footloosefotography / Tandem Stock

Text: Steve Howe

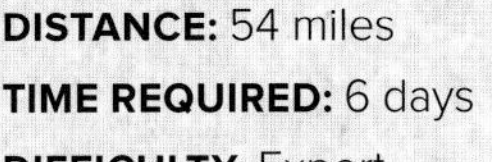

DISTANCE: 54 miles

TIME REQUIRED: 6 days

DIFFICULTY: Expert

CONTACT: Glacier National Park, (406) 888-7800; nps.gov/glac

THE PAYOFF: As big and bold as adventurers can get in Glacier.

TRAILHEAD GPS: 48.4921684265137, -113.365798950195

FINDING THE TRAILHEAD: Drive through the campground at Two Medicine Lake and park at the bridge over the outlet stream.

WAYPOINTS & DIRECTIONS

GPS:48.492168, -113.365799 Cross bridge and turn right onto Oldman Lake Trail (Pitamakan Pass Trail).

GPS: 48.514332, -113.377998 Turn left at T with trail sign, climbing toward Old Man Lake. After 5.8 miles, keep hiking straight, past a recovering burn zone, to the pass.

GPS: 48.517220, -113.462502 Pitamakan Pass. Swing north, switchbacking down to the turquoise Pitamakan Lake.

GPS: 48.540779, -113.457703 Beautiful campsite near Morning Star Lake. Continue roughly north along the Fork Cut Bank Creek.

GPS: 48.575569, -113.448196 Turn left onto Triple Divide Trail.

GPS: 48.573978, -113.461800 Keep right at Medicine Lake Trail junction.

GPS: 48.575581, -113.481003 Continue west, slanting toward the northeast side of Triple Divide Peak.

GPS: 48.574249, -113.513702 Triple Divide Pass. Drop north to Hudson Bay Creek.

GPS: 48.635681, -113.530602 Turn right at Red Eagle Creek and hike to Red Eagle Creek and campsites.

GPS: 48.645451, -113.509804 Campsites near Red Eagle Lake framed by stellar southwest views of the Continental Divide. Return to Red Eagle Creek trail junction and head north up the feeder stream—this begins the stout cross-country traverse of Red Eagle Pass.

GPS: 48.636978, -113.534698 Head west.

GPS: 48.634998, -113.537804 Safe stream crossing.

GPS: 48.631729, -113.537399 Marker waypoint.

GPS: 48.627750, -113.546303 Bear south-southwest.

GPS: 48.625149, -113.548103 Cairn marks the route.

GPS: 48.620571, -113.552399 Good stream crossing.

GPS: 48.614769, -113.559898 Trace the S side of Red Eagle Creek.

GPS: 48.609718, -113.568604 Look for logs to cross creeks.

GPS: 48.603130, -113.584602 Vast beaver ponds. Climb northwest.

GPS: 48.605228, -113.590897 Cut west across slope.

GPS: 48.603630, -113.598396 Super steep game trails. Go slow, and avoid when wet.

GPS: 48.604061, -113.600899 Pick up faint trail again, bearing west.

GPS: 48.601181, -113.604500 This vast alpine plateau yields fine camping.

GPS: 48.592480, -113.606499 Stay south.

GPS: 48.582581, -113.602303 The best route up the pass is a 200-foot climb on east side of creek.

GPS: 48.577499, -113.594704 Red Eagle Pass. The old, overgrown, pre–World War II route goes east, then down drainage. The best route now is a goat trail to the south.

GPS: 48.575680, -113.594902 Navigate goat path down through cliff bands.

GPS: 48.570549, -113.591698 Best to stay south of the runoff.

GPS: 48.567619, -113.594002 Go left around falls through blowdown, then find game trail to lower bench.

(*continued*)

GPS: 48.562279, -113.603996 The real work begins on this steep slope covered with slide alder and deadfall all the way to Nyack Trail. Move carefully, and expect 3 hours for the next 0.9 mile. Tip: Wear sunglasses for eye protection, and pack plenty of water.

GPS: 48.556000, -113.606400 Continue south. More blowdown ahead.

GPS: 48.550171, -113.605598 Nyack Trail. Turn left. Your reward is excellent hiking along turquoise Nyack Creek.

GPS: 48.549999, -113.586403 Campsites near the Nyack Creek.

GPS: 48.549278, -113.573303 Ford the creek.

GPS: 48.538898, -113.537300 Veer left, staying north and above a nameless fork of the Nyack.

GPS: 48.538490, -113.483299 Climb to pass. This north-facing slope is often covered in snow, even in midsummer, and the route changes slightly. Pick your way carefully across.

GPS: 48.520420, -113.472298 Cut Bank Pass; backpack south along Continental Divide then wrap west around Mount Morgan.

GPS: 48.487228, -113.472000 Dawson Pass; descend east into Bighorn Basin.

GPS: 48.479851, -113.448997 No Name Lake campsite.

GPS: 48.481121, -113.445702 Turn right, heading east.

GPS: 48.477661, -113.419899 Keep left, staying on Dawson Pass Trail and the north side of Two Medicine Lake. It's 3.1 miles back to the trailhead.

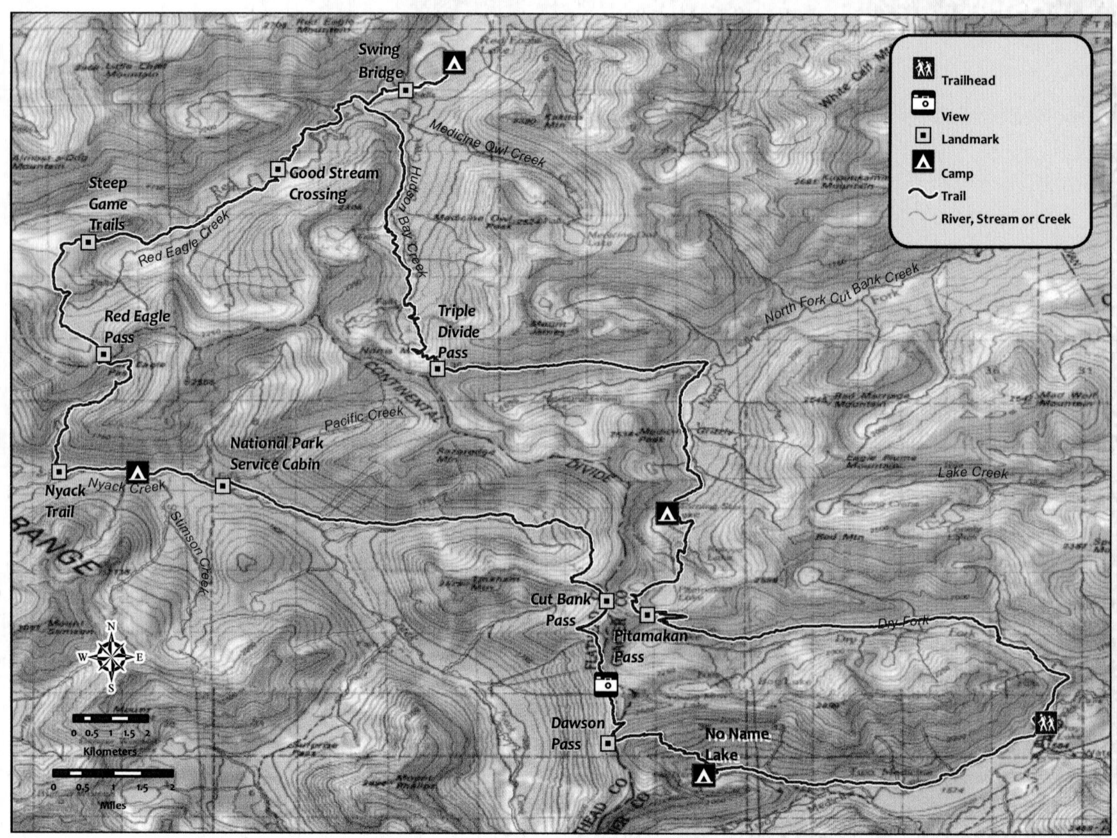

Beware when crossing streams

HOW TO CROSS A RIVER

Forget bears and lightning. The most common and dangerous backcountry hazard is a river crossing. Here's how to do it safely.

MARK CROSSINGS AS YOU PLAN YOUR ROUTE, and call ahead to check water levels. Carry a tide chart if you'll be hiking coastlines.

ALWAYS CROSS A RIVER AT ITS WIDEST POINT; narrow spots are deeper and faster. Check your map for forks, which contain less water and are potentially easier to cross. On glacial rivers, many braids means easier wading.

IN MUDDY OR SILTY RIVERS, LOB A ROCK INTO THE CURRENT. A hollow "ker-ploop" indicates deep, possibly dangerous water. If the rock moves downstream before sinking or you hear rocks rolling downstream, don't ford—the current is too powerful.

LOOK FOR A DIFFERENT PLACE TO CROSS if you're in deeper than your knees. Scout downstream if you encounter rapids, waterfalls, or obstacles such as fallen trees.

CROSS GLACIAL RIVERS EARLY IN THE DAY when possible, to avoid the higher runoff volume that comes with afternoon melting.

KEEP YOUR BOOTS DRY by wearing sandals or dirty socks instead. Only ford a sandy, gentle river barefoot.

USE TREKKING POLES to balance and probe.

FOR FAST-MOVING WATER, CROSS AT A SLIGHT ANGLE, heading downstream but facing upstream. Lean slightly into the current, and step sideways.

UNBUCKLE YOUR PACK'S HIPBELT before fording fast-moving rivers.

FOR A DIFFICULT CROSSING, FORD AS A GROUP WITH EVERYONE LOCKING ARMS. For three people, form a tripod (everyone facing in, arms locked) and shuffle across. Alternatively, if you have a sturdy rope, tie one end to a tree and send a strong party member across to tie off the other end. Clip in to cross; the last member brings the rope.

IF YOU FALL, DON'T PANIC. Remove your pack if it hinders you from getting up. If the current takes you, flip on your back with your feet downstream. When you reach calm water, swim to shore.

Photo: HagePhoto/ Tandem Stock

Toroweap Point, Grand Canyon National Park, Arizona
Photo: Chris Moore / Tandem Stock

GRAND CANYON
NATIONAL PARK

Tanner Trail

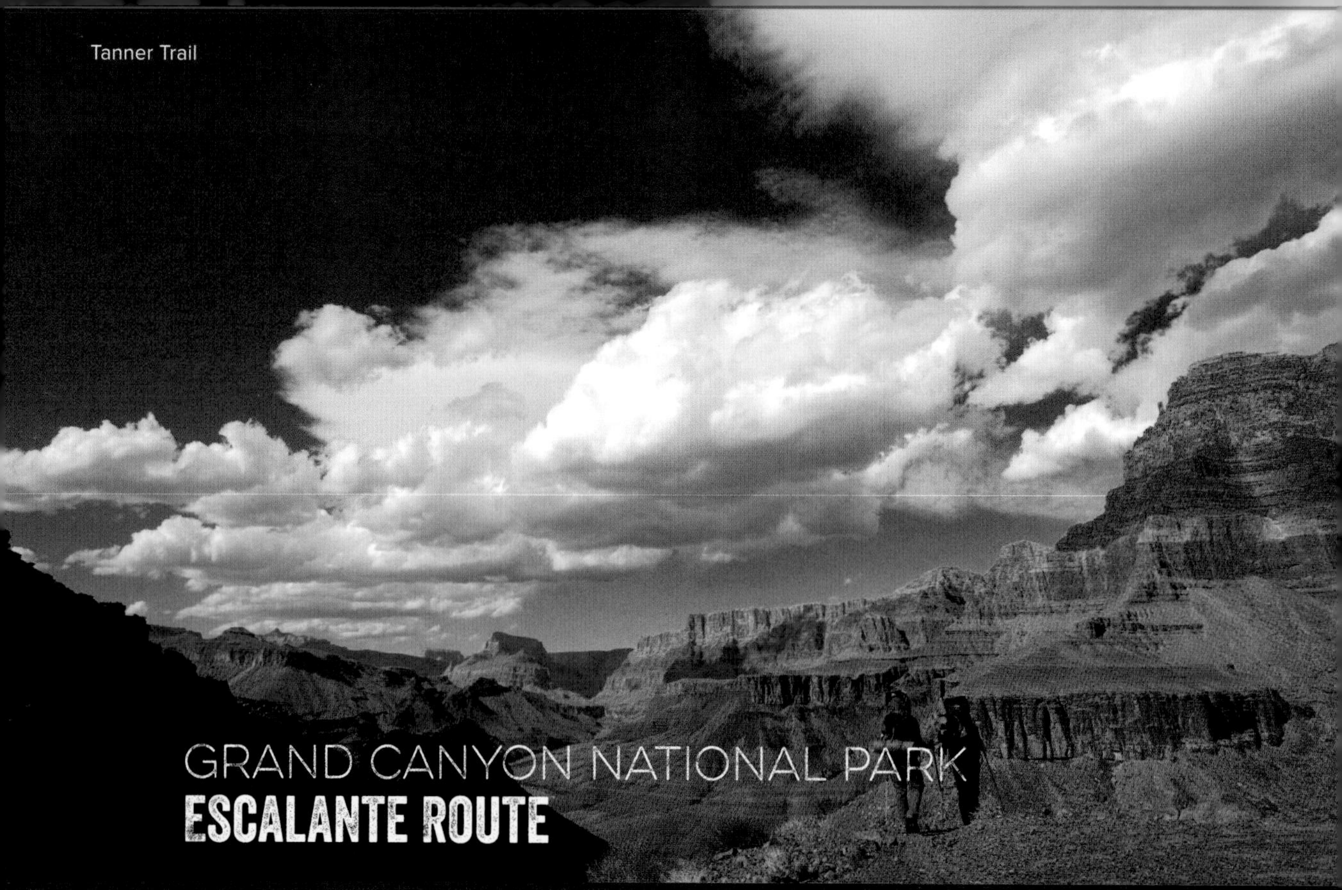

GRAND CANYON NATIONAL PARK
ESCALANTE ROUTE

If you've hiked the park's established paths, it's time to raise your game. Explore the South Rim's wilder side with this off-trail trek. The challenges: Route-finding, exposure, Class 3 scrambling. The rewards: Riverside beach camps, big views, solitude.

Grasping the full scope of the Grand Canyon's nearly 2-billion-year-old geologic grandeur would take a thousand lifetimes and even more trail miles. But you can get darn close on this 6-day, extended-play version of the epic Escalante Route that serves up supersized scenery and unlimited refills of solitude. Start at Lipan Point on the Tanner Trail, where the first 1.2 miles of this unmaintained, primitive path drop a brutally steep 1,300 feet down a scree-filled gully. Pass Escalante and Cardenas Buttes, then switchback down the near-vertical Redwall formation; watch your step on fine scree, but at mile 3.5, don't miss views of Palisades of the Desert, the undulating rock wall across the canyon. The final stretch of this 7.2-mile day reaches the cobblestone bed of Tanner Canyon and a riverside beach at Tanner Rapids, your camp for the next two nights.

On day two, day-hike upriver 3.5 miles northeast on the Beamer Trail to explore around Lava Canyon Falls, where boaters navigate rapids. Acrophobes beware: This side-trip's first 0.5 mile, a two-boots-wide path cutting a 200-foot-high cliff, might be a challenge. En route, get a glimpse of the tilted red shale and hardened black lava, a rare slice of the

Photo: Bennett Barthelemy / Tandem Stock

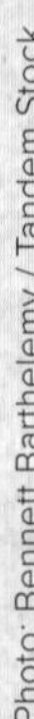

Text: Kelly Bastone and Elisabeth Kwak-Heferan

1.2-billion-year-old Grand Canyon Supergroup layer lining the lower gorge. After riverside rambling, reach the mouth of Palisades Creek and explore the talus slopes above Lava's churning whitewater milkshake, tumbling 37 feet in 200 yards. Backtrack to camp.

On day three, pack up and flex your navigation skills on a 9.8-mile stomp west on the unmaintained Escalante Route, which provides a highlight reel of tight slots, steep climbs, and field-level gorge views. Go 2.6 miles along the river to dry Cardenas Creek. Side-trip on a 30-foot scramble to Unkar Rapids Overlook, where you hover 1,000 feet above the Class 4–7 rapids on the river and below the canyon's fiery cliffs. Across the river, look for the rectangular outlines of several ancient Puebloan ruins written into the cliff sides. Then wind 3.6 miles around unnamed drainages and over narrow scree slopes to the east fork of Escalante Canyon. Here, cairns mark various high and low routes, as erosion is constantly altering the path on the canyon's west side. Walk downcanyon a few hundred feet before climbing out above a pouroff. Follow cairns contouring above the drainage, then head upcanyon into the scramble-filled crux of the route: Seventyfive Mile Creek, a 300-foot-tall labyrinthine squeeze of a slot with sparkling, quartz-studded walls and a polished cobblestone floor. At the head of the canyon just above the river, reach a 30-foot downclimb and lower packs (no rappel required). Drop to the bottom and hike 0.6 mile to camp alongside the waves at Nevills Rapids.

Day four brings a full-body workout via the 7.4-mile hike to Hance Creek. Start by following ledges west above the river, but sticking as close to the banks as possible. At the mouth of Papago Creek, follow cairns out of the drainage. Contour up cliff bands to a 30-foot climb with secure hand- and footholds (more pack hauling involved), then follow a 200-foot-high, boulder-strewn slope to the river. From Hance Rapids, march up the dunes on the East Tonto Trail and wind around the rim of Mineral Canyon below Ayer Point. Make camp next to the perennial waters of Hance Creek east of Horseshoe Mesa. Alternative clutch spot (before Hance Creek): Overnight at the mouth of Red Canyon, a beach campsite enlivened by the roar of Hance Rapids.

On day five, follow a well-marked, 4.9-mile stretch of the Tonto Trail to Cottonwood Creek, another perennial stream with a shady camp. Your last day packs a punch, starting with a 1,200-foot, 1.6-mile climb to crest Horseshoe Mesa near Last Chance Mine. Take in views, but budget time for the three-mile, 2,400-foot lung-buster on the Grandview Trail up to your car.

DISTANCE: 41.1 miles

TIME REQUIRED: 6 days

DIFFICULTY: Strenuous

CONTACT: Grand Canyon National Park, (928) 638-7875; nps.gov/grca

THE PAYOFF: Plumb the wildest depths of the Big Ditch.

TRAILHEAD GPS: 36.071683, -111.831825

FINDING THE TRAILHEAD: Lipan Point (the Tanner trailhead) is 2.3 miles west of Grand Canyon's east entrance. Take the park bus back from Grandview Point when finished, or leave a car at Grandview Point and take a shuttle to your start at Lipan Point.

WAYPOINTS & DIRECTIONS

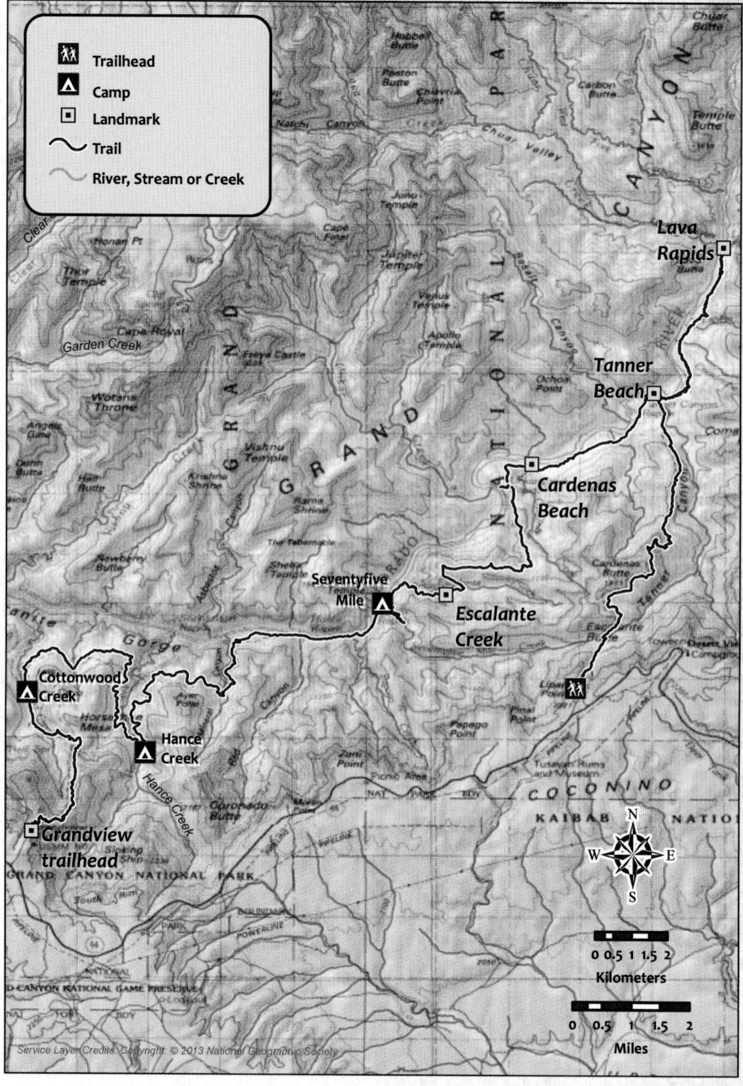

GPS: 36.032590, -111.852495 Tanner trailhead. Head north toward the Colorado River, hugging the cliffs of the Escalante and Cardenas Buttes as you descend.

GPS: 36.103109, -111.833315 Tanner beach. Turn right to head northeast on the Beaver Trail to Lava Rapids.

GPS: 36.137875, -111.816187 Lava Rapids. Head back south on the Beaver Trail to Tanner Beach and continue southwest along the south bank of the Colorado River.

GPS: 36.086009, -111.863523 Cardenas Beach.

GPS: 36.056212, -111.880324 Cross Escalante Creek.

GPS: 36.054616, -111.887512 After hiking along the southern cliffs of the Colorado River, the trail crosses Seventyfive Mile Creek. In order to make a safe crossing, head upstream a good distance.

GPS: 36.052534, -111.900687 Seventyfive Mile Camp on the shore of the Colorado by Nevills Rapids. From here, head southwest along the river before veering left into Mineral Canyon on the Tonto Trail.

GPS: 36.016763, -111.959392 Hance Creek Camp. Continue on the Tonto Trail heading north from the campsite on the west side of Hance Creek, staying right at the fork and looping counterclockwise around Horseshoe Mesa.

GPS: 36.030993, -111.988855 Cottonwood Creek Camp.

GPS: 36.020093, -111.975657 Turn right on Grandview Trail and fork right before Last Chance Mine.

GPS: 35.998033, -111.987656 Grandview trailhead. Turn around and survey the majesty of the landscape you just hiked.

GRAND CANYON NATIONAL PARK
SOUTH KAIBAB TO BRIGHT ANGEL LOOP

Trek to the bottom of the Grand Canyon on a shuttle hike that tours rugged canyons, visits the Colorado River, and features stunning cliffside views.

New to the Big Ditch and want to pack a weekend of adventure into one huge day? String together corridor and threshold trails on this view-filled hike into the guts of the canyon—with an option to bail out across the canyon's midsection. You'll have plenty of company at the start and end, but empty stretches on the Tonto Plateau and along the bottom offer ample breaks from crowds. **NOTE:** Don't attempt this hike in summer's heat, spring and fall are best.

Begin at dawn, descending on the South Kaibab Trail into the belly of the canyon. Fill bottles at the trailhead; it's the only reliable water until mile 8.7. Pass the informally named Ooh Aah Point at the 0.8-mile mark and scan northeast across the canyon to Zoroaster

Temple; by now, morning light will bathe the iconic, eroded spire. Continue switchbacking through off-white Coconino Sandstone and head north along Cedar Ridge through the Supai Group's blood-red shale. Wind behind 6,071-foot O'Neill Butte and drop 300 feet to the saddle below 5,210-foot Skeleton Point, where you'll hear the distant roar of the Colorado River flowing a half-mile below. Look up toward the north-northwest and you can see Natural Arch at the top of the butte. The trail travels across the Tipoff, the trail's steepest section and the beginning the descent into the inner canyon. Here, buttes and points fan out in every direction. Continue straight on the South Kaibab Trail at the next two intersections with Tonto West Trail and Tonto East Trail. Take your group's pulse: If you're feeling gassed, detour left at mile 8.4 to follow the Tonto Plateau onto the Bright Angel Trail and hike 0.3 mile to Indian Gardens. If you're feeling strong, continue to your first views of the Black Bridge spanning the Colorado River.

Soak up views of the Colorado River as you descend into banks of otherworldly Vishnu schist—dark, green-black rocks shot with pink granite and other colors—that make up the basement of the canyon. Walk across Black Bridge. To the west, you can see the Silver Bridge, as well as Bright Angel Campground. Below, whitewater rafters and kayakers take breaks on the beach next to the Colorado River. Follow the trail on the opposite side of the river to pass 800-year-old ruins along the banks. Turn left at a three-way intersection to cross Silver Bridge. Potable water (seasonal) and a bathroom are available here. After the bridge crossing, turn right at the T intersection. The sandy path ahead may slow your pace. Continue straight at a three-way intersection on the Bright Angel Trail (the right trail leads down to the Pipe Creek Beach). Pass the River Resthouse and begin a steep climb up to Indian Gardens. Once there (the aforementioned bailout point), break creekside in groves of cottonwoods and admire the vermillion-streaked, cathedral-like walls. Tank up here before the 4.7-mile, 3,000-foot ascent to the rim.

Pace yourself on Jacob's Ladder, a set of steep switchbacks rising through the Redwall Formation between the 1.5-Mile and 3-Mile Resthouses. After nearly 12 hours of hiking, you'll reach the rim—just in time for victory steaks at the Bright Angel Lodge.

DISTANCE: 13.7 miles

TIME REQUIRED: 1 day

DIFFICULTY: Strenuous

CONTACT: Grand Canyon National Park, (928) 638-7875; nps.gov/grca

THE PAYOFF: This canyon classic packs park highlights into one big day.

TRAILHEAD GPS: 36.0534096, -112.0835495

FINDING THE TRAILHEAD: From S. Lake Powell Boulevard and US 89 in Page, head southwest on US 89. In 81.5 miles, turn right onto AZ 64. In 53 miles, turn right onto S. Entrance Road. In 2.7 miles, turn left onto Village Loop Drive. In 0.2 mile, bear left at Village Loop Drive. In 0.2 mile, turn right to stay on Village Loop Drive. In 100 feet, turn left to stay on Village Loop Drive. Go 500 feet and park in Lot E at the South Rim Backcountry Information Center. Take a free shuttle bus to the trailhead.

Text: Trung Q. Le and Annette McGivney

WAYPOINTS & DIRECTIONS

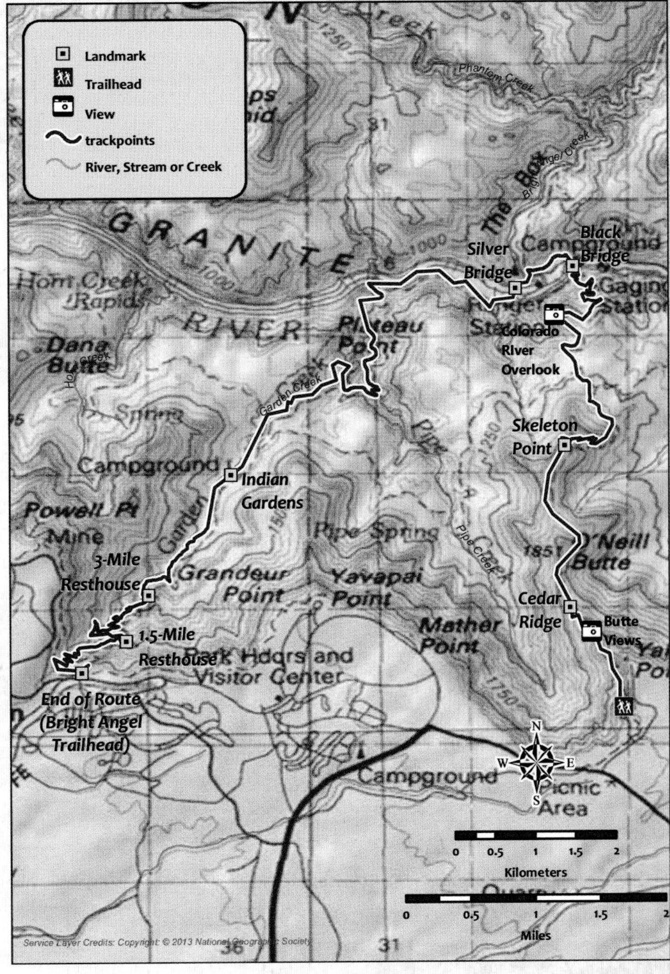

GPS: 36.053410, -112.083550 Head north from the South Kaibab trailhead. From May to mid-October, fill water bottles at the spigot near the bus stop. Caution: There are no other water sources along the South Kaibab Trail.

GPS: 36.064053, -112.089485 Head north along Cedar Ridge, a wide ridge that resembles a plateau (stunning bird's-eye views of the canyon). There are established composting toilets here.

GPS: 36.081291, -112.089996 Skeleton Point, which offers the first views and sounds of the Colorado River. Look down to the east to see the numerous switchbacks ahead.

GPS: 36.085462, -112.086371 Look up toward the north-northwest and you can see Natural Arch at the top of the butte.

GPS: 36.090066, -112.088903 The trail travels across the Tipoff. (***Note:*** There is a phone here that could be used in an emergency.) Continue straight on South Kaibab Trail at the next two intersections with Tonto West Trail and Tonto East Trail.

GPS: 36.096248, -112.086650 First views of Black Bridge, a suspension bridge over the Colorado. Look down on the series of switchbacks to come.

GPS: 36.099342, -112.088871 Stay right at Y intersection on South Kaibab Trail as the River Trail enters on the left.

GPS: 36.100435, -112.089064 Walk across Black Bridge. To the west, you can see the Silver Bridge, as well as Bright Angel Campground. Below, whitewater rafters and kayakers take breaks on the beach next to the Colorado.

GPS: 36.099842, -112.093971 The trail passes 800-year-old ruins along the banks of the Colorado. Turn left at three-way intersection to cross Silver Bridge.

GPS: 36.098122, -112.095406 Cross the Colorado River on the Silver Bridge, a suspension bridge with views of the raging water below. After the bridge crossing, turn right at the T intersection.

GPS: 36.098541, -112.111748 Continue straight at three-way intersection on the Bright Angel Trail. Trail passes the River Resthouse and steeply climbs through the canyon up to Indian Gardens.

GPS: 36.081951, -112.124550 Continue straight on Bright Angel Trail at three-way intersection. Tonto East Trail enters on the left.

GPS: 36.065552, -112.136231 3-Mile Resthouse. Take a break at this shelter. (***Note:*** Emergency phone available). Only three miles of trail remain to the South Rim. The route continues to climb up switchbacks; views extend into the canyon to Indian Gardens.

GPS: 36.060680, -112.138733 1.5-Mile Resthouse. There are two shelters here; one of them has potable water and a bathroom. Next, the trail continues to climb up switchbacks, but becomes noticeably flatter as it approaches the South Rim.

GPS: 36.057312, -112.143631 The route ends at the Bright Angel Trailhead.

GRAND CANYON NATIONAL PARK

THE KIDS ARE ALRIGHT

The only thing you'll regret about taking the brood backpacking is not doing it sooner—and more often.

"How much farther?" It's a question young kids seem hardwired to ask, whether on a car ride or a hike. My kids were no different. All three boys started camping before they could talk, then backpacking as soon as they could walk, and I'm pretty sure that was one of their first sentences. But really, is there anything to be gained from telling the truth?

In my twenties, as a wilderness guide for teens, I developed an "educational" strategy to address this inevitable question, and I adopted the same policy with my kids, Milo, Zig, and Tate, from the outset: No matter where we were—a few minutes from the trailhead, a few minutes from camp, or anywhere in between—when they asked how much farther, I'd respond: "We're halfway." Admittedly, that answer didn't always lead directly to smiles, and it probably delayed their grasp of distances by a couple of years. But early on, they learned to stop dwelling on when we'd "get there" and start enjoying the hiking part of backpacking, because that's the real hurdle with kids. (Playing in the dirt, climbing rocks, eating s'mores, and wrestling in a tent don't need a hard sell.) In the beginning, expect some trial and error. There were plenty of times that we started too late and found ourselves pleading with preschoolers—"Keep hiking, you can do it"—in order to make camp before dark. (Tip: There's no shame in candy bribes.) But mostly, it's just fun. All of it.

Case in point: On a weekend trip in Colorado's Indian Peaks Wilderness, we tackled a route that climbs about 2,000 feet in 3 miles. Milo, Zig, and Tate were 8, 6, and 4 years old at the time, and I expected them to poop out, well, about halfway up the steep trail. Instead, my wife, Jen, told a Batman story, the boys stopped to explore an abandoned silver mine, and we all took a break to throw rocks in a scree field. They were surprised when we arrived at the pass on the Continental Divide so "fast," and ran down to the lake on the other side. Like true backpackers, they knew instinctively that the pine- and meadow-fringed basin was a magical place simply because we'd walked to it. That evening, a swirling, low-hanging cloud caught light from the setting sun and filled the cirque with a red glow. Moisture in the cloud reflected the light, so it felt like we were camping in the middle of an electric snow globe. Will they remember playing cards amid that otherworldly light? Doesn't matter. I'm convinced it left an imprint that will last a lifetime—on all of us.

"My pack's too heavy." Not a surprising complaint from a 5-year-old. So when Tate announced that he couldn't carry his pack another step, I ignored him. We were hiking up a trail in the Rockies in October, amid aspens turned a dozen shades of gold. Jen, Milo, and Zig continued up the trail ahead of us, ascending along a creek. I slowed down and walked next to Tate, my youngest. I figured he was just tired from his school field trip. He had gone to a farm near Boulder, Colorado, where he and his classmates had been encouraged to pick all the potatoes, onions, carrots, turnips, and pumpkins they could carry. He came home dirty and exhausted but excited about his haul.

The next day, we had this season-ending weekend in the high country on the schedule. We performed the normal fire drill getting out the door, haranguing the kids to pack their gear. They've been responsible for getting their own stuff together since they could carry the smallest packs, starting with the little things—a book, a headlamp—and growing into the heavier items. We figure if they're responsible for packing, they can't complain about what they don't have. (Admittedly, the rule has resulted in a few missing items.) On this trip, Milo and Zig were responsible for all of their gear, and Tate, the kindergartner, was charged with carrying everything but his bag and pad. That's why I felt comfortable dismissing his whining. How heavy could a kid-size fleece and a comic book be?

But when he stopped to complain yet again, dropping his pack to the ground and leaning against a boulder to rest, I was torn. Like any parent who wants his kid to love the outdoors, I didn't want to let one moment undermine everything that had come before.

"Please," he asked, "can you carry my pack for a little bit?"

"OK," I relented, knowing we still had a couple of hours to go. "Just for a bit." I reached down and grabbed the pack—and nearly lost my balance trying to lift it. "What in the world do you have in here?" I asked. "Just my pumpkin," Tate answered, as if it was one of the 10 Essentials. Another reason to take your kids backpacking: You think you've seen it all, and then find yourself hanging a pumpkin in a bear bag.

Challenging kids—without pushing too hard—requires constant recalibration as they get older. You want to see them experience the triumph of achievement without overdoing the agony of defeat.

We had something like that in mind when we hiked to the bottom of the Grand Canyon for Christmas, a couple months after the pumpkin episode. Not surprisingly, the kids breezed down the South Kaibab Trail, gaping over the views and the trailside drops. We pitched our tinsel-draped tent at Bright Angel campground, where a ranger convinced the boys that a satellite passing overhead was Santa's sleigh, and we joined a group of carolers at Phantom Ranch. Mission accomplished? Not quite.

As every Grand Canyon hiker knows, getting in is the easy part. On the hike out, along the Bright Angel Trail, the boys slowed to a snail's pace. Every time they looked at the rim far, far above, they might as well have been contemplating the moon. Tate needed more superhero stories per mile than usual. But their little legs kept churning away. Over two days, we inched our way upward, and they started hiking stronger as the inner gorge receded below. And thanks to backpacking, we experienced another parenting moment that's hard to beat: when your kids have every right to complain but don't.

We were nearly at the top when we passed an older hiker, perhaps in this sixties, bent under a heavy load, resting beside the trail. "How much farther do you think it is?" he asked as we passed.

"Looks like we're about halfway," Milo responded, without hesitation.

I couldn't have been more proud.

—Dennis Lewon

Elves Chasm

GRAND CANYON NATIONAL PARK

ROYAL ARCH LOOP

The best view in the Grand Canyon can't be seen from the rim. Brave the trek to Royal Arch, hidden deep in the gorge, and your world will never look the same.

This 34-mile loop packs explores canyons and cliffs, and leads to a 20-foot technical rock climb on day three. Starting at the South Bass trailhead, descend 1.2 miles north to a three-way junction to begin a counterclockwise loop. Go straight on South Bass Trail and drop into Bass Canyon, descending more than 2,000 feet in 2.5 miles between two towering sandstone buttes that pinch the gorge tight. Bear left onto the Tonto Trail and go 1.5 miles to a plateau campsite under the 4,800-foot red walls of Tyndall Dome.

Start day two by 8 a.m. to avoid the midday scorch—it's 11.5 miles to a primo campsite on the Colorado River, the trip's first dependable water source. Follow the Tonto Trail west to the bottom of Copper Canyon, where you might find water in potholes after a rain. The route veers around 4,700-foot Fiske Butte and traces sheer sandstone cliffs above Walthenberg Rapids, which roar through Granite Gorge. After 10 miles, the Tonto Trail ends in Garnet Canyon. Head west on an unmaintained trail dotted with cairns. End at the sandy banks of Toltec Beach, your second camp at mile 17.5.

On day three, leave your pack at camp for a 2.1-mile out-and-back to Elves Chasm, a secluded, waterfall-rich grotto at the mouth of Royal Arch Creek. Backtrack to camp and lay

Photo: iStockPhoto.com / tonda

Text: Annette McGivney and Elias Butler

over or finish the day's remaining six miles with a stiff ascent to a roughly 20-foot rock wall and the technical crux of the trip. Pack a harness, 40-foot dynamic rope, locking carabiner, and 20 feet of webbing for belays and for hauling up packs; someone in your party should feel comfortable leading this short, stiff climb. From the top of the cliff, the route climbs gradually for 1.7 miles before dropping into Royal Arch Creek. Then descend the rocky creekbed to Royal Arch, the Grand Canyon's largest natural rock bridge. (There's a reliable spring upstream.) Hike back upstream 3.2 miles to a set of smooth potholes carved into the creekbed and your last campsite.

The final day ascends past Montezuma, Toltec, and Chemehuevi Points. After 7.3 miles, reconnect with the South Bass Trail and climb 1,200 feet to your starting point.

You can reverse this route to make the technical 20-foot wall a rappel rather than a climb. But increase your water capacity and expect heavier packs, since the 2-day, mostly uphill stretch from Toltec Beach to the South Rim has no reliable water sources.

DISTANCE: 34 miles

TIME REQUIRED: 4–5 days

DIFFICULTY: Strenuous to Expert

CONTACT: Grand Canyon National Park, (928) 638-7875; nps.gov/grca

THE PAYOFF: Tight slot canyons, hidden waterfall grottos, and up-close views of the park's largest natural bridge.

TRAILHEAD GPS: 36.183853, -112.3766613

FINDING THE TRAILHEAD: From Tusayan, go west on FR 328 (off AZ 64) for 6 miles. Veer northwest onto FR 328A for another 17.6 miles to Pasture Wash Road. Turn right and continue to the parking lot.

WAYPOINTS & DIRECTIONS

GPS: 36.183853, -112.376661 Drop off the rim on the South Bass Trail.Good view of Mount Huethawali.

GPS: 36.192720, -112.374172 Head north on South Bass Trail; you'll return to this junction on the last day.

GPS: 36.203015, -112.373639 Trail descends the Supai Formation.

GPS: 36.216406, -112.355247 This is just above the junction of the South Bass Trail and the Tonto Trail. Keep left following cairns for Tonto Trail.

GPS: 36.231639, -112.348788 Camp 1. Very good views of the Colorado River, Tyndall Dome, the North Rim, and the Grand Canyon looking up- and downstream. No water here.

GPS: 36.227900, -112.378313 Here the Tonto Trail crosses the bottom of Copper Canyon. You might find water in potholes here after a rain.

GPS: 36.232920, -112.413955 Good view above Walthenburg Rapids and the Colorado River. The Tonto Trail skirts the edge of a cliff formed by Tapeats Sandstone, making for excellent views.

GPS: 36.214346, -112.421036 This is where the Tonto Trail officially ends at Garnet Canyon. The trail descends to the bed of Garnet. Look for a footpath to continue heading west below the Tapeats Sandstone. This path is marked by rock cairns and begins to slowly descend along a talus slope toward the Colorado River.

GPS: 36.200720, -112.432065 This is Toltec Beach, the first good water (at the Colorado River) since leaving the South Bass trailhead. Good camping on sandy flat spots. Hikers should leave their packs here and then head downstream toward Elves Chasm (the mouth of Royal Arch Creek). then return the same way. (*continued*)

GPS: 36.197603, -112.450647 This is the mouth of Royal Arch Creek and the entrance to the grotto named Elves Chasm. To get to this spot, hikers must head west along a cairned path from Toltec Beach that follows the talus slope above the Colorado. It is a rough path and will take 1.5 hours to cover due to the up-and-down nature or catch a ride with passing boaters. Turn back here to retrieve your pack.

GPS: 36.196966, -112.436206 A 20-foot cliff must climbed here in order to continue. Sometimes a knotted rope is already in place, but don't count on it. Pack your own rope, harness, and anchors. To reach this spot, leave Toltec Beach and ascend the sandy trail that begins immediately to the south. This trail ascends steeply toward the prominent travertine cliff above the Colorado River and leads to the climbing spot.

GPS: 36.183991, -112.451162 Take this steep route for access into Royal Arch Creek from the Tonto Platform.

GPS: 36.191300, -112.453802 Here is Royal Arch, the largest natural bridge in Grand Canyon. Great camping and good water, a special place for those who love beauty and stillness.

GPS: 36.188979, -112.455068 This is the best water to be had on the entire loop.

GPS: 36.164672, -112.443932 Great last-night camp. Reliable water in potholes and nice views. Continue east and northeast past Toltec and Montezuma Points before closing the loop at the South Bass Trail.

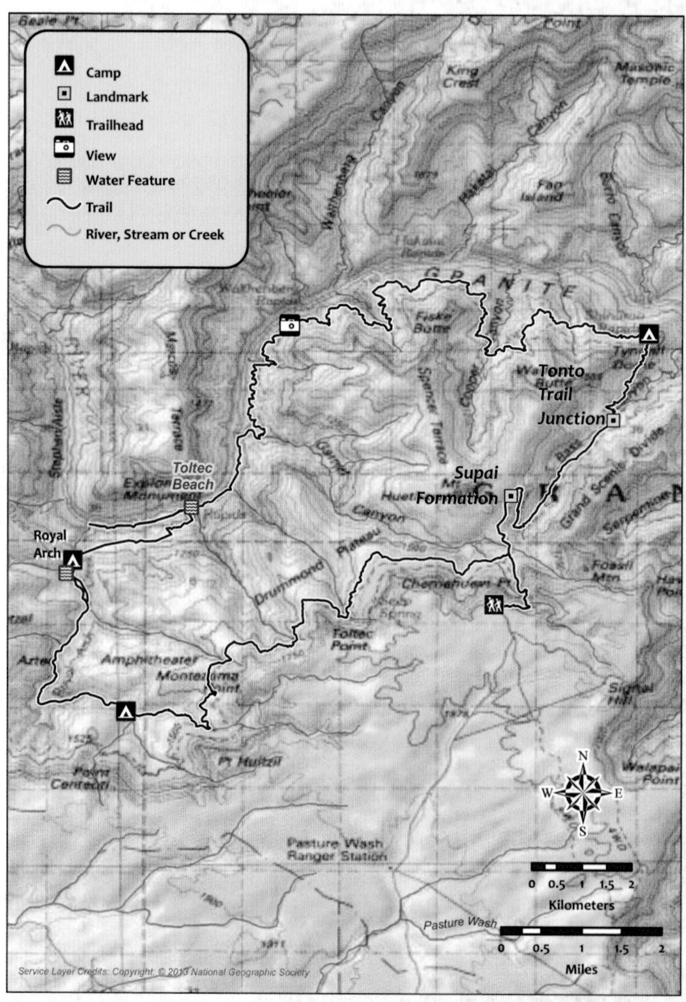

The Colorado River
Photo: Chad Case / Tandem Stock

GRAND CANYON NATIONAL PARK
POWELL PLATEAU

Follow the footsteps of John Wesley Powell to iconic views above the Grand Canyon on this backcountry trek.

Naturalist John Wesley Powell famously endured three months of disasters—including near drownings, mutiny, and wrecked equipment—on his first cartographic exploration of the Grand Canyon in 1869. Thanks in part to his beta, well-prepared hikers don't have to share Powell's hardships. But you will share the same crowd-free vistas of the Grand Canyon that he saw on this out-and-back to Powell Plateau, a remote, pine-forested tableland that rises a mile above the Colorado River near the canyon's North Rim. It's only 2.5 miles from the trailhead to the plateau, but you'll want to spend at least 2 days exploring the 10 miles of secluded trail along the rim. Start by switchbacking down 1 mile and 800 feet from Swamp Point trailhead to an unsigned junction at Muav Saddle. Tank up on water here. Continue straight and descend to a slightly lower saddle, then climb 900 feet over 1.5 miles to reach the plateau. (The trail is faint in places.) Camp here: The rimside perch lies on a Powell Plateau ledge, where the tent-door view looks west across gaping Bedrock and Galloway Canyons. At the plateau's western edge, you'll find numerous ledges like this one. When you reach the rim, follow the trail south for one magnificent view after another. Campsites are plentiful in the ponderosa forest; water, however, is scarce. Powell Plateau offers an excellent side-trip option: Stay

Photo: iStockPhoto.com / KimberlyDeprey

here your first or last night on a four-day, 27-mile out-and-back on the classic, very remote North Bass Trail down to the Colorado River. Autumn is the best time to go; the North Rim remains snowbound and inaccessible until late spring, when the inner canyon already approaches oven temps.

DISTANCE: 5 miles

TIME REQUIRED: 2 days

DIFFICULTY: Intermediate

CONTACT: Grand Canyon National Park, (928) 638-7875; nps.gov/grca

THE PAYOFF: Solitude and exploration on the canyon's forested North Rim.

TRAILHEAD GPS: 36.3356285095215, -112.349716186523

FINDING THE TRAILHEAD: From Jacob Lake, go 26.5 miles south on AZ 67. Turn right on FR 22, left on FR 270, then right on FR 223. Go 5.8 miles, then veer left on FR 268 and left again on FR 268B and into the park. Go 7.8 miles to Swamp Point Trailhead. High-clearance vehicles only.

WAYPOINTS & DIRECTIONS

GPS: 36.335629, -112.349716 Swamp Point Trailhead. Head roughly west, taking some switchbacks descending toward Mauv Saddle.

GPS: 36.333761, -112.360868 Fill up all of your water bottles here.

GPS: 36.333070, -112.370739 Camp anywhere along Powell Plateau in established campsites; explore the entire rim from here. Retrace your steps back to the trailhead.

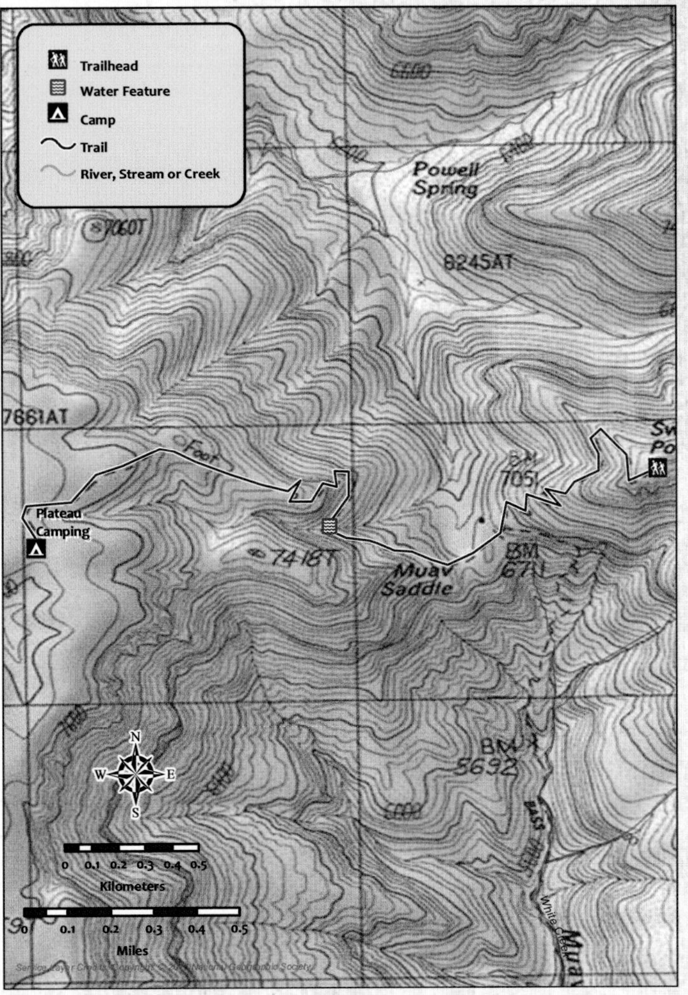

GRAND CANYON NATIONAL PARK
THE JEWELS ROUTE

Hopi Point, Grand Canyon National Park, Arizona

Drop into America's belly on a little-known hike that dips in and out of four different canyons, each blessed with gurgling springwater.

Life gets pared down quickly on the West Tonto. Even on milder spring days on this arid shelf, your world is reduced to walking and water. Or, more specifically, walking to get to water. For five days, that is what you'll do. It's all you'll do. And it will be the best five days of your life.

The trek that Grand Canyon regulars call the Jewels descends the South Bass Trail for 4 miles through brush-choked Bass Canyon to the Tonto Plateau, an exposed and undulating balcony perched 2,000 feet above the Colorado River. Rather than continuing down Bass to the rapids, you'll hang a right on West Tonto Trail. Here, the people are few and water is sparse. But each source is conveniently spaced a day's walk apart in side canyons all named after precious gems: Ruby, Turquoise, Sapphire, and Agate.

The bumpy, 25-mile dirt road to South Bass trailhead weeds out many would-be hikers. (That, and the mandatory car shuttle to Hermits Rest trailhead at the end of your hike.) And since most of this trek is a lateral ramble across the Grand Canyon's panoramic mezzanine level, goal-oriented endurance hikers tend to stick to more difficult and crowded rim-to-river trails. Heading east from the South Bass junction, the barely discernable West Tonto Trail winds through a sunbaked, low-lying obstacle course of blackbrush and prickly pear. The canyon falls away to your left, dropping thousands of feet straight down into a tight corridor of black schist and green river. Across the gorge, an archipelago of pastel-colored buttes and temples rise from an ocean of space stretching some 20 miles to the canyon's North Rim. Within two miles from the junction, you'll reach the twisting folds of Serpentine Canyon, your first night's camp. If you're lucky, the tiny seep at the canyon's

Photo: iStockPhoto.com / ventdusud

Text: Annette McGivney

bottom will be running, producing a trickle of the cold, sweet water that emerges from an ancient aquifer. Depending on seasonal precipitation, Serpentine can be dry. Be prepared to dry camp your first night. Carry in 6 to 8 liters per person.

Your second day, it's another 6 achingly beautiful miles on the Tonto to Ruby Canyon, the next water source. As you circumnavigate the deep drainage from the Tonto's high perch, you'll spot the glint of water. Near the head of the canyon, the trail meets a sandy streambed and a series of shallow, clear pools that are fed by a bubbling spring. Mission accomplished. Guzzle up.

On day three, continue connecting the dots, hiking 6 miles from Ruby to Turquoise Canyon and another water-blessed camp. Between the jewels, take in the space and solitude, venturing to the lip of the plateau to look down at the Colorado. Day four brings Sapphire and Agate—each a lush oasis. After 14 long miles, you'll reach flowing Boucher Creek. Camp here, next to what seems like an obscene amount of water. On your fifth and final day, you'll climb 10 steep miles out of the canyon on the Boucher and Hermit Trails to Hermits Rest trailhead, where your car is parked. (Note: Reliable water on this route can usually be found in Ruby and Turquoise Canyons and Boucher Creek. Depending on seasonal precipitation, water may also be found in Serpentine, Sapphire, and Agate Canyons. A high-clearance, 4WD vehicle is required.)

If this sounds too remote and committing, there is Plan B. Although the 30-mile East Tonto Trail is not as remote as West Tonto, it retains the far-as-the-eye-can-see, 360-degree vantages found atop the Tonto Plateau. It is also significantly less crowded than the popular corridor trails like the South Kaibab and Bright Angel. Hike down the South Rim's brutally steep and rocky New Hance Trail to the river and camp on the beach near Hance Rapid, then ascend the scree-filled slopes of the Colorado River gorge, turning west on the East Tonto Trail toward Hance Creek and hulking Horseshoe Mesa. You can climb up the east side of this red monolith via the Page Springs Trail or continue on East Tonto to Cottonwood Creek. Have lunch on the mesa and soak in the panoramic views; if you're not claustrophobic, take a peek inside Cave of the Domes near the Cottonwood Trail junction. From Horseshoe Mesa, it's 3 steep miles to the South Rim via the Grandview Trail.

DISTANCE: 50 miles

TIME REQUIRED: 5 days

DIFFICULTY: Intermediate

CONTACT: Grand Canyon National Park, (928) 638-7875; nps.gov/grca

THE PAYOFF: Discover the Canyon's best-kept secrets on the secluded West Tonto Trail.

TRAILHEAD GPS: 36.183853, -112.376533

FINDING THE TRAILHEAD: From Flagstaff, drive northwest on US 180/Fort Valley Ranch Road. for 49 miles. Turn right on US 180/AZ 64, and go 27 miles to Grand Canyon Village. Drive through the village on Village Loop Drive, merge onto West Rim Drive, and park a shuttle car at Hermits Rest Trailhead (the end of the road). Backtrack to three-way junction with West Rim Drive and an unnamed road; turn right on the unnamed road and go 400 feet. Turn right onto another unnamed road; follow it 19.5 miles to South Bass Trailhead.

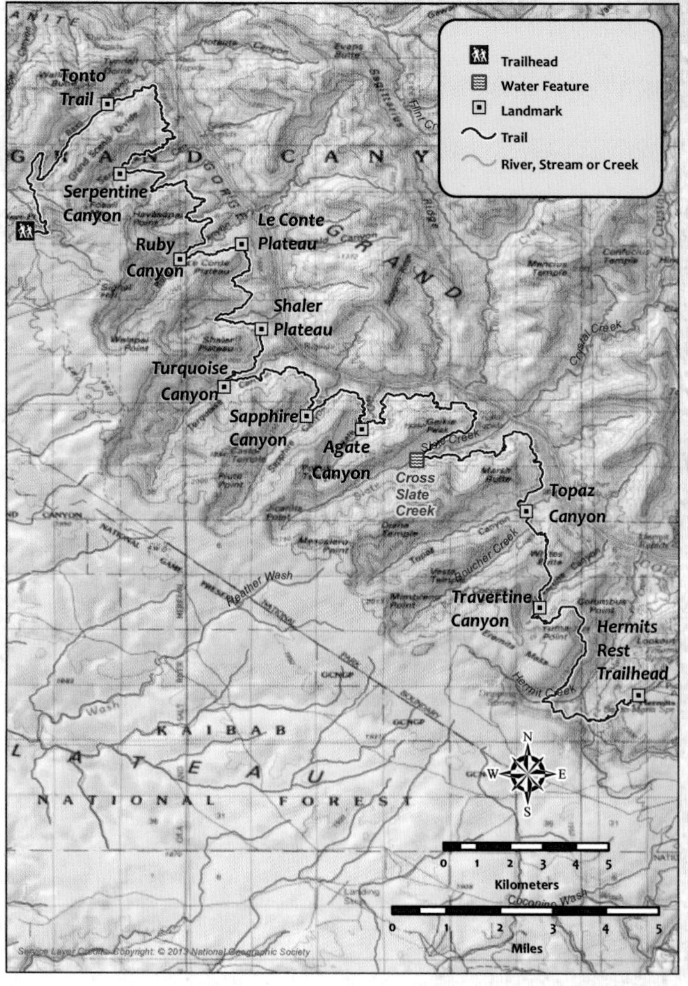

WAYPOINTS & DIRECTIONS

GPS: 36.183853, -112.376533 South Bass trailhead. Good view of Mount Huethawali; drop off the rim on the South Bass Trail.

GPS: 36.192703, -112.374065 Go north on South Bass Trail.

GPS: 36.217500, -112.354342 Bear west onto Tonto Trail. The route follows this trail for the next 29 miles.

GPS: 36.222223, -112.341471 Trail swings to the south above Granite Gorge and the Colorado River.

GPS: 36.208612, -112.335845 Look down onto the Serpentine Rapids before turning southwest into Serpentine Canyon.

GPS: 36.176752, -112.334561 Ruby Canyon.

GPS: 36.180704, -112.317780 Hike south across the Le Conte Plateau.

GPS: 36.158355, -112.312503 Hike south across the Shaler Plateau.

GPS: 36.143095, -112.322563 Drop into Turquoise Canyon—it's likely you'll find running water here.

GPS: 36.135533, -112.300165 Sapphire Canyon.

GPS: 36.131966, -112.285402 Agate Canyon.

GPS: 36.123824, -112.270592 Cross Slate Creek, one of the more reliable water sources. Look for campsites nearby.

GPS: 36.130700, -112.241349 The trail curves to the south, traversing the base of Marsh Butte.

GPS: 36.110439, -112.240984 Topaz Canyon.

GPS: 36.104615, -112.236843 Turn right onto Boucher Trail at T junction and begin a switchback climb. Whites Butte rises directly to the southeast.

GPS: 36.085037, -112.237315 Travertine Canyon.

GPS: 36.060119, -112.236546 Turn left at T junction and hike east.

GPS: 36.055587, -112.224441 Continue straight on Hermit Trail.

GPS: 36.055015, -112.221308 Continue straight on Hermit Trail.

GPS: 36.062109, -112.210318 Hermits Rest trailhead.

Fire brings warmth and comfort

HOW TO BUILD A NEVER-FAIL CAMPFIRE

Where campfires are allowed, it's important to know how to build—and put out—flames properly.

Backcountry bonfires are as yesterday as neon tracksuits. Even small campfires, where they aren't banned outright—as in popular sections of the Sierra high country—are strongly discouraged elsewhere. Still, there are special circumstances in which knowing how to perform one of humankind's first true skills can save your butt. Like when you're soaked to the bone after a day of sea kayaking in Glacier Bay's 70-mile Muir Inlet and the cold rain just won't let up.

Find Fuel Use driftwood or deadfall; an armload of twigs and sticks (thumb-width or skinnier) will get the fire going, and a couple of armloads of wrist-thick wood will last the evening. Search for dry wood under rock overhangs, near fallen logs, and at the bottom of driftwood piles. If necessary, shave off wet bark with your pocketknife to get to the dry stuff underneath.

Make a Pit By the water, scoop out gravel or sand below the high-tide mark to create an Leave No Trace–approved fireplace. It's harder to be low-impact on land, but you can still dig (or better yet find) a small pit and surround it with wind-breaking rocks.

Rig a Tarp This shelter will shield you, your woodpile, and your fire.

Build It Up Place a handful of firestarter on a bed of sticks. Leave gaps for air to fuel the flames. Good fire starters include dryer lint and egg cartons filled with wood shavings and coated in wax, which light even after they've been dunked. You can even use tortilla chips.

Ignite Place a fist-size stack of tinder (wood shavings, twigs, paper) over your fire starter, then flick your Bic. (Matches are fine as a backup, but waterproof them by dipping the heads in melted paraffin.)

Add Fuel Carefully supply more tinder and larger sticks without smothering your nascent fire. Protect it from the wind, and blow on it gently to fan the flames.

Burn the wood to ashes if possible, leaving them for the incoming tide to scatter.

Photo: Ethan Welty/Tandem Stock

The Grand Tetons in Grand Teton National Park, Wyoming
Photo: iStockPhoto.com / MartinM303

GRAND TETON
NATIONAL PARK

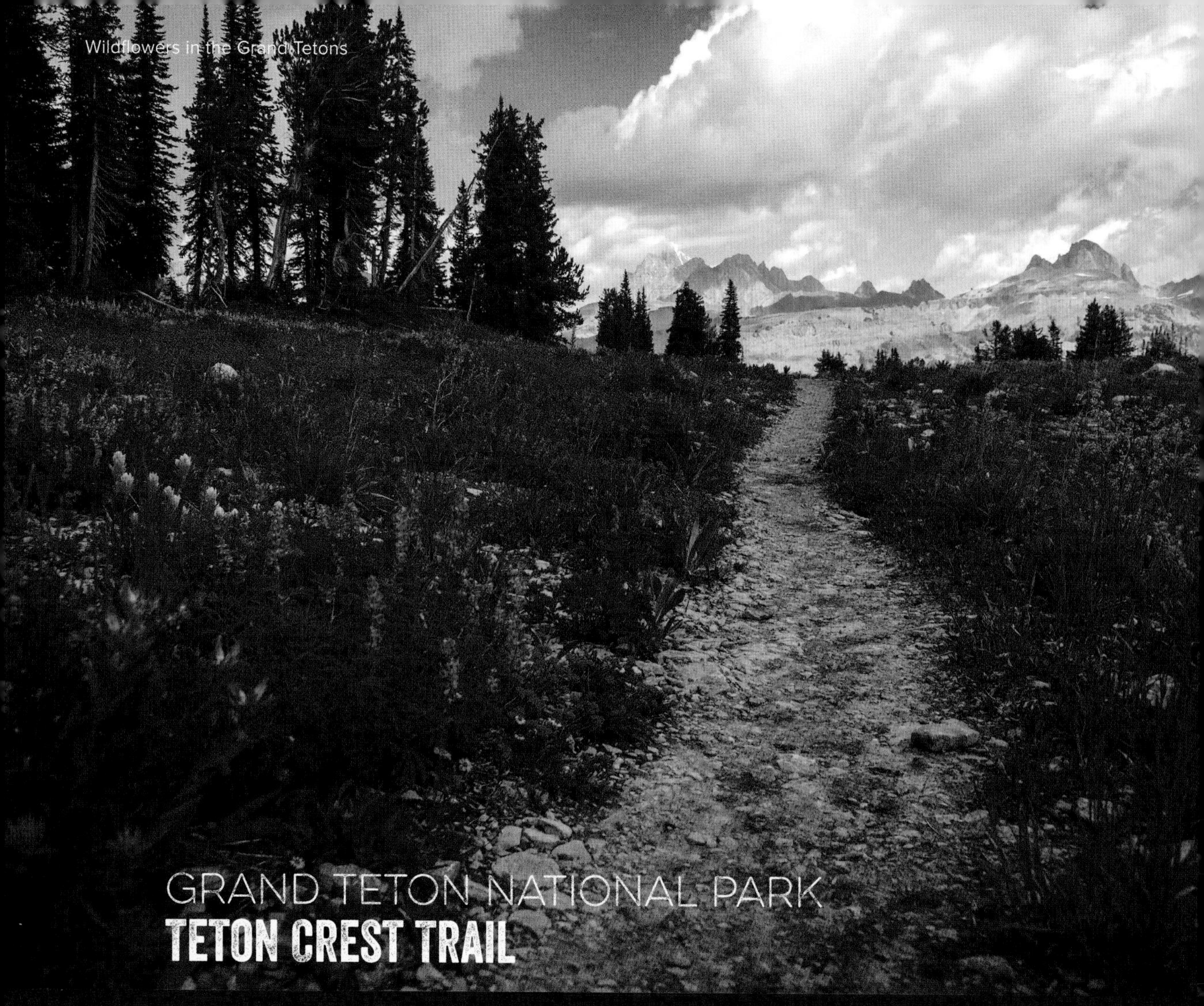

Wildflowers in the Grand Tetons

GRAND TETON NATIONAL PARK
TETON CREST TRAIL

Trace the crest of the Tetons on this classic point-to-point that rarely sinks below 8,000 feet.

Think the view of the mighty Tetons is impressive from the park road? Wait until you see them from the backcountry. The Teton Crest Trail runs through the scraggy alpine zone west of the summits, dishing out vistas that somehow make 12,325-foot Teewinot, 12,804-foot Middle Teton, 12,928-foot Mount Owen, and 13,700-foot Grand Teton look even bigger. "With all due respect to the John Muir Trail," declares former *Backpacker* Northwest editor Michael Lanza, "the Teton Crest will forever be my all-time favorite. Its combination of constant, incredible scenery, great campsites, abundant wildlife, and accessibility for all types of backpackers is simply unmatched." Rarely dipping below 8,000 feet, this high route crosses tundra bejeweled with paintbrush and

Photo: iStockPhoto.com / skiserge1

Text: Mike Lanza and Elisabeth Kwak-Heferan

larkspur, offers mesmerizing and constant views of jagged peaks, and lets you camp with center-balcony views of everything—the perch on Death Canyon Shelf will make you want to homestead right there.

The full route links Teton Pass on WY 22 to String Lake in Grand Teton National Park, but other approaches are also popular: Take the Teton Village tram and hike to Marion Lake to pick up the trail at mile 10 and save 2,500 feet of climbing, or start at the Coal Creek or Moose Creek trailheads. Hiking south to north includes more elevation gain, but saves the best views for last.

From Teton Pass, head north to Phillips Canyon and Phillips Pass, climbing switchbacks to a 9,085-foot saddle before descending to Middle Fork Granite Creek. Climb out of the tiered basin to pass turquoise Marion Lake (and potential campsites) on a grassy bench. Ahead, watch for elk roaming through the next lonely, five-mile stretch. Cross a small saddle at mile 15.2, and continue north for less than 2 miles to Fox Creek Pass, a meadow with sweeping northeast views of the Tetons' vaulted skyline. In July, lupine and columbine splash the scene with blue, purple, and yellow. From here, traverse north-northeast to reach Death Canyon Shelf, a 3-mile-long, 900-foot-wide ledge. A 500-foot-tall cliff band rises to the west and a 200-foot ledge drops into Death Canyon to the east. There are year-round springs and several campsites, all with views of the Grand Teton and other peaks. Find second-night campsites by a creek with some low trees for wind protection.

The next morning, take the gentle, 200-foot climb over 9,726-foot Mount Meek Pass (you may not even notice it), then descend the Sheep Steps switchbacks into Alaska Basin. Pass popular campsites at Basin Lakes in Alaska Basin, speckled with granite and a cluster of lakes. Continue north past Sunset Lake to cross a high plateau. Linger at 10,372-foot Hurricane Pass for top-of-the-world views of the Grand, Middle, and South Tetons, which rise just 2 miles to the east. Here is where the vistas reach their climax. Descend past Schoolroom Glacier, a remnant ice field next to a teal-colored lake. Turn right at the three-way junction, heading south, to grab one of the uppermost sites in South Fork Cascade Canyon. Or descend switchbacks into South Fork Cascade Canyon and turn left to wind south through the evergreen forests of North Fork Cascade Canyon, where roughly 1 later you can claim one of the first established camps for neck-cramping views of the Grand, 5,500 feet overhead.

Get an early start the next day to beat the afternoon heat on the relentless, 2,000-plus-foot climb to 10,720-foot Paintbrush Divide, where you'll get slap-in-the-face views of the Grand. Pass Lake Solitude, set in a stone cirque. Ahead, Mount Owen and Teewinot explode into view; it's a wildflower heaven in summer. (Got an extra night? Camp in the upper reaches of the canyon.) Next, descend 8.3 miles past cliffs striped in browns, grays, and muted reds. Cross String Lake and then turn right, heading south, to find the end of the route at the trailhead east of String Lake. Shuttle back to your car, where you can revel in having seen the full glory of the Tetons by getting up close and personal.

DISTANCE: 38.1 miles

TIME REQUIRED: 3–5 days

DIFFICULTY: Strenuous

CONTACT: Grand Teton National Park, (307) 739-3343; nps.gov/grte

THE PAYOFF: Traverse the nation's most photogenic range.

TRAILHEAD GPS: 43.509250, -110.923526

FINDING THE TRAILHEAD: From Jackson, go north 12 miles on US 191, then turn left on Teton Park Road. In 8.5 miles, turn left on Jenny Lake Road. In 2.5 miles, turn left on String Lake Road. In 0.3 mile, park shuttle car. Return to Jackson via US 191, and turn right to go west on WY 22/Teton Pass Highway. In 9.5 miles, take a sharp right onto Phillips Canyon Trail. Go 0.4 mile to the trailhead.

WAYPOINTS & DIRECTIONS

GPS: 43.509250, -110.923526 Hike north from the trailhead.

GPS: 43.516222, -110.917754 Stay right at the fork, continuing north.

GPS: 43.539309, -110.917068 Turn left on Phillips Canyon Trail.

GPS: 43.548222, -110.931981 At Phillips Pass, turn right and trace the crest of the ridge east, then north.

GPS: 43.589965, -110.923204 Turn right, and climb switchbacks to a 9,085-foot saddle.

GPS: 43.592825, -110.921359 Descend to Middle Fork Granite Creek.

GPS: 43.601030, -110.921316 Continue straight at the three-way junction.

GPS: 43.613457, -110.927787 Continue straight at the three-way junction.

GPS: 43.618179, -110.929804 Once again continue straight at the three-way junction, and climb out of the tiered basin.

GPS: 43.622734, -110.927603 Pass turquoise Marion Lake (and potential campsites) on a grassy bench. Ahead, watch for elk roaming through the next lonely, 5-mile stretch.

GPS: 43.628651, -110.927196 Cross a small saddle at mile 15.2, and continue north for less than 2 miles to Fox Creek Pass.

GPS: 43.646091, -110.910094 Cross Fox Creek Pass, then traverse north-northeast.

GPS: 43.650004, -110.905523 Death Canyon Shelf. Traverse this 3-mile-long, 900-foot-wide ledge. A 500-foot-tall cliff band rises to the west and a 200-foot ledge drops into Death Canyon to the east.

GPS: 43.654033, -110.900317 Campsite. One of the park's most spectacular (and remote) backcountry camps.

GPS: 43.657583, -110.898700 Reliable spring.

GPS: 43.684074, -110.874753 Make the gentle, 200-foot climb over 9,726-foot Mount Meek Pass (you may not even notice it), then descend into Alaska Basin.

GPS: 43.691925, -110.868187 Descend the Sheep Steps switchbacks.

GPS: 43.706042, -110.855699 Continue straight, heading north.

GPS: 43.709793, -110.857174 Continue north past Sunset Lake (possible tent sites on flat slabs) and cross a high plateau.

GPS: 43.728253, -110.850719 Linger at 10,372-foot Hurricane Pass for top-of-the-world views of the Grand, Middle, and South Tetons, which rise just 2 miles to the east. Descend past Schoolroom Glacier.

GPS: 43.731147, -110.838921 Campsites. Turn right at the three-way junction, heading south, to grab one of the uppermost campsites in South Fork Cascade.

GPS: 43.733669, -110.835090 Descend switchbacks into South Fork Cascade Canyon.

GPS: 43.764462, -110.816903 Turn left into North Fork Cascade Canyon. Roughly a mile later, claim one of the first established camps. Get an early start in the morning to beat the heat on the grueling hike up the Paintbrush Divide.

GPS: 43.791977, -110.841494 Pass Lake Solitude, set in a stone cirque.

GPS: 43.793092, -110.818105 Crest Paintbrush Divide. Next, descend 8.3 miles past cliffs striped in browns, grays, and muted reds to your shuttle car.

GPS: 43.789406, -110.801325 Keep right at the three-way junction.

GPS: 43.788631, -110.790768 Keep right at the junction continuing the descent into Paintbrush Canyon down a series of switchbacks.

GPS: 43.796453, -110.738626 Swing left.

GPS: 43.797336, -110.729098 Cross String Lake, then turn right, heading south, and continuing to stay right to stay close to the shore of String Lake.

GPS: 43.788670, -110.730638 The route ends at the trailhead east of String Lake. Pick up your shuttle car to return to the Phillips Canyon trailhead.

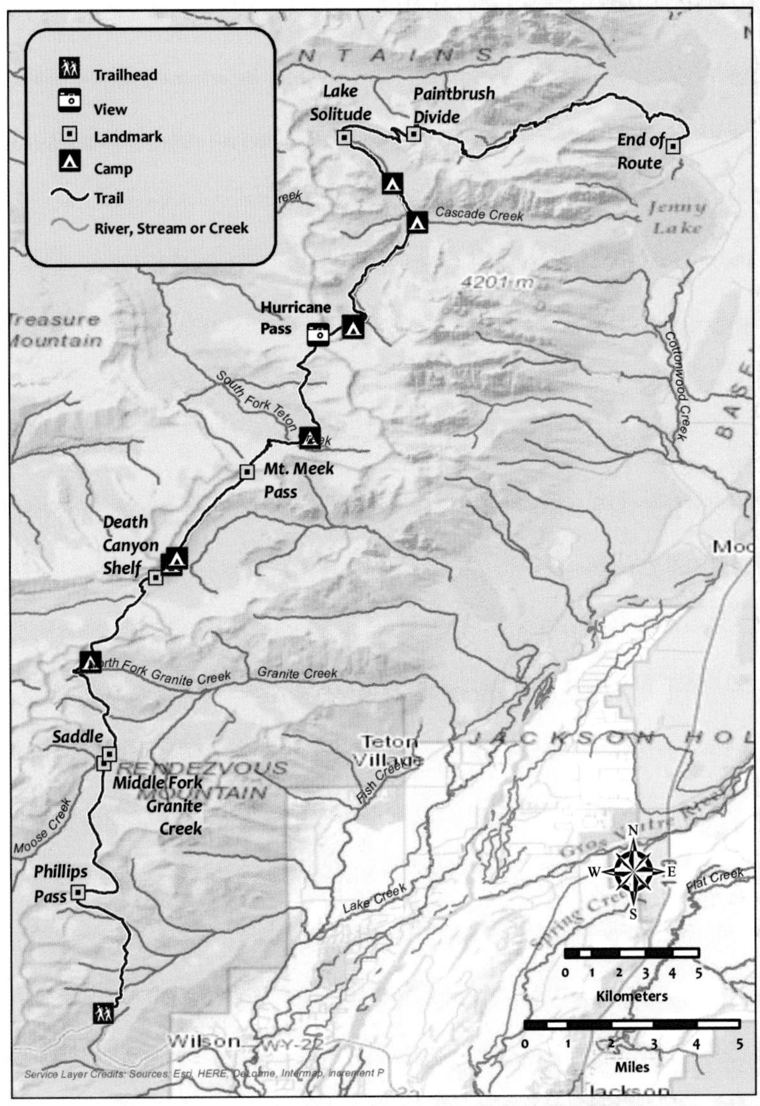

GRAND TETON NATIONAL PARK

DEATH CANYON LOOP

Rise above the crowds to sleep in a lake-dotted basin, scale an 11,000-foot peak, and earn solo views of elk, wildflowers, and summit sunsets.

Consider this route a lesson in investments. While hikers focused on short-term gains jostle for permits to the more accessible (and, yes, gorgeous) loop of Cascade and Paintbrush Canyons, venture a little more sweat equity and embark from Death Canyon trailhead instead. The payoffs are astounding. You'll score solitude and million-dollar views of the Teton spires—and you won't have to motor from camping zone to camping zone to nab the best sites. The route links Open Canyon, Mount Hunt Divide, Granite Canyon, Alaska Basin, and Static Peak Divide to delve deep into the big, open country of the wildlife-packed southern Tetons, a less-visited area of rugged canyons, wildflower-strewn plateaus, endless mountain vistas—and empty campsites.

Start at the Death Canyon trailhead and hike west (ignore initial company; other hikers soon vanish). The first mile climbs gently through conifers to a 7,202-foot perch overlooking the deep blues of Phelps Lake. Keep an eye out for moose at the lake's edge. While cruising on the Open Canyon and Teton Crest Trails, look for the distinctive spire of 10,131-foot Spearhead Peak.

Descend the next mile to the mouth of Death Canyon, where black bears gorge on juicy huckleberries in late summer, and continue west into the canyon on switchbacks that gain more than 1,100 feet in a 2-mile stretch to a small patrol cabin. Scan the sheer granite walls for rock climbers scaling some of the park's most renowned multipitch climbs.

From the cabin, go straight at the three-way junction for another 4.5 miles along the gently inclined valley floor, which brims with Indian paintbrush, columbine, and monkshood in July. Sleep in the upper reaches of the canyon near the edge of the Death Canyon camping zone.

The next day, hike half a mile to the head of the valley and start the 0.8-mile, 700-foot push to Fox Creek Pass at 9,600 feet. As you climb higher, the surrounding cliffs transition from granite to pocketed walls of limestone, remnants of the ancient sea that once submerged the area.

Cruise north from the pass along the Death Canyon Shelf, a broad, boulder-riddled ledge with skybox views of the Tetons. (Alternate option: Camp on Death Canyon Shelf to hear elk bugle startlingly close to your tent at night. Wake at dawn to stroll to the canyon rim, where you sip coffee and scan the valley 1,000 feet below for moose).

Next, 3 miles later, cross 9,726-foot Mount Meek Pass and descend the Sheep Steps switchbacks to campsites in Alaska Basin, which neighbor lakes, granite slabs, and wildflower nooks.

Death Canyon

You'll tick off 12.9 miles on the last day: Hike north about a mile, then turn right for a 2.2-mile climb that leaves the lush basin for stark, high-alpine terrain. At 10,550-foot Buck Mountain Divide, contour 1.1 miles southeast. Drop your pack on Static Peak Divide for a 0.5-mile out-and-back to Static's 11,303-foot summit, where the views grow from great to greater. Descend 4.1 miles through whitebark pines to the cabin and return to the trailhead.

DISTANCE: 28.2 miles

Time **REQUIRED:** 2–4 days

DIFFICULTY: Strenuous

CONTACT: Grand Teton National Park, (307) 739-3343; nps.gov/grte

THE PAYOFF: Craggy peaks, wildflowers, and alpine lakes without the crowds.

TRAILHEAD GPS: 43.655766, -110.781066

FINDING THE TRAILHEAD: From Jackson, go north 12 miles on US 191. Turn left on Teton Park Road. In 0.7 mile, turn left on Moose Wilson Road. In 3.1 miles, turn right on Whitegrass Ranch Road. Bear left after 0.7 mile. Park in 0.9 mile.

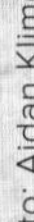

Text: Mike Lanza and Molly Loomis

WAYPOINTS & DIRECTIONS

GPS: 43.655766, -110.781066 Start at the Death Canyon trailhead and hike west. The first mile climbs gently through conifers to a 7,202-foot perch overlooking the deep blues of Phelps Lake.

GPS: 43.657007, -110.799441 At this high point, stare down at Phelps Lake, a popular hangout for moose and black bears. Next, descend to the mouth of Death Canyon.

GPS: 43.655061, -110.809839 Continue west at the mouth of Death Canyon, where black bears gorge on juicy huckleberries in late summer. Ahead, the trail gains more than 1,100 feet in a 2-mile stretch to a small patrol cabin.

GPS: 43.664115, -110.831065 From the cabin, go straight at the three-way junction for another 4.5 miles.

GPS: 43.651289, -110.893765 Sleep in the upper reaches of the canyon near the edge of the Death Canyon camping zone. The next day, hike 0.5 mile to the head of the valley and start the 0.8-mile, 700-foot push to Fox Creek Pass, at 9,600 feet.

GPS: 43.646927, -110.910066 Summit Fox Creek Pass, a meadow with sweeping northeast views of the Tetons' vaulted skyline. From here, traverse north-northeast.

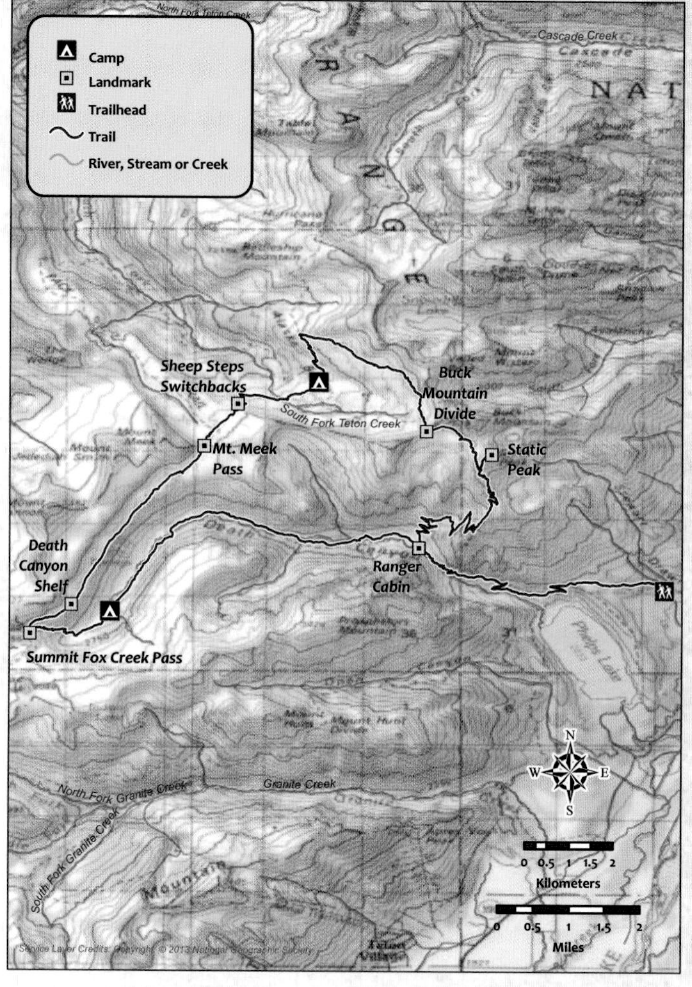

GPS: 43.652656, -110.901489 Death Canyon Shelf. Traverse this 3-mile-long, 900-foot-wide ledge. A 500-foot-tall cliff band rises to the west and a 200-foot wide ledge drops into Death Canyon to the east. There are year-round springs and several campsites, all with views of the Grand Teton and other peaks.

GPS: 43.684045, -110.874749 Cross 9,726-foot Mount Meek Pass and continue north.

GPS: 43.692456, -110.867969 Drop down the Sheep Steps switchbacks.

GPS: 43.696731, -110.851579 Your campsite in Alaska Basin, neighboring lakes, granite slabs, and wildflower nooks. You'll tick off 12.9 miles on the last day: Hike north about 1 mile, then turn right for a 2.2-mile climb that leaves the lush basin for stark, high-alpine terrain.

GPS: 43.706136, -110.855614 Turn right at the three-way junction, and climb out of Alaska Basin.

GPS: 43.687147, -110.829553 At 10,550-foot Buck Mountain Divide, swing 1.1 miles southeast.

GPS: 43.679576, -110.818583 Drop your pack on Static Peak Divide for a 0.5-mile out-and-back to the summit.

GPS: 43.682552, -110.816179 Static Peak (11,303 feet). Descend 4.1 miles through whitebark pines back to the cabin.

GPS: 43.664207, -110.831032 Turn left and retrace your steps to the trailhead.

String Lake

GRAND TETON NATIONAL PARK

JENNY LAKE AND HANGING CANYON LOOP

Circle a glacial lake, see a waterfall, and explore a forgotten trail on this big-view loop.

Visitors to the Tetons shouldn't miss seeing the range's serrated profile reflected in at least one of the park's mirror-smooth lakes. Only one problem: Come summer, the established trails near Jenny Lake can be hiker magnets. Your solution: This 12.4-mile circuit that tours several of the park's must-see sights before ducking onto an unofficial trail that doesn't appear on area maps. From the ranger station near Jenny Lake Campground, pick up the well-maintained Valley Trail around the lake's southern shoreline.

After 2.5 miles, bear left at the fork for a gentle climb up the Cascade Creek drainage to Hidden Falls, which plummets 200 feet down tiers of boulders. Next, cross a bridge over the creek and follow the switchbacks to Inspiration Point, a rocky pulpit overlooking the entire lake. From here, the trail curves west into Cascade Canyon for less than half a mile to a junction; turn right and descend to Jenny's western shore.

At mile 4.3, turn left on the Valley Trail and hike north for .1 mile. Immediately after crossing a stream (mile 4.4) on a small bridge, watch closely for an unsigned turnoff into Hanging Canyon; veer left here. Keep the stream on your left as you follow the obvious user path—soft with decomposing trees and crowded by ferns and towering stalks of purple monkshood—through lush terrain reminiscent of the Pacific Northwest.

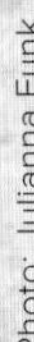
Photo: Julianna Funk

Soon after the route enters the canyon, the climbing ramps up (you'll notch 2,800 feet in the next 1.5 miles) as the trail switchbacks up a forested hillside slowly recovering from a wildfire nearly a decade ago. Pass Ribbon Cascade, where narrow bands of water plunge down tiered outcrops, and maneuver around intermittent stretches of thick deadfall caused by heavy snows in 2011.

At mile 5.3, contour southwest across patches of slabby granite to reach Arrowhead Pool, the first of the canyon's three lakes. Drop down a spur to the shore, then continue another three-quarters of a mile on a path that runs along the north side of Ramshead Lake to Lake of the Crags, tucked into a pinched cirque of towering rock walls. (Tempted to stay longer? There's one campsite per lake.) Descend back to the canyon's mouth and turn left. The final 4.5 miles wrap around the north and east shores of Jenny Lake to the ranger station.

DISTANCE: 12.4 miles

TIME REQUIRED: 1–2 days

DIFFICULTY: Strenuous

CONTACT: Grand Teton National Park, (307) 739-3343; nps.gov/grte

THE PAYOFF: Round the park's iconic lakes and explore secret canyons.

TRAILHEAD GPS: 43.751749, -110.722334

FINDING THE TRAILHEAD: From Jackson, go north 12 miles; turn left on Teton Park Rd. In 7.9 miles, turn left into the parking area near Jenny Lake Campground.

WAYPOINTS & DIRECTIONS

GPS: 43.751749, -110.722334 Start the Jenny Lake loop at the flagpole near the ranger station. Pick up an illustrated map at the sign board, and look for Teewinot Mountain views.

GPS: 43.752838, -110.723391 Fork left at this paved junction (right leads to Jenny Lake Campground). Views of Cascade Canyon, Mt. St. John and Rockchuck Peak over Jenny Lake.

GPS: 43.753137, -110.723712 Turn left to begin the clockwise loop.

GPS: 43.751513, -110.725461 Cross the bridge at the boat dock.

GPS: 43.749808, -110.729528 Pass the drive-in boat ramp.

GPS: 43.747822, -110.736220 Keep straight on the main trail at the Bradley Lake trail junction.

GPS: 43.748460, -110.739087 Continue straight. ***Side Trip:*** Turn left onto the Moose Ponds trail for a short side loop around marshy ponds. Keep an eye out for moose at the viewpoint over the pond.

GPS: 43.750101, -110.739478 At the horse trail junction, head right to continue along the shoreline.

GPS: 43.765007, -110.745070 Take a quick side trail to an overlook above Cascade Creek.

GPS: 43.765082, -110.745406 Bear left and start a gentle climb along Cascade Creek. The trail on the right leads to the boat dock.

GPS: 43.764989, -110.750180 Bear left for the quick trip to see Hidden Falls.

GPS: 43.765066, -110.751151 Hidden Falls: Popular 200-foot cascade visited by scores of tourists. Return to the turnoff and turn left across the bridge.

Text: Eli Boschetto and Molly Loomis

GPS: **43.766921, -110.748349** Rocky switchbacks lead to this perch on Inspiration Point. From here, follow the trail west for 0.5 mile to the three-way junction.

GPS: 43.767065, -110.754375 Turn right. The trail on the left leads into Cascade Canyon.

GPS: 43.768986, -110.744623 Back at the lakeshore, bear left to continue around Jenny Lake.

GPS: 43.770094, -110.743008 Immediately after crossing the creek on a small footbridge, turn left at the unmarked junction. (This trail does not appear on area maps.) Keep the stream on your left as you follow the well-beaten path through lush terrain.

GPS: 43.770908, -110.743550 Soon after entering the canyon, begin climbing.

GPS: 43.774905, -110.749698 Pass Ribbon Cascade, where narrow bands of water plunge down tiered outcrops.

GPS: 43.775974, -110.755792 At mile 5.3, contour southwest across patches of slabby granite to reach Arrowhead Pool, the first of the canyon's three lakes.

GPS: 43.775665, -110.758646 Drop down a spur to the shore, then continue another three-quarters of a mile on a path that runs along the north side of Ramshead Lake to Lake of the Crags.

GPS: 43.777205, -110.764027 Ramshead Lake.

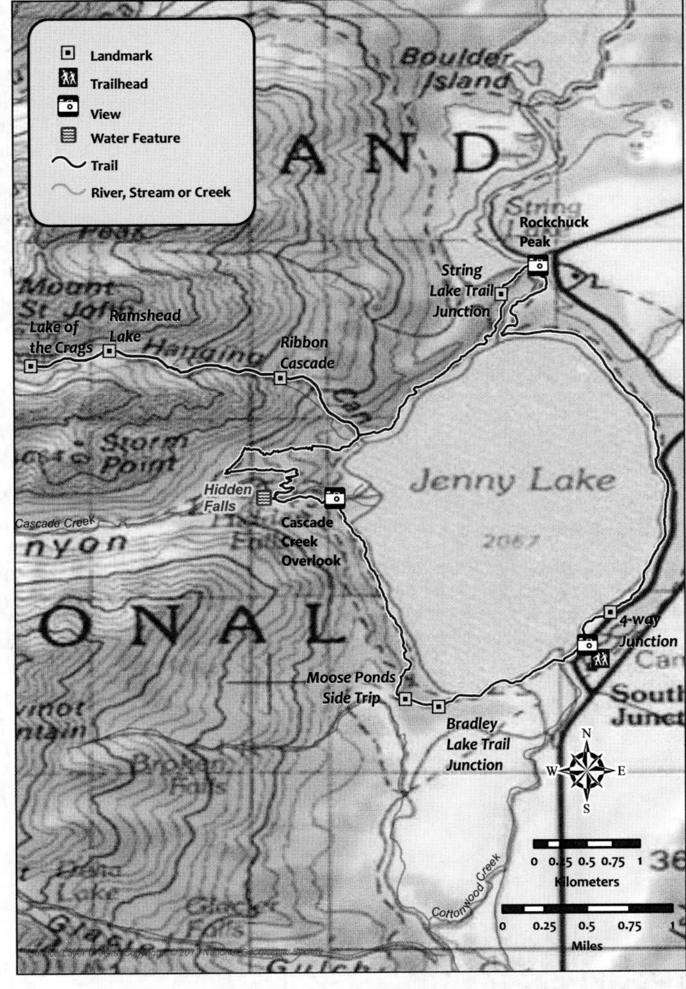

GPS: 43.776005, -110.770726 Lake of the Crags: This tarn is tucked into a pinched cirque of towering rock walls. Next, descend back to the mouth of the canyon and turn left.

GPS: 43.770180, -110.742617 Follow the lakeside trail to the northeast.

GPS: 43.781687, -110.730680 At the String Lake trail junction, bear right to continue around Jenny Lake.

GPS: 43.784010, -110.727490 From the bridge, enjoy a view of Rockchuck Peak towering overhead. After crossing String Lake outlet, turn right to continue around Jenny Lake.

GPS: 43.755531, -110.721454 Continue straight at the 4-way junction to complete the loop back at the ranger station.

Lehman Valley in Great Basin National Park, Nevada
Photo: Andrew Peacock / Tandem Stock

GREAT BASIN NATIONAL PARK

A bristlecone pine in Great Basin

GREAT BASIN NATIONAL PARK

PYRAMID PEAK LOOP

Climb out of the desert heat to breezy alpine solitude.

Between California's Sierra Nevada and Utah's Wasatch stretches a vast, high-and-dry country of broken earth known as the Great Basin. Easily dismissed as a desert wasteland, the heart of it—Nevada's Great Basin National Park, near the Utah border—possesses wonders of striking diversity. The high alpine hosts bristlecone pines (the oldest non-clonal organisms on the planet) and some of the darkest night skies anywhere. Here, rolling sagebrush plains collide with mountains levitating more than a mile above. Lucky for solitude-seeking hikers, Great Basin is no mirage. The park's peaks offer a summer escape to lakes and meadows with staggering desert views. This 12.7-mile overnight loop hits the best of the park.

Begin on a moderate ascent on mostly aspen-forested trail alongside Baker Creek. Continue west, and at mile 1.9 look for towering Pyramid, Baker, and Wheeler Peaks. The

Photo: iStockPhoto.com / AvatarKnowmad

Text: Eli Boschetto

latter, at 13,065 feet, is the park's tallest and Nevada's second highest. At mile 5.3, turn right to Baker Lake, a glassy, teal pool nestled near treeline in an amphitheater of sheer, glacier-carved stone set just below 12,298-foot Baker Peak. Camp on the northwest side of Baker Lake, with views southeast toward Pyramid Peak.

The next day, head south on a use trail, following large cairns through wide meadows and up a drainage lined with monkeyflower in late July. At mile 7, a 100-mile panorama includes arid basin and range country sprawling to the east. Here, peakbaggers who start early to avoid afternoon storms can scramble up 600 feet in 0.4 mile to summit 11,926-foot Pyramid Peak. After summit snacks and photos, return to the trail and veer uphill at mile 8.8 on the faint Snake-Baker Pass Trail. Climb steadily through groves of aspen into meadows of purple lupine and penstemon; the ridgetop flower meadows reach their peak at 9,871-foot Snake Pass. At mile 9.9, you'll emerge into a rolling meadow with views of Pyramid Peak's barren east slope. Follow South Fork Baker Creek at mile 11.4; a quick left turn at mile 12.6 takes you back to your vehicle. Don't be surprised if you never saw another soul.

DISTANCE: 12.7 miles

TIME REQUIRED: 2 days

DIFFICULTY: Intermediate

CONTACT: Great Basin National Park, (775) 234-7331; nps.gov/grba

THE PAYOFF: The best of this famously empty park's desert and mountain views.

TRAILHEAD GPS: 38.976645, -114.245578

FINDING THE TRAILHEAD: From Ely, take US 50 east for 56 miles, then turn right on NV 487. In 4.9 miles, turn right on NV 488. In 5 miles, turn left on Baker Creek Road, and in 3.4 miles park at road's end.

WAYPOINTS & DIRECTIONS

GPS: 38.976645, -114.245578 From the trailhead, begin a moderate ascent on mostly aspen-forested trail alongside Baker Creek.

GPS: 38.972462, -114.266068 Trail junction. Continue straight (west). (The trail left crosses a creek for a short loop option.)

GPS: 38.969002, -114.280858 Trail sign. Turn right and begin easy switchbacks.

GPS: 38.960572, -114.295644 Debris field. Notice wide avalanche debris path in basin.

GPS: 38.957478, -114.307869 Turn right to Baker Lake, nestled near treeline in an amphitheater of sheer, glacier-carved stone beneath 12,298-foot Baker Peak.

GPS: 38.957704, -114.311414 Camp on the northwest side of Baker Lake, with views southeast toward Pyramid Peak. The next day, head south on a use trail, following large cairns through wide meadows and up a drainage lined with monkeyflower in late July.

GPS: 38.945721, -114.300861 Pyramid Peak west ridge.

GPS: 38.948466, -114.295323 Option: Scramble up 600 feet in 0.4 mile to bag 11,926-foot Pyramid Peak. Start early to avoid afternoon storms.

GPS: 38.945283, -114.301039 The 100-mile panorama includes basin and range country sprawling to the east. Follow cairns to descend to Johnson Lake.

(*continued*)

GPS: 38.943748, -114.299321 Rusty gondola and mining equipment remains.

GPS: 38.941698, -114.285913 Nice campsite in trees.

GPS: 38.941649, -114.272982 Veer uphill on the faint Snake-Baker Pass Trail. Climb steadily through groves of aspen into meadows of purple lupine and penstemon.

GPS: 38.951991, -114.261452 Emerge into a rolling meadow with views of Pyramid Peak's barren east slope. Turn left (north), following signs for South Fork Baker Creek.

GPS: 38.967384, -114.262809 Trail fork; veer right (northeast), following South Fork Baker Creek.

GPS: 38.974477, -114.246101 Trail junction. Veer left (north), cross Baker Creek, and complete loop.

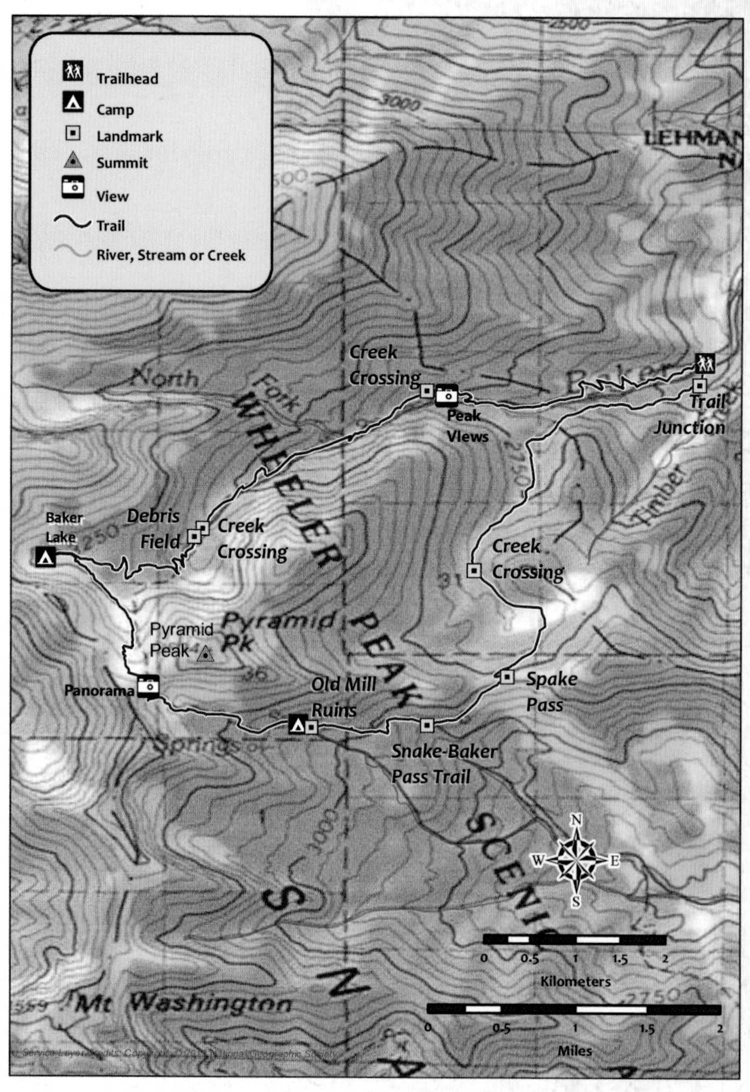

10 TIPS TO GO ULTRALIGHT

Boost comfort and miles with these field-proven tips for carrying less.

Mike Clelland not only wrote the book on slashing pack pounds, he also illustrated it: His *Ultralight Backpackin' Tips* ($15; falcon.com) draws on nearly a decade of practice hauling a pack with a sub-10-pound base weight. Here, the former National Outdoor Leadership School instructor offers his top tips for how you, too, can venture into the backcountry with a bag light enough to lift with one finger.

1. Weigh Everything Buy a 5-pound-capacity postal scale and write down the weight of every single item you plan to pack. When deciding between similar things, always choose the lighter one. "Let the scale make all the decisions," Clelland says.

2. Eat More Fritos When planning meals and snacks, target foods that pack about 125 calories per ounce—or more. Some examples: olive oil (248), peanut butter (165), cashews (155), dark chocolate (153), shortbread cookies (150), gorp (130), Triscuit crackers (120), and cheddar cheese (113).

3. Just In Case Don't give in to doomsday scenarios: only pack for the worst conditions you're likely to face. "The easiest way to get the weight down is to leave stuff behind."

4. Select Campsites Carefully You can ditch heavy comfort items like inflatable pads, big tents, and bulky bags if you know how to look. Look for level sleeping spots, ideally with a slight depression for your butt. Clear debris and lie down to test comfort. Avoid dips in the terrain, where cold air pools overnight, and seek dense trees for added shelter and insulation.

5. Leave the TP at Home No toilet, no paper. In a quarter century in the field, Clelland has never brought along this so-called essential. His top picks for all-natural bum-wiping materials:

- **Snow:** Squeeze a handful of the stuff into an oblong ball.
- **River rocks:** Gather smooth, egg-shaped stones.
- **Fuzzy leaves:** Find mullein, a weed common to sunny, disturbed areas. Its soft, strong leaves do the trick.

6. Save Ounces—and Pennies Ultralight doesn't have to mean ultra-expensive. Some gear swaps that will actually save money:

- **Canister stove:** DIY alcohol stove (learn how at backpacker.com/alcoholstove)
  Savings: about 3 oz. and $37
- **Two-person tent:** Tarp
  Savings: about 2 lbs. and $240
- **Knife:** Single-edge razor
  Savings: about 4 oz. and $23
- **Pillow:** Zip-top bags (7 partly inflated, quart-size, double-zipper bags in a stuffsack)
  Savings: about 0.4 oz. and $20

7. Hike All Day When not saddled by a heavy pack, the journey is the destination. Clelland hikes from dawn to dusk, with lots of stops for streamside meals, coffee, even naps. Bonus? At camp, you won't miss the little luxuries you left behind. "I simply lay down and fall right asleep."

8. Do Calisthenics On chilly nights, Clelland suggests doing jumping jacks immediately before hopping into the sack—raising your body temp right before bed will help you sleep warmer. If you get cold in the night, do a few minutes' worth of crunches right in your bag.

9. Carry Less Water Unless you're trekking across the desert, pack no more than 1.5 liters and plan your route around water stops, treating as you go with lightweight drops or tablets.

10. Keep an Open Mind "What you want is very different from what you need," Clelland says. "It's all mental. The only challenge that has to be overcome is your own attitude."

Fall in Great Sand Dunes National Park, Colorado
Photo: Patrick Myers / NPS Photo

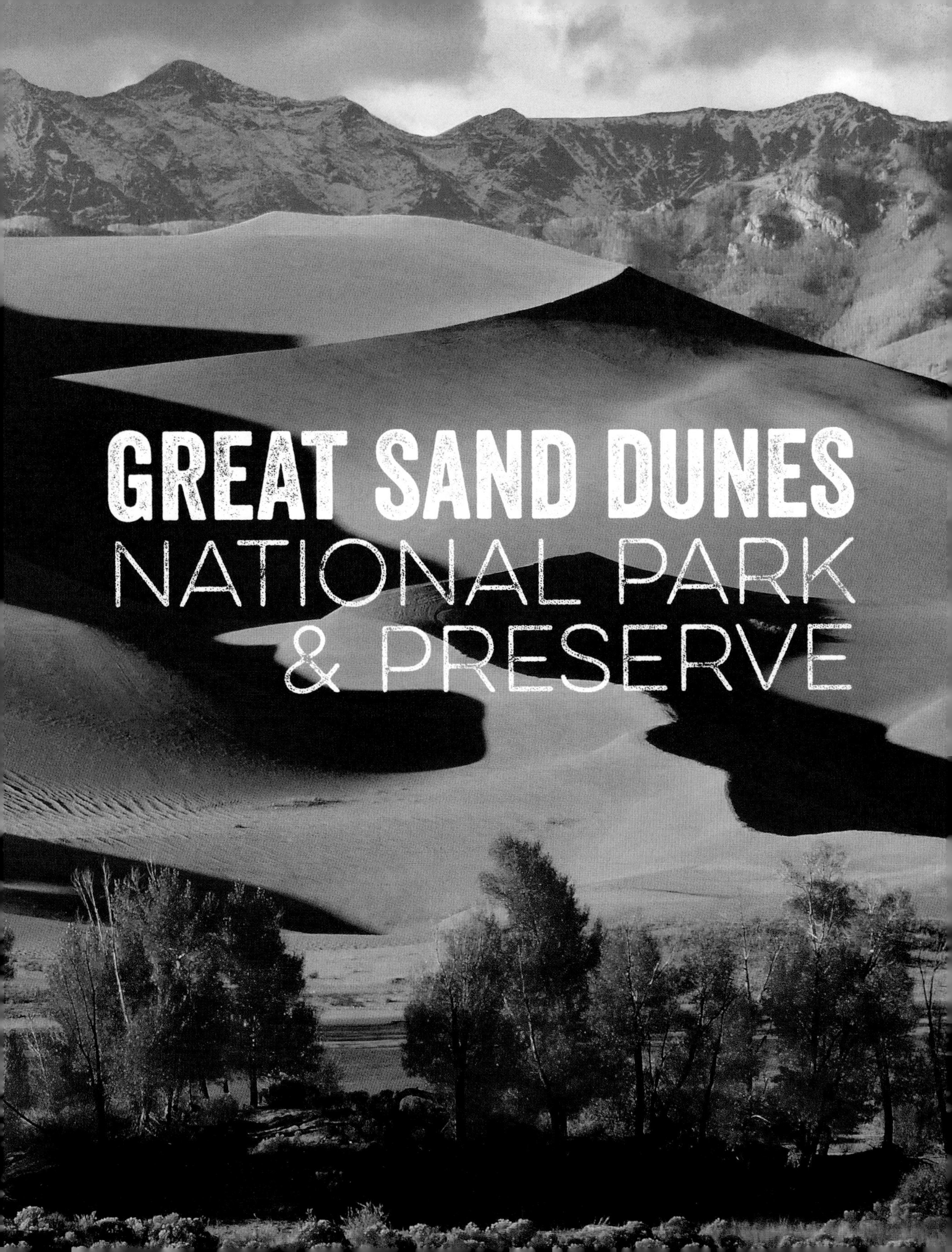
GREAT SAND DUNES
NATIONAL PARK
& PRESERVE

Sand dunes in the mountains

GREAT SAND DUNES NATIONAL PARK & PRESERVE

STAR DUNE LOOP

Ascend North America's tallest dunes for a day surrounded by alpine peaks, a desert valley, and shifting mountains of sand.

While most national parks protect the most incredible places on our planet, Great Sand Dunes' eerie juxtaposition of hulking, wind-whipped piles of sand shoved against precipitous mountains feels more like a preserve on an alien world. Once you crest the sprawling beige dunefield, it's easy to feel like you've crash-landed on a distant planet. The extraterrestrial visuals are abetted by spooky audio: The sand-muffled wilderness here is so silent that nighttime readings bottom out beyond the capabilities of the NPS Natural Sounds Program's ultra-sensitive instruments. Our earthbound physics can explain why: Sand dampens sound waves (some recording studios even use it), so it's safe to say that any peep in this 30-square-mile dunefield doesn't stand a chance. The dunes also offer one-small-step-for-mankind exploratory opportunities. There are no trails; hike more than 1.5 miles into it and you can camp anywhere. Claim your quiet and target Star Dune, the tallest dune in North America at nearly 1,000 feet, and listen as the sand vibrates beneath your boots, alternately sighing, whistling, grunting, groaning, and barking. Then hike about 4.5 miles northwest from Medano Creek; camp in the dunefield after and enjoy the silence.

Photo: iStockPhoto.com / ericfoltz

DISTANCE: 6.6 miles

TIME REQUIRED: 1–2 days

DIFFICULTY: Intermediate

CONTACT: Great Sand Dunes National Park and Preserve, (719) 378-6399; nps.gov/grsa

THE PAYOFF: Otherworldly dunes set against a classic Rocky Mountain backdrop.

TRAILHEAD GPS: 37.739334, -105.517548

FINDING THE TRAILHEAD: From Alamosa, take CO 17 south to turn left on CR 6N. Go 15.9 miles to CO 150. Turn left onto CO 150; go 6.2 miles to the visitor center. Then 1 mile past the visitor center, turn left into the parking lot. Park near Nature Trail signs at the northern end.

WAYPOINTS & DIRECTIONS

GPS: 37.739334, -105.517548 Hike through junipers to dunefield. Enter Medano Creek's "perched aquifer" area, the lifeblood of the dunes.

GPS: 37.743832, -105.521667 Reach foothills of dune and enter the sand sheet.

GPS: 37.749149, -105.533020 Here is the apex of High Dune—an example of a transverse dune, one that progresses forward via minuscule sand avalanches.

GPS: 37.747982, -105.538017 Panoramic views to the southeast of San Luis Valley.

GPS: 37.751148, -105.556503 Make the steep ascent up Star Dune, North America's tallest at 8,900-foot. At the summit, relax atop its ever changing peak. The snowy Sangre de Cristo Mountains lie to the east.

GPS: 37.751202, -105.557930 Descend Star Dune along the east ridge. Start looping back to main dunefield.

GPS: 37.749298, -105.558067 Turn left at the saddle of Little Star Dune to descend into the basin.

GPS: 37.740135, -105.549217 Turn right at Lookout Dune and observe Blanca Peak.

GPS: 37.736668, -105.543404 Turn left at the ridgeline.

GPS: 37.735569, -105.524864 Take a left at the terminus of dunes; follow Medano Creek back to the trailhead.

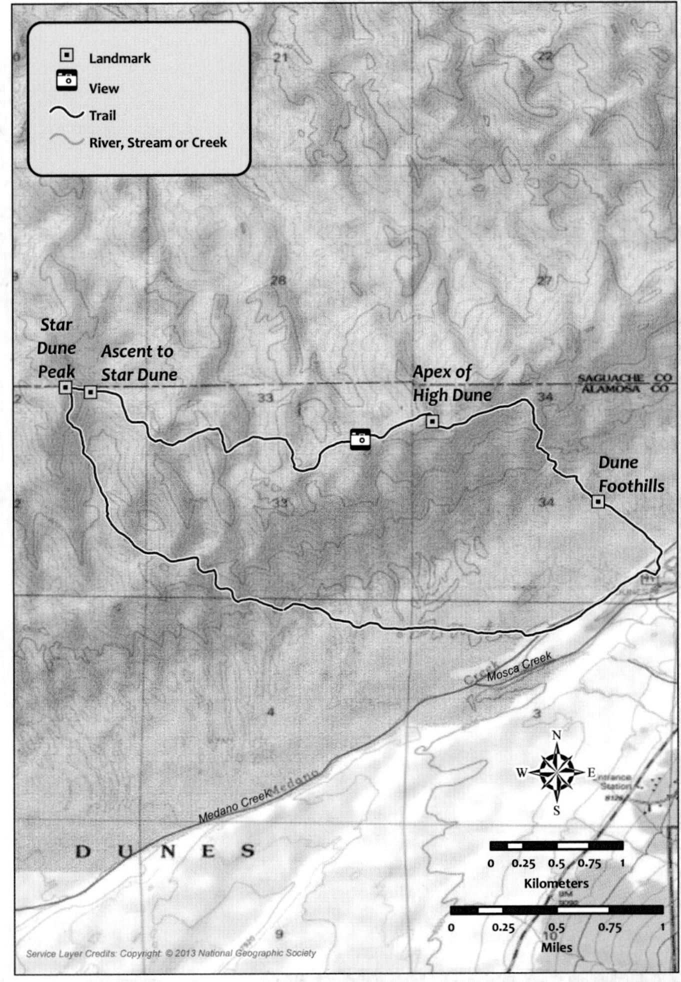

Autumn descends on Great Smoky Mountains National Park, North Carolina/Tennessee
Photo: iStockPhoto.com / Sean Pavone

GREAT SMOKY MOUNTAINS NATIONAL PARK

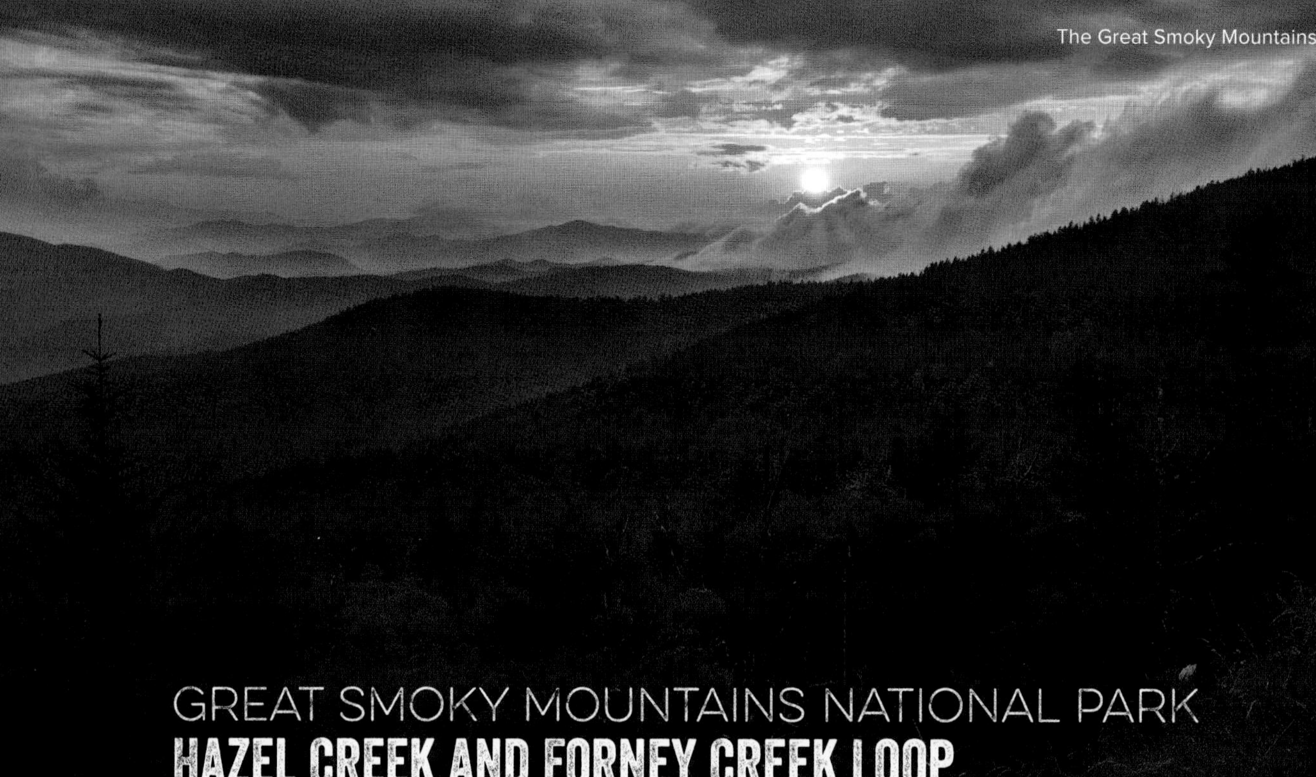

GREAT SMOKY MOUNTAINS NATIONAL PARK
HAZEL CREEK AND FORNEY CREEK LOOP

Graze blueberry patches, explore swimming holes, and tag the South's high points on this sultry hike.

Don't be fooled: Though the Smokies can be busier than a NASCAR stadium, the lush peaks and hazy mist that inspired the park's name hide a lifetime's worth of adventure. Packed into the park are verdant groves of tulip poplar and wind-whipped spruce-fir forests where elk and black bears roam. Three-foot salamanders swim beneath clouds of fireflies blinking in unison. On a typical multiday hike, you could pass more than 10,000 plant and animal species (though scientists believe 90,000 could live here). In this Eastern oasis, in the shadow of 300-million-year-old mountains that once soared as tall as the Rockies, life explodes in a shock of blooming, buzzing, slithering, and chirping—a rare escape where hikers can leave civilization and lose themselves in deep wilderness.

This challenging 5-night, 56.7-mile loop packs in long days, steep climbs, and tricky creek crossings to bring you deep into the heart of the last true Eastern wilderness. Get ready to kiss civilization goodbye: The North Carolina side of the Smokies sees just 15 percent of the park's total visitors, and you'll be wandering the area's most remote miles, where bobcats and red foxes linger beneath more than 100 different types of trees. Depart on a Sunday night for maximum solitude—and don't forget a quick-dry towel for swimming.

First stop: The Smokies' high point, 6,643-foot Clingmans Dome. Park just shy of the summit and stroll up the dome's observation tower for a stunning preview of the ridges and

Photo: Steve Perry / Backcountry Gallery

Text: Elisabeth Kwak-Heferan

valleys to come, then pick up the Appalachian Trail and follow it west. Peek through the trees for a glimpse of row upon row of gently undulating, blue-tinged mountains. Then turn to the trail's seasonal treats: an explosion of white spring-beauty wildflowers in March, plump blackberries in late summer, and a palette of fiery-toned foliage come fall. The real solitude starts at mile 5 as you take the Welch Ridge Trail to the Hazel Creek Trail. Stride on under the stately hardwood canopy, dropping sharply to Site 82 at mile 12. You're in primo trout territory here: Take a fly rod and wade about a mile upstream to reach a small cascade marking the boundary between native brookies and the more aggressive rainbows and browns downstream. (It's very unlikely that this site will be full, especially midweek. Even if you do have company, it's big enough for multiple parties to camp without being on top of each other.)

On day two, you'll descend 9.5 miles to the secluded shores of Fontana Lake. Believe it or not, this wilderness was a thriving community, complete with a sawmill and a movie theater, from the late 1800s until the 1940s. Stay straight when you come to the next junction past site 85 and detour 0.5 mile to a No Horses sign, where a footpath leads to an old cemetery with gravestones dating to the mid-1800s. Return to the junction and veer right to camp beneath white pines at Site 86. Take your pick of swimming spots: You'll be 0.25 mile from the lake's rocky shore, and right beside A-1 splashing in the 10-foot-deep pools tucked in Hazel Creek.

The next day's journey is an easy 12.3-mile cruise east on the Lakeshore Trail. Despite the name, this gentle roller coaster is more woods than water, leading through a pine-oak forest inhabited by scarlet tanagers and pileated woodpeckers, and 30 species of salamanders (look for them under rocks). In July, compete with bears for the trail's juiciest blueberries. For the better of the two tent areas at Site 76, turn right at the No Horses sign and follow the spur to sleep near Fontana's lapping waves. You'll want to spend the bulk of day four at Site 70, 12.5 miles on, where one of the Smokies' sweetest swimming holes awaits. Take the Lakeshore Trail to Forney Creek, then head north beneath a hemlock canopy. There's a mellow climb once you pass Site 71, but keep your eyes on the prize: Your site's rhododendron-shaded pool, a pocket where two small streams come together.

Day five is only 5.5 miles, but they're burly ones–you'll ford six major creeks, which can reach waist-level in high water. March and April bring the peak flows, but summer cloudbursts can also make the streams impassable. Go for it if the water is knee-deep or lower: Pack sturdy sandals, grab a walking stick, and feel your way over the stream's moss-covered boulders. You'll pass a 15-foot waterfall at Site 69 en route to your last night's rest at site 68, where water cascades 40 feet over a giant, slanting rock beside a birch grove. Your last day brings you back up to the high country—you'll gain nearly 2,000 feet in the first 2.5 miles. Hang a right on the Forney Ridge Trail and hike 0.7 mile south for one more iconic Smokies destination: Andrews Bald, a grassy, open patch with flame azaleas in late spring and abundant blueberries in August, plus killer views of the misty blue valleys you've just left. From this grassy vantage, vistas stretch over Fontana Lake and the Smokies' wrinkled ridges. Backtrack to the junction and climb 1.5 miles back to Clingmans Dome on Forney Ridge for one last look at southern hospitality the hiker's way.

DISTANCE: 56.7 miles

TIME REQUIRED: 5 days

DIFFICULTY: Strenuous

CONTACT: Great Smoky Mountains National Park, (865) 436-1200; nps.gov/grsm

THE PAYOFF: The South's best swimming-hole tour, complete with balsam-covered peaks and cascading creeks.

TRAILHEAD GPS: 35.556853, -83.496222

FINDING THE TRAILHEAD: From Gatlinburg, Tennessee, take US 441 into Great Smoky Mountains National Park. At mile 14.7, turn right onto Clingmans Dome Road and go 6.3 miles to the parking lot (closed from December through March).

WAYPOINTS & DIRECTIONS

GPS: 35.556853, -83.496222 Park just below Clingman's Dome; pick up the Appalachian Trail and take it west. In 5 miles, turn left onto Welch Ridge Trail. Follow the trail past Mule Gap, and then make a sharp right onto the Hazel Creek Trail.

GPS: 35.517173, -83.641877 Find your first camp, Site 82, after 12 miles of hiking. This area is known for its great trout fishing. The next day, continue to follow the Hazel Creek Trail as it winds southwest.

GPS: 35.472239, -83.725863 The second night's camp is underneath the white pines of Site 86. In the morning, pick up the Lakeshore Trail for an easy 12.3 mile day along the shores of Fontana Lake.

GPS: 35.447875, -83.636341 Third camp at Site 76. For the better of the two tent areas, turn right at the No Horses sign and follow the spur to sleep near Fontana's lapping waves.

GPS: 35.513156, -83.558128 To reach your fourth camp, take the Lakeshore Trail to Forney Creek, then head north beneath a hemlock canopy. There's a mellow climb once you pass Site 71, but campsite 70 is the better location—look for a rhododendron-shaded pool where two small streams come together.

GPS: 35.515391, -83.553343 Begin the first of five or six creek fords, but only attempt if the water is knee-deep or lower.You'll pass a 15-foot waterfall at Site 69 en route to your last night's rest at Site 68. In the morning, wend your way along Forney Creek Trail before taking a left at the T junction, heading north on Forney Ridge Trail back to Clingmans Dome.

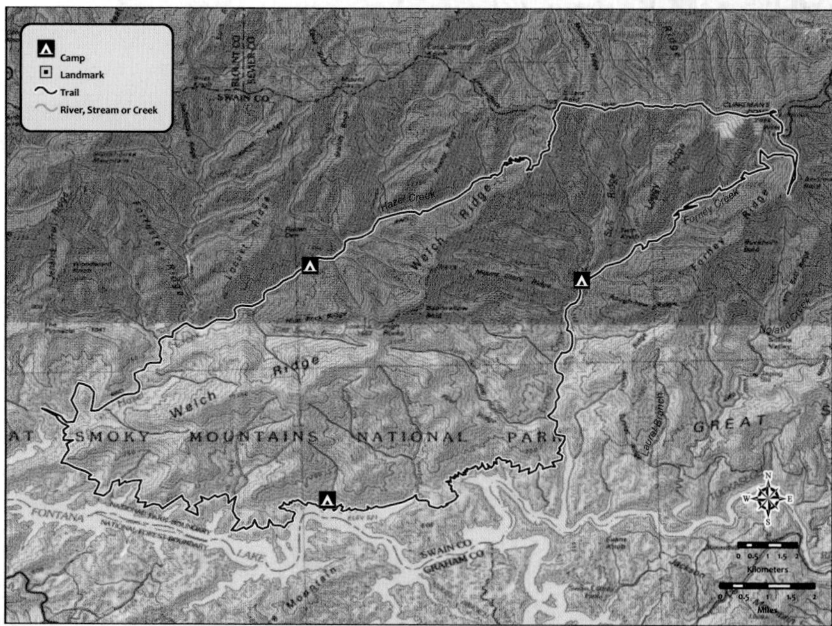

Black bear cub

GREAT SMOKY MOUNTAINS NATIONAL PARK

MID-SMOKIES CIRCUIT

String together the Appalachian, Benton MacKaye, and Mountains-to-Sea Trails for an instant classic that hits the park's best views and backcountry campsites.

Tick off Smoky Mountains must-sees and sample hidden gems on an unforgettable 6-day trip tiptoeing across lofty ledges, dense forests, and everything in between.

From the Noland Divide trailhead on Clingmans Dome Road (closed December through March), descend the ridgeline west of 5,150-foot Roundtop Knob. Pass through patches of rhododendron and mountain laurel (blooming in June) into stands of hardwood-hemlock forest. At mile 3.7, turn left onto Pole Road Creek Trail and head downhill, past trickling springs. Cross a log bridge and turn left onto Deep Creek Trail at mile 6.8. Nearby Burnt Spruce Campsite (#56) offers six creekside, first-come, first-serve tent spots in the valley.

On day two, continue along Deep Creek before turning left onto Martin's Gap Trail. Meander through boggy hemlock stands by way of boardwalks and ascend 1,000 feet to Martin's Gap and the intersection with Sunkota Ridge Trail. Turn left for a 5-mile ridge walk with intermittent views into forested valleys; you'll gently ascend to 5,000 feet. Stay on the Sunkota Ridge Trail at the intersection with Thomas Ridge Trail and reach the Newton Bald Campsite (#52) at a grassy saddle on the flank of its namesake peak. Here, synchronous fireflies stage a dazzling, bioluminescent flash mob during peak mating season, from early- to mid-June. Viewing tip: The show starts after 9:30 p.m. and lasts until midnight. Look for males as they fly and flicker; females remain stationary and shine in return.

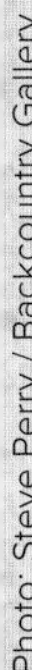
Photo: Steve Perry / Backcountry Gallery

The next morning, traverse just below the crest of the 5,160-foot peak before hitting the Newton Bald Trail. Turn left here to begin a 4.7-mile, 2,500-foot descent through forest dominated by towering tulip poplar and dotted with ferns and rhododendrons. Emerge at US 441, jog left, then cross the bridge toward Smokemont Campground. Continue past another bridge and turn left onto the Bradley Fork Trail. Reach Lower Chasteen Creek Campsite (#50) at the confluence of the fork and the creek.

On day four, prepare to regain the altitude you lost yesterday with a 500-foot rise on the Bradley Fork Trail. After 2.8 miles, turn right to stay with the Bradley Fork Trail and begin the real test: a 3.3-mile, 2,000-foot climb up Tawya Creek through mature beech, oak, and maple. Reach Hughes Ridge and turn left to continue climbing via the Hughes Ridge Trail. After 1.8 miles, look for your accommodations: Pecks Corner Shelter, below the trail to the right.

On day five, start with a steep, 0.3-mile push that takes you from hardwood stands to the spruce and fir on the high ridgelines. Turn left at the intersection with the Appalachian Trail to begin one of the most iconic ridge walks of the Smokies: 6 miles of uninterrupted ridgeline provide back-and-forth vistas into North Carolina and Tennessee while winding along Laurel Top and The Sawteeth. A signed, 0.6-mile side trail leads to Charlies Bunion, a can't-miss rock outcropping with vertigo-inducing views to the valleys below and clear shots east to Mount LeConte. Back on the Appalachian Trail, pause after a mile for the 0.4-mile detour to the Jumpoff, a secluded perch with big drops and Instagram-worthy views of Porters Mountain. Continue 0.4 miles to Icewater Spring Shelter and stop for the night.

The next day, rejoin the Appalachian Trail through stands of wind-stunted fir, hemlock, and beech. Hike a 2.7-mile stretch through a meditative tunnel of green before reaching the bustle of Newfound Gap, the only road-crossing along the 100-plus miles of the Smokies' crest. Continue following white blazes across US 441 and back into dense evergreens.

Cross the 6,000-foot line twice on this 7.5-mile section over Mount Collins and Mount Love, and emerge on the 6,643-foot summit of Clingmans Dome, the highest point in the park (and on the whole Appalachian Trail). Climb the spiral observation tower for near-100-mile vistas—if a mist hasn't enshrouded the lookout. Descend 0.8 mile to the Clingmans Dome Parking Area and walk 1.5 road miles to your car.

DISTANCE: 48 miles

TIME REQUIRED: 6 days

DIFFICULTY: Strenuous

CONTACT: Great Smoky Mountains National Park, (865) 436-1200; nps.gov/grsm

THE PAYOFF: Get lost on a high tour of the Smokies' best and wildest spots.

TRAILHEAD GPS: 35.567179, -83.481629

FINDING THE TRAILHEAD: From Gatlinburg, Tennessee, take US 441 south. In 15 miles, turn right on Clingmans Dome Road. Continue 5.5 miles to the Nolan Divide trailhead. If full, go 1.5 miles to the Clingmans Dome parking area.

Text: Peter Rives and Andrew Matranga

WAYPOINTS & DIRECTIONS

GPS: 35.567179, -83.481629 Head southeast from the Noland trailhead.

GPS: 35.532225, -83.454251 Take a left at Pole Road Creek Trail.

GPS: 35.529187, -83.422622 Cross a log bridge and turn left onto Deep Creek Trail.

GPS: 35.524888, -83.419879 Burnt Spruce Creek campsite offers six first-come, first-serve tent spots in the valley, right next to the creek. Continue along Deep Creek Trail in the morning.

GPS: 35.520804, -83.419448 Turn left onto Martins Gap Trail.

GPS: 35.519282, -83.408134 Turn left on Sunkota Ridge Trail.

GPS: 35.541605, -83.367411 Bypass Thomas Ridge, staying on the Sunkota Ridge Trail.

GPS: 35.544155, -83.363339 Find Newton Bald Campsite along a grassy saddle on the flank of its namesake peak.

GPS: 35.541846, -83.358804 The next morning, traverse just below the crest of the 5,160-foot peak before hitting the Newton Bald Trail. Turn left here to begin a 4.7-mile, 2,500-foot descent.

GPS: 35.552639, -83.309781 Emerge at US 441, jog left, then cross the bridge toward Smokemont Campground. Continue past another bridge and turn left onto the Bradley Fork Trail.

GPS: 35.577060, -83.312998 Reach Camp 3, the Lower Chasteen Creek campsite (#50) at the confluence of the Bradley Fork and the Chasteen Creek.

GPS: 35.606629, -83.332504 Start the next morning with a brisk 500-foot climb on the Bradley Fork Trail. After 2.8 miles, turn right to stay with the Bradley Fork Trail and begin the real test: A 3.3-mile, 2,000-foot climb up Tawya Creek.

GPS: 35.629794, -83.304945 Reach Hughes Ridge, and turn left to continue climbing via the Hughes Ridge Trail.

GPS: 35.650701, -83.308527 Find camp, Peck's Corner Shelter, below the trail to the right, 1.8 miles past the Hughes Ridge turn.

GPS: 35.655201, -83.308447 Turn left on the Appalachian Trail to begin one of the most iconic ridge walks of the Smokies.

GPS: 35.637936, -83.373938 Take a 0.4-mile detour to the Jumpoff, a secluded perch with big drops and stunning views of Porters Mountain.

GPS: 35.629522, -83.386463 Camp at the Icewater Spring Shelter, 0.4 miles beyond the Jumpoff detour.

GPS: 35.610890, -83.424852 In the morning, hike 2.7 wooded miles before reaching the bustle of Newfound Gap. Continue following white blazes across US 441 and back into dense evergreens.

GPS: 35.563096, -83.498193 Climb the spiral observation tower of Clingmans Dome for sweeping vistas—if a mist hasn't enshrouded the lookout. Descend 0.8 mile to the Clingmans Dome Parking Area and walk 1.5 road miles to your car.

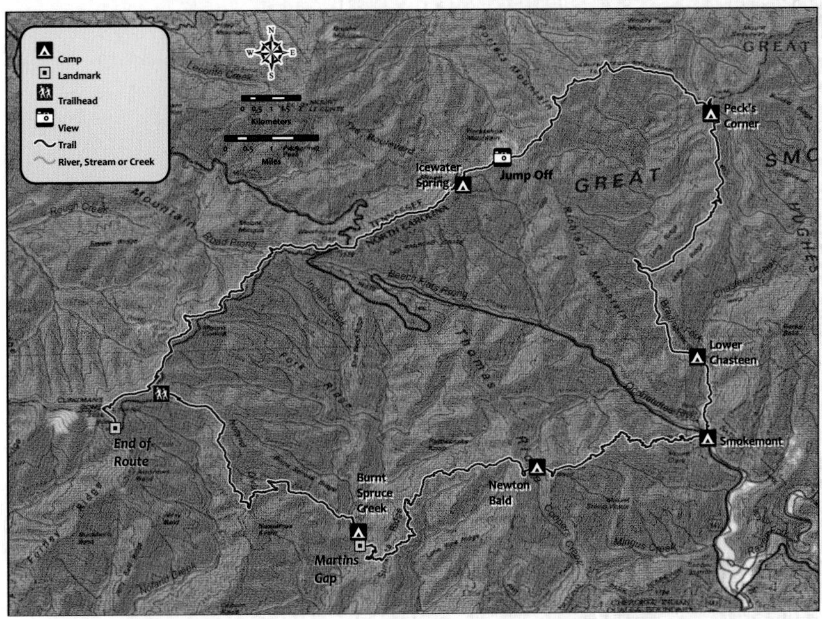

View from Clingmans Dome

GREAT SMOKY MOUNTAINS NATIONAL PARK

CHARLIES BUNION LOOP

Pack a camera for this lollipop loop to one of the best mountain views in the park: A sit-awhile panorama, atop a 5,565-foot knob with thousand-foot drop-offs on three sides, that stretches from Mount LeConte to the jagged peaks of the Sawteeth Range.

A mere footnote in the geologic record, Charlies Bunion may lack the fame other Smoky Mountain hikes. But stand on this weatherworn promontory and peer past the dizzying 1,000-foot dropoffs to a quintessential Smokies skyline, and there's no doubt: This is a destination worth getting up early for.

In fact, a predawn alarm isn't a bad idea, since you'll be bagging the standout summit in the most visited U.S. national park. There's a reason the softshell-clad masses trek through an evergreen tunnel along the spine of the Appalachians: A jaw-dropping panorama stretches from Mount LeConte eastward to the jagged peaks of the Sawteeth Range. A 1925 wildfire that incinerated the slopes of this 5,565-foot knob is responsible for the exceptional views—and the peculiar name. Noted outdoorsman Horace Kephart named the bulbous peak in 1929 after observing its resemblance to his hiking companion's inflamed big toe.

Set off from the Newfound Gap parking lot on the Appalachian Trail heading north. At mile 1.6, turn right onto the Sweat Heifer Creek Trail and begin a 1,404-foot descent to the stream. Keep an eye out at mile 3: The trail cuts northeast here at an old logging road landing. A

Photo: iStockPhoto.com / RichardBarrow

Text: Thomas Wilmes and Shannon Davis

DISTANCE: 12.8 miles

TIME REQUIRED: 2–3 days

DIFFICULTY: Intermediate

CONTACT: Great Smoky Mountains National Park, (865) 436-1200; nps.gov/grsm

THE PAYOFF: Quick access to the high reaches of the Smokies.

TRAILHEAD GPS: 35.610933, -83.425219

FINDING THE TRAILHEAD: From Asheville, North Carolina, take I-40 west for 16.7 miles. Make a slight right onto US 74, and drive 4 miles. Take exit 103 onto US 19 and head 24.1 miles. Turn right onto US 441 and drive 19 miles to trailhead parking.

WAYPOINTS & DIRECTIONS

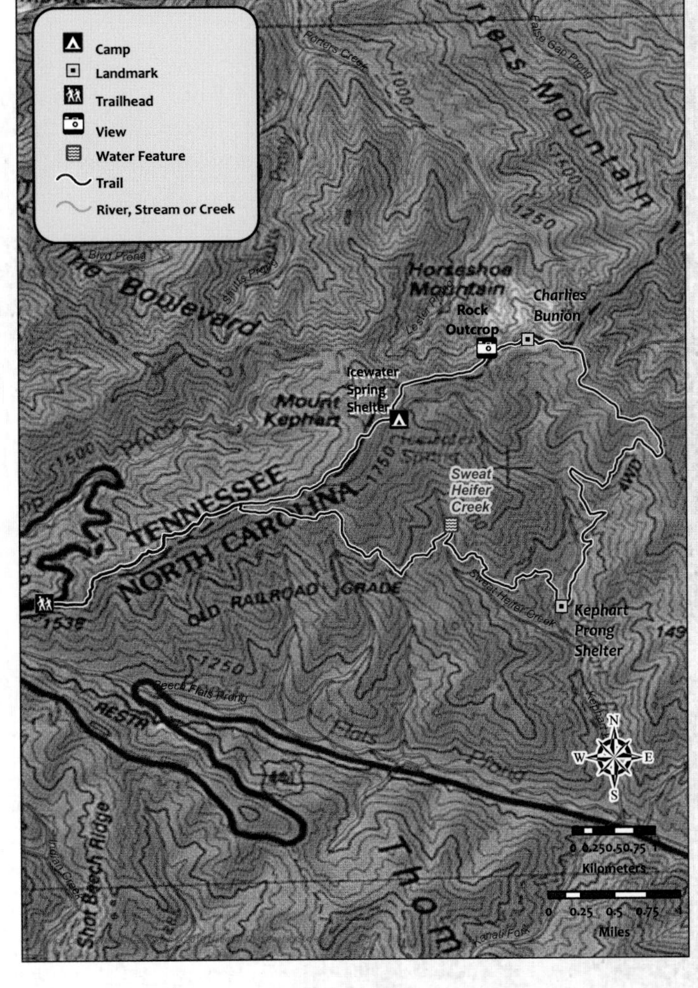

GPS: 35.610933, -83.425219

Hike northeast along the Appalachian Trail from the trailhead at Newfound Gap.

GPS: 35.621109, -83.403801

Turn right at T junction onto Sweat Heifer Creek Trail.

GPS: 35.613670, -83.386253

The trail cuts to the northeast at an old logging landing; continue descent to creekbed.

GPS: 35.610229, -83.368683

Pass Kephart Prong Shelter, a large stone hut tucked into a glade. Turn left at T and follow the Grassy Branch Trail north.

GPS: 35.626019, -83.357590

Turn left at the T for steady ascent up the Dry Sluice Gap Trail.

GPS: 35.638130, -83.369133

Turn left at T junction onto the Appalachian Trail.

GPS: 35.638405, -83.372253

Traverse the southern edge of Charlies Bunion, a bare, rocky bluff with 1,000-foot drop-offs to the north.

GPS: 35.637497, -83.376785

Rock outcrop provides views of layered Smoky Mountain ridgelines; traverse ridgecrest to the southwest.

GPS: 35.628380, -83.390671

Stay straight on Appalachian Trail at three-way intersection with Boulevard Trail. Follow the North Carolina-Tennessee state line southwest to descend on the lush ridgeline back to the Sweet Heifer Creek Trail junction and continue west to the trailhead.

little more than 0.5 mile later, cross Sweat Heifer Creek and ignore the gross name: It's a fern-lined stream with pools deep enough for swimming. Pass the Kephart Prong Shelter, which sleeps eight. It's popular—aim to arrive early if you plan to overnight here. Continue on by turning left at the junction onto Grassy Branch Trail. Turn left onto Dry Sluice Gap Trail to begin a gentle ridgewalk to return to the AT. Turn left onto the AT for the 0.2-mile stretch to Charlies Bunion. Turn right to reach The Bunion. Traverse the rocky bluff north to reach a cliff with 1,000-foot drop-offs. A series of rock outcroppings at mile 9 offer views of layered Smoky ridgelines to the north. Nearly a mile later, pass the Icewater Spring Shelter. (It sleeps 12 and has a privy). Stay straight on the AT at the junction with Boulevard Trail. Follow the North Carolina-Tennessee state line on a southwest descent on lush ridgeline back to the beginning of Sweat Heifer Creek Trail. Then continue to your car, a hop, skip, and jump 2.6 miles away.

HOT TIP: Spring brings the thru-hikers, and summer and fall bring everyone else. Visit the Bunion in winter and you'll enjoy even better views through the leaf-bare trees, plus you'll likely avoid a bottleneck at the outcrop. A bonus: The low humidity and cool, dense air help confine that famous Smoky Mountains fog to the valleys.

YELLOWSTONE NATIONAL PARK

HOW TO LIVE IN A NATIONAL PARK—AND WHY YOU'D WANT TO

A national park vacation is great, but the real fun starts when you get to call the park home.

The summer I lived in Yellowstone National Park, I saw bison out my kitchen window—regularly. I passed a mama moose every day on my way to the office. I averaged 30 miles a week of hiking, much of it part of my job as a Student Conservation Association intern.

And I learned a secret: The best way to really get to know a park is to live there. As a resident, I had the time, knowledge, and access to truly explore. On my days off, I was in prime position to hit the trail. I knew the best tricks for getting permits and the coolest out-of-the-way corners. In one summer, I hit nearly every park highlight, bagged a dozen peaks, and discovered hot springs that aren't on any map.

It was so amazing, I decided to do it again the next year. That time, I signed up for an Americorps position as a crew leader with the Utah Conservation Corps. Over the next year and half, I had the privilege of spending months at a time in Capitol Reef and Zion National Parks, working alongside park staff on various projects. Again, I did some of the best exploring of my life. —*Rachel Zurer*

TRY IT

The unparalleled access is worth the time, whether between jobs, after you retire, or as a permanent way of life. Here are some resources to get you started.

Student Conservation Association Ages 15 and up; semivolunteer placements on public lands nationwide. thesca.org

Volunteers in Parks All ages; some positions provide housing. volunteer.gov

CoolWorks Clearinghouse Paid positions with park concessionaires. coolworks.com

National Park Service Federal jobs can be tough to get; many are seasonal. usajobs.gov

The Alum Cave Trail

GREAT SMOKY MOUNTAINS NATIONAL PARK

ALUM CAVE TO GREENBRIER COVE

Trek into the past on this 6-day route linking a rock arch, 5,000-foot balds, old settler homesites, and hundred-year-old cemeteries.

The Smokies have high-mountain views and astonishing biodiversity, but unlike many Western parks, they also house preserved remnants from residents whose arrival predates the park's 1934 inauguration by decades (and centuries, especially in the case of the Cherokee). This 50-mile hike winds past highlights from Mother Nature and humankind.

Begin at Alum Cave trailhead off Newfound Gap Road, a 20-mile shuttle from the end point. Shortly after the start, ascend slippery stone steps through Arch Rock, a large black chunk of slate weathered into a natural arch. Next, pass a heath bald to traverse a steep slope beneath 4,950-foot Alum Cave Bluff. At mile 4.8, top out on Mount Le Conte (6,593 feet), the third-highest peak in the park and home to the plank-board sided LeConte Lodge. Overnight here (check rates at lecontelodge.com) or camp a few strides later at Le Conte Shelter.

Photo: CSP_hilltop341 / AGE footstock

The next day, hike above 5,500 feet on the Boulevard Trail to the Appalachian Trail. Swing northeast, and trek 1.1 miles to a spur trail up the treeless 5,565-foot knob of Charlies Bunion. Look out into a collage of forest-green ridgelines and rounded mountains. Continue on the AT, linking a ribbon of ridgetops. In 3.4 miles, cross Laurel Top for more views. Go 2.6 more miles and turn right onto Hughes Ridge Trail to descend to Pecks Corner Shelter.

An easy day three straddles the Tennessee-North Carolina border, crosses Mounts Sequoyah and Chapman, and ends at the recently renovated Tricorner Knob Shelter.

The next morning, follow the AT for 6.1 miles and turn left onto Snake Den Ridge Trail. In 0.7 mile, turn left onto the Maddron Bald Trail. Ahead are long-stretch views from the crown of Maddron Bald (5,212 feet). Descend 600 feet and pitch a tent at Campsite 29 near the sloping banks of Otter Creek.

The trail continues west under the giant maples, beeches, and tulip trees in Albright Grove; see trunks with a 20-foot girth. Turn left onto Old Settlers Trail, passing stone walls marking old land boundaries. Around lunchtime, detour north to the Tyson McCarter barn, built in 1876 (its shingled roof and log walls remain intact). Stay on Old Settlers Trail and pass several derelict chimney stacks. Campsite 33—your final night's stay—marks the homesite of Perry Ramsey, who lived in the park until 1930. The last day climbs over Copeland Divide and ends 6.4 miles later at Greenbrier Cove.

Spring and autumn are ideal trip times: April and May are best for wildflower blooms, while fall brings brilliantly colored leaves and drier weather.

DISTANCE: 50 miles

TIME REQUIRED: 6 days

DIFFICULTY: Intermediate

CONTACT: Great Smoky Mountains National Park, (865) 436-1200; nps.gov/grsm

THE PAYOFF: Go deep into the park's rich history and grandest views.

TRAILHEAD GPS: 35.629159, -83.450940

FINDING THE TRAILHEAD: From Gatlinburg, Tennessee, take Highway 321 N for 6 miles. Turn right on gravel Greenbrier Road. Go 4 miles, until it dead-ends at a trailhead. Park a shuttle car here (or arrange a shuttle pick-up). Return to take US 441 S for 6 miles, then merge left onto US 441 S. Continue on US 441/Newfound Gap Road for 11 miles to Alum Cave trailhead.

Text: Marcus Woolf

WAYPOINTS & DIRECTIONS

GPS: 35.629159, -83.450940 Follow the Alum Cave Trail east from the trailhead.

GPS: 35.638817, -83.445343 Traverse a steep, dusty slope beneath the massive Alum Cave Bluffs.

GPS: 35.654140, -83.440540 At Y junction, bear right and travel south on the Boulevard Trail.

GPS: 35.653312, -83.438764 The Le Conte Shelter lies to the right of the trail.

GPS: 35.628309, -83.390647 At Y junction, bear right and descend on the Appalachian Trail.

GPS: 35.636799, -83.376736 At Y junction, bear left to reach Charlies Bunion, a large rocky knob with great views of rounded peaks.

GPS: 35.655251, -83.308446 Turn right onto Hughes Ridge Trail and descend to reach Pecks Corner Shelter. A water source lies downhill, south of the shelter.

GPS: 35.693516, -83.257178 At Y junction, bear left to ascend and continue on the Appalachian Trail. The trail to the right descends to Tricorner Knob Shelter.

GPS: 35.727040, -83.238972 At T intersection, turn left onto Snake Den Ridge Trail and descend, traveling west.

Side Trip: Turn right onto Snake Den Ridge Trail and descend to Cosby campground.

GPS: 35.732161, -83.246219 Turn right onto Maddron Bald Trail and descend narrow path through small hemlocks.

GPS: 35.729674, -83.253692 Reach Campsite 29, which lies in a ravine at 4,560 feet, next to Otter Creek.

GPS: 35.755614, -83.271850 At four-way junction, turn left onto Old Settlers Trail and travel southwest.

GPS: 35.758721, -83.303161 At four-way junction, turn right at sign for T. McCarter Barn and walk 500 feet to reach the barn.

GPS: 35.748414, -83.344378 Reach Campsite #33. A stone chimney from an old homesite lies a few yards east of the campsite.

GPS: 35.707778, -83.380067 End hike at Greenbrier Cove. Turn right on Ramsey Prong Road, then left on Greenbrier Road for 1 road mile to your shuttle.

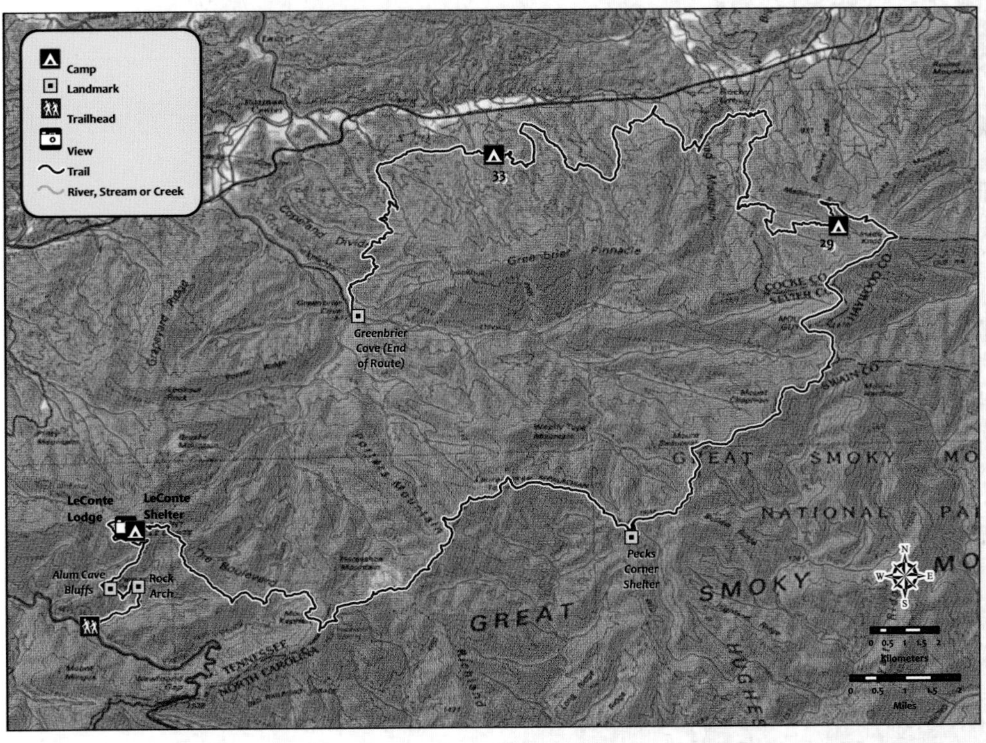

The Guadalupe Mountains' El Capitan
Photo: iStockPhoto.com / Sean Pavone

GUADALUPE MOUNTAINS NATIONAL PARK

El Capitan

GUADALUPE MOUNTAINS NATIONAL PARK
MCKITTRICK CANYON TO PINE SPRINGS

Traverse Guadalupe Mountains National Park to the state's airiest perch.

Alpine adventure in the Lone Star State? You bet. Towering over lowland scrub are the Guadalupe Mountains, a 65-mile-long range with limestone walls that shoot thousands of feet above the Chihuahuan Desert. Trout swim in one of the region's only perennial streams, and the state's highest point, Guadalupe Peak (8,749 feet), rises like a pyramid above it all. Hit the loftiest peaks by traversing the park on this point-to-point hike from the McKittrick Canyon visitor center to the Pine Springs visitor center. You'll gain and then lose 2,600 feet along the 25.7-mile route, and packing for a hike in this West Texas park is a challenge: Do you prepare for the open desert, rugged canyons, or high mountains? All three, actually, which is why some aficionados call this the best-kept secret in the national park system. Stay overnight in the backcountry, and you've found the secret inside the secret. The park's remote location and lack of water (it's strictly BYO for backpackers) mean you'll have the place virtually to yourself. On the weekend traverse you'll sample all of Guadalupe's diversity: Yucca- and agave-dotted desert, breezy limestone and sandstone ridges overlooking sheer-sided, multifingered canyons, and cool-air mountaintops with Texas-size vistas.

Photo: iStockPhoto.com / DenisTangneyJr

Text: Michael Lanza

DISTANCE: 25.7 miles

TIME REQUIRED: 3–7 days

DIFFICULTY: Intermediate

CONTACT: Guadalupe Mountains National Park, (915) 828-3251; nps.gov/gumo

THE PAYOFF: Climb from sublime desert to pine forests and peaks with 100-mile views.

TRAILHEAD GPS: 31.976192, -104.750004

FINDING THE TRAILHEAD: Start at McKittrick Canyon trailhead, which is 3.5 miles off US 62/180, 108 miles east of El Paso). End at Pine Springs trailhead, 0.25 mile off US 62/180 (7 miles southwest on 62/180).

WAYPOINTS & DIRECTIONS

GPS: 31.976192, -104.750004 Enter a narrow, cactus-lined ravine at McKittrick Canyon trailhead.

GPS: 31.966908, -104.788799 The Grotto, a cavern with stalactites, is a great picnic site.

GPS: 31.966344, -104.788606 Begin a series of switchbacks up 1,600 feet in about 1.5 miles to reach McKittrick Ridge.

GPS: 31.973425, -104.807510 Spend the night at McKittrick Ridge Campsite, with sunset views of the range's highest peaks.

GPS: 31.962248, -104.847336 Bear left to stay on the Mckittrick Canyon Trail at the Tejas Trail junction.

GPS: 31.918620, -104.845448 Spend the night at the Pine Top Campsite before ascending Guadalupe Peak in the morning. Bear left during the ascent to avoid the slower pack-trail route.

GPS: 31.892024, -104.860511 Take in the views from the Guadalupe Peak Summit before descending either to your shuttle at Pine Springs or, if you wish to hike longer and reverse your route, Guadalupe Peak Campground (GPS: 31.893481, -104.851971).

GPS: 31.896142, -104.826307 Await the Pine Springs shuttle here.

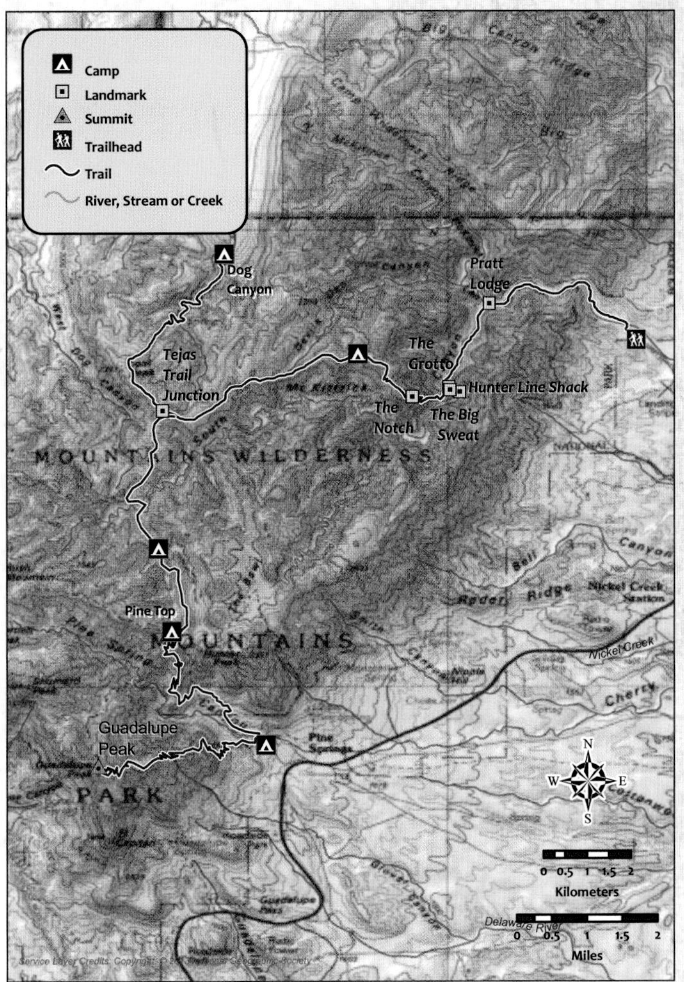

This pleasant hike through the canyon—the northernmost canyon in the park—is an easy escape from the dry, desert surrounds. This route begins at the visitor center and enters a narrow, cactus-lined ravine before rounding a small hillside and then crossing a big, rocky wash that exposes the canyon's geology. As you continue winding up and over the canyon's bends, the trail alternates between dry and riparian landscapes. The reliable canopy of oak, Texas madrone, and big leaf maple is one of the things that makes this such a popular trail—it's lauded as one of Texas's most beautiful fall-color displays. At 2.4 miles, you'll reach Pratt Cabin, a homestead built in the 1930s. In another 1.1 miles, you'll find the Grotto, a cavern with stalactites. Then switchback up 1,600 feet in just over 1.5 miles to McKittrick Ridge. Cruise the pine-covered spine of the Guadalupes to the Tejas Trail junction (mile 11.1). Camp at the McKittrick Ridge Campsite the first night—it has sunset views of the range's highest peaks.

The next day, continue south on the Tejas Trail down a gentle slope, passing junctions with Blue Ridge/Marcus Trail (mile 12.6), Juniper Trail (mile 13.7), and Bush Mountain Trail (mile 15.2). Pack binoculars and scope for some of the park's 300 bird species. A 3.7-mile home stretch brings you to the Pine Springs tent sites and cold running water. Wake early on day three to nab Guadalupe Peak, 4.2 miles and 3,000 vertical feet above. A pack trail splits 0.1 miles from camp, then rejoins it at mile 0.8; go left at both junctions to save time. The highest campground in Texas, Guadalupe Peak, is a mile from the top at 8,150 feet. Plan a feturn shuttle from Pine Springs for a 3-day trip or, if you want more high-country rambling, reverse your route for a 5- to 7-day trek.

Photo: iStockPhoto.com / David Parsons

The Guadalupe Mountains

HOW TO WIN THE BATTLE AGAINST BLISTERS

Death, taxes, and blisters? Not so fast. Here are 10 ways to avoid every backpacker's pet peeve.

1. Be Proactive Five miles into your hike should not be the first time you worry about blisters. The best way to avoid them is to prepare. Have you tied your boots correctly to prevent rubbing? Are you carrying moleskin, duct tape, or other first-aid implements, just in case?

2. Toughen Up Some people get blisters just because they have soft feet. At home, try taking off your shoes and walking around barefoot to harden soles.

3. Choose the Right Shoes Boot fit is the single most important way to prevent blisters on the trail. Don't order your next pair sight unseen: Go to a retail store and try on multiple pairs while wearing a fully loaded pack to give yourself a true simulation.

4. And Socks Just like shoes, not all socks are the same. Choose synthetic or wool socks that wick moisture and fit snug without any bunching in the heel or toe.

5. Layer Up Don't want to splurge on pricey double-layer socks? Try wearing two thinner pairs at the same time. The extra cushion will prevent rubbing, and a technical fabric will wick moisture away from your feet.

6. Get Insoles The insoles that come in boots can be the main cause of a lot of blister problems: They wear out sometimes they just aren't a very good fit for your foot. You can buy new boots, but the more cost-effective solution is to replace the insoles with better ones.

7. Prep with Moleskin These preventative adhesive patches can be a lifesaver—if you know where hotspots are likely to develop in advance. Put 'em on before your hike and enjoy knowing that blisters won't pop up in the usual trouble spots.

8. Pack Duct Tape It fixes everything, including blisters. If you feel a hotspot, take some duct tape and cover it securely. It's adhesive enough to stay put and slippery enough to reduce friction from your boot.

9. Keep Dry Moisture buildup causes skin to swell and rub awkwardly, so do your best to stay out of puddles. Choose boots that are waterproof yet breathable. If you get wet, take off your boots and socks in camp to let them air out.

10. Keep Clean Hikers' feet won't win any beauty contest, and a little grime comes with the territory. But over the long haul, dirty feet can contribute to blisters and cause existing sores to become infected. Rinse and dry feet whenever you come across a source of running water.

Photo: Eric Johnson

Haleakala Crater, Haleakala National Park, Hawaii
Photo: iStockPhoto.com / Dirk90425

HALEAKALA NATIONAL PARK

Haleakala Crater

HALEAKALA NATIONAL PARK
KA LU'U O KA 'O'O CINDER CONE

Drop into the muzzle of the world's largest dormant volcanoes.

Haleakala means "house of the sun" in Hawaiian, and one could easily believe the sun beds down here: Scorched earth stripes this 10,023-foot volcano in multicolored washes; it shifts underfoot to reveal highlights cast in volcanic sand. But these hues were forged from fires within the Earth, far from any celestial body. Now they're exposed on top of a massive shield volcano that occupies 75 percent of Maui.

Drop into the Haleakala Crater on this 5.5-mile trip that circles the rim of the colorful Ka Lu'u o Ka 'O'o cinder cone and features jaw-dropping views across the crater floor and Ko'olau Gap. From the visitor center parking area, pick up the Sliding Sands Trail, marked by a large sign. Contour around a large outcrop, then begin the long, steady descent into the crater on loose, sandy trail. As you descend, study the colors of the landscape, which change with the angle of the sun.

After a mile, stop at Na'ena'e Overlook for long views across the crater floor to the Kaupo Gap, then continue the descent, passing small patches of 'ahinahina (silversword). At mile 2, cool off behind two large rock outcrops, one of the crater's few shady spots, and turn right onto the short, 0.6-mile spur to circumnavigate a Lu'u o Ka 'O'o, a cinder cone with bands of red, orange, yellow, green and brown. (Caution: The trail is narrow and loose; do not descend into the crater.)

At the end of the spur trail, turn right and continue north to an overlook of the Ko'olau Gap, Kalahaku Pali, and the numerous other cinder cones within Haleakala. Pull up a rock, have a snack, and soak up the striking landscape. When you're ready, follow the same route back to the trailhead.

Photo: iStockPhoto.com / peanut8481

Text: Eli Boschetto

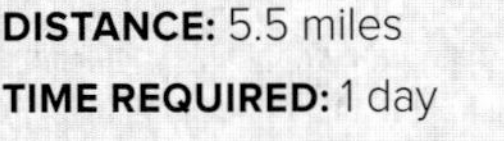

DISTANCE: 5.5 miles

TIME REQUIRED: 1 day

DIFFICULTY: Intermediate

CONTACT: Haleakala National Park, (808) 572-4400; nps.gov/hale

THE PAYOFF: Descends into the Haleakala Crater, circle the Ka Lu'u o ka 'O'o cinder cone, absorb views of volcanic landscapes.

TRAILHEAD GPS: 20.714416, -156.250431

FINDING THE TRAILHEAD: From Kahalui, Head west on HI 37, following signs to Haleakala. Turn left on HI 377. In 6.2 miles, turn left on HI 378. Go to the road's end at the summit and visitor center.

WAYPOINTS & DIRECTIONS

GPS: 20.714416, -156.250431 From the visitor center parking lot, walk south on the path that parallels the road to reach Sliding Sands trailhead.

GPS: 20.712025, -156.249930 At the Sliding Sands trailhead, continue southeast. Look for the Big Island's Mauna Kea peak, 80 miles to the southeast.

GPS: 20.710389, -156.242087 Na'ena'e Overlook. Stop and take in the views over Haleakala Crater and Kaupo Gap.

GPS: 20.713252, -156.238095 At this switchback, you'll find more views across Ka Lu'u o ka 'O'o Crater and the Ko'olau Gap.

GPS: 20.711056, -156.233279 Bear left (north) at the large rock outcrop, taking the spur trail to Ka Lu'u o ka 'O'o Crater.

GPS: 20.716500, -156.233547 Bear right at the three-way junction for a quick loop around the rim of Ka Lu'u o ka 'O'o Crater.

GPS: 20.719350, -156.233053 Stop for lunch at this viewpoint overlooking the Haleakala Crater floor and XX Gap. Turn around and retrace steps back to the parking area.

GPS: 20.709977, -156.253138 After your hike, catch the sunrise or just more breathtaking views at the Haleakala's summit—follow route 378 a bit farther south to the access on the right side of the road.

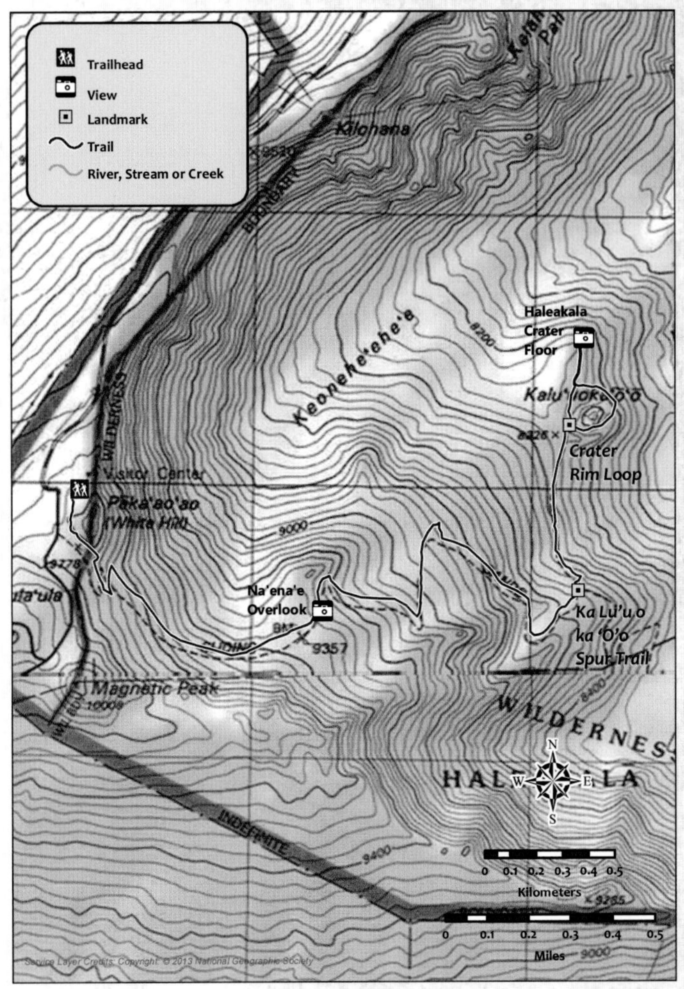

Clouds roll over Haleakala Crater

See shooting stars from a five-star backcountry observatory.

With negligible light pollution, high-altitude (read: clear) atmosphere, and horizon-to-horizon views, astronomers rank Hawaii's volcano summits to be among the top ten spots in the world to witness a meteor shower. Any time of year offers a banquet of meteors crisscrossing constellations. But the Geminids, in December, offer an especially vivid and prolific show, with streaks of white, green, and blue flashing at a rate of more than one per minute.

From the Haleakala National Park visitor center at 9,740 feet, pick up a free permit the day of your trip. Then drive back to the Halemau'u trailhead to begin the 7.5-mile, one-way hike to the night's camp. Continue straight through the three-way junction on the Halemau'u Trail. Just beyond the junction you'll see your first view over the blown-out side of the massive volcano. Crest the volcano's lip, taking in superb views as you switchback 1,000 feet to the crater floor. Pass cliff bands of jagged and scissor-sharp black lava on the way. Be careful: The rock is sharp enough to slash hiking shoes. Look out to long views of the often cloud-spotted Ke'anae Valley, where ecological zones from cinder-ash deserts to lush rainforests thrive. You'll see the Pacific Ocean glittering blue beyond.

Next, you'll descend through cemented lava flows and ash fields. Finally, you'll reach the bottom of the crater at Ko'olau Gap (6,700 feet). Take a moment to snapshot the hillsides and lava mounds streaked in reds, browns, and greens. Then continue south another mile: You'll reach camping at the 25-person capacity Holua Campsite (6,940 feet), which has water and pit toilets nearby. Pitch a tent, get in a catnap, and wait for the evening's entertainment, which peaks around midnight.

Photo: iStockPhoto.com / Global_Pics

Text: Charlie Wood

The shower reaches its most intense flurry on just a few days in December, but the sky here lights up a week before and after, so schedule your trip close to a new moon for the darkest sky.

DISTANCE: 15 miles

TIME REQUIRED: 2 days

DIFFICULTY: Intermediate

CONTACT: Haleakala National Park, (808) 572-4400; nps.gov/hale

THE PAYOFF: Sleep under some of the best starry sky in the country.

TRAILHEAD GPS: 20.752357, -156.228295

FINDING THE TRAILHEAD: From Kahului, take Haleakala Highway (which becomes Crater Road) for 28.3 miles into the park. After picking up a permit at the trailhead, continue to the Halemauʻu trailhead.

WAYPOINTS & DIRECTIONS

GPS: 20.752560, -156.228607 Head northeast on Halemauʻu Trail.

GPS: 20.755697, -156.222275 Go straight at three-way juncture with Supply Trail, staying on Halemauʻu Trail. Take your first view over the blown-out side of the massive volcano that forms more than 75 percent of the island.

GPS: 20.755751, -156.218964 Crest volcanic lip (superb views), then start switchbacking 1,000 feet to the crater floor.

GPS: 20.755741, -156.215027 Pass cliff bands of jagged and scissor-sharp black lava (be careful not to slash your hiking shoes).

GPS: 20.755203, -156.212997 Clouds drift over the Keʻanae Valley, where various ecological zones (from cinder ash deserts to lush rainforests) thrive.

GPS: 20.753677, -156.214661 Look down for a view of cemented lava flows and ash fields that lie below.

GPS: 20.752155, -156.213150 Koolau Gap (6,700 feet). Photograph hillsides and lava mounds streaked in reds, browns, and greens before heading back to the trailhead. Campers: Continue south for another mile to Holua Campground.

GPS: 20.740021, -156.217840 Holua Campground.

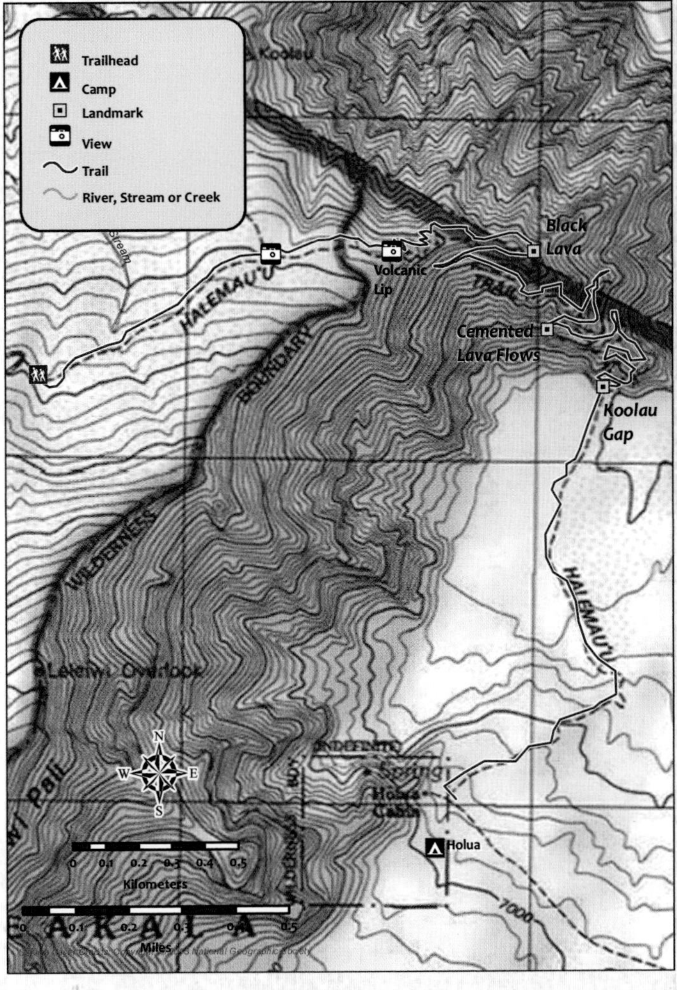

Kilauea eruption, Hawaii Volcanoes National Park, Hawaii
Photo: iStockPhoto.com / theartist312

HAWAII VOLCANOES NATIONAL PARK

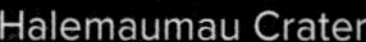
Halemaumau Crater

HAWAII VOLCANOES NATIONAL PARK

KILAUEA THREE WAYS: IKI, HALEMA'UMA'U CRATER, AND PU'U O'O TRAILS

Plunge from rainforest to caldera and see Hawaii's famously explosive national park three different ways.

Flash back to your childhood imaginings of lava belching forth from the guts of the earth. What you see in your mind's eye is reality at Hawaii Volcanoes National Park, where two of the world's most active volcanoes—Kilauea and Mauna Loa—spew Day-Glo orange rivers of molten rock that cool into bizarre shapes in an ever shifting landscape. Intrepid hikers can wander into eruptions in real time in three unique ways.

With three hours available, the Kilauea Iki Trail drops visitors into a caldera on a day hike that ventures from a tropical rainforest dripping with life to a scorched and barren lava field. This 4-mile loop hits you with the best of both extremes, winding through thick vegetation before descending 400 feet into a steaming crater. From the Kilauea Iki Overlook located near the Thurston Lava Tube, head out onto the Kilauea Iki Trail. In just over a mile, the trail descends black rock slabs to the crater's flat, crunchy bottom. This 1.5-mile section is smooth, with buckled lava flow flanking the sides. You'll pass the source of the highest-recorded lava fountain in Hawaii's history, 1,900 feet in 1959, as you close the loop.

Photo: iStockPhoto.com / mbdement

Text: Kellie Schmitt

Got five hours? Explore the Halema'uma'u Crater, which exploded in March 2008 for the first time since 1924; survey the aftermath on a 5-mile hike. From the Kilauea Visitor Center, cross Crater Rim Drive and hang a right onto Crater Rim Trail to cruise through pointed ferns and red tufted ohia trees. Just 1 mile in, steam billows upward from the fractured earth, the air hot enough to fog sunglasses. Continue 1.2 miles to the Jaggar Museum overlook to watch plumes rise from Halema'uma'u, the fabled home of the Hawaiian fire goddess, Pele. A white cloud, evidence of a lava pond deep below the vent's rim, often billows a mile high before arcing in the wind.

Hikers with nine hours to blow reap the finest trip of all on a trek to a remote crater. The volcanic vent Pu'u 'O'o has erupted continuously since 1983, making it Kilauea's most active fissure in 600 years. Stop at the Kilauea visitor center for a Napau Trail permit (free) then drive on Crater Rim Drive east to reach the trailhead. The 14-mile round-trip route starts atop a 1974 lava flow. Eerie remnants like contorted trees and channels linger where lava once gushed. At 0.75 mile, ascend the Pu'u Huluhulu cinder cone for views of three volcanoes—Kilauea, Mauna Kea, and Mauna Loa. As you curve around the Makaopuhi Crater, ferns and rosy ohelo berries brighten the landscape. Backtrack after watching the steam show at fuming Pu'u 'O'o vent at the Napau Crater overlook.

DISTANCE: 4, 5, and 14 miles

TIME REQUIRED: 3, 5, and 9 hours

DIFFICULTY: Intermediate

CONTACT: Hawaii Volcanoes National Park, (808) 985-6000; nps.gov/havo

THE PAYOFF: Active lava flows, steam vents, jungle scenery.

TRAILHEAD GPS: 19.429525, -155.257072

FINDING THE TRAILHEAD: From Hilo, take HI 11 south for 30.1 miles to the Kilauea visitor center.

WAYPOINTS & DIRECTIONS

Kilauea Iki loop (3 hours)

GPS: 19.417068, -155.242981 From the Kilauea Iki trailhead just west of the Thurston Lava Tube, wind through thick vegetation before descending 400 feet and walking through the steaming crater.

GPS: 19.413599, -155.238800 Walk in the dark through Nahuku, known as the Thurston Lava Tube.

GPS: 19.415022, -155.236862 Emerge blinking in the sunlight at the end of Nahuku.

GPS: 19.416439, -155.242950 Complete the hike by closing the loop around the crater rim of Kilauea Iki by going right (east) at the T on Crater Rim Trail.

Crater Rim Trail (5 hours)

GPS: 19.429525, -155.257072 From park headquarters, cross Crater Rim Drive and go right on Crater Rim Trail.

GPS: 19.419994, -155.288550 Continue 1.2 miles to the Jaggar Museum overlook to watch plumes rise from Halema'uma'u. At the junction with the Halema'uma'u trail at the south end of the Kilauea Crater, hang a left onto the Halema'uma'u Trail and follow it north through the crater, taking in the volcanic landscape before closing the Crater Rim Trail loop at the visitor center.

Napau Trail (9 hours)

GPS: 19.365081, -155.215616 Drive southeast on Crater Rim Drive from the entrance. The Napau Trail begins atop the remnants of a lava flow from 1974.

GPS: 19.370790, -155.204759 At 0.75 miles, ascend the Pu'u Huluhulu Crater, to gain long views of Mauna Kea, Kilauea, and Mauna Loa.

GPS: 19.363138, -155.174589 Near Makaopuhi Crater, Look for ferns and rosy 'ohelo berries brightening the lava-scarred landscape.

GPS: 19.369292, -155.156221 Remnant lava flows from the 1960s reach the trail.

GPS: 19.373624, -155.148046 After gazing at the steaming crater, backtrack from here.

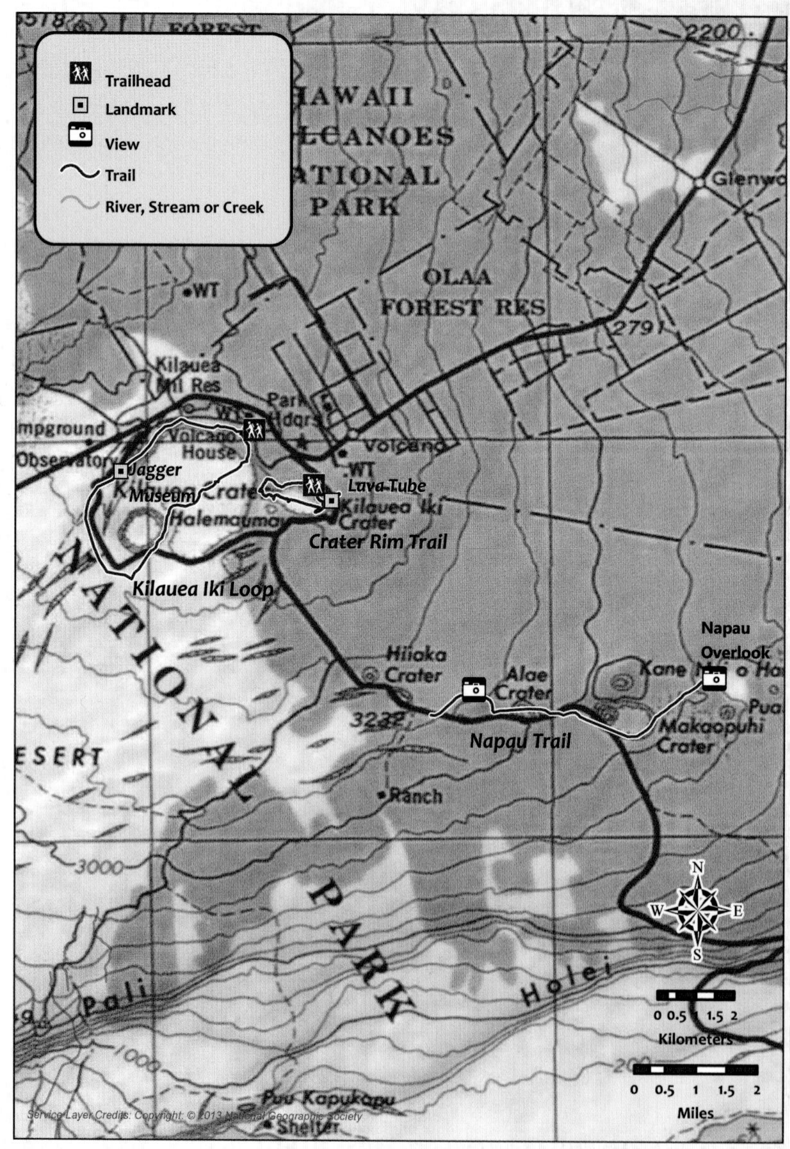

HOW TO PACK A BACKPACK THE RIGHT WAY

Pack right, and light

Want to pack more efficiently? Follow these tips on how to pack a week's worth of gear into your regular weekend pack.

DON'T PACK PIECEMEAL. Lay out everything you think you'll need to bring and strategize from there.

GET BIG ITEMS SITUATED FIRST. Keep weight low and centered. Liquid fuel should be placed outside or at the very bottom of a pack in case of a leak.

LOOK AT THE AMOUNT OF CLOTHING YOU PLAN TO BRING, THEN CUT IT IN HALF. It's not a wilderness experience otherwise! Pick baselayers that can provide both breathability and warmth. Roll, don't fold—or better yet, use a compression sack.

COMPRESSION SACKS ARE YOUR BEST FRIEND for slimming down puffy items, like sleeping bags. Bonus: they provide water protection in case of a downpour.

DEFLATE DRY-FOOD PACKS WITH A PIN AND COVER THE HOLE WITH TAPE. Put survival items in the brain of the pack for fast emergency access.

CARABINER LIGHTER ITEMS TO THE FRONT OF YOUR PACK, taking care to balance out each side. Use external loops and straps to secure awkwardly shaped items like tent poles and sleeping pads.

STUFF SHELLS AND OUTERWEAR in the front and side pockets.

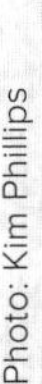

Photo: Kim Phillips

Text: Abbey Dufoe

Rock Harbor, Isle Royale National Park, Michigan
Photo: iStockPhoto.com / Posnov

ISLE ROYALE
NATIONAL
PARK

ISLE ROYALE NATIONAL PARK

SCOVILLE POINT LOOP

A rugged coastline hike soundtracked by howling wolves and keening loons might be the best in the Midwest.

Take everything there is to love about upper-Midwest hiking—serene forests, rocky bluffs, the soundtrack of howling wolves and lilting loons, and above all, those glorious lakes—turn it up to 11, and you have Isle Royale. The island's charms are in full force on its northeastern tip, where the trail hugs the shoreline for constant lake views. It's here, where dry land's victory over the water's countless incursions of bays, inlets, and waves never seems totally assured, that you'll best appreciate the drama of this rugged refuge. Start on the Stoll Memorial Trail and hike 4 miles east through the spruce-fir woods to the stony finger of Scoville Point for horizon-gazing across Lake Superior. Look for moose on the return hike along Tobin Harbor, a sheltered cove sprinkled with evergreen-furred islands of its own.

Photo: Chris Miele/Tandem Stock

Text: Elisabeth Kwak-Heferan

DISTANCE: 4 miles

TIME REQUIRED: 1 day

DIFFICULTY: Easy

CONTACT: Isle Royale National Park, (906) 482-0984; nps.gov/isro

THE PAYOFF: Raw coast, wolf wildlife, wide views.

TRAILHEAD GPS: 48.103765, -88.567016

FINDING THE TRAILHEAD: Get to the island via the *Voyageur II* ferry from Grand Portage, Minnesota.

WAYPOINTS & DIRECTIONS

GPS: 48.146417, -88.484058 From Snug Harbor, go right (east) on the Stoll Memorial Trail through spruce-fir woods.

GPS: 48.163223, -88.450627 At the stony finger of Scoville Point, the far point of the trail, gaze across Lake Superior. On the return trip, take the right, western fork to hike along Tobin Harbor.

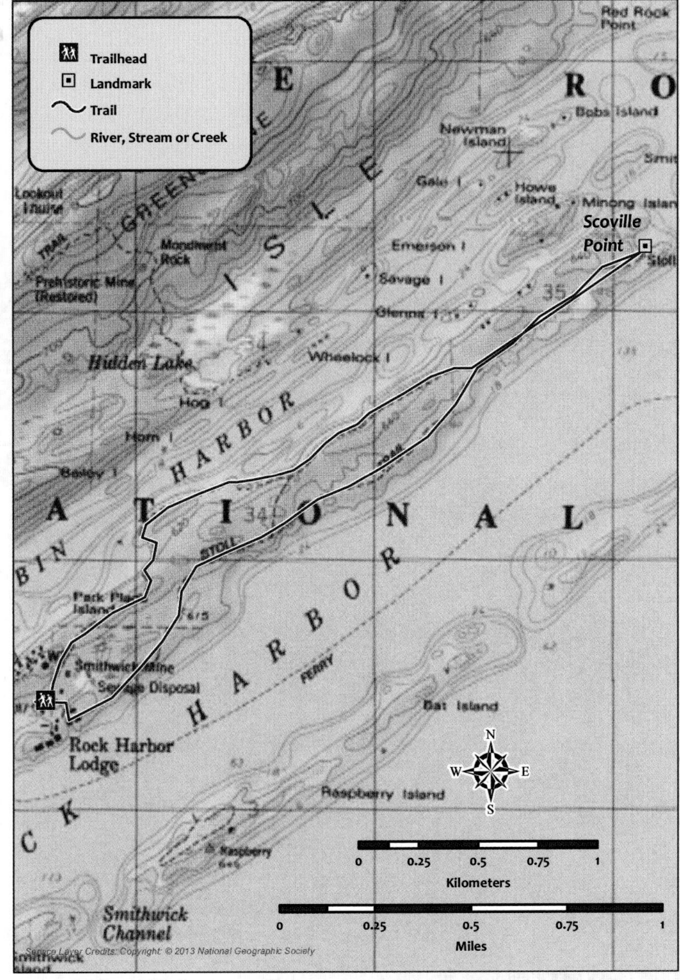

West Chickenbone Lake Campground

ISLE ROYALE NATIONAL PARK
GREENSTONE RIDGE TRAIL

Go high above this tiny Lake Superior island for solitude, views, and one of Michigan's most incredible ridge hikes.

Lake Superior acts like a 31,800-square-mile moat that keeps the sightseers away—this island park gets fewer visitors in a year than Yosemite gets on a busy midsummer day. One 7-hour ferry plus a 42-mile trail equals zero crowds. The precious few who make it here and actually go backpacking rightfully target Greenstone Ridge, the backbone of the island and home to its highest landmark, 1,365-foot Ishpeming Point. Thanks to boat-only access, the Greenstone Ridge Trail, which bumps along the view-draped spine of Isle Royale National Park, dishes up Alaska-style solitude. Jump in at either end (mapped here done west to east, Windigo to Rock Harbor) and emerge having snarfed thimbleberries by the handful, swum in remote lakes, and walked grassy heights with lookouts sweeping to shores 50 miles distant. Most Greenstone Ridge Trail hikers skip the 5 miles from Lookout Louise to Mount Franklin. Big mistake: At the Rock Harbor visitor center, arrange for a water taxi to Hidden Lake Dock. The views on this stretch are tops. Go in mid-August through September to catch the first blush of fall color and skip the park's legendary mosquitoes and blackflies.

DISTANCE: 42 miles

TIME REQUIRED: 4–5 days

DIFFICULTY: Intermediate

CONTACT: Isle Royale National Park, (906) 482-0984; nps.gov/isro

THE PAYOFF: High views, Alaska-quality solitude.

TRAILHEAD GPS: 47.911847, -89.157741

FINDING THE TRAILHEAD: Take the ferry from Grand Portage to Windigo, on the southwest end of the island. The Western trailhead begins at the visitor center.

Photo: Alex Messenger / Tandem Stock

Text: Jim Gorman and Mike Lanza

WAYPOINTS & DIRECTIONS

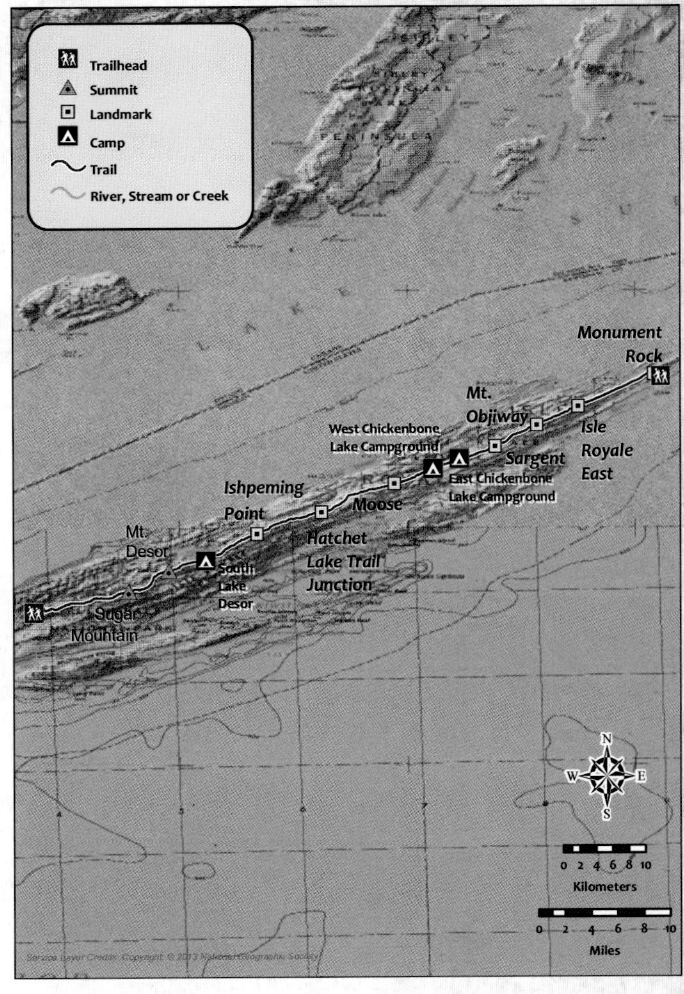

GPS: 47.911847, -89.157741 Start at the western trailhead, right by the Windigo visitor center.

GPS: 47.917824, -89.149504 Turn left onto the Greenstone Ridge Trail, one of the best ridge treks in the country.

GPS: 47.933850, -89.055117 Summit Sugar Mountain, taking in the beauty and solitude of your surroundings.

GPS: 47.935050, -89.043328 At this junction with the Island Mine Trail, turn right for a campground or continue on to the Greenstone Ridge.

GPS: 47.955746, -89.011701 Eastern (and higher) summit of two-tipped Mount Desor.

GPS: 47.966093, -88.970744 Turn left for camping at the South Lake Desor Campground.

GPS: 47.994346, -88.915426 Ascend the lookout tower at Ishpeming Point. The Ishpeming Trail leads south to Eagle Harbor and the Malone Bay Campground at the island's south side.

GPS: 48.017345, -88.843939 At this junction with the Hatchet Lake Trail, continue straight on the ridge trail or turn left to find camping north on Hatchet Lake.

GPS: 48.062204, -88.722377 Turn left for a quick spur to the West Chickenbone Lake Campground.

GPS: 48.072766, -88.693436 Hike 0.1 mile north at this junction to the East Chickenbone Lake Campground.

GPS: 48.098467, -88.629646 Bear left at the junction with Daisy Farm Trail.

GPS: 48.108390, -88.607417 Summit Mount Objiway (1,133 feet), a peak with its own lookout tower.

GPS: 48.152805, -88.502043 Continue straight.

GPS: 48.163502, -88.481281 Turn southeast with the Greenstone Ridge Trail and begin the final descent.

GPS: 48.158908, -88.471938 Here is the eastern trailhead, overlooking Hog Island and Wheelock Island to the South. Arrange a water taxi to pick you up at Hidden Lake and transport you to Rock Harbor through the Rock Harbor visitors center.

Granite formations in Joshua Tree National Park, California
Photo: iStockPhoto.com / sborisov

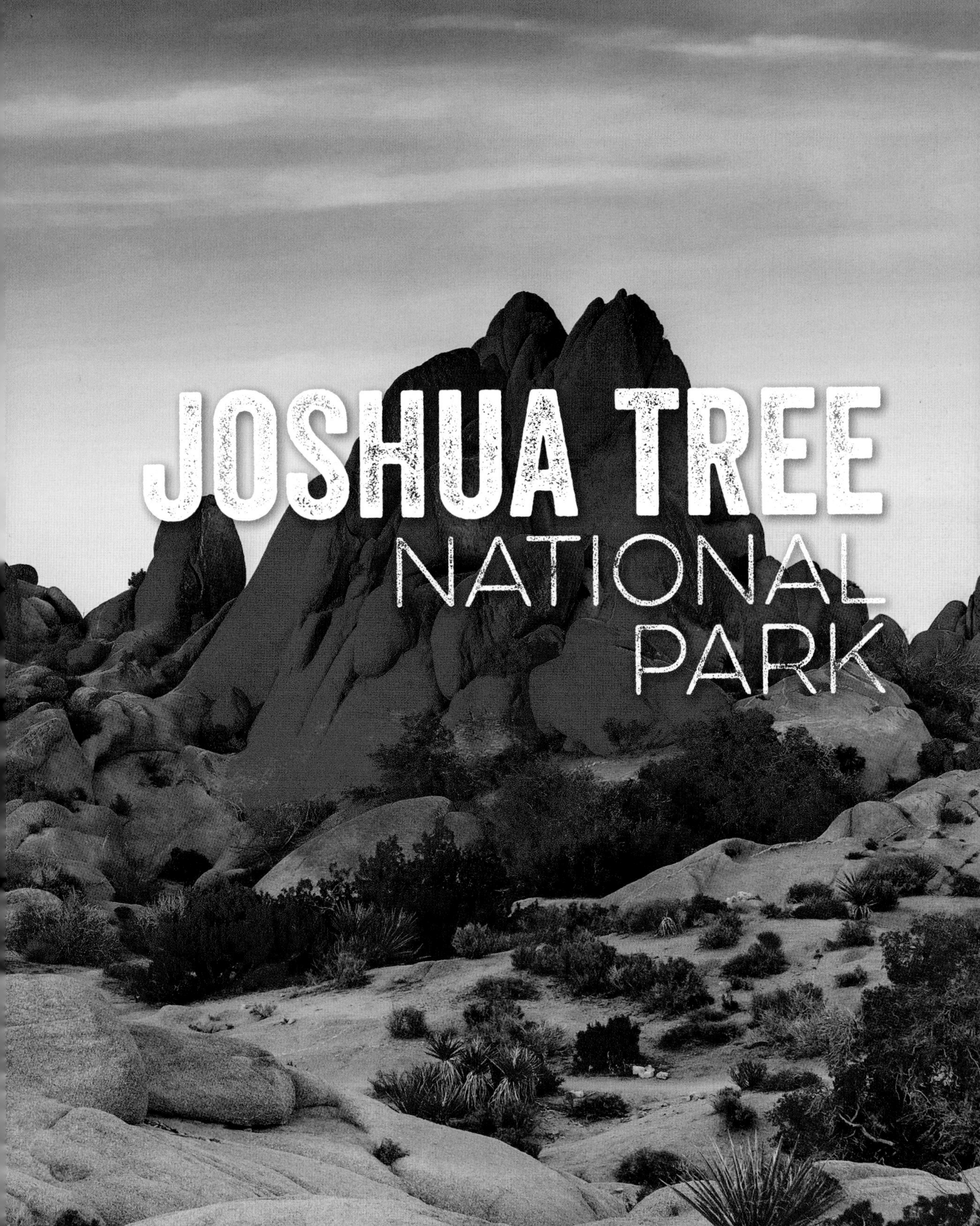
JOSHUA TREE
NATIONAL
PARK

Blooming cholla in "J-Tree"

JOSHUA TREE NATIONAL PARK

INDIAN COVE TO BOY SCOUT TRAIL TO RATTLESNAKE CANYON

Journey through a desert to bear witness to some of the loveliest wildflowers you'll ever see.

We think of deserts as desiccated landscapes of raw earth populated only by the heartiest of life forms. Joshua Tree National Park—with its piles of topsy-turvy boulders and scrubby washes studded with namesake trees reaching for the sky—certainly fits the bill. But it's also a place to witness some of the loveliest wildflowers you'll ever see.

Some years, during the height of spring bloom season, the flowers are so thick that the colors roll all the way across the usually bleak landscape and vanish into the horizon. Other times, you have to seek the blooms out one at a time, like little treasures. At night, huge, ghostlike blossoms open to the moon and later wither with the sun. Then the ephemeral colors are gone, and you'll wonder if the whole thing wasn't just a mirage.

Given the desert's fickle patterns of rain and temperature, you can't always predict when, where, or even if the flower show will occur. But plan a likely route anyway, then be prepared to change those plans and go where the flowers may be.

A spectacular and rugged 16-mile loop in Joshua Tree National Park will entertain you even if the blooms aren't peaking. From Indian Cove, hike the Boy Scout Trail to a camp not far from Willow Hole (watch for bighorn sheep). Then scramble and boulder-hop to Rattlesnake Canyon in the Wonderland of Rocks, and descend back to Indian Cove.

Photo: iStockPhoto.com / ericfoltz

Text: John Harlin

DISTANCE: 16 miles

TIME REQUIRED: 1–3 days

DIFFICULTY: Intermediate

CONTACT: Joshua Tree National Park, (760) 367-5500; nps.gov/jotr

THE PAYOFF: Spectacular wildflowers, wild rock formations.

TRAILHEAD GPS: 34.112799, -116.156301

FINDING THE TRAILHEAD: From Twentynine Palms on the edge of Joshua Tree National Park, drive 10 miles west on CA 62, and go south at the signed entrance to the Indian Cove campground and trailhead.

WAYPOINTS & DIRECTIONS

GPS: 34.112799, -116.156301 Begin at the Boy Scout Trail next to the Indian Cove backcountry board.

GPS: 34.101500, -116.199131 Here, the Boy Scout Trail turns south.

GPS: 34.103987, -116.184540 Enter large boulder piles.

GPS: 34.058135, -116.179562 At 6.8 miles, you'll meet the junction with Willow Hole Trail. Turn left (northeast).

GPS: 34.069298, -116.152396 In wet seasons, you can find pools of water and lush vegetation.

GPS: 34.072142, -116.147547 Difficult scrambling leads into Rattlesnake Canyon.

GPS: 34.073564, -116.144714 Oh-ba-yo-yo, a structure built from rocks by locals, is sometimes stocked with supplies.

GPS: 34.085507, -116.140423 At Rattlesnake Canyon Picnic Area, follow the road 1.3 miles back to Indian Cove.

GPS: 34.093753, -116.155701 At Indian Cove, follow the road 1.4 miles back to the Boy Scout trailhead.

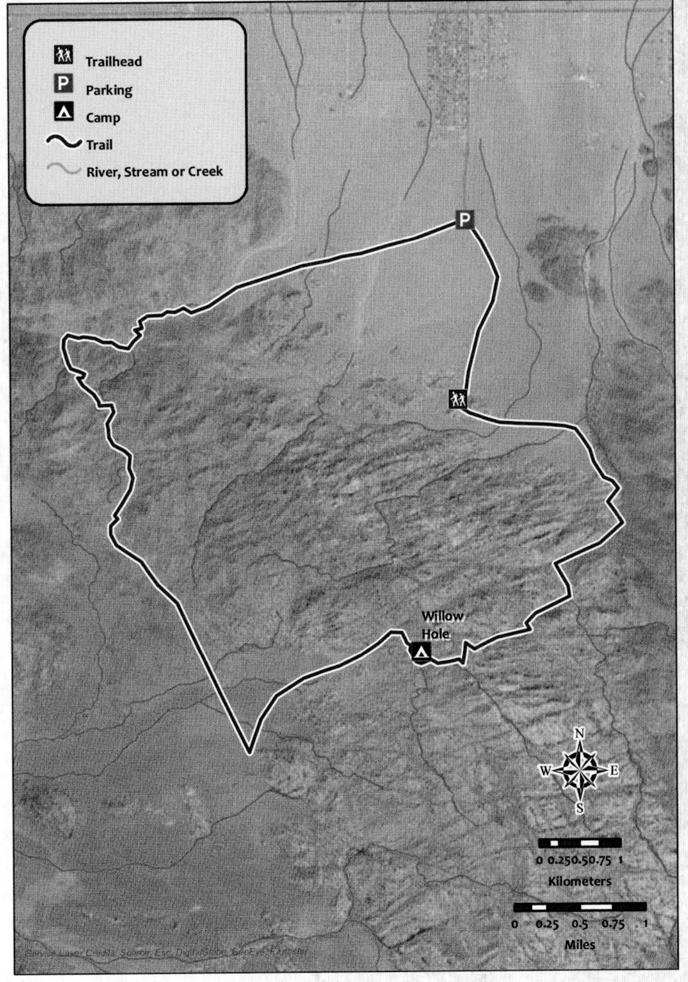

JOSHUA TREE NATIONAL PARK

LOST PALMS OASIS

Roll over hills dotted with spiky yuccas, ocotillos, and cactus before dropping into the lush Lost Palms Oasis.

Home to the largest stand of fan palms in Joshua Tree National Park, the Lost Palms Oasis is a refreshing reward for hikers on this 7.4-mile desert trek. Starting near the southern border of the park at Cottonwood Spring Trailhead, the hike climbs to the southeast through scrub-covered desert. Watch for hummingbirds that dart around the surrounding yuccas, chollas, and ocotillos. (In early summer, red flower clusters adorn the tips of the ocotillo plants.)

Massive boulder piles and rocky gullies become more common as the trail nears Lost Palms Oasis. At mile 2.3, turn right into a wash and follow the sandy trail through a mazelike wall of rocks. Next, descend into a small canyon lined with gullies and gorges and continue hiking southeast. One mile later, turn right onto a short spur trail that leads to bird's-eye views of the green, shaggy-topped fan palms. After 3.5 miles, a short, downward scramble drops down to the oasis, a prime spot for picnicking and bouldering. After relaxing at the oasis, retrace the route back to the trailhead.

Photo: Chuck Graham

Text: Amy Balfour

DISTANCE: 7.4 miles

TIME REQUIRED: 1 day

DIFFICULTY: Intermediate

CONTACT: Joshua Tree National Park, (760) 367-5500; nps.gov/jotr

THE PAYOFF: Massive boulder piles, fan palms.

TRAILHEAD GPS: 33.736916, -115.810656

FINDING THE TRAILHEAD: From Indio, take I-10 E about 25 miles to the Cottonwood Springs Road exit. Follow it north 7 miles to the Cottonwood visitor center. Turn right and follow Cottonwood Spring Road just over 1 mile to the parking area and trailhead.

WAYPOINTS & DIRECTIONS

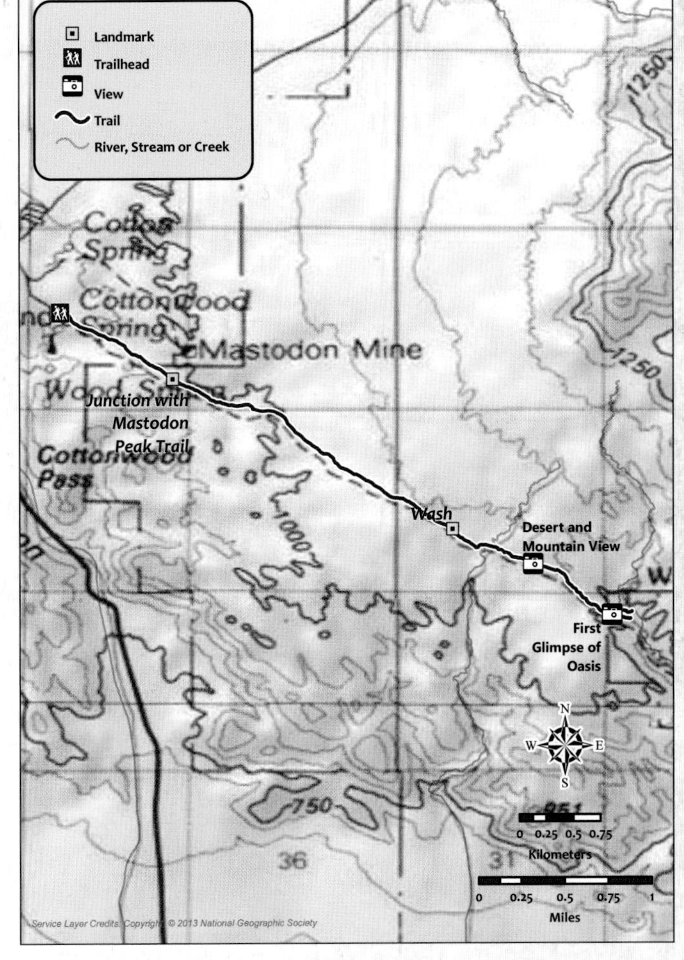

GPS: 33.736916, -115.810656 Cottonwood Spring. Once an important water-gathering spot for Cahuilla Indians and prospectors, the spring here now lures birdwatchers hoping to catch glimpses of ravens, flickers, cactus wrens, and hooded orioles.

GPS: 33.735264, -115.807595 Pass the first trail sign and continue southeast.

GPS: 33.731612, -115.801445 Stay straight at three-way junction. The Mastodon Peak Trail veers to the left.

GPS: 33.729580, -115.797002 Hike past the one mile marker.

GPS: 33.722359, -115.783560 Pass a Mile 2 marker, then meander southeast past the surrounding ridges and rock piles.

GPS: 33.719485, -115.777788 Turn right to follow a wash. The sandy trail winds through a craggy, maze-like wall of rocks.

GPS: 33.719389, -115.777630 Follow signs leading out of wash. The trail soon descends into a small canyon lined with gullies and gorges.

GPS: 33.715487, -115.768240 When you reach a ridge above a narrow gully, turn right off the ridge and drop onto a rock-bordered path. From here, the trail rolls across a series of hills and gullies.

GPS: 33.712614, -115.764978 There's no camping beyond this day-use sign. Bighorn sheep and other wildlife drink from the springs at night.

GPS: 33.712573, -115.764452 Look down the canyon for a first glimpse of the green, shaggy-topped fan palms. Before scrambling down to the oasis, turn right at three-way intersection to visit an overlook with bird's-eye views of the palms.

GPS: 33.712248, -115.762895 Take in the scene at Lost Palms Oasis Overlook, then backtrack and turn right. Descend 650 feet to Lost Palms Oasis.

GPS: 33.712817, -115.762776 Enter Lost Palms Oasis, which contains the largest number of fan palms in the park. When you're ready, turn around and follow the same route back to Cottonwood Spring.

Steller sea lions lounge on rocky cliffs in Kenai Fjords National Park, Alaska
Photo: iStockPhoto.com / jin_tang

KENAI FJORDS NATIONAL PARK

KENAI FJORDS NATIONAL PARK

HARDING ICEFIELD LOOP

The Harding Icefield

Hike to an ocean of ice—and escape the crowds by making it an overnight.

The Ice Age clings to life in Alaska's Kenai Fjords, where 40 glaciers pour from the Harding Icefield into inlets and bays swarming with whales, sea otters, and other marine life. Get a front-row seat of the glaciers in retreat on this challenging 8-mile out-and-back to the Harding Icefield. Best of all, no crampons or ice axes are needed during the summer months. Not that there isn't a price: this steep trail climbs 3,000 feet in 3.7 miles. But the reward is some of the most spectacular views in Alaska, with incredible vistas over endless plains of glacial ice punctuated by dozens of nunataks—isolated, conical rocky peaks that protrude through the ice and rise several hundred feet above it.

No surprise that Harding is a popular day hike. But very few visitors continue past the first major overlooks. So to enjoy the view in solitude—and make this trip an unforgettable overnight—just continue west 1.3 miles, across the obvious dark moraines, to more secluded viewpoints and choice tent sites, which offer seclusion, equally good views of the icefield, and reasonable access to water running over the nearby ice. The total one-way trip is 5.3 very strenuous miles; the trail is steep and slick in wet conditions, hot and exposed on sunny days. Keep an eye out for bears, mountain goats, and marmots.

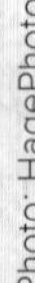
Photo: HagePhoto

Text: Steve Howe

DISTANCE: 10.6 miles

TIME REQUIRED: 1–2 days

DIFFICULTY: Intermediate

CONTACT: Kenai Fjords National Park, (907) 224-7500; nps.gov/kefj

THE PAYOFF: Up-close glacier views, temperate rainforest.

TRAILHEAD GPS: 60.189274, -149.629318

FINDING THE TRAILHEAD: From Anchorage, take AK 1 S (becomes the Seward Highway/AK 9 just south of Gilpatricks); in 127 miles, just outside Seward, turn west at the Glacier Road /FH 46 exit. Follow signs 8.4 miles to Exit Glacier trailhead; park in the lot.

WAYPOINTS & DIRECTIONS

GPS: 60.189274, -149.629318 Begin on Harding Icefield Trail, near the visitor center. (***Caution:*** Check trail conditions first).

GPS: 60.187751, -149.632673 Trail junction; continue straight through hemlock and spruce forest.

GPS: 60.184132, -149.649551 Cross bridge over glacier-fed creek.

GPS: 60.182976, -149.653061 Follow trail along Exit Glacier ridge. This is an excellent location to take photos in summer twilight.

GPS: 60.181816, -149.656311 Trail opens to views of Harding Icefield, a near- blinding spread of bowl-shaped glacial cirques covering half the park.

GPS: 60.181412, -149.663361 Turn left onto side trail for Exit Glacier overlook.

GPS: 60.183701, -149.665466 Follow switchbacks above cottonwood and alder treeline.

GPS: 60.184559, -149.684586 Follow orange markers; use caution crossing the first snowfield and watch for white mountain goats.

GPS: 60.182037, -149.702515 Pass small gray emergency cabin.

GPS: 60.178944, -149.706711 Reach Harding Icefield overlook; admire endless expanse of snow and ice. Retrace route to trailhead.

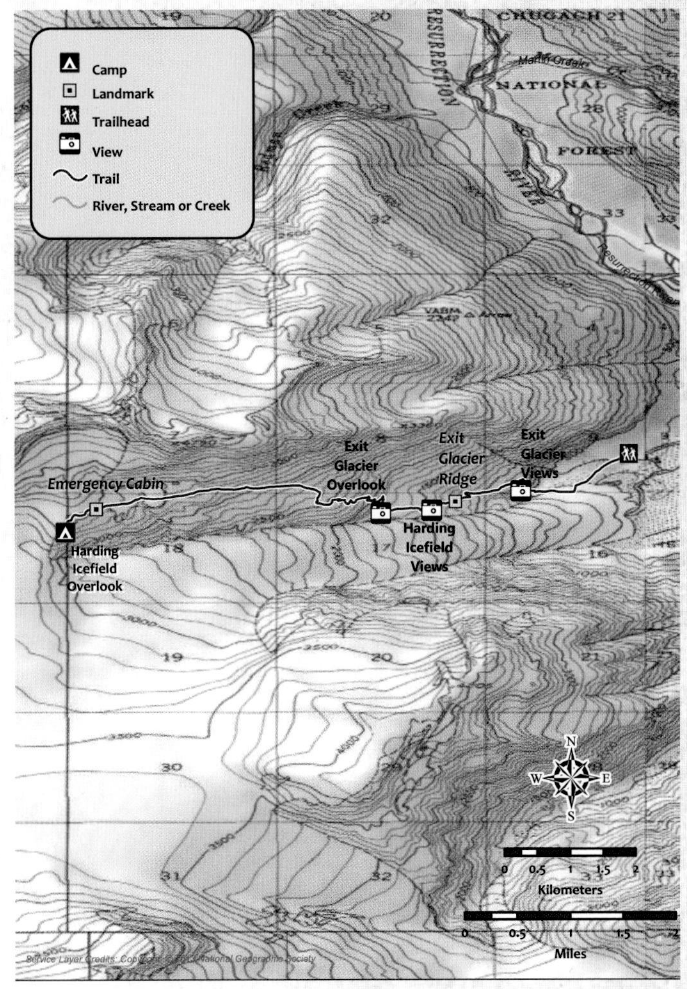

LAKE CLARK NATIONAL PARK AND PRESERVE

FEAR WALKED WITH ME

A once-in-a-lifetime solo hike through Lake Clark National Park and Preserve, where the midnight sun shines like candlelight on the mountains.

In June 1998, I spent a week in Lake Clark, backpacking across a breathtaking landscape of glacier-capped mountains, turquoise lakes, and caribou-nibbled tundra. Rarely have I felt so alive. Rarely have I been so miserable.

This is a story of fear and loneliness, and how I bit off more solitude, more wilderness, and more risk than I ultimately cared to chew.

It all started about three years earlier, when I was planning a trip to Denali National Park and Preserve. A return trip, to be exact, because I had unfinished business there. Ten days of rain, snow, bushwhacking, and bears the previous summer had chased my wife and me from the park. Denali slapped us silly, and I wanted satisfaction. I wanted to see the mountain on a clear, cloudless day. I wanted blue skies instead of soggy ground. I wanted the picture-book Alaska I expected to find the first time.

But something else, something more powerful, was also driving me to return: I wanted the kind of wilderness experience that turns amateurs into experts, a wild, challenging, solo trip through some of the most remote land in the world. Like most hikers who have plied well-worn trails, I'd fantasized about leaving partners and passersby behind and reveling in utter solitude and total self-reliance. I'd read about the intrepid adventurers who single-handedly blazed trails to the ends of the earth. Now it was my turn—two weeks, alone, in untracked, bear-infested tundra. This would be my breakthrough adventure.

Three days before my scheduled departure, I canceled the trip. It was a wise, rational decision, I told myself, made for all the right reasons. A 14-day solo hike was too ambitious, and the terrain required more advanced route-finding and survival skills than I possessed. Besides, the boss wanted me in the office, and my wife and 2-month-old daughter needed me at home.

Truth be told, I chickened out. Increasingly vivid daydreams of grizzlies, twisted ankles, and route-finding mistakes tied my innards in knots. Then there was the prospect of spending too much time alone, which made me so nervous I couldn't concentrate on such simple tasks as washing dishes. Would I come back in a dozen gnawed pieces? Would I turn into a big bowl of Fruit Loops out there on the high tundra?

Relieved, and a bit ashamed, I sat at home, burped my daughter, and wondered when—and if—I'd return to Alaska.

Three years later, standing on the gravel bar where I'd landed a half-mile upstream of Lake Telaquana, the sheer stupidity of my situation became obvious. Behind me lay hundreds of miles of uninhabited, mountainous terrain. Before me spread the vast, one-false-step-and-you're-dead wilderness of Lake Clark National Park and Preserve. I wanted to face the land unarmed, so I wasn't carrying a gun, bear spray, a radio, or signal flares. Only a pound of first-aid supplies, 12 pounds of food, and 45 pounds of camping gear stood between me and extinction.

A new job at *Backpacker* had given me the opportunity to return to Alaska, but with it came additional self-imposed pressure to earn my solo stripes. Now there was no turning back. My only link to civilization had already buzzed over the hills and wouldn't return for a week. Sitting tight on Lake Telaquana wasn't an option, either, because my pick-up point lay several drainages and many miles of bushwhacking to the south.

Solitude suddenly seemed much more menacing than I'd imagined from my leather armchair back home. As far as I knew, there were no other backpackers in the park and preserve's 4 million total acres. The nearest humans were two Russian biologists studying shorebirds on a lake about 20 brushy miles away. I remembered what Glen Alsworth, my affable, fiftysomething bush pilot, had said: "In an emergency, you could hike over to their camp. They probably have a radio, and you could use it to raise the Park Service, if the weather's good." It had been rainy and overcast for weeks.

I tried to tell myself that my upset stomach and quivering nerves were the result of the bumpy, 90-minute flight north from Port Alsworth. Twice the passenger door had popped open when Glen dipped the wing on my side to point out herds of caribou. Twice I'd cinched the seat belt tighter and wondered what I'd gotten myself into.

Thirty minutes on the ground eliminated any lingering doubts; I was, indeed, in a pretty precarious situation. Wading through a maze of willow thickets and abandoned beaver dams, I spooked a moose, tripped over the bleached bones of a caribou, stumbled across two sets of day-old grizzly tracks, and discovered what looked like a shrunken wolf skull but was really the shriveled head of a massive king salmon. Animals owned this place, and I didn't know whether the dense cover was hiding them or me.

When I finally emerged onto open lakeshore, I sat down in front of my video camera to tape a diary entry. Relief, worry, and awe mingled with breathless excitement, but also with the morbid realization that I wasn't merely taping a diary entry. I brought the video camera on a lark, but now I was using it to create evidence. This is how my family would piece together what had happened.

Five days of hiking took me from Lake Telaquana south to Turquoise Lake, my route skirting a jumble of jagged peaks fronted by 8,020-foot Telaquana Mountain. One full morning and another afternoon were spent thrashing through brush bordering the lakes; the remainder involved relatively easy cross-country hiking. The weather, typical for Lake Clark in early June, wasn't terrific. Rain came intermittently in sheets and drizzles, interrupted by one warm, sunny day. Constant strong winds had me battening down my rain gear and tent hatches. Snow fell almost daily above 3,500 feet; on day four, I trekked across 7 miles of largely featureless terrain in a snowstorm that reduced visibility to 100 yards or less.

Despite the weather, there was much to marvel at, from four-lane caribou highways worn 6 inches deep into the pebbly turf, to clusters of tiny yellow and pink flowers, to horizons cluttered with snow-clad giants and endless waves of rolling green tundra.

Known for its active volcanoes (Mount Redoubt last erupted in 1990, spewing ash as far as Anchorage) and plentiful glaciers, the park offers a dramatic landscape that testifies to the powers of fire and ice. But despite the ferocity of the landscape, wildlife thrives here. Bears, wolves, Dall sheep, caribou, delicate nesting birds that seem out of place in this hardscrabble environment—there are more varieties of animals than you can shake a trekking pole at. All in all, Lake Clark is a classic hiking destination with everything you could want and no competition for campsites.

Unfortunately, I was too busy looking over my shoulder to pay attention to geological formations and pretty birds. I had hiked solo before, traipsing all over New England in summer and winter, good weather and bad. I had also spent considerable time in bear country out West. But this wasn't New Hampshire or Montana, and the range of real and perceived threats was almost paralyzing. There were grizzlies, snowfields, loose rock, stream crossings, and threatening weather. But most of all there was the isolation, and with it the knowledge that one careless step, one surprise attack, and the critters hereabouts would hear a huge sucking sound as the land swallowed me whole.

The result was that I spent the entire trip, every waking moment, on full alert. I watched where I stepped and gingerly tested the depth of each snowfield. I took circuitous detours around sketchy talus slopes. I shouted myself horse yelling "Hey, bear!" every 20 seconds. The nervous energy expended left me mentally and physically exhausted at the end of each day. Unable to relax, I counted the hours until the flight home.

"We have nothing to fear but fear itself." Yeah, right. Ten to one that old FDR never heard a grizzly growling 20 feet away in dense brush. Or stared into a freshly excavated bear den after turning a blind corner in a one-way-out ravine. Or awoke to a chorus of wolves in a forest of 4-foot trees. And FDR had several hundred of his best buddies standing close by when he waxed eloquent about fear. There are certain undeniable benefits to having a hiking partner, the least of which is the perception of safety in numbers. Fear, on a solo hike, can become inescapable and overwhelming. When you're with a buddy or two, you can carve up the fear, pass it around, and digest it in manageable slices. Take away a partner and there's no one to share responsibility, administer first aid, run for help, or take the point position when bushwhacking starts to eat at your nerves. Take away a partner and you wind up pretty damn lonely.

From the get-go, I wished my wife had come along. We've hiked thousands of miles together; I've leaned on her, she's leaned on me, and so we've become a crack team. Without her beside me, I had less confidence, less fun. Lonely, tired, and still cussing myself for bumbling onto that bear den, I descended to Turquoise Lake and my last night's camp just as the sun burst out of the clouds to paint the surrounding peaks. The psychological effect was spectacular: A glowing alpine amphitheater ringing a dreamy blue, glacier-fed lake, with avalanches tumbling down 1,000-foot chutes as sun-warmed snow let loose from high on the shoulders of Telaquana and her sister mountains. With spirits lifted, I enjoyed my first leisurely meal of the trip and sat back to contemplate the lessons learned.

First and foremost, I decided that solo travel in the Alaskan bush produces more anxiety than I can handle. In the Lower 48, I know that help is never too far away. But in Alaska, where rescue may be days or weeks away, I felt for the first time in my life that I was flirting too closely with taking a father away from my daughter, a husband away from my wife, and a son away from my parents. Maybe I'll outgrow my anxieties, but this time out, fear kept me from fully appreciating Lake Clark.

Ironically—this may be difficult to believe—fear is also the reason I would consider repeating this trip. It put my system on alert like never before. Every step was wary and tentative, but also electric. In five years I'll probably need to try again, because the experience of living for a week on an emotional razor's edge purged my tanks and taught me a lot about who I am—and the kind of man I want to be. My sun-splashed reverie didn't last long. Within 2 hours, strong winds whipped through the valley, blowing whitecaps across Turquoise Lake and making me wonder if my pilot could land on a 30-yard gravel bar between 40-mile-per-hour gusts.

Then the final ignominy. Around midnight, sensing a momentary lull in the howl, I hopped out of the tent to relieve some pressure that had nothing to do with anxiety. Standing atop a hillock with my back to the wind, I surveyed the magnificent, wind-carved landscape and started to think that I'd actually conquered the place, that next time I would jump off the bush plane with less apprehension and a lot more confidence. Then a squirrelly gust wrapped around me, blowing an unwelcome reminder back in my face that it's good to be humble in a place like Lake Clark.

—Jonathan Dorn

View of a snow-covered Mount Lassen in Lassen Volcanic National Park, California
Photo: iStockPhoto.com / BurneyImageCreator

LASSEN VOLCANIC NATIONAL PARK

Volcanic rock

LASSEN VOLCANIC NATIONAL PARK

SUMMIT LAKES TRAIL

Pass sparkling alpine lakes on this easy weekend through volcanic high country.

Lassen Peak is the largest plug dome volcano in the world, and it marks where the Cascade volcano chain begins. This 10,457-foot hunk of extruded lava still burns: Hissing fumaroles and boiling mud pots ring its flanks. But it's water that marks this park's marquee trip. You'll hit eight forested pools on this 2-day, 19.1-mile lollipop in alpine terrain where the Sierra Nevada meets the Cascade Range. Even better: No crowds, because big-name neighbors (Shasta, Tahoe, and Yosemite) draw visitors away.

From the Summit Lakes trailhead, immediately cross vibrant Dersch Meadows—a frequent grazing spot for mule deer—over a 100-foot-long boardwalk. Dive into white pine and red fir forest, veering left at 0.3 mile and skirting the North Summit Lake Campgrounds. Walk 20 yards along the lake's northeast edge, forking left at the next junction and beginning a steady 400-foot climb to another junction at mile 1.3 atop a plateau. Here, the left fork leads to the Cluster Lakes—currently inaccessible following 2012's Reading Fire—so continue across the plateau and descend 250 feet over 0.6 mile, past azure Echo Lake. In 1.4 miles, walk under the steep, forested slopes along Upper Twin Lake's

Photo: Aidan Klimenko

Text: Kim Phillips

WAYPOINTS & DIRECTIONS

GPS: 40.498263, -121.427062 From the Summit Lakes trailhead, immediately cross the vibrant Dersch Meadows on a long boardwalk. Dive into a white pine and red fir forest, veering left and skirting the North Summit Lake campgrounds.

GPS: 40.494022, -121.421571 Walk 20 yards along the lake's northeast edge, forking left at the next junction and beginning a steady 400-foot climb to another junction atop a plateau.

GPS: 40.496580, -121.407580 Here, the left fork leads to the Cluster Lakes (currently inaccessible). Continue east across the plateau and descend past Echo Lake. In 1.4 miles, walk along Upper Twin Lake's north shore, and then contour around Lower Twin Lake.

GPS: 40.513864, -121.350024 From the shore of Rainbow Lake you can see the forested slopes of Fairfield Peak—one of Lassen's three cinder cones—mirrored on calm waters. Continue east into a bleached forest.

GPS: 40.506588, -121.317083 Begin a 1.3-mile-long descent (look for new undergrowth sprouting through the charred fir and pine) to the southwest shore of Snag Lake.

GPS: 40.508579, -121.316142 Go 0.1 mile north along the shore to find secluded campsites on the forested peninsula.

GPS: 40.473396, -121.332364 Stay right and continue following the meandering creek amid wide meadows. Hit the east shore of choppy Horseshoe Lake and spy Lassen Peak poking through the forested basin's horizon to the west.

GPS: 40.493549, -121.365160 Hike 0.5 mile and connect with the Pacific Crest Trail before returning to Lower Twin Lake and closing the loop, and turning left to return to the trailhead.

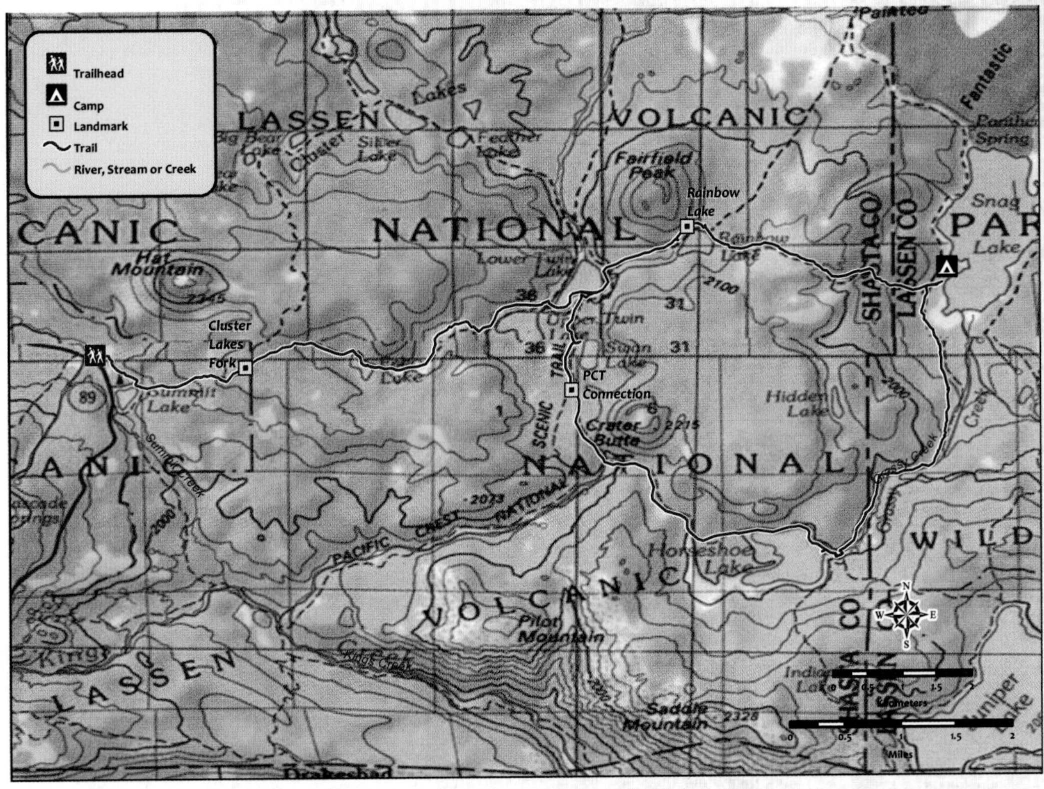

north shore, and then contour around the rocky southern shores of Lower Twin Lake. Hike east through currant and manzanita clusters and into thinning forest, alongside burnt stumps from a managed 2004 fire. At 5.2 miles, curl around Rainbow Lake, where you can see the forested slopes of 7,272-foot Fairfield Peak—one of Lassen's three cinder cones—mirrored on calm waters.

Continue east and delve into ghostly forest: Bleached tree skeletons and charred trunks litter the floor. Listen for skittering golden-mantled ground squirrels and one of Lassen's 216 bird species chirping and cawing in this 0.7-mile section of flash-burned forest. At 6.3 miles, begin a 1.3-mile-long descent (look for new undergrowth sprouting through the charred fir and pine) to the southwest shore of Snag Lake—one of the largest and shallowest (average 25 feet deep) lakes in the park. See 7,577-foot Ash Butte to the east and the bronze-streaked basalt Fantastic Lava Beds to the north. Venture 0.1 mile north along the shore to find secluded campsites on the forested peninsula, where you can take a dip and watch the setting sun paint the surrounding peaks in glorious alpenglow.

The next morning, continue 3.1 miles south on the main trail alongside Grassy Creek, hugging the hillside, and zigzag over the water on wooden bridges. At 9.6 miles, stay right and continue following the meandering creek amid wide meadows. Hit the east shore of choppy Horseshoe Lake and spy Lassen Peak poking through the forested basin's horizon to the west. Next, pass an unnamed pond surrounded by rolling meadowland. At 12.7 miles, trace the base of 7,267-foot Crater Butte, the second of the three cinder cones. (An overgrown, 0.4-mile-long trail ascends Crater Butte at a 35-degree angle, affording a panoramic view of the park over a small crater lake.) Hike 0.5 mile and connect with the Pacific Crest Trail at 13.6 miles. Return to Lower Twin Lake under a shady forest canopy, and turn left. Retrace your steps 4.4 miles past Upper Twin, Echo, and Summit Lakes to your car.

If Lassen Peak is covered in white this summer, it's probably not snow. Look for the endangered white and lavender Lassen Smelowskia flower (budding late July) clustered on peaks.

DISTANCE: 19.1 miles

TIME REQUIRED: 2 days

DIFFICULTY: Easy

CONTACT: Lassen Volcanic National Park, (530) 595-4480; nps.gov/lavo

THE PAYOFF: Eight placid, crowd-free pools where Sierra meets Cascade.

TRAILHEAD GPS: 40.498263, -121.427062

FINDING THE TRAILHEAD: From Redding, go 47 miles on CA 44 E to the park entrance. Continue 13 miles on CA 89 to the Summit Lakes trailhead.

RANGER PROFILE

JERRY BRANSFORD

The Living History
Mammoth Cave National Park, Kentucky

"Quite simply, he is the park's history." —Glen Everhart, *Backpacker* reader

Jerry Bransford's great-great-grandfather, Materson Bransford, was an explorer and tour guide of Mammoth Cave as a slave before the Civil War. When the war ended, the Bransford men continued that tradition until private guides were banned when the National Park Service took over in 1941. Eleven years ago, the Park Service asked Bransford to bring the family name back to the cave. His ancestors names are etched everywhere, from the walls of the cave to the park's gravestones. He says he will never get used to the feeling he gets when he passes one of those names.

FAVORITE SPOT: Sal Hollow Loop

This 11.7-mile loop over a rolling karst landscape smothered in beech, maple, and hickory trees proves the park's topside features are just as attractive as the caves. For a quiet overnight, trace the Sal Hollow Trail 7.1 miles to the Sal Hollow backcountry site. The next day, take the 0.3-mile spur to Miles-Davis Cemetery, a settler's graveyard dating back to the mid-1800s. Return via the Buffalo Creek Trail.

TRAILHEAD: Maple Springs

INFO: nps. gov/maca

Sunset at Reflection Lakes in Mount Rainer National Park, Washington
Photo: Ian Shive / Tandem Stock

MOUNT RAINIER
NATIONAL
PARK

Walking through wildflowers on Wonderland Trail

MOUNT RAINIER NATIONAL PARK

WONDERLAND TRAIL, FROM FRYINGPAN CREEK TO MOWICH LAKE

Explore Mount Rainier from nearly every angle on this classic weeklong stretch of the Wonderland Trail.

There are all other mountains in the Lower 48, and then there's Mount Rainier. A few other peaks are taller, sure, but no single summit can beat this 14,409-foot volcano, the jewel of Washington's Cascade Range, for top-to-bottom immensity. And with its necklace of showy wildflowers, glacier-draped crown, and waterfall after roaring waterfall spilling from its shoulders, we'll go ahead and say it—it's the prettiest one, too. The 93-mile Wonderland Trail that rings the peak serves up a full buffet of Mount Rainier's beauty, but if you want to skip to the main course, head to this weeklong trip. In just six days, this 57.5-mile, roller-coaster route racks up a total elevation gain of 19,301 feet (and a loss of 18,183 feet) as it wraps around Mount Rainier's glacier-chiseled terrain.

After leaving the Sunrise Park Road trailhead, start a sustained, nearly 3,000-foot climb that parallels the cascades of Fryingpan Creek. If it's late summer, look for ripe huckleberries to pop into your mouth along the way, until you rise above the trees to reach-out-and-touch-it views of the mountain. At the head of the valley, scale switchbacks that deliver you

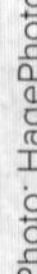
Photo: HagePhoto

 Text: Elisabeth Kwak-Hefferan, Evelyn Spence, and David Tate to Summerland, an open meadow doused with gentian, subalpine buttercups, aster, and dozens more summer blossoms.

Next, pass the Summerland Shelter, a rock and timber lean-to, and keep climbing southwest to 6,750-foot Panhandle Gap, the high point of the Wonderland Trail. Linger at the top with resident mountain goats for views that stretch across the enormous Fryingpan Glacier to distant glacier-capped Mount Adams and, on clear days, Oregon's Mount Hood.

Drop down the backside and traverse small snowfields above Ohanapecosh Park, passing a massive cirque streaked with a dozen waterfalls, before reaching yet another wildflower-dazzled basin at Indian Bar. At mile 8.3, cross Indian Bar, where the braided channels of the Ohanapecosh River vein the volcanic riverbed, then cross a bridge above Wauhaukaupauken Falls, gushing through a small slot canyon. Less than 200 feet later, drop your pack and spend the night at Indian Bar Shelter; deer and elk mingle in the adjacent meadows at dusk.

The next day, warm up with an 800-foot climb to a 5,930-foot high point on Cowlitz Divide. Trace the ridgeline southeast for 3miles, before descending to Nickel Creek and Box Canyon. Turn south at mile 15.3 and hike roughly 1.5 miles to the mouth of Stevens Canyon. Sleep at Maple Creek Camp near mile 18.

Climb out of the valley on day three, passing Sylvia and Martha Falls—and the crowd-pleasing Reflection and Louise Lakes at the head of the canyon. Begin the 5.8-mile descent into Paradise Valley and Longmire a mile later. Pause at mile 24 to stare at Narada Falls, a two-tiered waterfall that plunges 168 feet, then 20 feet over cliffs (ice climbers scale the upper falls in winter). Pitch your tent a mile from here in the forested Paradise River Camp.

On day four, pass back-to-back Madcap and Carter Falls at mile 25.2 and 25.5, and continue the southwest descent to Longmire, the park's former headquarters and the most popular place to start and finish the Wonderland Trail. Just north of the park buildings, the route swings north for a steep, 1,050-foot climb up forested Rampart Ridge (day-hiking crowds diminish in 1 mile). Less than 2 miles later, the trail rolls over the ridgetop and drops north into Kautz Creek. Sspringtime washouts are common; link the cairns to find log crossings. Then 0.5 mile later, cross Pyramid Creek, then climb 2.2 miles to Devils Dream Camp.

Rise early on the fifth day for the 1-mile stretch to Indian Henrys Hunting Ground. Spend some downtime in the sprawling, wildflower fields, backdropped by Rainier's southwest face, before starting the 1.1-mile, 1,050-foot descent to a suspension bridge slung high above Tahoma Creek's broad and rocky riverbank. After two more rigorous climbs and two knee-jarring descents, cross the bridge over the North Puyallup and sleep at its same-name camp (mile 45).

On the last day, climb past the flowery meadows and clusters of lakes that dot Sunset Park (black bears come here in the fall for the huckleberries) before descending into the Mowich River valley. Cross the South and North Mowich Rivers and begin the final 3.2-mile, 2,330-foot climb to the bustling Mowich Lake Campground and your shuttle car.

Only have a weekend to hike the Wonderland Trail? No problem. Sample the best stretch on a 15.4-mile point-to-point highlight from Fryingpan Creek to exit at Box Canyon. (Drop your shuttle car at this trailhead instead.)

DISTANCE: 57.5 miles

TIME REQUIRED: 6 days

DIFFICULTY: Strenuous

CONTACT: Mount Rainier National Park, (360) 569-2211; nps.gov/mora

THE PAYOFF: Wildflower meadows, life-list glacier views, wildlife galore.

TRAILHEAD GPS: 46.920662, -121.883993

FINDING THE TRAILHEAD: For the shuttle car drop, drive southeast on WA 410 E. In 11 miles, turn right onto Mundy Loss Rd. In 1.2 miles, turn left onto WA 162 E. In .3 mile, go straight on WA 165 S. Go 25 miles to parking at Mowich Lake Campground. **To reach the trailhead,** return to the WA 162/WA 165 junction; turn right to stay on WA 165. In 1.6 miles, turn right onto WA 410 E. In 41.4 miles, bear right onto Sunrise Park Rd./ White River Rd. Go 4.3 miles to parking pull-out.

WAYPOINTS & DIRECTIONS

GPS: 46.888369, -121.610667 Hike southwest from Sunrise Park Road along Fryingpan Creek and continue straight at the three-way junction.

GPS: 46.855434, -121.645349 Crest Panhandle Gap, the highest point along the Wonderland Trail at 6,750 feet.

GPS: 46.826095, -121.639124 Continue straight at the three-way junction. Turn right to sleep at Indian Bar Shelter. This historic shelter has a fireplace (filled with rocks) and ten bunk beds.

GPS: 46.776349, -121.606373 Turn right (southwest) for a wooded descent past the Nickel Creek Shelter to Nickel Creek.

GPS: 46.765832, -121.634998 The trail meets Stevens Canyon Road in Box Canyon. Turn right and descend to a footbridge over the Cowlitz River.

GPS: 46.760411, -121.661352 Maple Creek Camp (2,815 feet). Spend the second night at this site in Stevens Canyon (mile 17.6).

GPS: 46.770235, -121.703322 Carefully cross Stevens Canyon Road.

GPS: 46.770117, -121.723233

Turn right at this three-way junction overlooking Reflection Lakes (west) and Louise Lake (east).

GPS: 46.774763, -121.737231 Continue straight at this saddle below the Mazama Ridge for the descent into Paradise Valley.

GPS: 46.778955, -121.737054 Turn left (southwest) toward Narada Falls, then cross the highway. The wide, well-traveled trail descends to Narada Falls and parallels the Paradise River.

GPS: 46.769237, -121.758604 After crossing the Paradise River, spend the third night at forested Paradise River Camp (mile 25; 3,805 feet). The next day, continue southwest descent past Madcap and Carter Falls.

GPS: 46.766501, -121.791343 Turn left at this junction just east of Cougar Rock Campground. Continue descent southwest to Longmire.

GPS: 46.751678, -121.811864 The trail skirts the historic district of Longmire, the park's former headquarters and the most popular place to start and finish the Wonderland Trail. Turn right, heading north, for a steep, 1,050-foot climb up Rampart Ridge. (***Tip:*** To decrease the amount of food you must haul on the first three days, leave a food cache at the Longmire Wilderness Information Center before starting the trip.)

GPS: 46.766819, -121.808807 Turn right (north) for a descent to Kautz Creek.

GPS: 46.773553, -121.811605 Springtime washouts are common along this stretch of Kautz Creek's bed. Link the series of cairns to find log crossings over the creek.

GPS: 46.780108, -121.811686 Cross Pyramid Creek, then start the second climb of the day, ascending 1,600 feet in the next 3 miles to Indian Henrys Hunting Ground.

GPS: 46.782753, -121.834517 Spend the fourth night at the forested Devils Dream Camp. Refill water bottles in Devils Dream Creek, which flows through a gorge to the east.

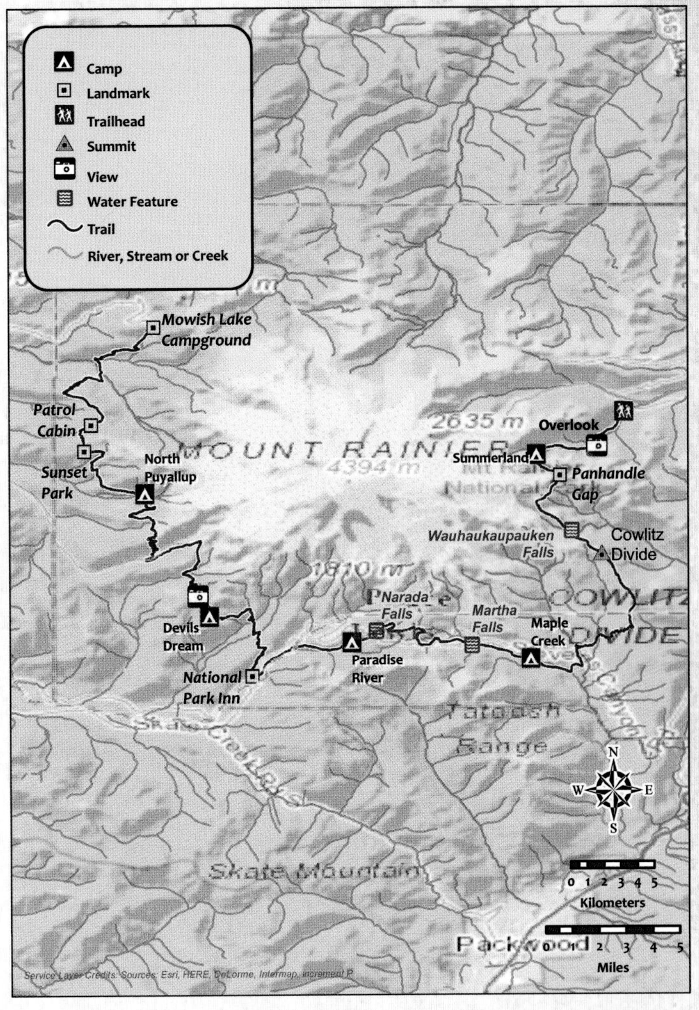

GPS: 46.795593, -121.841600 Turn left at three-way junction and drop 1,050 feet in 1.1 miles to Tahoma Creek. (***Side Trip:*** The trail on the right leads 0.5 mile to Mirror Lakes, which reflect Rainier on calm days.)

GPS: 46.804732, -121.848297 Cross a long, one-hiker-wide suspension bridge high above Tahoma Creek's wide and rocky banks.

GPS: 46.811812, -121.868843 Turn right, then cross the South Puyallup River.

GPS: 46.812720, -121.868806 Prepare for a steep, 2,000-foot grind up back-to-back switchbacks to St. Andrews Park.

GPS: 46.835356, -121.877469 Turn right at Aurora Lake and Klapatche Park, a grassy bench above the North Puyallup valley to the north.

GPS: 46.840376, -121.868847 Descend tight switchbacks into the North Puyallup valley.

GPS: 46.846573, -121.868935 After crossing the bridge over the North Puyallup, spend the fifth night at the same-name camp (mile 45). The next day, hike west above the river, then north toward Sunset Park.

GPS: 46.898820, -121.911941 Crest the ridgetop, then descend switchbacks through mossy forest (losing 2,000 feet of elevation) to the South Mowich River.

GPS: 46.908851, -121.892921 Scout out the best place to ford the South Mowich River. (***Caution:*** Water levels can be high in spring and later in the day due to meltwater from the South Mowich Glacier.)

GPS: 46.915712, -121.893954 Cross the North Mowich River, then begin the final 3.2-mile, 2,330-foot climb out of the valley to Mowich Lake.

GPS: 46.918058, -121.890262 At the three-way junction, bear right. The trail on the left climbs to Paul Peak.

GPS: 46.932829, -121.863959 The route ends at the bustling Mowich Lake Campground, on the southern edge of Mowich Lake. Pick up your shuttle car to return to the trailhead.

Dawn patrol

MOUNT RAINIER NATIONAL PARK
SUMMIT VIA DISAPPOINTMENT CLEAVER

This challenging climb on Mount Rainier gains almost 2,000 feet per mile.

Need proof that Washington's iconic peak deserves its reputation as the Lower 48's biggest and baddest mountaineering challenge? Ponder these two figures: 9,000 feet, the height it rises above the lush foothills where you start hiking, and 26, the number of glaciers on the massif, many of which you'll see from very, very close up.

First-time climbers typically follow the Disappointment Cleaver Route, the mountain's most popular and least technical ascent. But you'll still need avalanche smarts and advanced glacier-travel and rescue skills. No experience? Go with a guide, like one from RMI Expeditions (rmiguides.com).

The DIY plan: Ascend to Camp Muir, a mountaineers' camp at 10,000 feet. Start early (by 2 a.m.) to crest the crater rim by mid-morning, and get out before afternoon sun melts all that ice deadly.

From the parking lot trailhead, take the Skyline Trail 1.5 miles to Panorama Point. Avoid the numerous social paths branching out into the meadows. At mile 2.3, stay west of 7,385-foot McClure Rock and plant a crampon in Muir Snowfield. In another 1.2 miles, you'll reach Camp Muir—the unofficial halfway point with a stone hut, a tent area for climbers (guide companies have their own digs), and well-used toilets. Sidestep across the Cowlitz Glacier and walk out onto the Ingraham Flats, a broad, wind-stung area. Pitch a bomber tent here for a head start on Camp Muir campers.

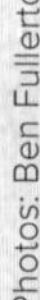
Photos: Ben Fullerton

Text: Shannon Davis

The next day, set your alarms for an early alpine start. You'll reach the bottom of the Disappointment Cleaver at about mile 5.2. It's aptly named: Steep, ice-covered rocks are the route's crux. Don't linger: There's no room to pass, and ice conditions can deteriorate later in the day. You'll reach the top of the grueling Cleaver in a just under 0.5 mile; rest after climbing the 45-degree slopes of rock and ice, and grab a snack. The guide's rule of thumb: Eat 200 calories per hour to maintain energy.

The summit crater comes at mile 6.5. After a tricky passage over and around crevasses and ice bridges, it's a relatively easy 20-minute stroll to the official summit at 14,410-foot Columbia Crest. Plan to summit by 9 a.m. Shoot hero video for post-trip bragging rights, but keep it short and stay sharp for the return. You'll want to descend before afternoon temperatures increase avalanche and crevasse danger and soft snow makes plunge-stepping a knee-busting slog.

DISTANCE: 13 miles

TIME REQUIRED: 2–3 days

DIFFICULTY: Expert

CONTACT: Mount Rainier National Park, (360) 569-2211; nps.gov/mora

THE PAYOFF: Bag the greatest summit in the Lower 48.

TRAILHEAD GPS: 46.786206, -121.735652

FINDING THE TRAILHEAD: From Seattle, take I-5 S to exit 154A to I-405 N to exit 2 to WA 167 S to WA 161 S to WA 7 S to Elbe. From here, head southeast on National Park Highway. In 14.8 miles, turn right at Paradise-Longmire Road. Follow 16.3 miles to parking at Paradise.

Glacier travel

WAYPOINTS & DIRECTIONS

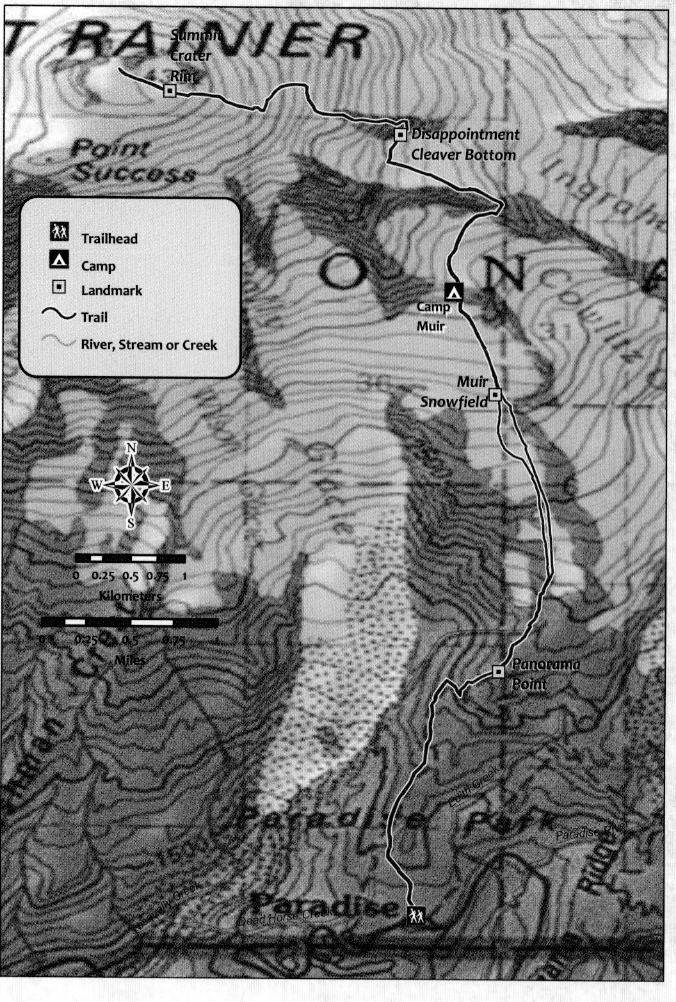

GPS: 46.786206, -121.735652 From the Paradise parking lot, take the Skyline Trail 1.5 miles to Panorama Point.

GPS: 46.805535, -121.729004 Continue on the broad ridge above Panorama Point, staying west of McClure Rock to reach the Muir Snowfield.

GPS: 46.813302, -121.724571 Leave the official trail and begin climbing on snow to the Muir Snowfield and Camp Muir.

GPS: 46.835463, -121.732797 Camp Muir. Most climbers stop here to prepare for their summit assault.

GPS: 46.844656, -121.734633 After crossing the Cowlitz Glacier and rounding the rocky corner at Cathedral Gap, you'll reach the Ingraham Flats on the Ingraham Glacier. If Camp Muir is too crowded (and you have a bomber four-season tent), this is a fantastic, flat place to camp. You'll hike westerly navigating crevasses to gain the Cleaver via a ledge system above the Flats. (***Note:*** high rockfall danger here.)

GPS: 46.847894, -121.737227 Bottom of Disappointment Cleaver. Steep, ice-covered rocks are the route's crux. Don't linger; there's no room to pass, and ice conditions can deteriorate later in the day.

GPS: 46.849449, -121.742079 After negotiating the 30-to-45-degree slopes of the icy and rocky Cleaver, you'll reach a flat area at the top, perfect for a quick rest. Try to get at least 200 calories every hour to maintain energy on your ascent. (***Note:*** The Ingraham Direct Route meets the Disappointment Cleaver Route just beyond here.)

GPS: 46.851246, -121.756299 You'll reach the rim of the summit crater after tackling the 25-to-30-degree slopes of the Ingraham and Emmons Glaciers, navigating gaping crevasses and unstable snow bridges on the way.

GPS: 46.852944, -121.760494 Conditions permitting, ditch your pack, unclip your rope, and cross the crater to the Columbia Crest, the official high point of Mount Rainier. It'll take about 20 minutes to cross. Turn back and retrace your steps for the decent.

Approaching the summit of Mt. Rainier

MOUNT RAINIER NATIONAL PARK

COLD COMFORT

There's no better way to get hooked on backpacking than a sufferfest.

As a child, camping meant staking out a luxurious acre inside the Ted Shed: my family's Ted Williams Signature tent, a Taj Mahal of canvas from Sears and Roebuck that could have sheltered a football team. When I fled the nest after college, I left behind the massive tarp and bought myself a real backpacking tent: A four-person, three-season REI dome that weighed five times what any experienced adventurer would have considered. To me, after the Shed's heft of two-stone-eleven, it seemed featherlight. For its first real test, I shouldered it on a September trek around Mount Rainier on the Wonderland Trail. After I set off alone into the forest, it began to rain. And rain. And then it poured. By the time I reached my first campsite, the properly christened Devils Dream, I was soaked. Worry and fear set in. My cold fingers fumbled with the grommets and poles. An hour was lost in the simple act of stove ignition. Dinner was freeze-dried and tasted it. Pooling water lapped at the edges of my tent. I tried to read my book. It was one I'd always meant to get to: Thomas Mann's *The Magic Mountain*. It sucked. Capsuled inside a teddy-thin sleeping bag, I passed the night slowly in a wakeful shiver. And then finally, blessedly, dawn and a few rays of sun arrived. I had survived. Looking back now, after 20 years of adventures to the far north, to the South Pacific, to Central America, I realize I did nearly everything wrong that night at Devils Dream. But I have no regrets. Your first night doesn't have to be perfect. In fact, it rarely is, but how else will you learn? Long ago, I rubbished that sheer sleeping bag in favor of a superwarm fatty. My tent now weighs less than my shoes. I carry food that's real and delicious. My only books are old favorites—James Ellroy is my go-to guy. Nowadays, when I hunker down in a tent, I'm warm and dry and home—and that awful night at Devils Dream was the first step to getting there.

—Bruce Barcott

On route to Camp Muir

MOUNT RAINIER NATIONAL PARK

CAMP MUIR

Experience this world-class, glaciated peak in a day on an 8.4-mile out-and-back that climbs 4,600 feet to a high-altitude camp above the Muir Snowfield.

Want a taste of Mt. Rainier without actually climbing it? You'll still need to be prepared for hazardous alpine conditions, but this challenging, 8.4-mile out-and-back climbs to a high-altitude base camp above the Muir Snowfield and comes within two miles of the mountain's 14,410-foot crown. Start at the upper parking area, next to the Paradise Jackson Visitor Center, and follow the wide paved path northeast to the signed Skyline Trail, a well-worn dirt trail directly across from the ranger station. Stop at the visitor center for general information, exhibits, guided ranger programs, bookstore, and cafeteria. Recommended gear: Mountaineering boots, crampons, and trekking poles.

Turn left off the main footpath and climb northwest through Paradise Park. A spiderweb of trails crisscrosses the meadows—and violet patches of lupine and bright red Indian paintbrush drown out the grass in July and August. Keep straight at the next two four-way intersections, following signs for Camp Muir and Skyline Trail. Resident marmots may track your progress from the tops of armchair-size boulders.

Less than a mile in, crest a grassy ridgeline separating calf-deep Dead Horse and Edith Creeks, and continue on Skyline Trail. At the junction near mile 1.1, pick your preferred route: 1) Bear left to crest Glacier Vista, a 6,336-foot ridgetop high above a valley scored by the Nisqually Glacier to the west (across the chasm of ice, thinly braided waterfalls flow out of the Wilson Glacier and over the adjacent cliffs). 2) Bypass the ridgetop by veering right. The trails reconnect just ahead. At mile 1.6, turn left at a signed junction toward Pebble Creek and Camp Muir. Rock-hop across Pebble Creek at mile 2.1, then keep climbing north past 7,385-foot McClure Rock, which resembles a pyramid-shaped pile of plywood-size rock slabs.

Photo: Ben Fullerton

Text: David Tate

The official trail ends near 7,300 feet. The remaining, upward trudge to Camp Muir crosses permanent snowfields interspersed with rock, sand, and piles of pumice and volcanic ash that turn the snow a muddy red in places. At 8,640 feet, round a rock promontory, which forms the leading edge of a ridge that connects to the aptly-named 9,584-foot Anvil Rock (0.5 mile to the north-northeast). Keep this ridge to your right as you climb up the Muir Snowfield. In late summer, the exposed ice of the Muir Glacier melts into small rivulets of water; crampons or mountaineering boots required.

Up next: Ascend 1,440 feet in the next 1 mile. Take your time: Crevasses (roughly two to four feet wide) become more prevalent the higher you climb. Follow the most obvious path across the snowfield (look for wire wands with fluorescent tape that mark the best route; give a wide berth to small holes in the snow). As you near Camp Muir, the blue tints of the Nisqually Glacier become apparent. Listen for the loud cracking sounds of massive, jumbled blocks of ice calving off the glacier.

After 4.2 miles, drop your pack at Camp Muir. Perched between the Muir Snowfield and the Cowlitz Glacier, this 10,080-foot base camp consists of a ranger station and a rock warming hut. In summer, the camp can be bustling with climbers and day hikers. Stake out a little patch of rock and savor hard-earned views of 12,281-foot Mount Adams's flat-topped summit, the Tatoosh spires to the south, the Cowlitz Glacier, and Cathedral Rock. Descend the same route back to the trailhead. Whiteouts can occur here any time. To stay on course, know the compass bearings between landmarks (though they alone can't safeguard against crevasses, cliffs, or other hazards). Basic true-north bearings from key landmarks can be found on the national park website.

DISTANCE: 8.4 miles

TIME REQUIRED: 1 day

DIFFICULTY: Strenuous

CONTACT: Mount Rainier National Park, (360) 569-2211; nps.gov/mora

THE PAYOFF: Get a taste of Rainier's grandeur.

TRAILHEAD GPS: 46.786206, -121.735652

FINDING THE TRAILHEAD: From Ashford, drive east on WA 706. In roughly 7 miles, turn right onto Paradise Road E (toward Longmire). In 11.4 miles, turn left to stay on Paradise Road E. In 2.8 miles, turn left to stay on Paradise Road E. Go 2.1 miles to the parking area near the Paradise Jackson visitor center.

WAYPOINTS & DIRECTIONS

GPS: 46.786338, -121.735807 Start at the upper parking area, next to the Paradise Jackson Visitor Center, and follow the wide paved path northeast.

GPS: 46.787041, -121.735017 Turn left off the main footpath onto the signed Skyline Trail, a well-worn dirt trail directly across from the ranger station. Climb northwest.

GPS: 46.788358, -121.736153 Continue straight on Skyline Trail at the four-way junction. A spiderweb of trails crisscrosses the meadows of Paradise Park.

GPS: 46.788780, -121.736903 Keep straight at the four-way intersection, following signs for Camp Muir and Skyline Trail.

GPS: 46.794118, -121.736227 Crest a grassy ridgeline separating calf-deep Dead Horse and Edith Creeks. Continue on Skyline Trail.

GPS: 46.798185, -121.735372 Pass the trail junction to Dead Horse Creek. Continue straight on Skyline Trail.

GPS: 46.799622, -121.734990 You've got two options here: 1) Bear left to crest Glacier Vista, a 6,336-foot (*continued*)

ridgetop high above a valley scored by the Nisqually Glacier to the west (across the chasm of ice, thinly braided waterfalls flow out of the Wilson Glacier and over the adjacent cliffs); 2) Bypass the ridgetop by veering right. The trails reconnect just ahead.

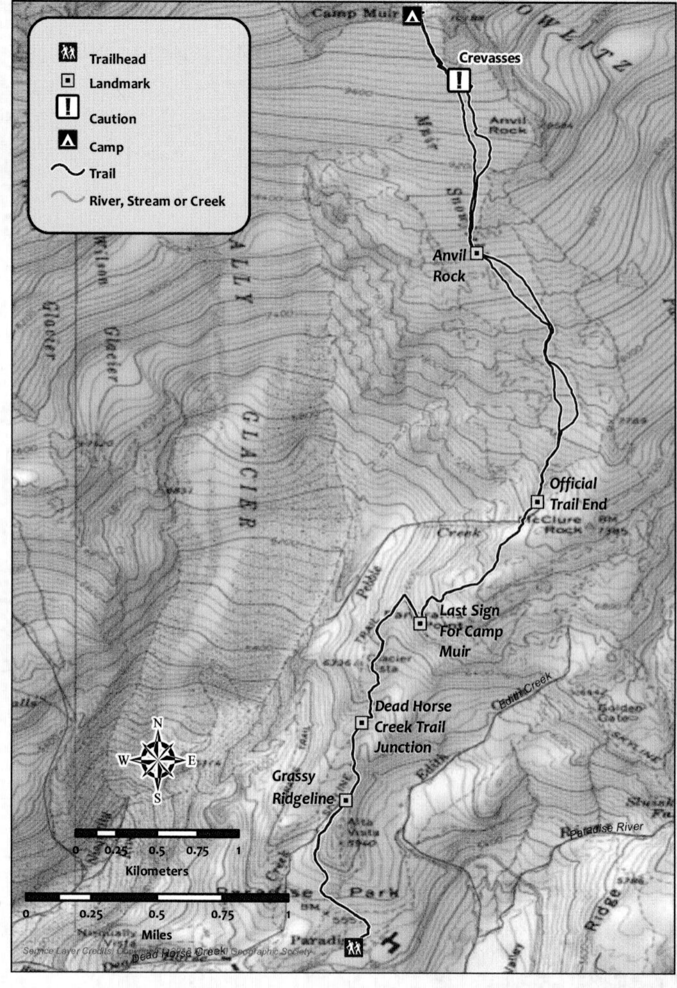

GPS: 46.801466, -121.734712 The two trails reconnect here; continue straight.

GPS: 46.803433, -121.732222 Turn left at this signed junction toward Pebble Creek and Camp Muir. This is the last sign for Camp Muir; follow signs for Pebble Creek ahead. (***Note:*** If you miss this turn, you'll continue heading southeast on Skyline Trail. Although it eventually rejoins Pebble Creek Trail, it will add time and mileage to your hike.)

GPS: 46.804841, -121.730983 Pass a warning sign that lists the possible dangers of continuing on to Camp Muir. (***Caution:*** You may encounter whiteout conditions, crevasses, and other hazards ahead.)

GPS: 46.805601, -121.728934 Continue straight at the Pebble Creek-Skyline Trail junction, marked by a sign on the right.

GPS: 46.808852, -121.726629 Rock-hop across Pebble Creek and continue climbing north. Keep 7,385-foot McClure Rock, which resembles a pyramid-shaped pile of plywood-size rock slabs, to your right.

GPS: 46.809859, -121.725779 The official trail ends near 7,300 feet. The remaining, upward trudge to Camp Muir crosses permanent snowfields interspersed with rock, sand, and piles of pumice and volcanic ash that turn the snow a muddy red in places.

GPS: 46.822945, -121.729128 At 8,640 feet, round a rock promontory, which forms the leading edge of a ridge that connects to the well-named Anvil Rock (0.5 to the north-northeast). Keep this ridge to your right as you climb up the Muir Snowfield, an arm of the Nisqually Glacier. In 0.3 mile, pass Moon Rocks, a mounded island of boulders and rubble usually swept free of snow by the wind. In late summer, the exposed ice of the Muir Snowfield melts into small rivulets of water; attach crampons for better grip.

GPS: 46.832038, -121.730114 Ascend 1,440 feet in the next mile. Take your time: Crevasses (roughly 2 to 4 feet wide) become more prevalent the higher you climb. Follow the most obvious path across the snowfield (look for wire wands with fluorescent tape that mark the best route; give a wide berth to small holes in the snow).

GPS: 46.835421, -121.732676 Camp Muir. Perched between the Muir Snowfield and the Cowlitz Glacier, this 10,080-foot base camp consists of a ranger station and a rock warming hut. Stake out a little patch of rock and savor hard-earned views of 12,281-foot Mount Adams's flat-topped summit, the Tatoosh spires to the south, the Cowlitz Glacier, and Cathedral Rock. Descend the same route back to the trailhead.

Tatoosh Mountains

MOUNT RAINIER NATIONAL PARK

TATOOSH RANGE

This backcountry trek serves up two mountain lakes, intimate views of Mount Rainier, and some off-trail scrambles in the Tatoosh Range.

The mileage is minimal on this route—only about 8 clicks round-trip—but they're steep miles with huge vistas of Mount Rainier to the north and neck-craning views of the Tatoosh Range's jagged spires all around you. The best time to visit is from mid-August through September, when the huckleberries are ripe and the weather is most stable. The best way to experience this country is to keep hiking past the designated campsites at Snow Lake (they're beautiful, but lack Rainier views) and camp high in the backcountry zone below Unicorn Peak or the Castle.

These are two of the major summits in the eastern half of the Tatoosh Range, and their ridges and drainages offer plenty of exploring on faint climbers paths and through sparse forest pocked with wildflower meadows. With solid navigation and scrambling skills, you can also complete a full traverse of the Tatoosh Range; usually done east to west, it's a high, spectacular, and very arduous hike that's worthwhile (and safe) only with a good forecast. Note: Use caution when climbing the talus-filled gulley that leads from Snow Lake into the Unicorn Creek bowl; the footing is steep and loose, and it's easy to dislodge rocks onto hikers below you.

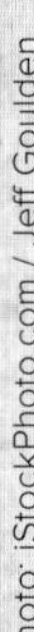

Photo: iStockPhoto.com / Jeff Goulden

Text: Jonathan Dorn

DISTANCE: 8 miles

TIME REQUIRED: 2 days

DIFFICULTY: Strenuous

CONTACT: Mount Rainier National Park, (360) 569-2211; nps.gov/mora

THE PAYOFF: Go rugged and remote in this rarely visited subrange of Rainier.

TRAILHEAD GPS: 46.767617, -121.707981

FINDING THE TRAILHEAD: From the Longmire park entrance, near Ashford, follow signs to the Longmire visitor center. Follow signs to Paradise, but stay straight at the final left-hand turn to Paradise on Stevens Canyon Road. You'll soon pass Reflection Lakes, a spot that rivals Rainier's summit as the most-photographed scenic point in the park. Just beyond, turn right in the parking area for Bench and Snow Lakes.

WAYPOINTS & DIRECTIONS

GPS: 46.767617, -121.707981 Begin hiking southeast from Snow Lake trailhead.

GPS: 46.762013, -121.699604 Veer right at Y. Going a few yards left leads to the first views of Rainier. Farther on, Snow Lake sits in a forested bowl below the trail.

GPS: 46.758664, -121.698715 Stay right at T where trail reaches Snow Lake. Trail leads to two designated campsites that must be reserved at Longmire, plus a toilet with a million-dollar view of the mountain. The route continues straight up toward the first talus field beyond Snow Lake; a narrow climbers' path picks up where official maintained trail ends. Follow it along the left edge of talus until directly below obvious chute leading up to the second bowl.

GPS: 46.754665, -121.702386 Climbers path ends. Use caution crossing the rocks to the bottom of the chute, as many are precariously balanced and big enough to do some damage to a fallen hiker.

GPS: 46.751774, -121.705685 Bottom of chute. Stay right for the first half of the 200-foot climb up, then pick whichever side looks the most promising for the top half. The chute is only a Class 3 walk-up, but be careful not to climb directly below other hikers to avoid falling rocks.

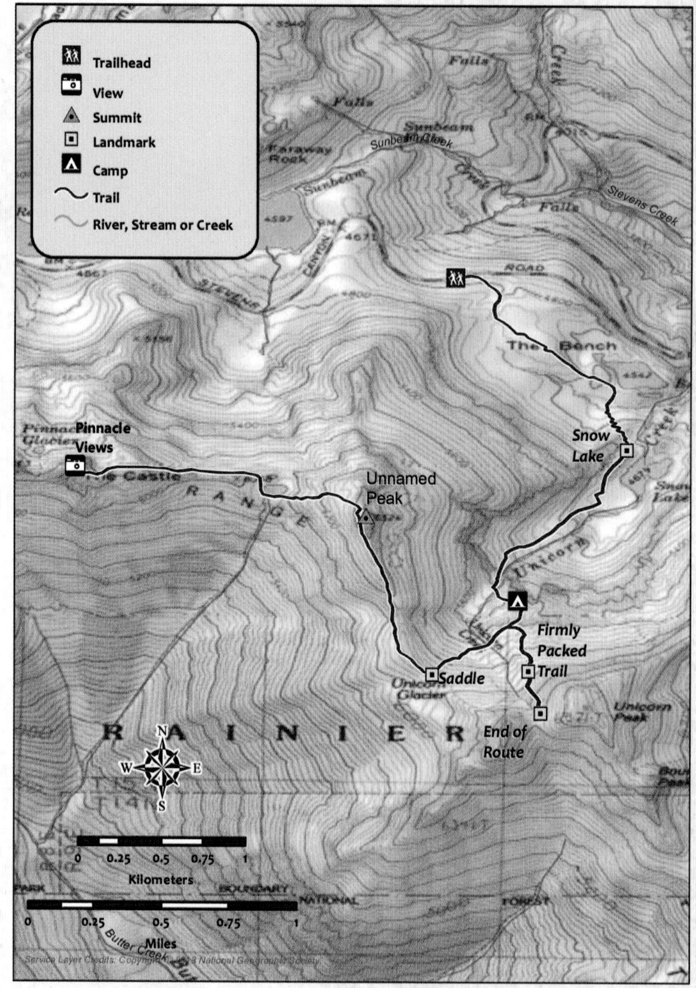

GPS: 46.751581, -121.705812 Top of chute. Be prepared for a blast of wind, which can either feel great (after a stiff ascent on a hot day) or chilling (any other time). Scout for the climbers path leading up steep switchbacks of the left wall. After reaching the first plateau, continue either straight up toward Unicorn Peak and numerous campsites, or veer left and contour around the base of the small, steep hill.

GPS: 46.750748, -121.704549 This location could well be one of the best campsites in the park. The ground may be wet early in the summer because of poor drainage, but there's room for two or three tents and plenty of flat rocks for lounging. If staying here, keep a strict Leave No Trace camp. From here, there are several options for exploring the east part of the Tatoosh Range. If indecisive, try going west first.

GPS: 46.748390, -121.706189 After climbing a few hundred feet above camp on the steep hillside behind it, turn right and traverse down the talus bowl through which Unicorn Creek flows. Then pick a route and tiptoe up and across boulders through the main draw.

GPS: 46.746885, -121.709145 From the saddle, head due north on thin, dirt trail that follows the crest of a knife-edge ridge.

GPS: 46.755178, -121.712783 Summit of unnamed peak. Descend the peak's west slope, carpeted with huckleberry bushes, to a broad saddle with a snowmelt pond that was dry in early September. Climb opposite slope, rising steeply through grass and rock toward The Castle.

GPS: 46.757747, -121.728449 Reach obvious notch in The Castle's crenellated summit ridge and enjoy exquisite views of the Pinnacle. A short Class 4 scramble to the right, around the backside of the Castle's upper ridge, leads to its airy summit. Retrace your steps toward camp.

GPS: 46.749314, -121.705120 Bear right at this point on the descent back to camp for an out-and-back toward Unicorn Peak. A climbers path appears now and again while threading through rock and huckleberry bushes.

GPS: 46.747889, -121.704054 Continue following climbers path, heading straight uphill and avoiding the band of talus to the right.

GPS: 46.747080, -121.703968 Reach a firmly packed trail through talus that lies above the hillside's last vegetation. Turn right and follow path as it contours beneath the west face of Unicorn Peak toward the saddle.

GPS: 46.744866, -121.703302 This is the farthest point to proceed safely without climbing gear. Though the left wall features easy Class 5 climbing, it could be a death fall and would be very difficult to downclimb. Retrace steps along Snow Lake Trail to car. (***Caution:*** Rockslide danger.)

Photo: OLOS/Shutterstock

Wild deer in the foothills of Mt. Rainier

Hiker in Spray Park

MOUNT RAINIER NATIONAL PARK

SPRAY PARK

This backcountry trek serves up two mountain lakes, intimate views of Mount Rainier, and some off-trail scrambles in the Tatoosh Range.

Almost any hike in this national park offers knockout views of Rainier's glacier-clad slopes. But Spray Park is where the cognoscenti flock to see a spectacular wildflower show against the mountain backdrop. The 8.2-mile hike begins at Mowich Lake, passes a 0.5-mile side trip to Spray Falls, and climbs to broad meadows carpeted with pink heather, lilies, and Indian paintbrush.

From the Mowich Lake trailhead parking area, cross the outlet of Mowich Lake by the bathrooms, and head straight to find the Wonderland Trail. Go left at the junction to leave the Wonderland Trail and begin the hike toward Spray Falls and Spray Park. Huge old-growth forest and a few beautiful mossy creeks decorate the gentle stroll ahead. Cross a small bridge over Lee Creek. Walk through moss-covered landscapes, then pass an open avalanche slope littered with columbine and other lovely wildflowers. Pass Eagle Camp on the right, but stay straight. Pass a junction on the right that leads to Spray Falls. This worthwhile 0.5-mile side trip showcases a wild view of one of the biggest waterfalls in the park. Return and hike straight to continue on to Spray Park. Climb up steep switchbacks in less than 1 mile. Soon first views of Rainier appear as you cross the first meadow on a wooden set of steps. Hike past magenta paintbrush and lupines.

The trail levels out and passes a small tarn, then passes through meadows thick with avalanche lilies. The route winds past a faint boot path that contours up to Knapsack Pass, a gap in the Hessong Rock ridge to the north.

Pass a few more tarns (and millions of wildflowers). Turn left to check out a small viewpoint with tremendous views to the east across Seattle Park. Crest this high point, and turn left for a short climb (don't begin the descent into Seattle Park). Other options: Turn right and follow boot paths for a climb toward Observation Rock and views down on Seattle Park. Retrace your steps back to your car.

Photo: Stephen Matera / Tandem Stock

Text: Mike Lanza and Alan Bauer

DISTANCE: 8.1 miles

TIME REQUIRED: 1 day

DIFFICULTY: Strenuous

CONTACT: Mount Rainier National Park, (360) 569-2211; nps.gov/mora

THE PAYOFF: Kaleidoscopic flowers and constant views of Rainier's glacier-clad slopes.

TRAILHEAD GPS: 46.93342, -121.865536

FINDING THE TRAILHEAD: From Sumner, drive east on WA 410. In 9 miles, turn right at Mundy Loss Road. In 1.2 miles, turn left at WA 162 E/Pioneer Way E. In 0.3 mile, continue onto WA 165 S. Go 25.2 miles to the trailhead.

WAYPOINTS & DIRECTIONS

GPS: 46.933420, -121.865536 Leave the trailhead parking area, cross the outlet of Mowich Lake by the bathrooms, and head straight to find the Wonderland Trail.

GPS: 46.930836, -121.862648 Go left at the junction to leave the Wonderland Trail and begin the hike toward Spray Falls and Spray Park.

GPS: 46.924463, -121.858895 Cross a small bridge over Lee Creek. Walk through moss-covered landscapes, then pass an open avalanche slope filled with columbine and other lovely wildflowers.

GPS: 46.915853, -121.847350 Pass Eagle Camp here on your right. Stay straight.

GPS: 46.916153, -121.845076 Pass a junction on the right that leads to Spray Falls. (***Side trip:*** A quick 0.5-mile spur leads to impressive, 354-foot Spray Falls). Stay straight to continue on to Spray Park, and be ready to start a very steep climb up switchbacks in less than a mile.

GPS: 46.922890, -121.825198 Pass a few more tarns (and millions of wildflowers). Turn left to check out a small viewpoint with tremendous views to the east across Seattle Park.

GPS: 46.921587, -121.816663 Crest this high point, and turn left for a short climb (don't begin the descent into Seattle Park). Other option: Turn right and follow boot paths for a climb toward Observation Rock.

GPS: 46.923483, -121.818132 This knob offers new views down on Seattle Park. Scan the landscape for bears. Return to the trailhead along the same route.

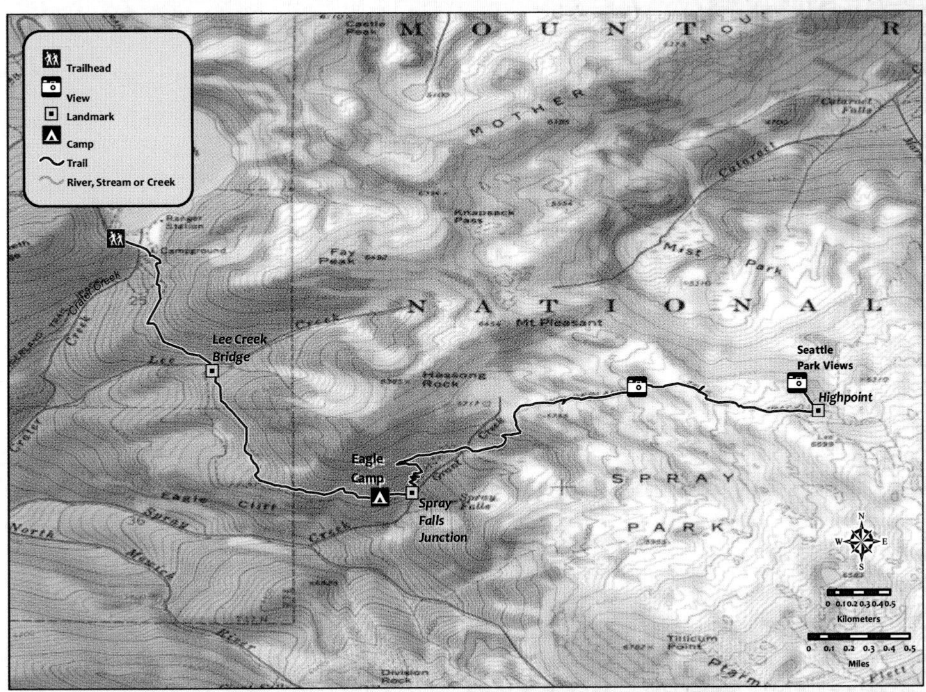

Whatcom Pass, North Cascades National Park, Washington
Photo: Alasdair Turner / Tandem Stock

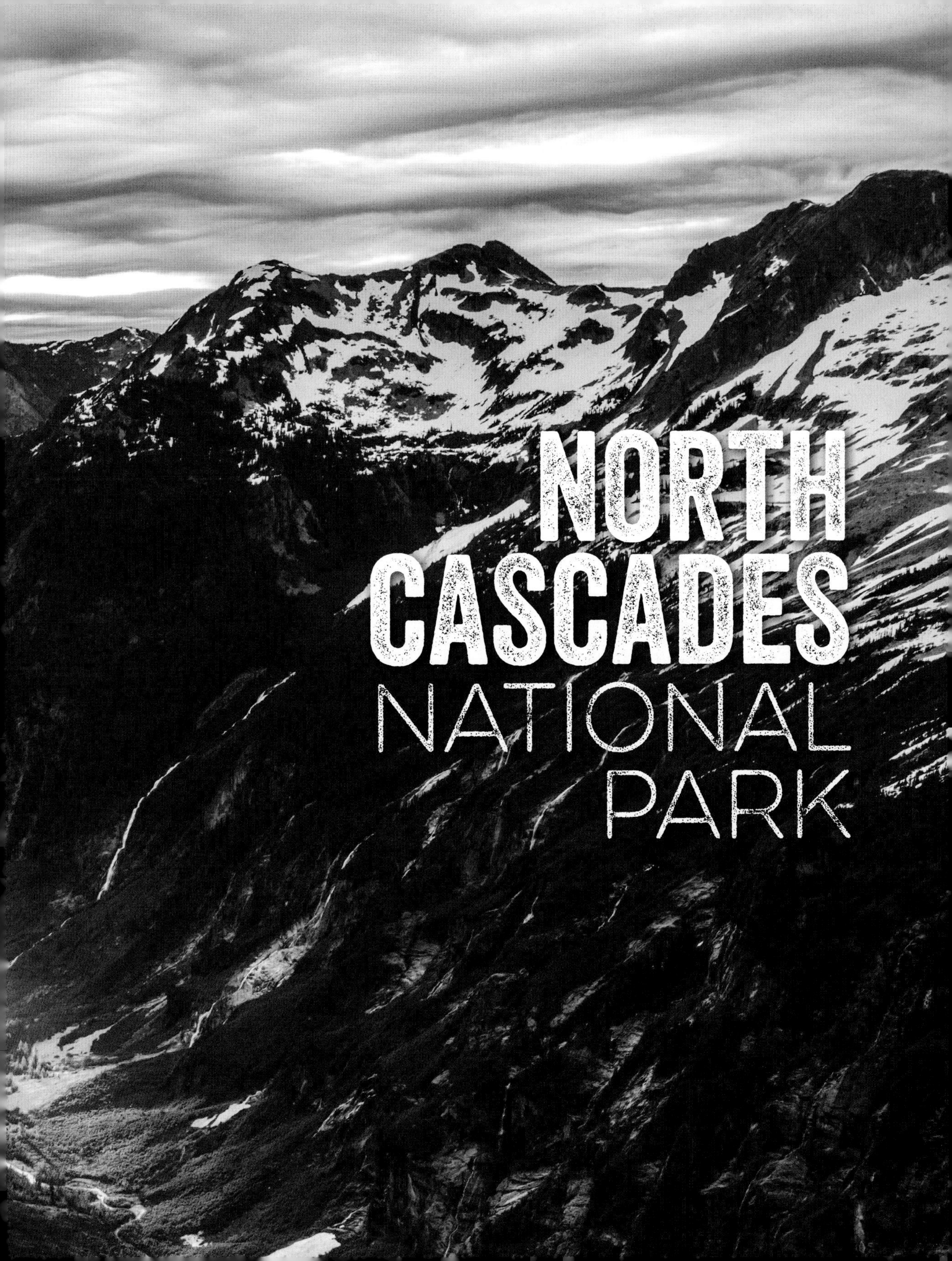
NORTH
CASCADES
NATIONAL
PARK

NORTH CASCADES NATIONAL PARK
COPPER RIDGE LOOP

Copper Ridge

Come for the sheer, glaciated peaks, but be mesmerized by rain-fed waterfalls that pour down on all sides along this weeklong trip.

Scores of mountains that rise 3,000 feet in the last horizontal mile to their summits. At least 77 peaks that tower 6,000 feet or more above adjacent valleys. The highest concentration of glaciers in the Lower 48. These are just a few of the features cited by those who believe that North Cascades is the wildest park in the continental United States. We only need one to make the case: The combination of vertical relief, remote location, and rugged approaches rebuffed exploration for so long that the heart of the park wasn't mapped by the U.S. Geological Survey until 1989. Think about it: We landed men on the moon two decades before we finished mapping this park.

Still not convinced? Consider the famously stormy weather. The legendary climber Fred Beckey, who made hundreds of first ascents in the region, once wrote, "Weather in the Cascades is actually highly predictable: Either it is raining, or it will be shortly." That, plus the wild topography, yields the perfect recipe for life-list scenery and zero crowds. This route connecting Hannegan Pass, Copper Ridge, Chilliwack, Brush Creek, Little Beaver, and Big Beaver Trails and linking camps at Egg Lake, Indian Creek, Whatcom, and Luna Camps serves up a giant bite of North Cascades adventure.

Photo: Kim Phillips

Text: Kim Phillips

Almost immediately after leaving the trailhead, the route runs below nine glaciated peaks that punctuate the Nooksack Ridge. By mile 5, you'll ascend Copper Ridge on one of the park's rare high-elevation trails (most hug valley bottoms). The path climbs to 6,268 feet and arrows northeast roughly eight miles on the open ridge. On the way up, look for black bears—and maybe even one of the park's extremely rare grizzlies—munching on blueberries and huckleberries that will help sustain them through winter. Hike on for another 2 miles to descend into the basin cupping Egg Lake, your first night's camp. In the morning, climb at sunrise to reveal exhilarating, eye-level views of toothy peaks cloaked with hanging glaciers stretching to the Canadian border, a mere 7 miles away. The Copper Ridge lookout tower marks the high point of the ridge. Next, stay to the right of the snowfield, heading northeast. (Don't hike toward the cairn.) First views of Copper Lake (Kool-Aid blue) suddenly appear to the north. Descend a slew of switchbacks to reach its shores.

Prepare for a long (3.5 miles) and steep (your knees will ache) descent into the Chilliwack River Valley. Along the way, hike through a field of gargantuan, car-size boulders. Look back over your shoulder to see distant views of the Copper Ridge lookout to the southwest. When you round the next big ridge, views of the mountains to the north pop into view (look for finger-shaped Chilliwack Lake, which lies just north of the border in British Columbia).

Follow the overgrown trail and ford a few creeks to reach your second camp at Indian Creek, where tent sites are protected by thick, old-growth canopy. The next morning, continue tramping along the Chilliwack River, where the forest is lush even by Pacific Northwest standards. Eighty-four inches of annual rainfall makes for a cedar and fir canopy so dense it repels raindrops like a thatched roof. Thick carpets of cushy moss, frilly ferns, and an *Alice in Wonderland* variety of mushrooms grow in profusion.

Leave the forest shelter for the final, exposed miles to camp at 5,206-foot Whatcom Pass. Views extend across Brush Creek to Easy Ridge with waterfalls pouring down the steep slopes. Look south for views of glaciers on Easy Ridge and cross cascading Tapto and Brush Creeks. After another 0.5 mile, turn left onto spur trail to reach Whatcom Camp, tucked into a small stand of trees just before the pass. The next day, scale the remainder of Whatcom Pass; the ridge that rises to the south from this small pass tops out on 7,574-foot Whatcom Peak. Begin a steep, switchback descent into the Little Beaver Creek Valley. Catch intermittent views of Little Beaver Creek as you cross a slew of creeks. Be careful: Rainfall can swell the creeks. At about mile 37, you'll cross unsigned Beaver Pass; a sheltered campsite lies just beyond. Camp here, or push on to Luna Camp another 3.5 miles beyond.

Your final day, track through gigantic Western red cedars and sandy beaches along the shore of electric-teal Ross Lake to reach the Big Beaver trailhead. Wait on the dock for your 4.1-mile water-taxi ride to Ross Dam; reserve ahead of time with Ross Lake Resort. After landing, it's a little over 1 road mile back to your shuttle car and the end of your wild Cascades ramble.

DISTANCE: 51 miles

TIME REQUIRED: 5–7 days

DIFFICULTY: Strenuous

CONTACT: North Cascades National Park, (360) 569-2211; nps.gov/noca

THE PAYOFF: Lonely alpine lakes, colossal peaks frosted with glaciers, far-flung valleys hiding bears and wolverines. Perhaps the wildest park in the Lower 48.

TRAILHEAD GPS: 48.910208, -121.59169

FINDING THE TRAILHEAD: To reach the eastern trailhead/end to drop a shuttle car, drive east from Marblemount on WA 20. In 0.9 mile, turn left on WA 20 and go 28 miles to Ross Dam parking pull-out. To reach the western trailhead/start from Marblemount, go 39 miles west on WA 20. Turn right on WA 9 N. In 22 miles, turn right on WA 542 E. In 32 miles, bear left on NFD 32. Go 5.3 miles to the Hannegan Campground trailhead.

WAYPOINTS & DIRECTIONS

GPS: 48.910208, -121.591690 The route begins at the eastern edge of Hannegan Campground. Follow the trail east, paralleling Ruth Creek.

GPS: 48.881376, -121.538280 Hike past the turn-off for Hannegan Campground on the right.

GPS: 48.882910, -121.534416 At Hannegan Pass, keep left and follow the sign to Boundary Camp. Ahead, the route descends switchbacks into the Chilliwack River Valley.

GPS: 48.887825, -121.524014 Veer left at the junction to Copper Ridge. The ridgeline climb begins here.

GPS: 48.897790, -121.503553 Keep an eye out for bears munching on berries in the bushes. (If you think you see a grizzly bear, tell a park ranger about your observations.)

GPS: 48.895809, -121.481400 Turn left to descend to Egg Lake on a narrow, rocky trail.

GPS: 48.900050, -121.484478 Make your first camp at this campsite perched above the small, turquoise Egg Lake.

GPS: 48.908487, -121.462591 The Copper Ridge lookout tower marks the high point of the ridge. Next, stay to the right of the snowfield, heading northeast. Don't hike toward the cairn.

GPS: 48.917254, -121.448167 At the junction, keep right to continue on the trail or bear left to visit the lake.

GPS: 48.927198, -121.444473 Hike through a field of gargantuan, car-size boulders.

GPS: 48.945208, -121.427770 Prepare for a long (3.5 miles) and steep (your knees will ache) descent into the Chilliwack River Valley.

GPS: 48.949718, -121.398658 Creek crossing. The trail is overgrown and hard to follow at this point. Follow the rocky creekbed, heading south, to reconnect with the trail.

GPS: 48.946508, -121.400031 Ford the creek. Pick up the trail directly across the stream.

GPS: 48.946112, -121.398049 Second ford. It's tricky to find the trail on the other side of the crossing. If you don't spot it, bushwhack up the bank and head east until you intersect the trail.

GPS: 48.944302, -121.393382 Turn right at T junction, heading south.

GPS: 48.934793, -121.394040 Turn left into Indian Creek Campsite to make your second camp.

GPS: 48.906578, -121.421678 Turn left onto the Brush Creek Trail/Pacific Northwest Trail.

GPS: 48.872933, -121.382972 Cross cascading Tapto Creek.

GPS: 48.873867, -121.376463 Cross Brush Creek.

GPS: 48.875079, -121.369237 Turn left onto spur trail to reach the third camp, Whatcom, which is tucked into a small stand of trees.

GPS: 48.875638, -121.363708 The ridge that rises to the south from this small pass tops out on 7,574-foot Whatcom Peak. Begin a steep switchback descent into the Little Beaver Creek Valley.

GPS: 48.872728, -121.350807 Creek crossing. Prepare to get your feet wet along this stretch of trail. (***Caution:*** After it rains, the crossings can be swollen with runoff.)

GPS: 48.893063, -121.269233 In October 2010, Little Beaver Creek washed out a short stretch of trail starting at this point. Bear left, uphill, to bypass it.

GPS: 48.893293, -121.268753 The trail continues here on the other side of the washout.

GPS: 48.897025, -121.253293 Turn right at three-way junction, heading south on Big Beaver Trail.

GPS: 48.880142, -121.254108 Snow marker. This marks the otherwise unsigned Beaver Pass.

GPS: 48.874910, -121.248644 Either camp here at Beaver Campsite for your fourth night or push ahead to Luna Camp, another 3.5 miles down the trail.

GPS: 48.835158, -121.201260 Turn right for tent sites in Luna Camp, which is tucked below towering old-growth trees.

GPS: 48.804498, -121.143107 Keep left, heading east. The trail is lined with reeds and bamboo stalks as you wend your way alongside Big Beaver Creek.

GPS: 48.775862, -121.065995 Follow the boardwalk.

GPS: 48.775633, -121.065605 Bear left and follow the trail along the shores of Ross Lake toward Big Beaver Camp.

GPS: 48.775230, -121.059782 Bear left, heading to the route terminus at Big Beaver trailhead.

GPS: 48.775423, -121.058123 Wait on the dock for your 4.1-mile water-taxi ride to Ross Dam (reserve ahead of time with Ross Lake Resort).

GPS: 48.735337, -121.061722 The water taxi will drop you off at the dock just north of Ross Dam. Follow the road, heading southwest, for 0.4 mile.

GPS: 48.730743, -121.065590 Turn left onto the trail and begin a 0.7-mile switchback climb to the parking area.

GPS: 48.727782, -121.062782 Ross Dam parking area: Pick up your shuttle car in this large pull-out.

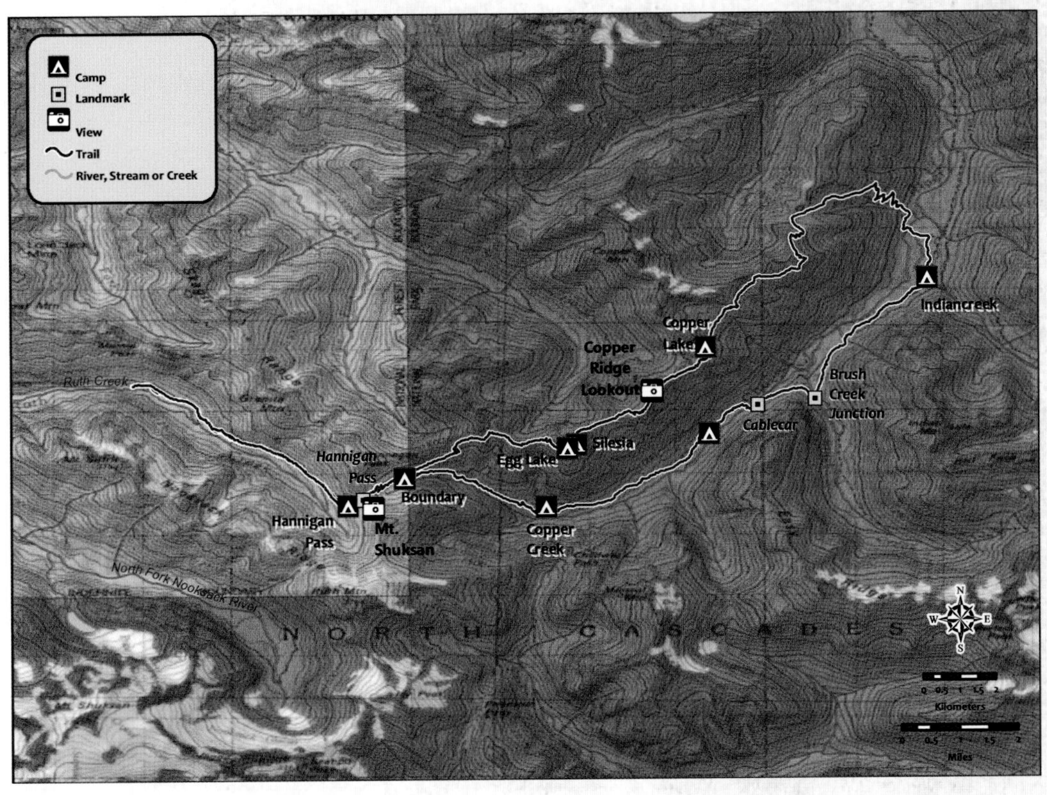

Sahale Glacier Camp

NORTH CASCADES NATIONAL PARK
CASCADE PASS TO SAHALE GLACIER CAMP

Satisfy your wanderlust on this 5.4-mile out-and-back, which offers stop-and-gawk panoramas of the jagged Cascades blanketed by glaciers.

Neck-craning views begin in the parking lot, where hulking granite masses of Cascade Peak, the Triplets, and Johannesburg Mountain block out the sky here. Hanging waterfalls course down the steep faces in thin ribbons. Trace the ridge east and you can spot the gap that is your destination: Cascade Pass, a mere 3.35 miles from the parking lot.

The trail begins by switchbacking up through the trees for 2.6 miles. According to the park rangers, this is the most heavily visited trail in the park.

Wide-open views break the treescape at the 2.75 mile mark. Traverse an open hillside loaded with heather and blueberries until you reach Cascade Pass in 0.5 mile. From the vantage point at the pass, look southeast down the Stehekin River Valley to see prominent peaks like Magic Mountain and Glory Mountain. Most folks stop here for lunch, but keep pushing: A left turn heads up to Sahale Arm, a polished rib of rock that ramps to the base of the Sahale Glacier. At about 4.15 miles, the trail winds through sparse alpine meadows that bloom with paintbrush, lupine, and asters in summer.

Beyond here, the trail grows rocky and views get bigger. Steep river valleys drop off 5,000-plus feet on either side of the arm, framed by glacier-cut peaks. Continue climbing along the faint trail; follow cairns across a jumbled scramble for the final 300 yards.

At 7,686 feet, you'll reach Sahale Glacier Camp, the park's highest designated site, sitting at the brink of a 2,000-foot drop-off overlooking a sea of razor peaks smothered in snow and ice. You'll likely share the view with mountain goats and hoary marmots, but not hiker hordes. There are six tent sites, each atop widely spaced talus mounds. Got a night to spare? Nab a permit at the visitor center in Marblemount to sleep on top of the world.

Photo: Mitch Pittman

DISTANCE: 11.8 miles

TIME REQUIRED: 1–2 days

DIFFICULTY: Intermediate

CONTACT: North Cascades National Park, (360) 569-2211; nps.gov/noca

THE PAYOFF: Big views of glaciers, thousand-foot waterfalls, toothy peaks.

TRAILHEAD GPS: 48.475503, -121.075001

FINDING THE TRAILHEAD: From Seattle, take I-5 N to Burlington; go right on WA 20 E. At Marblemount, go right on Cascade River Road; go 23.1 miles to Cascade Pass Trailhead. (A forest pass is required for parking along the road.)

WAYPOINTS & DIRECTIONS

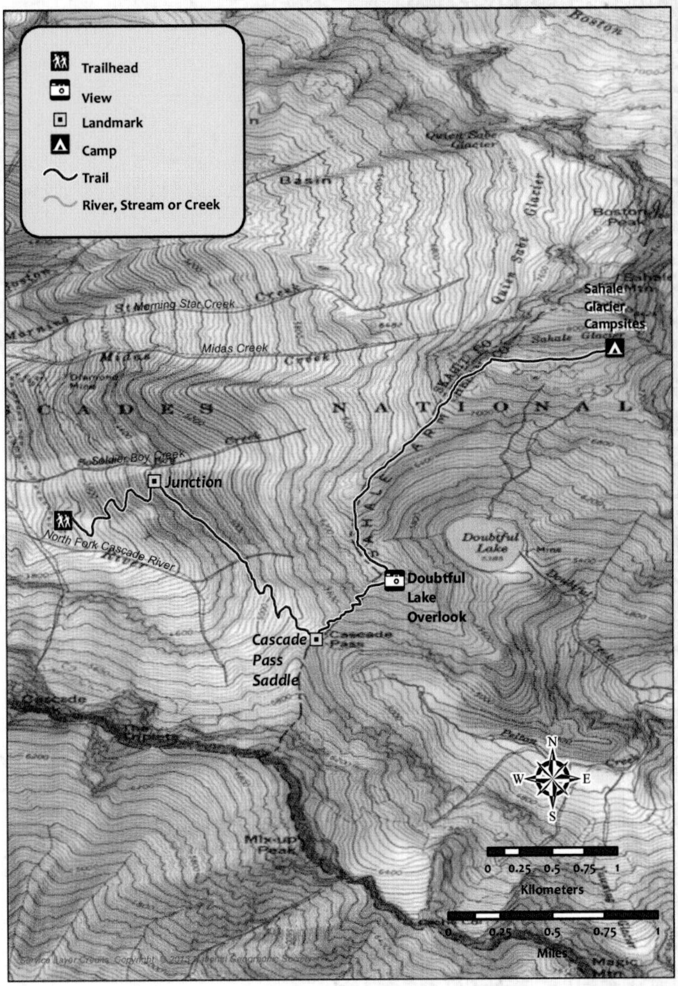

GPS: 48.475623, -121.076397 From the trailhead, begin switchbacking through the trees, starting the first ascent of the day.

GPS: 48.478200, -121.070156 At the T junction, turn right, heading south-southeast.

GPS: 48.467760, -121.059255 Turn left at the saddle of Cascade Pass to ascend the ridge. Look southeast down the Stehekin River Valley to see prominent peaks like Magic Mountain and Glory Mountain.

GPS: 48.471556, -121.053888 Reach the Sahale Arm and follow its ridgeline as it curls north-northeast. Pause for overlooks of Doubtful Lake.

GPS: 48.486816, -121.038565 Sahale Glacier Camp, the park's highest designated site, sits at the brink of a 2,000-foot drop-off overlooking a sea of razor peaks smothered in snow and ice. Depending on conditions, you may need to cross snow to reach this clutch of six campsites. Either retrace your steps back to the trailhead, or if you've obtained a permit, spend the night.

Only have a day to see the North Cascades? This big-and-burly hike—4,100 feet of gain in just over 5 miles—should be at the top of your priority list: The base camp for climbers at the foot of Sahale Peak serves up the hands-down best done-in-a-day view in the North Cascades.

Park Creek Pass

NORTH CASCADES NATIONAL PARK

EASY PASS TO THUNDER CREEK

This 25-mile point-to-point in North Cascades National Park weaves past electric wildflower displays and climbs to an airy, 6,525-foot alpine pass.

The North Cascades' rough and remote reputation keeps even the hint of crowds away, making it a cinch to score big-ticket solitude and scenery even on a short schedule. Here's your weekend plan: Beeline to the easier-access South Unit for this 25-mile highlight reel that weaves past electric wildflower displays in July, climbs to an airy, 6,525-foot alpine pass, and tracks through giant western hemlock and Douglas fir.

Drop a car at the Thunder Creek trailhead before starting at the Easy Pass trailhead. The trail zigzags along its namesake creek, then scales the eastern flanks of Ragged Ridge, gaining nearly 3,000 feet of elevation to the misleadingly named Easy Pass. At the top, pause for front-row views of Mount Logan's glaciated slopes framed by stands of sub-alpine larch (golden in fall).

Next, descend roughly 30 switchbacks into Fisher Creek Basin—home to black bears and the occasional moose. Just past Fisher Camp, the route dips back into forest on the 11.3-mile stretch to Junction Camp. The next day, descend 10.2 miles north through Thunder Creek Valley to your shuttle car.

Photo: Andy Porter

DISTANCE: 25 miles

TIME REQUIRED: 2 days

DIFFICULTY: Strenuous

CONTACT: North Cascades National Park, (360) 569-2211; nps.gov/noca

THE PAYOFF: North Cascades' perfect weekend.

TRAILHEAD GPS: 48.588205, -120.803068

FINDING THE TRAILHEAD: Thunder Creek trailhead/end: From Marblemount, go 25 miles east on WA 20. The trailhead is 20 minutes southeast of Ross Dam; parking is on the right-hand side. Easy Pass trailhead/start: From Marblemount, go 46 miles east on WA 20. Trailhead parking is on the right-hand side.

WAYPOINTS & DIRECTIONS

GPS: 48.588205, -120.803068 From the Easy Pass trailhead, hike south, then southwest.

GPS: 48.585777, -120.804784 Start switchback climb along Easy Creek, which ascends the eastern flanks of Ragged Ridge. Prepare to gain nearly 3,000 feet of elevation to the misleadingly named Easy Pass.

GPS: 48.572007, -120.843451 Easy Pass. At the top, pause for front-row views of Mount Logan's glaciated slopes framed by stands of subalpine larch (golden in fall). Next, descend roughly 30 switchbacks into Fisher Creek Basin.

GPS: 48.567989, -120.853499 End of switchback descent. From here, the route turns west and follows Fisher Creek. Fisher Camp is located in this basin.

GPS: 48.574364, -120.987303 Cross Logan Creek.

GPS: 48.584806, -121.018466 Continue straight at three-way junction. Spend the night at Junction Camp, located at this intersection with Thunder Creek Trail. In the morning start the descent north on through Thunder Creek Valley on the Thunder Creek Trail.

GPS: 48.671650, -121.068609 Continue straight at three-wayjunction as the Fourth of July Trail joins the Thunder Creek Trail.

GPS: 48.673573, -121.072203 Turn left and cross footbridge over Thunder Creek.

GPS: 48.684416, -121.092081 Bear left at Y junction.

GPS: 48.688556, -121.096362 Route ends at Thunder Creek trailhead and parking area. Shuttle back to the Easy Pass trailhead.

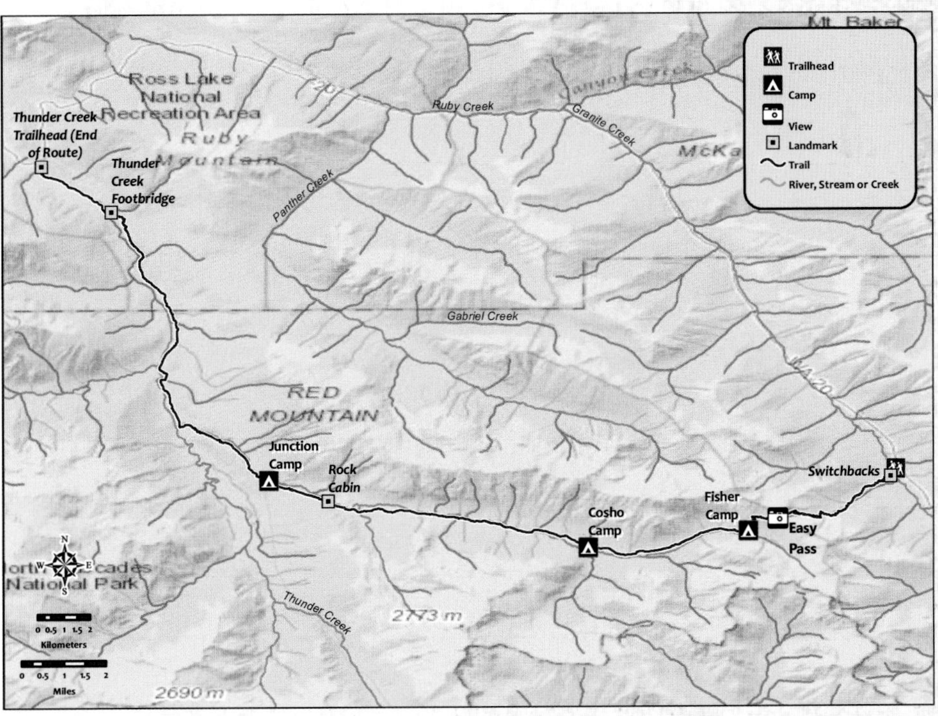

Rialto Beach
Photo: Dave Costello

OLYMPIC NATIONAL PARK

Shi Shi Beach

OLYMPIC NATIONAL PARK

SHI SHI BEACH TO CAPE ALAVA

These 15 miles of beachfront property are among the best miles of trail in the whole national park system.

With due respect to the sugar-sand beaches of the world, we like our coastal treks wild, rugged, and with more than a chance of rain.

You could parachute into any of the park's 73 miles of coastline and have the trip of a lifetime, but the very northern tip of the beach gets the nod for its density of sea-sculpted rocks, gritty scrambling, and the oasis of Shi Shi Beach.

After 2 miles of Sitka spruce and Western hemlock forest on the Shi Shi Beach Trail, shimmy down a 50-foot bluff to pop out on Shi Shi Beach, with wide swaths of sand, Jenga-like towers of rock topped with trees called sea stacks, and tide pools rich in starfish and hermit crabs.

Point of the Arches, at the beach's southern boundary, offers a mile-long parade of pinnacles, boulders, and precariously balanced sea arches. For the next 2 miles, the Pacific swallows the beach at several vertical headlands during high tide (carry a tide table and round them only when the tide ebbs).

After the last crossing (around mile 7), the route widens into 4 miles of driftwood-scattered beach end-capped by the Ozette River, a shin-deep ford that swells to an impassable flood at high tide. Once across, stroll 2 miles to the turnaround at Cape Alava.

Camping is allowed at seven designated sites along the route—you can't go wrong with any of them. Reserve permits for sites south of Point of the Arches starting March 15. The trip also requires a $10 Makah Recreation Pass.

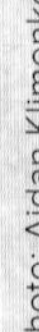

Text: Elisabeth Kwak-Hefferan

DISTANCE: 30 miles

TIME REQUIRED: 3–5 days

DIFFICULTY: Intermediate

CONTACT: Olympic National Park, (305) 565-3100; nps.gov/olym; $10 Makah Recreation Pass (makah.com/activities)

THE PAYOFF: Tide pools, sea stacks, the wildest coast in the Lower 48.

TRAILHEAD GPS: 48.319167, -124.675556

FINDING THE TRAILHEAD: From Port Angeles, take US-101 west for 5 miles. Turn onto SR-112 west for 64 miles to Neah Bay. Continue on Bayview Avenue for 1 mile and then turn left on Fort Street, turn right on Third Street, and turn left on Cape Flattery Road. Drive 2.5 miles and turn left on Hobuck Road. Drive 4.3 miles, following signs for the fish hatchery to the trailhead and day-use parking. Overnighters should park about 0.6 mile back at a private home. Bring cash: It's $10 per day for every day you will be parked there.

WAYPOINTS & DIRECTIONS

GPS: 48.319167, -124.675556 From the trailhead, travel 2 miles down Shi Shi Beach before shimmying down a 50-foot bluff to pop out on Shi Shi Beach.

GPS: 48.247283, -124.700747 Point of the Arches offers a mile-long parade of pinnacles, boulders, and precariously balanced sea arches. For the next 2 miles, the Pacific swallows the beach at several vertical headlands during high tide, so use a tide table to plan accordingly.

GPS: 48.185832, -124.703321 The camping option at North Ozette is one of seven designated sites along the shore that allows camping with a permit.

GPS: 48.181482, -124.708214 Crossing the Ozette River is usually a shin-deep ford but swells to an impassable flood at high tide.

GPS: 48.178049, -124.718599 Southside Ozette Camping is another option for spending the night on the beach.

GPS: 48.160246, -124.730959 Cape Alava marks the turnaround point; take in the view of Ozette Island across the water before heading back north to the trailhead.

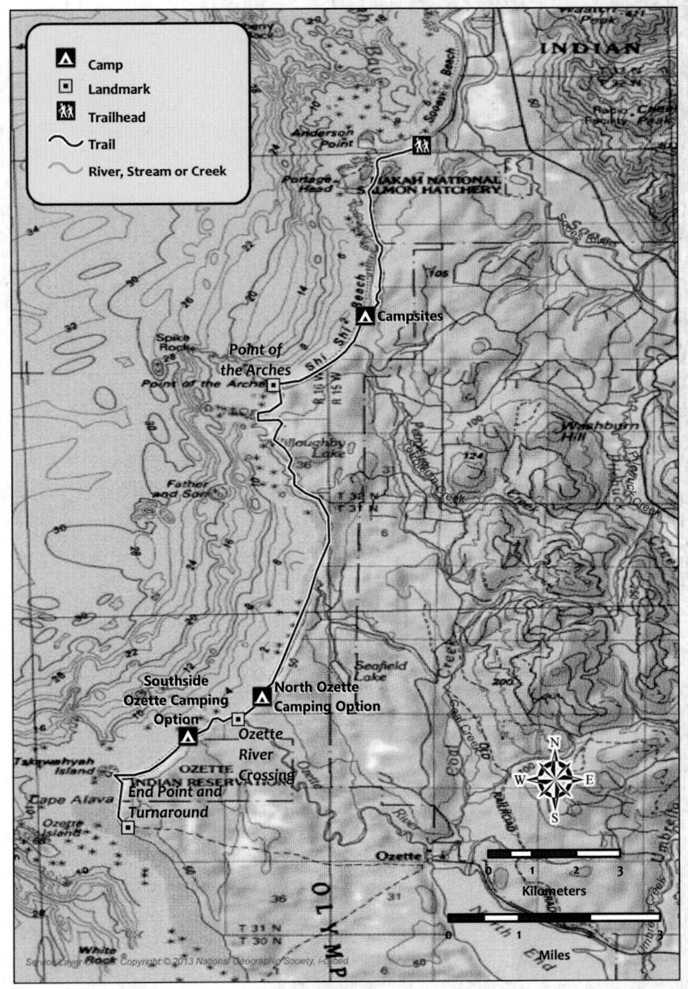

OLYMPIC NATIONAL PARK

HOH LAKE AND HEART LAKE VIA HOH RIVER TRAIL

Link lush, mossy forests with alpine lakes and meadows on this thigh-busting backpacking trip.

Hike into the wild green heart of the Northwest on this 35.2-mile tour de ecosystems in Olympic National Park.

Start from the Hoh Ranger Station, north of the Hoh Rain Forest Campground and hike northeast on the Hoh River Trail. For the next 9.5 miles, sunlight stabs through dripping, moss-hung rainforest. Then turn left as the trail climbs 4,000 feet on 22 switchbacks from riverside through Sitka spruce to the wildflower-filled alpine meadows (the season's first are avalanche lilies, in May) of the Seven Lakes Basin and the jagged, snow-capped High Divide. Find a string of aquamarine ponds shimmering below the High Divide's glaciated peaks at CB Flats, forage for huckleberries (starting to ripen in mid-July) in sprawling patches (watch out for black bears), and ogle hulking Mount Olympus. Pack an extra memory card for Hoh Lake at mile 13.9: The photo ops here (4,539 feet) include a wide alpine tundra and the glacier-laced flanks of 7,929-foot Olympus.

Next, cruise 4.3 miles to heath-lined Heart Lake. Camp lakeside in this small cirque, or hike north to the Heart Lake Shelter. The next day, retrace your route back to the trailhead at your pace.

Photo: Justin Baillie

DISTANCE: 35.2 miles

TIME REQUIRED: 3–5 days

DIFFICULTY: Intermediate

CONTACT: Olympic National Park, (305) 565-3100; nps.gov/olym

THE PAYOFF: An eye-popping tour of Olympic's rainforest and mountain ecosystems.

TRAILHEAD GPS: 47.860311, -123.934214

FINDING THE TRAILHEAD: From Forks, take US 101 S. In 13.1 miles, turn left at Upper Hoh Road. Go 18.1 miles to the trailhead.

GPS: 47.860311, -123.934214 Start from the Hoh Ranger Station (north of the Hoh Rain Forest Campground). Hike northeast on the Hoh River Trail.

GPS: 47.861204, -123.933291 Bear left at Y junction, and continue hiking northeast toward the Hoh River.

GPS: 47.868545, -123.829758 Hike past Happy Four Shelter. Ahead, the trail continues southeast, then rounds to the northeast.

GPS: 47.877712, -123.767311 Nice campsite by the river.

GPS: 47.878419, -123.754828 Bear left onto Canyon Creek Hoh Trail at the signed Y junction. Ahead, the trail leaves the river and climbs north up 22 steep switchbacks, toward Hoh Lake.

GPS: 47.889960, -123.783002 Pass the last campfire site. Keep climbing.

GPS: 47.893845, -123.790383 C.B. Flats, where you'll find group campsites and shimmering ponds.

GPS: 47.897655, -123.788856 Best site at Hoh Lake. You'll find incredible views of Mount Olympus.

GPS: 47.904217, -123.778517 On the small saddle beneath Bogachiel Peak, bear right onto Deer Lake Trail. The trail to the left leads to Seven Lakes Basin.

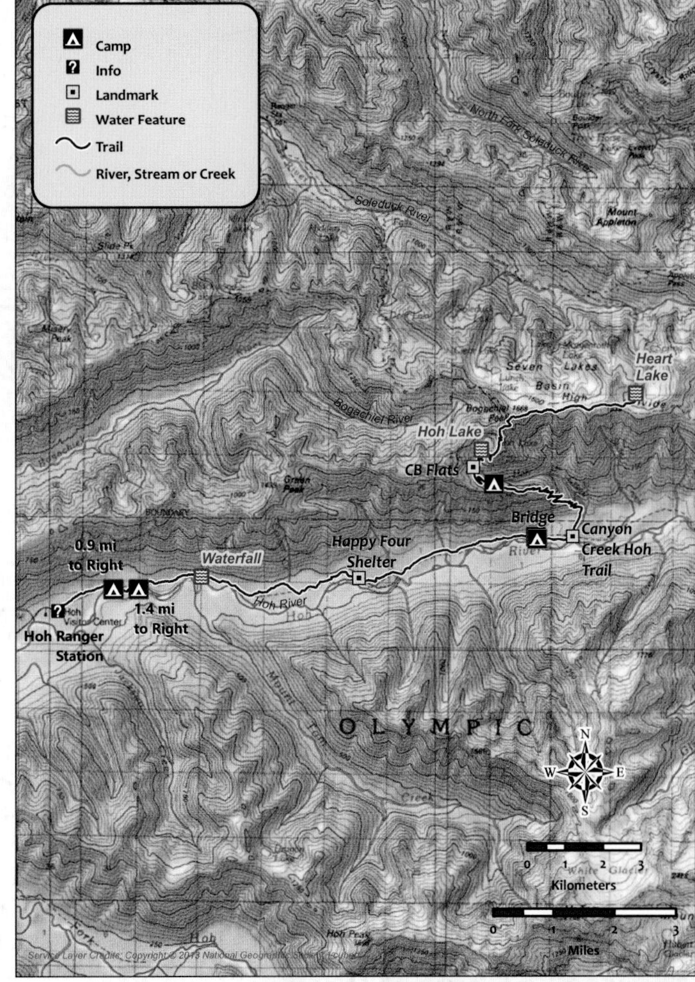

GPS: 47.905094, -123.775169 Keep right at three-way junction for a traverse along the High Divide. (***Side Trip:*** to climb Bogachiel Peak, turn left at junction.)

GPS: 47.907822, -123.738236 Bear left at Y junction. Leave the High Divide for a descent to Heart Lake.

GPS: 47.910834, -123.733177 This aptly named lake resembles a heart and is tucked at the foot of a small cirque. Camp here or continue north to Heart Lake Shelter. Retrace steps to the trailhead.

OLYMPIC NATIONAL PARK

SEVEN LAKES LOOP

Explore old-growth rainforest, ascend 5,474-foot Bogachiel Peak, and reap stunning views of Mount Olympus from High Divide's ridgeline on this 17.5-mile lasso loop around a breathtaking lake basin.

Sol Duc Falls

Olympic National Park's variety is its hidden ace: Few hikes in the world take you from stands of 200-foot-tall, centuries-old trees to wildflower meadows with views of glaciated peaks. Hikers who scale this airy, 5,000-foot ridgeline will trek above lake-filled basins and score unrivaled views of 7,965-foot Mount Olympus—the tallest peak in the Olympics. Get there about midway through a 17.5-mile lasso loop starting on the Sol Duc River Trail. Hike southeast 0.8 mile to Sol Duc Falls, where the river splits into three parallel channels and plummets into a pinched, moss-dusted gorge. The rainforest of the Sol Duc River is every bit as magnificent as the Hoh, but without the train of hikers.

From here, the route climbs up the valley another 4.6 miles, then bends south, gaining nearly 1,400 feet in 2.1 miles to a meadowy campsite near Heart Lake. The next day, ascend the grassy basin for less than half a mile, past thinning patches of subalpine firs and avalanche lilies, to the crest of the ridge.

Now comes the big show: Trace the spine of the High Divide west for 2 miles, grabbing aerial shots of teal-colored Sol Duc, Long, and Lunch Lakes to the north and unbroken views of ice- and snow-shrouded Olympus towering above the Hoh River valley to the south. At mile 9.7, take a 0.25-mile round-trip, nontechnical detour to 5,474-foot Bogachiel Peak for final views of Olympus. Drop 1,900 feet to Deer Lake, then finish off the loop with a 3.3-mile descent along Canyon Creek.

Photo: Andy Porter

DISTANCE: 17.5 miles

TIME REQUIRED: 2–4 days

DIFFICULTY: Intermediate

CONTACT: Olympic National Park, (305) 565-3100; nps.gov/olym

THE PAYOFF: Walk from lush rainforest to wide-open glacier views.

TRAILHEAD GPS: 47.860311, -123.934214

FINDING THE TRAILHEAD: Take US 101 W from Port Angeles for 27 miles. Turn left on Sol Duc Hot Springs Road. Follow to the end of the road and park at the trailhead.

WAYPOINTS & DIRECTIONS

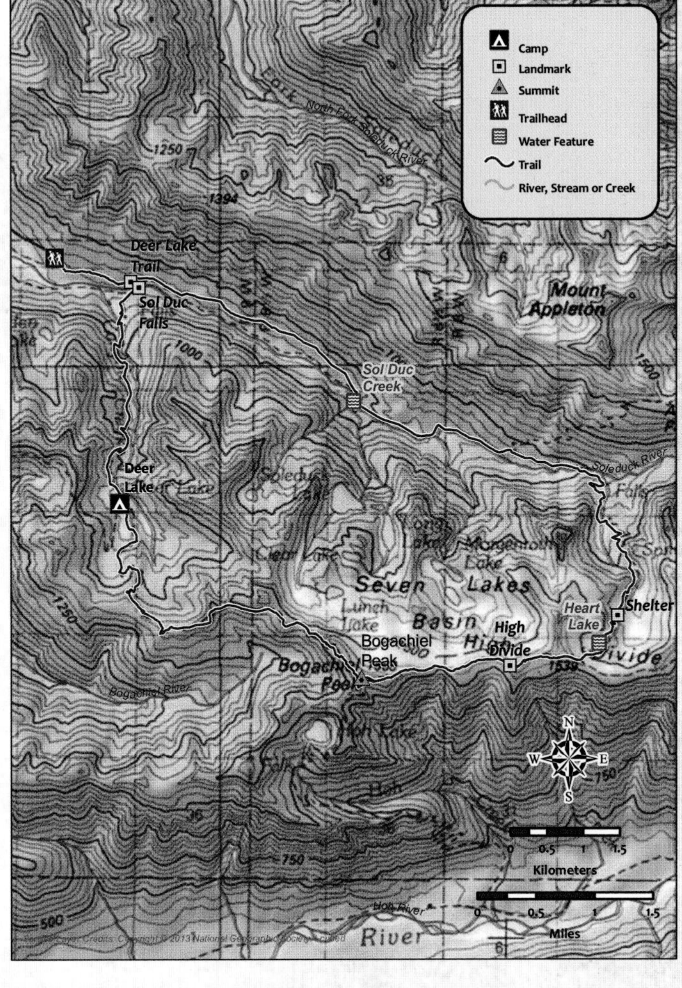

GPS: 47.954844, -123.834779 Begin hiking east from Sol Duc trailhead.

GPS: 47.952139, -123.820939 Continue straight on Sol Duc Trail at the junction with Deer Lake Trail.

GPS: 47.938195, -123.779615 Trail passes through valley along Sol Duc Creek.

GPS: 47.932306, -123.750554 Continue straight at the three-way junction; the trail gently ascends east. Ahead, pass 7-Mile Shelter on the right.

GPS: 47.909828, -123.734290 Find a great campsite with mountainous views along the shore of Heart Lake.

GPS: 47.907846, -123.737528 Turn right at T junction. (***Side Trip:*** Add a day and visit Cat Basin; turn left here onto the Cat Basin spur trail.)

GPS: 47.907069, -123.750564 Hike along High Divide, a long ridgeline overlooking Seven Lakes Basin to the north and Hoh River Valley to the south.

GPS: 47.905457, -123.777745 Summit Bogachiel Peak at 5,474 feet. Look north for great views to the north of Sol Duc, Long, and Lunch Lakes, and look south to see Mount Olympus. Continue along the ridgeline.

GPS: 47.925794, -123.822600 Deer Lake has a superb campsite. Turn right to stay on Deer Lake Trail and follow it north back to Sol Duc Trail.

GPS: 47.952071, -123.820660 Turn left and retrace route back to the trailhead.

OLYMPIC NATIONAL PARK

HOH RIVER TO THIRD BEACH

Trace the rugged coastline past dozens of sea-carved rock formations on this five-star weekend trip along the Olympic Peninsula.

Is it a hike or an army obstacle course? Both, actually, which you'll find out as you negotiate ladders and ropes through upland rainforest and rocky beach on this 16.1-mile trek. At the Oil City trailhead, take the South Coast Trail along the river. Two rights lead to the coast; cruise past a bleached driftwood graveyard to Jefferson Cove. Note: Cross the area only at tides lower than two feet. Get charts at the ranger station.

Head inland near a small waterfall and scale a 60-foot cliff on two fixed ropes. The 3.5-mile upland trail winds through a high-canopy forest, and begins a roller-coaster section up log steps and down into the mossy forest. Take the boardwalk over the marshy area to Mosquito Creek and camp on a bluff overlooking the Pacific.

The next morning, don your sandals and ford Mosquito Creek at its mouth. Walk the beach north for 2 miles past sea stacks. At low tide, hike on the beach to the left side of the rocky sea stack. At high tide, clamber over driftwood on the right. Turn inland at bull's-eye marker, head up a hillside, and hike through a leafy trellis of salal, salmonberry (edible but bland), thimbleberry (rich and juicy), and devil's club.

Stay straight to ford 20-foot-wide Goodman Creek, and reenter the woods. Pass massive red cedars to Falls Creek's low cascade. Descend a 30-foot trail ladder and head north to Toleak Point, watching for bald eagles. At Toleak and Strawberry Points, receding tides leave islands of sea water, rich with life-sustaining nutrients from Pacific upwelling, a process that carries deep-sea particulates to the surface. Tide pools support an amazing diversity of sea creatures—including the sunflower starfish, anemones, mollusks, multicolored sea slugs, and plant life—that you'd normally need scuba gear to view. Traverse a rocky stretch, and head past Giants Graveyard, a cluster of sea stacks and pinnacles.

Ford Scott Creek and traverse a forested hillside (use trail ropes if needed) to the beach. At the bull's-eye trail marker, climb 90 steps into the forest. After 14.2 miles, descend to Third Beach on stairs and ladders and pick up the dirt path to Third Beach parking area and your shuttle.

DISTANCE: 16.1 miles

TIME REQUIRED: 2 days

DIFFICULTY: Intermediate

CONTACT: Olympic National Park, (305) 565-3100; nps.gov/olym

THE PAYOFF: Mossy rainforest to wave-bashed coast in a weekend

TRAILHEAD GPS: 47.749164, -124.417832

FINDING THE TRAILHEAD: Start: From Port Angeles, head southwest on US-101. In 54.2 miles, turn right onto La Push Rd./WA 110. Go 11.6 miles to parking lot to leave your shuttle car. Return to US-101 and continue 15.8 miles (70 from Port Angeles) to turn right on onto Lower Hoh Road/Oil City Road. Go 10.3 miles to parking area.

Text: Kari Bodnarchuk

Third Beach.
Photo: iStockPhoto.com / RonGreer

WAYPOINTS & DIRECTIONS

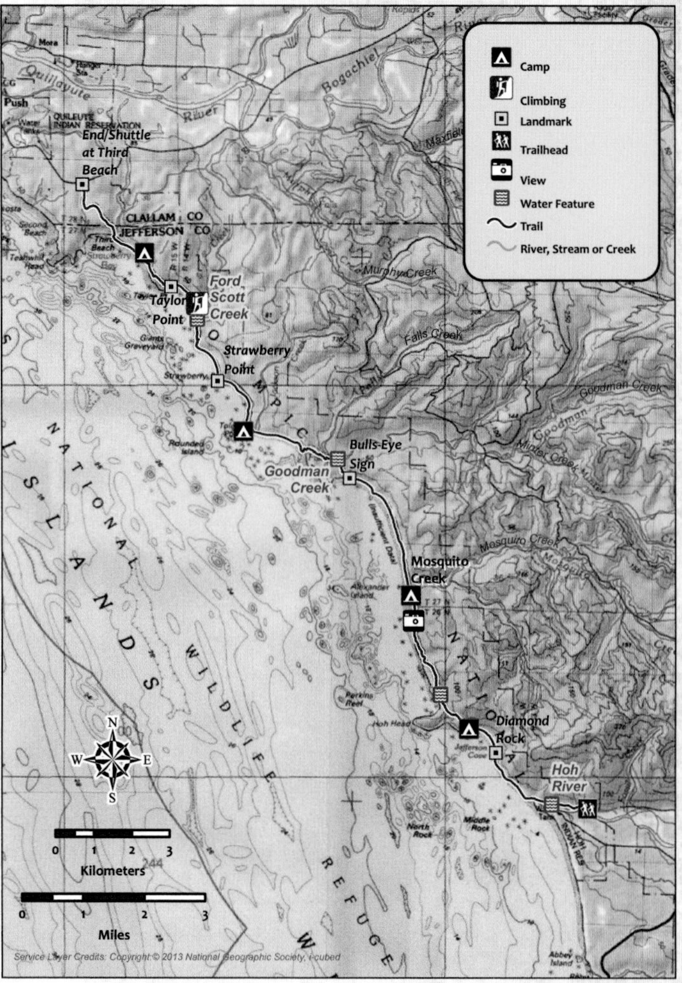

GPS: 47.749164, -124.417832 From the trailhead on the northwest side of parking lot, head west along the dirt and pine-needle singletrack.

GPS: 47.750000, -124.430748 Trail emerges from forest next to the swift-moving Hoh River. Turn right and follow rocky, pebbly beach along the riverbank to the ocean and turn right again, heading north.

GPS: 47.761600, -124.450546 Trail skirts a headland marked by Diamond Rock, a triangular sea stack (***Caution:*** Pass only at low tide.) Next, enter Jefferson Cove and walk along beach blanketed in tiny pebbles.

GPS: 47.766788, -124.456749 Trail veers inland for 3.5 miles at the end of Jefferson Cove. Look for trail marker at the foot of the headland on the right, near the waterfall and rocks.

GPS: 47.774700, -124.470268 Cross stream (a good water source), then tackle a very steep switchback climb up log steps.

GPS: 47.797344, -124.481213 Refill water in creek close to the Mosquito Creek Campsite. From camp, head north through the woods and drop onto the beach and ford Mosquito Creek.

GPS: 47.798832, -124.482414 Walk north along the beach for about 2 miles. Savor views of the flat-topped Alexander Island to the west, sea stacks and headlands to the north, and a hillside blanketed in dense vegetation to the east.

GPS: 47.814018, -124.487717 Depending on the tides, you'll either scramble over giant driftwood to the right of the tree-topped sea stack or hike along a sandy stretch to the left of the sea stack.

GPS: 47.824148, -124.503357 Turn right at the red-and-black, target-shaped Olympic headland marker sign located to the right of rocky bluff (you can see a hole in the rock at low tide). Leave the beach and begin a steep scramble that switchbacks up the hillside to an overlook with stunning views of beach, islands, and rock pinnacles.

GPS: 47.828405, -124.507638 Ignore the trail on the right and continue straight. Ford the 20-foot-wide Goodman Creek. Reenter woods and hike through dense forest alongside Goodman Creek (on the left). The trail passes a small, plunging waterfall on the right. Ahead, ford Falls Creek and continue hiking uphill.

GPS: 47.831848, -124.521767 Descend 30 feet down a rock face on a vertical ladder (***Caution:*** Slippery when wet). Head north along the sandy beach toward Toleak Point.

GPS: 47.853668, -124.558250 Hike around headland on very rocky shore (***Caution:*** 4-foot tide); take in views of Giants Graveyard, a cluster of sea stacks, islands and rock pinnacles.

GPS: 47.860016, -124.558107 Ford Scott Creek (another good water source) on logs or by rock-hopping, and then turn right at the bull's-eye marker and head inland for a short, steep climb around Scotts Bluff.

GPS: 47.863529, -124.558139 Use the provided ropes to rappel down the steep hillside to the beach below and head north along the beach.

GPS: 47.867382, -124.567520 Taylor Point. Plan to get into the cove at low tide (***Caution:*** 4.5-foot tide) to access the trail that heads inland (look for bull's-eye marker on tree). Climb up roughly 90 steps that lead out of the cove.

GPS: 47.874907, -124.577140 Pass a campsite on the hill before descending through forest; climb down two sets of stairs and ladders to the southern end of Third Beach. Follow the wide, sandy beach north looking to the right for the bull's-eye marker indicating where the trail disappears inland again.

GPS: 47.878033, -124.588036 Turn right onto trail that crosses a small creek and heads inland. Switchback up the wide, well-trodden dirt and gravel path to the Third Beach parking area and shuttle back to the trailhead.

RANGER PROFILE

BRYAN BELL

The Backcountry Guru
Olympic National Park, Washington

"The man is an encyclopedia of backcountry knowledge."
—Michael Lanza, *Backpacker* Contributor

Bryan Bell's first hikes were through rainforest. When he was young, he used to hike to Lake Quinault, just north of where he grew up in Aberdeen, Washington, and to this day the trek remains his favorite. Over time, Bell built a mental map of the park's expansive back-country—from beach to rainforest to mountaintop—and applied his knowledge to search-and-rescue operations for years. Now he uses it to match backpackers with the right places and itineraries, what he calls "preventative search and rescue." And that, he says, is a team effort: "No one person is a super ranger."

FAVORITE SPOT: Lake Quinault, Enchanted Valley

Enchanted Valley is right: In this idyllic area, 13 miles up the East Fork Quinault River Trail, waterfalls careen down the sides of sheer peaks to a verdant haven frequented by black bears. On the way, you'll hike under an electric-green canopy of enormous evergreens near a rushing cobalt river.

TRAILHEAD: East Fork Quinault River

INFO: nps.gov/olym

Text: Mike Lanza and Dan Nelson

STAY DRY IN ANY WEATHER

Rainy weather doesn't have to ruin your big day out. Here's how to go waterproof.

On the Trail

HIKE WET, CAMP DRY. During days and days of constant rain, you're going to get wet. But your body heat will keep you warm while you're moving. (If not, you need to stop and make camp). Divide your clothes into "sacrifice" layers and "sacred" layers, advises Judd Rogers, a National Outdoor Leadership School instructor who once experienced 60 days of rain on a 75-day course in Chilean Patagonia. Hike in your sacrifice layers and store them wet, in your vestibule. Keep your sacred layers dry. Always.

DOUBLE BAG. Use waterproof stuffsacks or line your pack with trash-compactor bags. Pack covers reduce the water weight absorbed by your pack but tend to flap in the wind and snag if you're bushwhacking.

WALK, DON'T RUN. Simply put, the harder you run to avoid the rain, the wetter you're likely to get.

KEEP YOUR COOL. When waterproof-breathable shells get steamy, dial down your pace or wear the jacket like a vest: Stick your arms through the pit zips and tuck the sleeves into pockets.

CARRY AN UMBRELLA. They're easy to pack, improve visibility and hearing (compared with a hood), and provide a dry refuge for eating a snack or shooting photos.

REST WHEN THE RAIN STOPS. Forget your schedule; in extended bad weather, take advantage of dry spells to eat.

AVOID RAISING YOUR ARMS. In a downpour, water will enter at your cuffs and wick up your sleeves. Using trekking poles? Shorten the length to minimize wrist exposure. In the worst conditions, consider hiking in a paddling jacket. The neoprene cuffs and secure wrist enclosures help keep water out.

WEAR NEOPRENE SOCKS AND GLOVES. Rogers uses plastic boots—which absorb no water—to avoid chronically soggy feet.

In Camp

CHOOSE A DOUBLE-WALL TENT (best at reducing condensation) with at least one large vestibule. Or, pack an extra tarp and string it up over your tent. Even the best tents get soggy in the worst weather

MAKE SURE SEAMS ARE TAPED and seal any that show wear. Check for UV damage to your tent fly, says Rogers, by trying to suck air through it. If you can, replace it.

DON'T PITCH YOUR TENT IN A DEPRESSION OR ANYWHERE WATER MIGHT COLLECT. Even if your tent floor doesn't leak, the floorless vestibule will be over a puddle. Also: Keep the inner tent dry by pitching it in a sheltered area without staking it, then drape the fly over and move the tent as needed to level ground.

TIGHTEN SAGGING RAINFLIES. you want a taut pitch that separates fly and tent, which increases air circulation and reduces condensation. Use an adjustable trucker's hitch so you can easily retighten guylines. And pack gear you leave in the tent in waterproof stuffsacks if you won't be there to protect it.

RIG A KITCHEN TARP. It's more comfortable than vestibule cooking, and in bear country you want to keep food away from your tent anyway. An A-frame affords maximum weather protection, while a lean-to affords more headroom and a better view. No trees? Use trekking poles guyed out in two directions for stability.

WARM UP WITH SUPER COCOA: 4 tablespoons cocoa; 2 tablespoons each of powdered milk, brown sugar, and peanut butter; and 1 ounce of cheese. Add hot water to taste.

Text: Mike Lanza and Dan Nelson

Deer grazing along Grand Valley Loop

OLYMPIC NATIONAL PARK
GRAND VALLEY LOOP

The best way to see all that Olympic's drier northeast quadrant has to offer.

British sea captain John Meares might have raised expectations a little in 1788 when he named Washington's Mount Olympus after the mythological den of the Greek gods, but most backpackers would agree that the guy was on the mark. Few mountain ranges harbor such a variety of terrain—from rainforest to glaciated peaks—as the Olympic Mountains yet remain so accessible that you can sample them all in a weekend.

For a taste of what the Olympics have to offer, head to the park's northeast corner, which sees relatively less rain and snowfall than the rest of the park. There you'll find valleys thick with towering Douglas firs, hemlocks, and cedars. In the alpine zones, wildflowers carpet the meadows in July, and the views of Olympus, Mount Anderson, and the Needles will give you a Zeus-like perspective. This rigorous 3-day, 27-mile loop hike is the best way to get next to godliness.

From the end of the Obstruction Point Road, near the east end of Hurricane Ridge, trek about 3 miles along Lillian Ridge (6,200 feet) before dropping a mile to Grand Lake (4,750 feet) in the heart of Grand Valley. Then you face a high-mountain rambler's dilemma: One pass or two? That's your choice as you leave Grand Lake and climb south to the meadow-lined shores of Moose Lake. You'll soon enter a high-angle world of windswept ridges,

Photo: iStockPhoto.com / Sam Camp

endless views, and glacier-clad mountains. At Grand Pass, admire snowy vistas northwest to Hurricane Ridge and the spires of the Needles at the end of the Gray Wolf Range. Turn back for a round-trip of 5 miles or continue south for a 16-miler, descending into the forested Cameron Creek Valley before climbing to Cameron Pass beneath Mount Cameron (7,190 feet).

Day two's wildflower walk heads north through Grand Valley to its junction with Badger Valley, so named from the blunder of early explorers who mistook marmots for badgers. Turn and climb into the meadow-flecked basin, and plunge knee-deep into an explosion of color. Above Badger Walls, walk the open shoulder of Elk Mountain, enjoying close-ups of purple aster, heather, and lupine against panoramic backdrops reaching from Canada to Mount Olympus. Reach the 6,773-foot summit about 6 miles from camp.

Grand views and gaggles of wildlife are all well and good, but Olympic National Park is best known for its trees. Check out some of the tallest on this old-growth sampler that heads south over Cameron Pass to the deep, cathedral forests of Cameron Valley. Expect to be dazzled by the lush, emerald world of ancient hemlocks and dwarfed by cedars.

You'll also find bigleaf maples sporting long, drooping beards of moss. Where the forest thins, rhododendron tangles and tunnels fill the void. You'll end back at your car near Obstruction Point Road.

DISTANCE: 27 miles

TIME REQUIRED: 3 days

DIFFICULTY: Intermediate

CONTACT: Olympic National Park, (305) 565-3100; nps.gov/olym

THE PAYOFF: Sample rainforest and high alpine meadows and glaciated peaks in one weekend.

TRAILHEAD GPS: 47.918370, 123.381937

FINDING THE TRAILHEAD: From Port Angeles, take Hurricane Ridge Road south 17. 5 miles to Obstruction Point Road. Turn left (east) on Obstruction Point Road to reach the Grand Pass trailhead, in 7.6 miles.

WAYPOINTS & DIRECTIONS

GPS: 47.918370, 123.381937 From the trailhead, stay right to trek south along the Lillian Ridge before dropping a mile to Grand Lake, in the heart of Grand Valley.

GPS: 47.891715, -123.347111 Camp at Grand Lake. In the morning, climb southwest past the meadow-lined shores of Moose Lake.

GPS: 47.866098, -123.356380 At Grand Pass, admire snowy vistas northwest to Hurricane Ridge and the spires of the Needles at the end of the Gray Wolf Range. Turn back for a round-trip hike of 5 miles or continue south for a 16-miler, descending into the forested Cameron Creek Valley.

GPS: 47.853487, -123.350115 There are several camping options along Cameron Creek for hikers who wish to extend their trip.

GPS: 47.825171, -123.358526 Take in the views from Cameron Pass beneath Mount Cameron. Return to Grand Lake. The next day, head north through Grand Valley to its junction with Badger Valley. Veer right into the Badger Valley before hiking up the valley walls and taking a sharp left onto the ridge trail along the open shoulder of Elk Mountain. Continue to follow the contour of Elk Mountain and then Obstruction Peak west and southwest until you arrive back at your car near Obstruction Point Road.

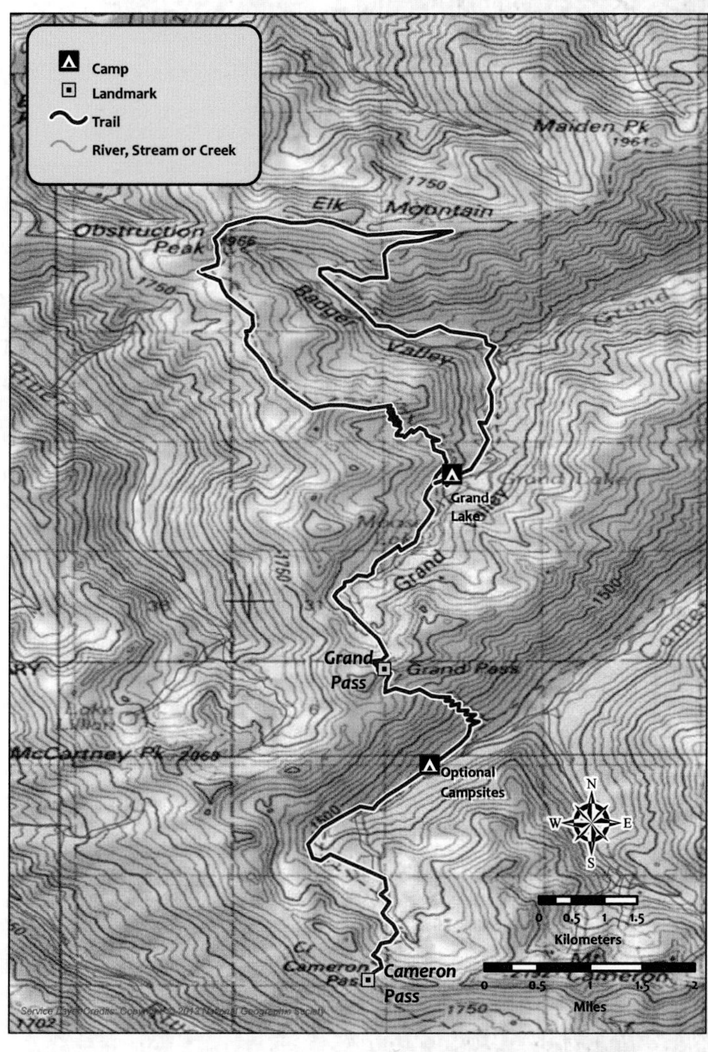

Conglomerate stone juts out of the rolling hills in Pinnacles National Park, California
Photo: Kaare Iverson / Tandem Stock

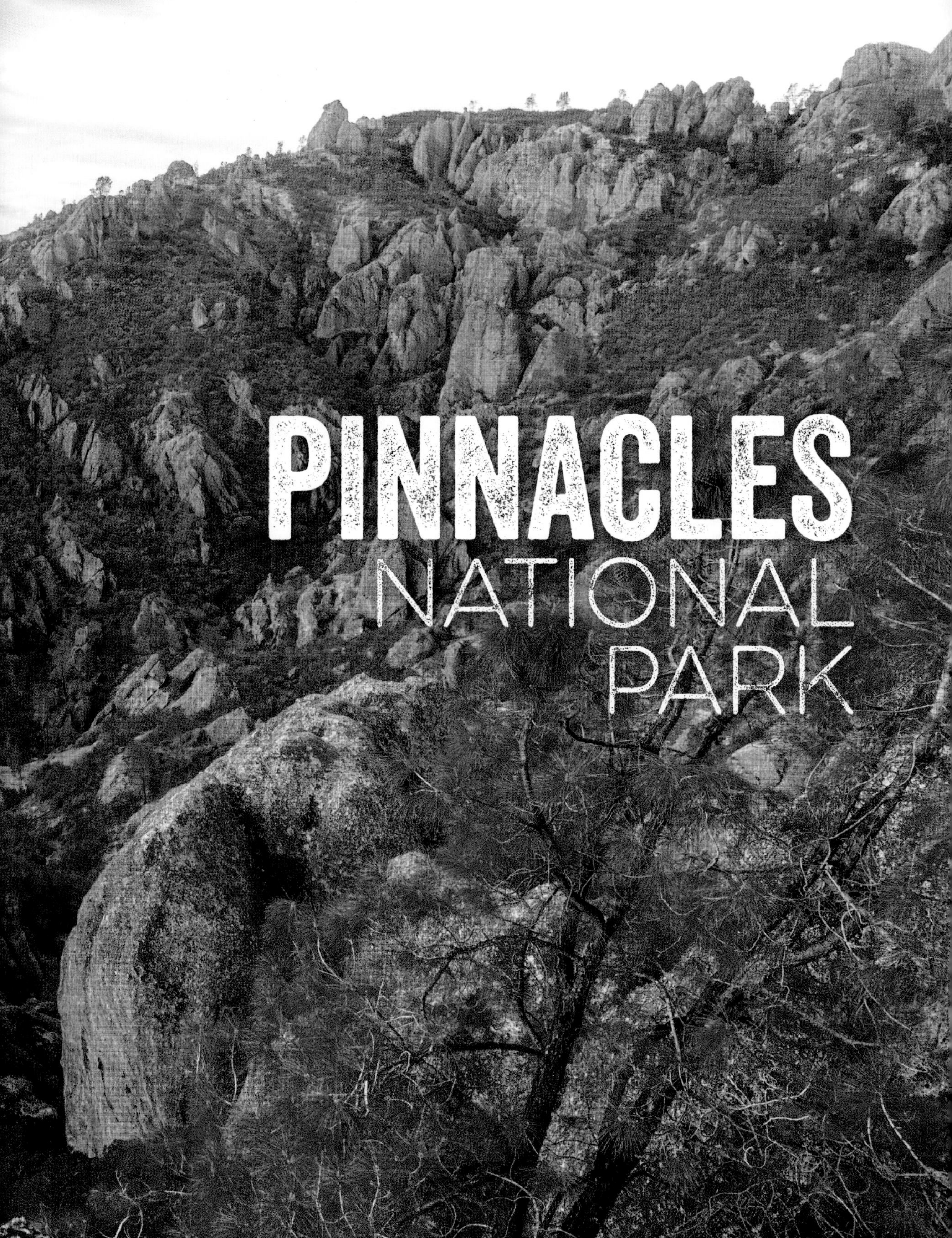
PINNACLES
NATIONAL
PARK

PINNACLES NATIONAL PARK

HIGH PEAKS LOOP

See the result of millions of years of tectonic movement on this 7.9-mile loop beneath massive volcanic monoliths harboring soaring condors. Bring a flashlight for optional cave trails.

America's newest national park is a testament to violent geological history: Pinnacles' raw materials of andesite and rhyolite formed in eruptions 23 million years ago. The San Andreas Fault then chopped and moved the rock bed 195 miles north. All the while, water and wind whittled the stone into fingers and bored narrow caves into the interior. In between, chaparral, scrub oak, and grassland provides ideal habitat for birds of prey—including the endangered California condor.

Hikers can glass for the giant birds commuting between here and Big Sur while scrambling into the park's rough-hewn interior. Start from the Chaparral trailhead by following blazes for Juniper Canyon Trail. As switchbacks steepen, look for the gnarled digits of the Fingers to the west and the blocky gray summit of Scout Peak to the south. After a wide view of the Salinas Valley at a five-way junction, turn left on the High Peaks Trail to get vertical. Hold onto metal railings and chains as you ascend tiny rock steps chipped into the pockmarked pink stone. Continue following High Peaks Trail signs toward Chalone Ranger Station. After, the trail flattens, then descends to reach the Old Pinnacles Trail along creek bed; cross bridges and follow signs for Old Pinnacles Trail.

Take a turn at a three-way junction onto the Balconies Cliffs Trail; switchbacks head up toward a giant breccia rock face. Across Pinnacles, deep, narrow gorges swallow toppled boulders that get stuck to create roofs for talus caves. With headlamps, hikers can explore them on the way. Take a right at the three-way junctiononto Balconies Trail; cross bridge immediately, bear right at a y to reach Machete Ridge and an east spur trail. A left at the next three-way junction leads to the Balconies Caves Trail. Use your headlamp in the cave, the trail becomes very narrow, dark and steep. Follow painted arrows as you clamber over and squeeze past truck-size boulders. Natural skylights allow shafts of sun to pierce the black, illuminating house-size chunks of granite caught mid-fall and squeezed by the rock. After marching up a narrow staircase, go left at a Y onto a rock path; right at another three-way junction leads back to the Juniper Canyon trail and your car.

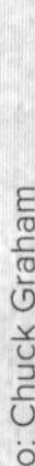

DISTANCE: 7.9 miles

TIME REQUIRED: 1 day

DIFFICULTY: Intermediate

CONTACT: Pinnacles National Park, (831) 389-4485; nps.gov/pinn

THE PAYOFF: Condors, caves, and impressive spires in America's newest national park.

TRAILHEAD GPS: 36.4855766296387, -121.200973510742

FINDING THE TRAILHEAD: From Soledad, take CA 146 E for 12.3 miles to the Chaparral trailhead. Trailhead parking will be on the right.

WAYPOINTS & DIRECTIONS

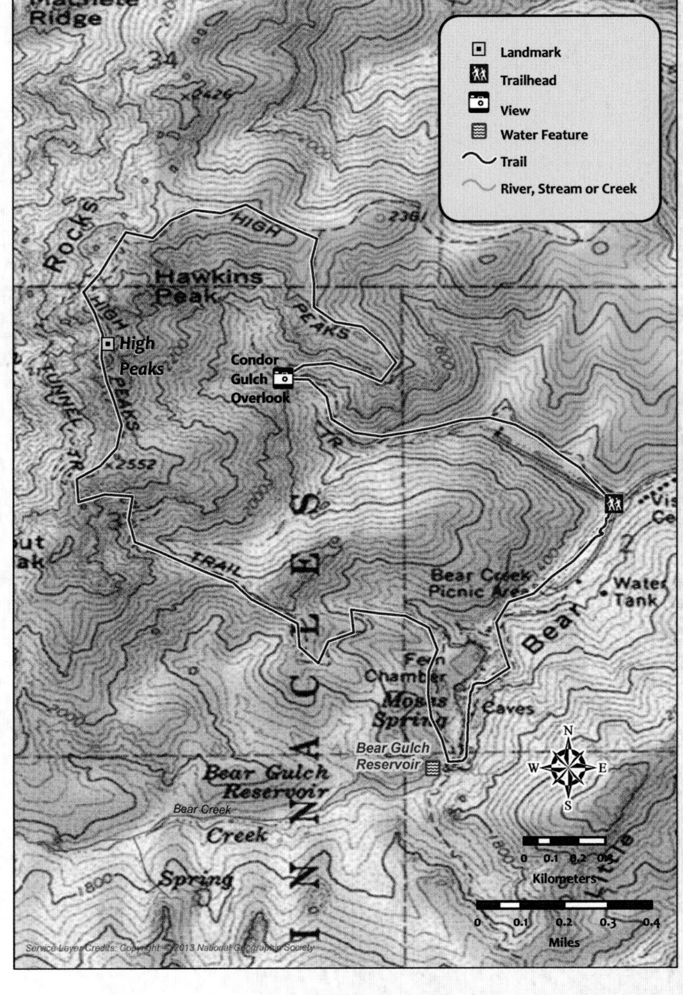

GPS: 36.481266, -121.181480 From Chaparral trailhead, head northwest up switchbacks on the Condor Gulch Trail.

GPS: 36.485249, -121.192368 From the ledge of Condor Gulch Overlook, peer south over eroded curves of the Little Pinnacles and north to Hawkins Peak. To continue, head east and then north along the ridge.

GPS: 36.489834, -121.191216 Turn left at the T onto High Peaks Trail; views open north over the Balconies, an 800-foot dome of cracked pink cliffs.

GPS: 36.488533, -121.198486 Veer left at the Y and begin traversing the jumbled formations of Pinnacle Rocks.

GPS: 36.486351, -121.198181 Cut across knife edge of the High Peaks on a dizzying section that has been chiseled out of breccia layers formed by lava and ash from the Pinnacles Volcano. (***Note:*** Not for acrophobes!)

GPS: 36.481617, -121.199265 Turn left at the T to start the steep descent of a narrow gorge.

GPS: 36.477215, -121.187263 Turn right at the Y onto the Rim Trail; in the spring, poppies and lupine streak the hillsides.

GPS: 36.472900, -121.187469 At Bear Gulch Reservoir, go left below the dam into a dark tunnel created by toppled boulders, now home to Townsend's big-eared bats. (***Note:*** Headlamp required.)

GPS: 36.475735, -121.186218 Take a right onto Moses Spring Trail at the T.

GPS: 36.477615, -121.185402 Veer right at the fork, and staying on Moses Spring Trail; continue 0.4 mile through sycamores to the car.

Towering redwoods in Redwood National Park, California
Photo: iStockPhoto.com / pawel.gaul

REDWOOD
NATIONAL PARK

Giant redwoods

REDWOOD NATIONAL PARK

REDWOOD CREEK TRAIL

Hike the quiet route to the iconic redwoods of Tall Trees Grove on this 16-mile out-and-back.

It's not usually satisfying to get cut down to size, but let Redwood National Park put you in your place—at the bottom of a 300-foot tree—and we guarantee you'll be happy with your flea-in-the-universe perspective. Hyperion is the world's tallest and most vexingly top-secret living tree: At 379 feet tall (about 70 feet higher than the Statue of Liberty), it was identified in 2006, and grows on a steep hillside flanking one of the streams that empty into Redwood Creek. You probably won't find it (and its location remains undisclosed to protect it from visitor traffic or potential vandals) but Hyperion grows in good company. Its grove and others situated along Redwood Creek are among the most truly breathtaking sights on earth. The Libbey Tree (363 feet high) and other giants dwell here.

Pay homage to that redwood and the species that sparked the national park's establishment and avoid the crowds of the shorter approach on this easy 16-mile out-and-back to Grove of the Giants. The route winds amid magically lush forest, and dispersed camping is permitted on Redwood Creek's gravel bars.

From the trailhead, hike south through spruce, hemlock, and yes, redwoods to the seasonal bridge over McArthur Creek at mile 1.5. The bridge is usually in place by Memorial Day. Follow meandering Redwood Creek, lined in spring with blooming trillium and skunk cabbage, another 6.5 miles to the grove, where several old-growth monsters approach 370 feet. This secluded sanctuary known as the Emerald Mile qualifies as a life-list hike:

Photo: iStockPhoto.com / pawel.gaul

Text: Kelly Bastone

Countless old-growth redwoods and Douglas firs line a deep gorge, building a natural tunnel that will keep your eyes endlessly drawn up, up, up. Turn back and camp anywhere along the creek's sandy gravel bar. Hike out along the same trail, keeping your eyes peeled for black bears, beavers, and Roosevelt elk.

Note: Winter stream crossings can be dangerous. Check with rangers for bridge and creek conditions.

DISTANCE: 16 miles

TIME REQUIRED: 1–2 days

DIFFICULTY: Easy

CONTACT: Redwood National Park, (707) 464-6101; nps.gov/redw

THE PAYOFF: Feel small among the world's tallest trees.

TRAILHEAD GPS: 41.207450, -124.012202

FINDING THE TRAILHEAD: From Orick, go north on US 101 for 1.3 miles. Turn right on Bald Hills Road. Drive 0.5 mile east, then turn right at the sign for the Redwood Creek trailhead.

WAYPOINTS & DIRECTIONS

GPS: 41.299137, -124.033592 From the trailhead, hike south through spruce, hemlock, and yes, redwoods.

GPS: 41.275775, -124.029250 The seasonal bridge over McArthur Creek is usually in place by Memorial Day. (***Note:*** Winter stream crossings can be dangerous. Check with rangers for bridge and creek conditions.)

GPS: 41.209462, -124.011140 Take in the majesty of the Grove of the Giants, where several old-growth monsters approach 370 feet (the current world-champion redwood measures 379 feet).

GPS: 41.207589, -124.009767 Turn back and camp anywhere along the creek's sandy gravel bar.

GPS: 41.207621, -124.014230 From Gravel Bar Camp, hike back to trailhead along the same route.

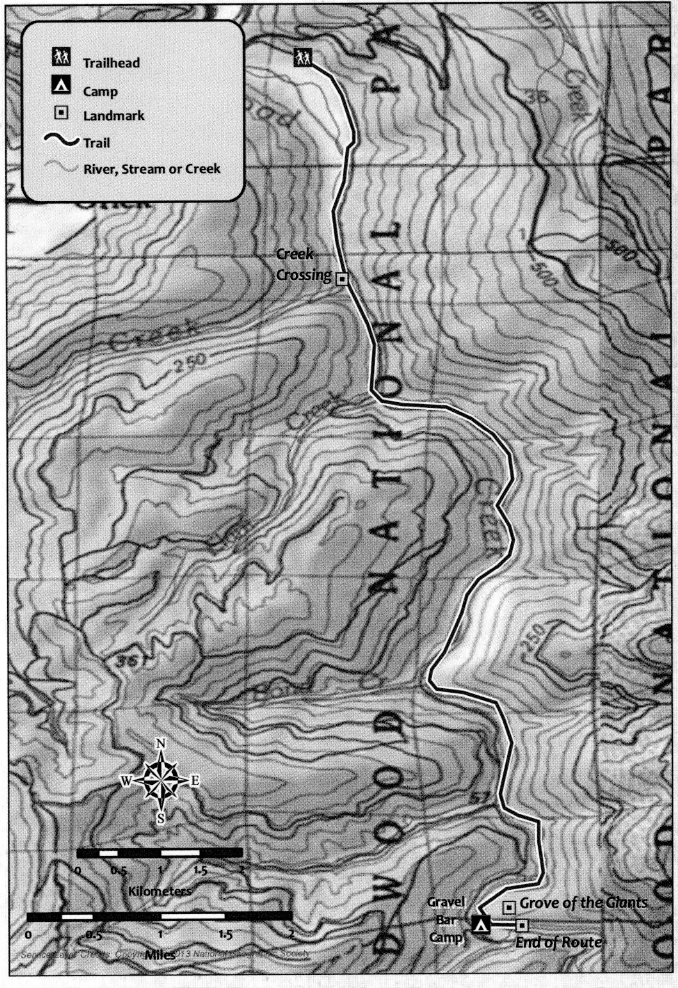

Fern Canyon

REDWOOD NATIONAL PARK

GOLDS BLUFF BEACH TO FERN CANYON LOOP

See towering forests, ocean waves, and fern-covered canyons at Redwood National and State Parks.

The life-list-worthy redwoods are reason enough to visit these combined national and state parks, but spring offers blooming skunk cabbage and swamp lantern, rushing mini waterfalls, and nine kinds of ferns along with the world's tallest trees. Explore the otherworldly coastal ecosystem on this moderate 15.7-mile shuttle hike, where you'll wind through spruce, alder, and hemlock and watch for wildlife like elk, black bears, and gray whales. From the Skunk Cabbage trailhead, hike west 2.5 miles for sweeping Pacific views, then continue north on the Coastal Trail. When the trail ends at mile 6.3, follow a dirt road along the beach to the developed Golds Bluff Beach Campground; Site 23 has been designated a backcountry site. Head back to the beach the next morning and hike north to Fern Canyon, a verdant paradise with 30-foot walls covered in ancient greenery. (Note: Check with rangers to see if seasonal footbridges are in place.) Take the James Irvine Trail to the Clintonia Trail, then hike out on the Miners Ridge Trail to the Elk Prairie Campground and your shuttle car.

Photo: iStockPhoto.com / zrfphoto

DISTANCE: 15.7 miles

TIME REQUIRED: 1–2 days

DIFFICULTY: Easy

CONTACT: Redwood National Park, (707) 464-6101; nps.gov/redw

THE PAYOFF: Giant trees, otherworldly coast.

TRAILHEAD GPS: 41.3060531616211, -124.045593261719

FINDING THE TRAILHEAD: From Orick, go 8 miles north on US 101. Take the Newton B. Drury Parkway exit; Elk Prairie campground is on the left, where you'll leave a shuttle car. Backtrack on US 101 for 6.2 mi. south to the Skunk Cabbage trailhead.

WAYPOINTS & DIRECTIONS

GPS: 41.306053, -124.045593 From the Skunk Cabbage Trailhead, hike west 2.5 miles, then continue north on the Coastal Trail. When the trail ends at mile 6.3, follow a dirt road along the beach to the developed Golds Bluff Beach Campground

GPS: 41.361092, -124.073818 Spend the night at the campground. In the morning, head back to the beach and hike north to Fern Canyon, turning onto the James Irvine Trail to hike east into the canyon. (***Note:*** Check with rangers to see if seasonal footbridges are in place.) Follow the James Irvine Trail but take the right fork at the junction with the Clintonia Trail. Hike out on the Miners Ridge Trail to the Elk Prairie Campground.

GPS: 41.357226, -124.030323 The hike ends at Elk Prairie Campground; pick up your shuttle car.

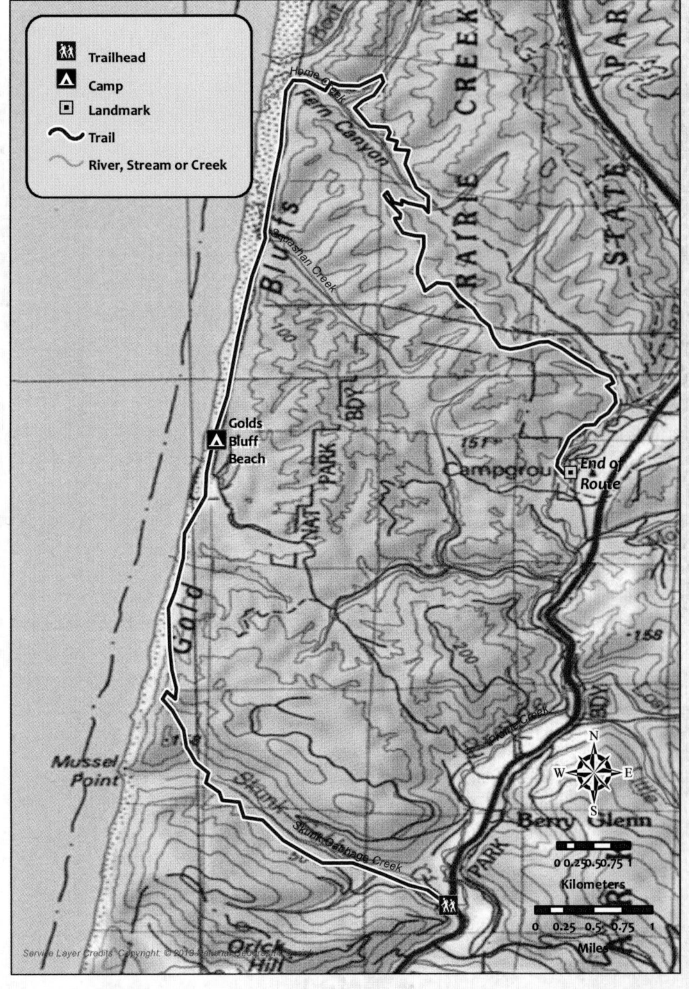

Longs Peak in Rocky Mountain National Park, Colorado
Photo: iStockPhoto.com / ryanwrightphoto

ROCKY MOUNTAIN NATIONAL PARK

The "keyhole" on Longs Peak

ROCKY MOUNTAIN NATIONAL PARK

LONGS PEAK VIA CLARK'S ARROW AND THE KEYHOLE

This stiff but nontechnical ascent leads to the highest point in Rocky Mountain National Park with unrivaled postcard views–and you can beat the crowds on a scrambly sneak route.

No fewer than 78 of the Rockies' 100 highest peaks lie in Colorado, but even with all of that competition, 14,259-foot Longs Peak is in a class by itself. Credit its striking profile, excellent rock, and spectacular approach. Its blunt crown beckons above every other summit in Rocky Mountain National Park, and its massive silhouette holds a hallowed standing among summitmongers. The "easiest" and classic route, the Keyhole charges 4,800 vertical feet past Tolkienesque features such as Goblins Forest and Chasm Junction, passes through the namesake Keyhole, and demands a serious scramble up the Trough. This nearly 14-mile out-and-back can easily chew up 16 hours, taxing your legs, lungs, and mental vigor. But the high is all Colorado—alpine lakes cupped by glacial rubble, an outrageous mountain skyline, and the noblest lunch spot of your life.

Not surprisingly, crowds of hikers storm the standard Keyhole Route in good weather. Avoid this bottleneck—and goose the adrenaline factor—by taking the 13-mile Clark's Arrow Loop. The clockwise traverse ascends 6,300 feet via the scrambly Loft and Clark's Arrow Routes and descends the Keyhole. Get a 3 a.m. start to reach the scrambly off-trail portion by sunrise. Follow East Longs Peak Trail up Alpine Brook to a three-way junction on Mills Moraine, where in summer ptarmigans are perfectly camouflaged against the grayish rocks. Bear left on the Chasm Lake Spur Trail toward the peak's sheer 1,000-foot Diamond Face.

If you're on pace, dawn will begin to drench the alpine landscape in rosy hues just as the trail ends east of Chasm Lake at mile 4. Climb a user trail southwest across rocky tundra

Photo: iStockPhoto.com / Skyhobo

Text: Jon Dorn and Dougald MacDonald

into the broad, boulder-filled gully below 13,911-foot Mount Meeker. You'll scale nearly 1,900 feet in the next 0.8 mile. Pick the path of least resistance through the stepped cliff bands and rock ramps at mile 4.6. If you venture into Class 4 terrain, you're off the route.

After cresting the Loft, a broad, slightly sloping boulder field between Meeker and Longs, connect cairns northwest to the top of a steep, loose Class 3 gully. Downclimb it nearly 200 feet to a ledge that runs to the base of the Palisades cliffs. Look for the faded Clark's Arrow, painted on a west-facing boulder by former park ranger John Clark.

Next, traverse gullies to Keplinger's Couloir and crawl up scree to a wide ramp that links to the Homestretch. Scale airy, cracked slabs of granite for the final 450 vertical feet to the summit of Longs. The peak's blunt, larger-than-a-football-field crown overlooks alpine lakes cupped by glacial rubble and Powell, McHenrys, and Chiefs Head Peaks—a ridgeline of Thirteeners two miles west that form the Continental Divide.

After cautiously crab-walking down the Homestretch, traverse exposed ledges to the Trough couloir, which typically holds snow into mid-July. Descend boulders (watch for rockfall), then contour north to the Keyhole's window-like rock notch. After a slow scramble down the 1.2-mile-long Boulder Field, turn right on Granite Pass; close the loop a mile later back at Mills Moraine.

DISTANCE: 13 miles

TIME REQUIRED: 1–2 days

DIFFICULTY: Strenuous to expert

CONTACT: Rocky Mountain National Park, (970) 586-1206; nps.gov/romo

THE PAYOFF: Bag the park's tallest peak.

TRAILHEAD GPS: 40.272232, -105.556786

FINDING THE TRAILHEAD: From Estes Park, take CO 7 E. Turn right toward Longs Peak Campground (marked by a brown National Park sign). Turn left at the Y, and park in the trailhead lot.

WAYPOINTS & DIRECTIONS

GPS: 40.272232, -105.556786 Get a predawn start to achieve the goal for the day: summiting Longs Peak before noon, when billowing thunderheads often charge the Front Range. Head west on East Longs Peak Trail under the glow of your headlamp. (***Note:*** Slower-paced hikers should get a 1 a.m. start.)

GPS: 40.275007, -105.564730 Stay on East Longs Peak Trail by veering left at the Y junction.

GPS: 40.273196, -105.580150 Cross two footbridges over Alpine Creek. This is a good spot to top off water bladders, grab an early morning snack, and soak your tired dogs on the return trip.

GPS: 40.265661, -105.592529 At the three-way junction on Mills Moraine, bear left (southwest) on Chasm Lake Spur Trail.

GPS: 40.259216, -105.600398 The maintained trail ends east of Chasm Lake. Continue past the lake on a user trail that climbs southwest across rocky tundra into the broad, boulder-filled gully. Keep the aptly named Ships Prow ridgeline to your right.

GPS: 40.256772, -105.602018 Stay to the left of the Ships Prow ridgeline and follow the user path that winds to the base of the Loft.

GPS: 40.251773, -105.605328 The seemingly vertical cliffs at the base of Mount Meeker pose a challenging route-finding problem. Pick the path of least resistance through the stepped cliff bands and rock ramps. (***Tip:*** If you venture into Class 4 terrain, you are off the route. Backtrack and try again.)

(*continued*)

GPS: 40.250446, -105.607238 Reach the broad and slightly sloping boulder field of the Loft, perched between Mount Meeker to the southeast and Longs Peak to the northwest. Hike northwest across this saddle, connecting cairns to the top of a steep, loose Class 3 gully on the Loft's western slopes.

GPS: 40.251326, -105.613916 Downclimb the gully for nearly 200 feet to a narrow ledge that runs below the Palisades Cliffs, and look for the faded Clark's Arrow—a white arrow inside a circle painted onto the west-facing rock face by former park ranger John Clark. Next, traverse west to Keplinger's Couloir.

GPS: 40.251658, -105.615799 Scramble up scree and boulders in Keplinger's Couloir toward the Notch, a deep gash separating the Palisades from the Longs summit block.

GPS: 40.253198, -105.614533 Before you reach the Notch, connect to the wide ledge that runs northwest and follow it to the bottom of the Homestretch.

GPS: 40.254237, -105.615416 The standard Keyhole Route joins up with Clark's Arrow Route at the Homestretch. Scale airy, cracked slabs of granite for the final 450 vertical feet to the summit.

GPS: 40.254846, -105.615986 Longs Peak (14,259 feet). The summit of offers unrivaled views a ridgeline of thirteeners—Powell, McHenrys, and Chiefs Head Peaks—that form the Continental Divide two miles to the west.

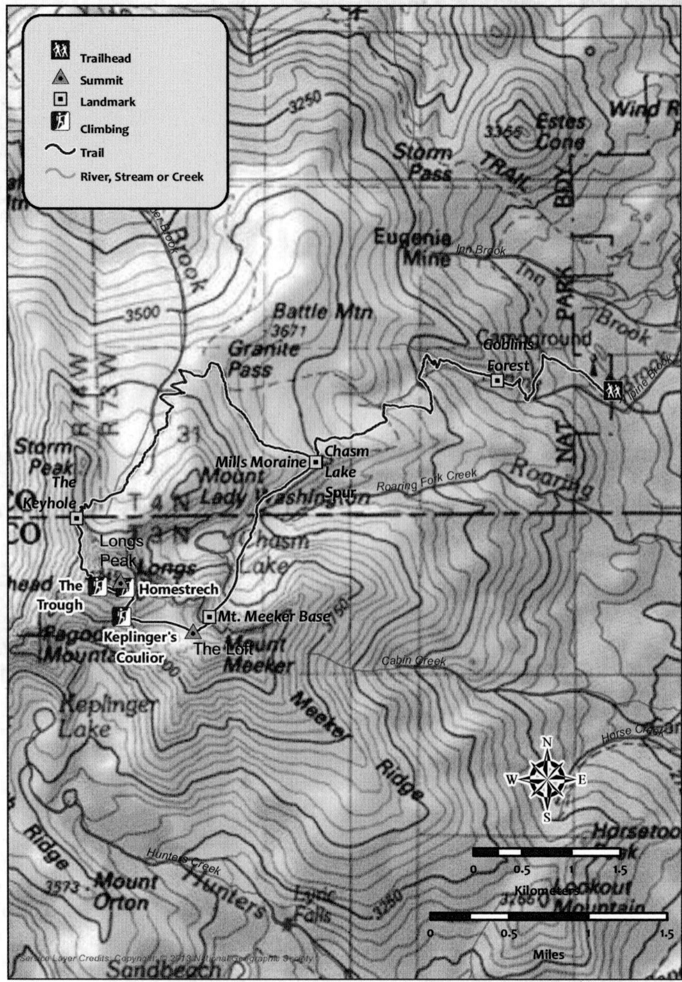

GPS: 40.254001, -105.615907 After cautiously crab-walking back down the Homestretch, bear left and traverse exposed ledges on the south face of Longs, which lead west to the Trough couloir.

GPS: 40.254344, -105.618696 Descend boulders and rocky rubble in the the Trough (watch for rockfall from hikers above), which holds snow into mid-July. (***Note:*** Check trail conditions on the park's website.)

GPS: 40.255949, -105.620617 Angle right and contour north along the Ledges's rock shelves to the Keyhole. The route is marked with painted yellow and red bull's-eyes.

GPS: 40.260517, -105.621239 Rest tired legs at the Keyhole before hiking east through the Keyhole and starting the slow scramble down the 1.2-mile-long Boulder Field.

GPS: 40.274177, -105.605427 Turn right at the Y junction on Granite Pass and descend a mile to close the loop back at Mills Moraine.

GPS: 40.265661, -105.592596 Close the loop back at Mills Moraine. Turn left at the three-way junction and backtrack to the trailhead.

Don't be afraid to use your hands

HOW TO SCRAMBLE SAFELY

Going off-trail on steep, rocky terrain? Follow these tips to stay steady out on the edge.

PACK HEAVY STUFF CLOSEST TO YOUR BODY. Don't tie anything outside—swinging water bottles and sleeping pads will throw off your center of gravity.

PUT AWAY TREKKING POLES. You'll need your hands for the ascent.

MAKE SURE THE ROUTE IS APPROPRIATE. Ask yourself these questions: If you encounter a tricky section, can you overcome it in just a move or two? If you slip, can you stop yourself from falling or tumbling more than a few feet? How hurt would you get if you fell?

CHECK YOUR SURROUNDINGS. When scrambling on unmarked terrain, take periodic looks around. Consult your map frequently or make sure to work toward a specific landmark.

MAINTAIN THREE POINTS OF CONTACT at all times on steep terrain.

TEST EACH BOULDER before committing your full weight.

TRUST YOUR FEET AND MAXIMIZE THE FRICTION between rubber and rock by keeping your center of gravity low, placing your foot flat with most of the rubber touching, and seeking bare, dry rock.

LEAN IN. On a more vertical climb (75 degrees or greater), keep your weight on your feet but lean in toward the rock.

USE POLES FOR BALANCE ON THE DESCENT. For the descent, take out one trekking pole to use for balance and, facing out, shift your weight back toward the slope to prevent tumbling forward.

FACE THE ROCK WHEN DOWNCLIMBING TRICKY SPOTS for better purchase and to keep your pack from bumping.

GOING DOWN IS HARDER THAN GOING UP. So if you're feeling maxed out on the ascent, you're pushing your comfort level for the descent.

Photo: Ben Fullerton

ROCKY MOUNTAIN NATIONAL PARK
SKY POND

Skirt wind-scoured lakes and scramble up the edge of a waterfall to arrive at Sky Pond, where crumbling spires stretch 2,000 feet into the air.

Alberta Falls

From Glacier Gorge Trailhead, follow the well-traveled path as it winds through a thick pine and fir forest with shivering aspens. Pass the crowds gathered at Alberta Falls (mile 0.6) and climb around boulders to a rocky point above the canyon formed by Glacier Creek. To the north, craggy peaks guard the mouths of Glacier Gorge and Loch Vale.

Enjoy a downhill stretch to the junction for Mills Lake and Loch Vale. Stay right and switchback up to the Loch, a gorgeous tarn with a backdrop of jagged peaks at mile 2.5. Pass the Loch on the northwest side as you continue the gradual climb south up Loch Vale. A half-mile above the Loch's shores, Cathedral Wall rises to your right; pause and search for climbers high on this popular crag.

Timberline Falls rushes below Lake of Glass, and reaching the lake requires a fun scramble up wet (or icy) rocks on its far west side. Top out the climb on the windy aquamarine shores of Lake of Glass, then look for cairns to the right that reveal an easy scramble to a trail on rock through krummholz—stunted, twisted fir and spruce trees—above the lake's western shore.

The Cathedral Spires dominate the skyline at Sky Pond. Find a comfy rock and kick back, have a snack, and break out the binoculars to spy on climbers on the Sharkstooth, Petit Grepon, and Saber (arrayed left to right).

Photo: Ben Fullerton

Text: Jenn Fields

DISTANCE: 8.1 miles

TIME REQUIRED: 1 day

DIFFICULTY: Intermediate

CONTACT: Rocky Mountain National Park, (970) 586-1206; nps.gov/romo

THE PAYOFF: Neck-craning views, waterfalls, peaceful alpine tarns.

TRAILHEAD GPS: 40.310556, -105.640197

FINDING THE TRAILHEAD: From the Beaver Meadows Entrance Station, go south on Bear Lake Road for 9 miles to the Glacier Gorge parking lot on the left.

WAYPOINTS & DIRECTIONS

GPS: 40.310556, -105.640197 From the Glacier Gorge trailhead, hike southwest toward Glacier Creek.

GPS: 40.308323, -105.642139 Cross a bridge over Glacier Creek.

GPS: 40.307717, -105.643265 Bear right at Y junction, following signs for Loch Vale.

GPS: 40.303847, -105.638480 The trail travels past the popular Alberta Falls. Stop to get a look at this photogenic waterfall that pours over massive boulders.

GPS: 40.297473, -105.646108 At the Y junction, veer right and follow signs for Loch Vale.

GPS: 40.294028, -105.654477 Turn right at Y junction.

GPS: 40.288054, -105.664380 Cross Andrews Creek, then continue left at the Y junction. The trail to Andrews Glacier enters on the right.

GPS: 40.283070, -105.665216 Climb up talus and rock ledges; water runs down the rocks along this stretch. (***Note:*** This can get icy in early fall, so exercise caution.)

GPS: 40.282505, -105.665281 Glass Lake is picturesque but windy. Plan to take your snack break elsewhere.

GPS: 40.278658, -105.667813 Sky Pond. Kick back in a wind-protected spot and enjoy the view of the Cathedral Spires to the west. Follow the same route back to the trailhead.

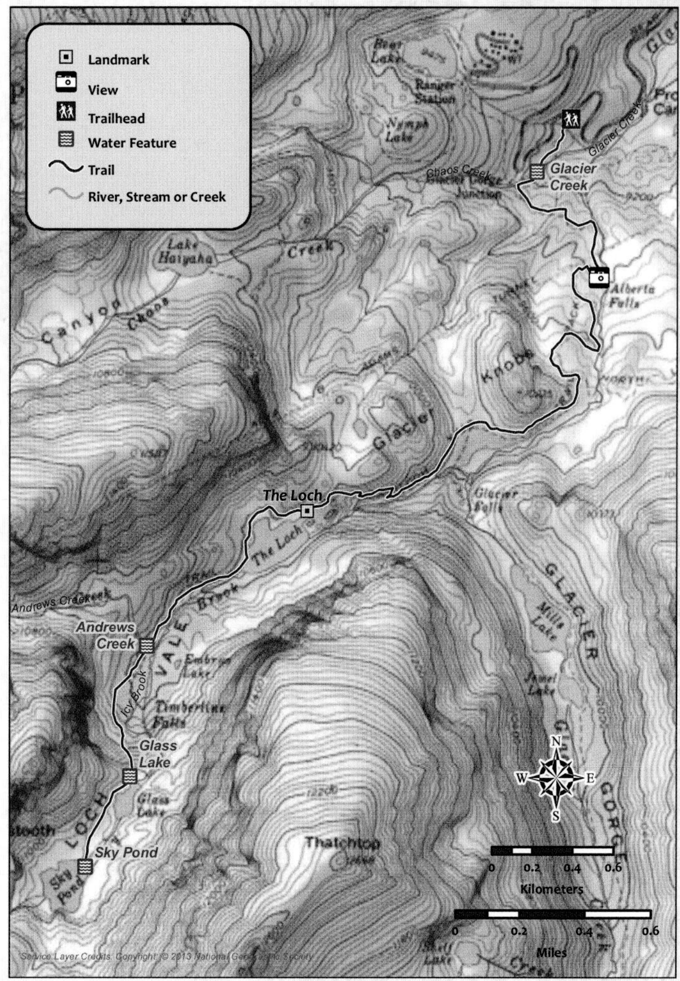

ROCKY MOUNTAIN NATIONAL PARK

CONTINENTAL DIVIDE LOOP

Tour glacial valleys and navigate to off-trail lakes and waterfalls on this 6-day circuit.

Want to see classic Rocky Mountain National Park landmarks and explore hidden pockets of wilderness? Do it on this 54-mile, best-of-both-worlds trek that crisscrosses the Continental Divide, linking the park's lesser-tracked high country west of the Divide with the well-loved lakes and waterfalls on the east side.

Start on the East Inlet Trail, roughly 2 miles from the town of Grand Lake, and hike east along its meandering namesake creek. Less than 0.5 mile in, take the quick 0.2-mile loop on the right to see Adams Falls, which cascades down boulders and plummets through a narrow gorge. As the trail runs up the valley, you'll skirt marshy meadows (look for moose munching in the willows in early morning) and meander through lodgepole pine and quaking aspen groves.

Five miles in, trace the southern shoreline of Lone Pine Lake, a forested pool protected by a cluster of 12,000-foot peaks, and climb east toward the head of the pinched valley. Pick up the user path at mile 6.4, where the maintained trail ends at Lake Verna, and follow it past Spirit and Fourth Lakes. From there, tackle a steep bushwhack, gaining 1,600 feet in 0.9 mile, to wind-blown 12,061-foot Boulder-Grand Pass on the crest of the Continental Divide.

Descend talus-filled gullies on the east side of the Divide and connect with the maintained trail at Thunder Lake; camp in the designated site just north of the lake.

Rise early on day two for a strenuous day of high-altitude cross-country travel that racks up 6,200 feet of elevation change in less than 5 miles. Leave the established trail 0.2 mile east of the Thunder Lake patrol cabin and navigate north past your own private

Photo: Ben Fullerton

Text: Dougald MacDonald

waterfall—watch misty Thunder Falls pour down a short cliff, then flow through a streambed of boulders.

About half an hour from the Thunder Lake Camp, cross the Lion Lake Trail in a spongy meadow and veer east to the granite-lined banks of Castle Lake, one of the most isolated in the park, with prime northwest views of Mount Alice's crags. Next, climb northeast above treeline to a broad, flat saddle on North Ridge, then descend the backside, crossing Hunters Creek at the outlet of a small pond below Keplinger Lake.

Past the lake, maneuver around boulders and bushwhack through stunted trees near the timberline to the base of Keplinger's Couloir on Longs Peak's south face (mile 13). Scramble up the couloir to about 13,500 feet, and traverse northwest on a rock ramp that leads to the 3-foot-wide Narrows ledge. (Don't miss: Scale the cracked granite slabs that rise 450 vertical feet directly in front of you to tag Longs Peak's summit on a 0.1-mile round-trip detour.)

Tightrope walk west, then downclimb boulders in the Trough couloir, angling north at 13,200 feet for a 0.3-mile traverse to the Keyhole notch and the Boulder Field. Sleep above treeline in one of nine campsites.

On day three, descend East Longs Peak Trail, and swing left at mile 20 near the park's eastern boundary to crest Storm Pass and the 11,006-foot pinnacle of Estes Cone. Descend 2.9 miles and spend the third night near beaver ponds at Upper Wind River Campsite.

Day four: Drop into Glacier Basin, and turn left at mile 30, passing the popular Alberta Falls (crowds fade ahead). Less than 1 mile later, turn right at the base of Glacier Knobs, two side-by-side granite domes, and skirt the north shore of the Loch, rimmed by cliffy, granite peaks. Pitch your tent 0.2 mile later in a spruce-fir stand at Andrews Creek Camp.

Hike past Chaos Canyon, Tyndall Gorge, and three more lakes (Dream, Nymph, and Bear) on day five. The last major climb (gaining 2,800 feet in 4 miles) starts at mile 37.7 from the eastern shores of Bear Lake and ascends steadily through shady spruce, fir, and aspen stands. Stop at an overlook midway up a series of tight switchbacks to peer into the depths of Tyndall Gorge; Tyndall Glacier, one of the park's most photographed, sits at the head of the cirque.

Near mile 42, you'll roll across 12,324-foot Flattop Mountain, a broad swath of alpine tundra where you're almost guaranteed the chance to hang with elk. Descend west to pick up North Inlet Trail at a three-way junction, and drop down 3.3 miles to the July Campsite near Hallett Creek. Close out the week with an 8.4-mile descent along North Inlet Creek to your car.

Only have a long weekend? Do an abbreviated version this loop over the Continental Divide by following the Tonahutu Creek Trail to Grand Lake and returning over Flattop Mountain via the North Inlet Trail, following creeks to a long alpine tundra traverse. In autumn, the forest floor beside the trail is covered with a golden carpet of bearberry and other ground cover. Allow 3 to 4 days to make the most of this superb, 34-mile tour of the west side. Get an early start over Flattop in both directions—you're exposed to severe weather for several miles above the treeline.

DISTANCE: 54 miles

TIME REQUIRED: 6 day

DIFFICULTY: Strenuous

CONTACT: Rocky Mountain National Park, (970) 586-1206; nps.gov/romo

THE PAYOFF: Link classic spots with empty wilderness.

TRAILHEAD GPS: 40.239406, -105.799839

FINDING THE TRAILHEAD: From Trail Ridge Road and W. Portal Road in Grand Lake, drive 1.1 miles northeast on W. Portal Road. Turn left on CR 663. Go 0.3 mile to the parking area and drop your shuttle car. Take CR 663 back to W. Portal Road and turn left. Drive southeast 1.2 miles to the East Inlet parking area.

WAYPOINTS & DIRECTIONS

GPS: 40.239406, -105.799839 Hike southeast on the East Inlet Trail from the trailhead at the eastern edge of Grand Lake.

GPS: 40.237117, -105.797497 Turn right onto the short loop trail that leads to a viewing platform near Adams Falls before continuing on the main trail.

GPS: 40.227416, -105.712144 Lake Verna. This long, whale-shaped lake has a sandy beach on its east shores. The maintained trail ends here; follow the path that runs along the northern shore of the lake.

GPS: 40.222993, -105.685043 At the northeast edge of Fourth Lake, start a steep bushwhack, next to a tiny creek, that ends on Boulder-Grand Pass.

GPS: 40.224795, -105.673456 Hike through grass hummocks in this shallow, wet gully near treeline. The remaining stretch across tundra to the pass (directly east of this point) is obvious from here.

GPS: 40.224631, -105.669100 Crest the wind-blown Boulder-Grand Pass, which links the East Inlet valley and Wild Basin.

GPS: 40.224664, -105.668628 Descend this gully (bypassing the permanent snowfield on the east side of the pass) to the banks of Lake of Many Winds.

GPS: 40.225376, -105.665731 This aptly named lake is perched on a gusty bench below Boulder-Grand Pass. From here, descend a boulder-filled gully paralleling the outlet stream to reach the north side of Thunder Lake.

GPS: 40.222305, -105.644982 Pass the Park Service patrol cabin, then turn left at the side trail to the forested Thunder Lake Campsites to camp the first night.

GPS: 40.221797, -105.641828 On the second day, the route leaves Thunder Lake Trail. Bear left (north) at this point (0.2 mile east of the lake) for a cross-country climb that passes Thunder Falls.

GPS: 40.229480, -105.637901 About 30 minutes from the Thunder Lake Campsite, you'll cross the Lion Lake Trail in a wet meadow. Continue cross-country, heading southeast to lily-pad-shaped Castle Lake.

GPS: 40.228983, -105.635058 Scramble through the gap in a small cliff band to reach Castle Lake.

GPS: 40.229022, -105.634747 Granite-lined Castle Lake offers prime views of Mount Alice's east face. From here, skirt the southern edge of the lake, then climb northeast to the broad, flat saddle on North Ridge.

GPS: 40.230571, -105.627141 The climb tops out above the treeline on North Ridge, which forms the southern slopes of Chiefs Head Peak. Next, descend North Ridge, heading north to the small pond below Keplinger Lake.

GPS: 40.235328, -105.626078 Cross Hunters Creek at the outlet of this small pond below Keplinger Lake. Next, climb northeast into the gully adjacent to the Keplinger Lake drainage. (***Note:*** It's tough going ahead through boulders and krummholz for about 0.5 mile.)

GPS: 40.247971, -105.616901 This point marks the entrance to Keplingers Couloir, the gully splitting the south face of Longs Peak. Keep climbing.

GPS: 40.249939, -105.616486 The gully forks here: stay left.

GPS: 40.253148, -105.614512 Below the Notch, follow a wide rock ramp to the northwest to reach the Homestretch.

GPS: 40.253656, -105.614877 Follow the ledges to the left (west) below the Notch here.

GPS: 40.254049, -105.616980 East end of the Narrows. The route traverses west along more exposed ledges.

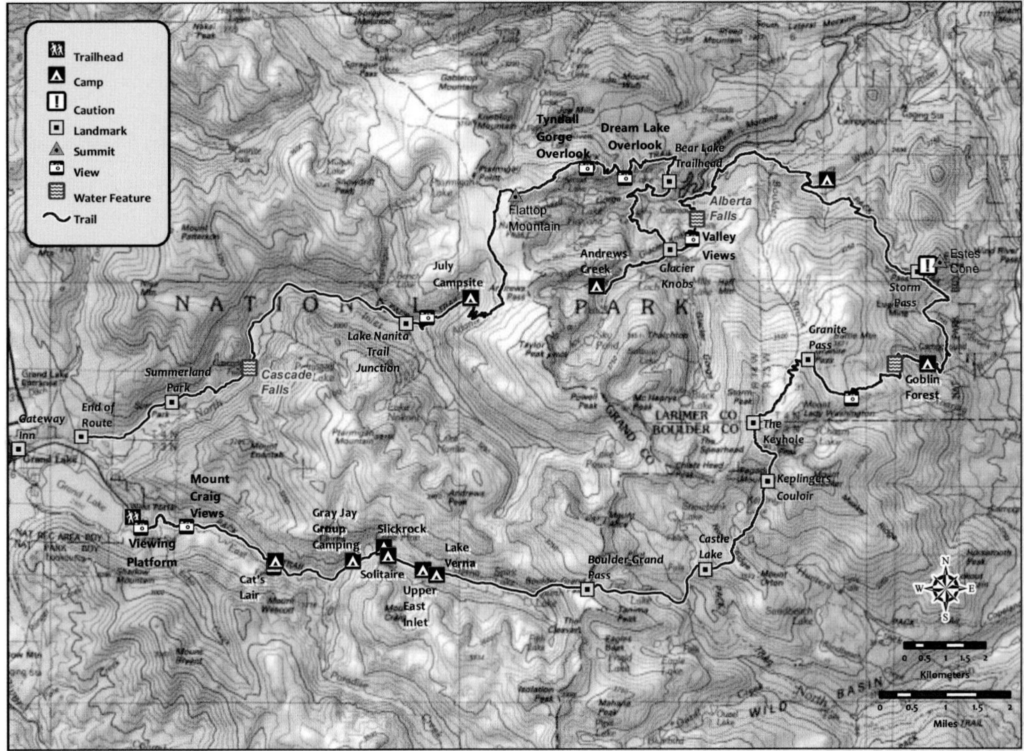

GPS: 40.254393, -105.618718 Top of the Trough, a huge northwest-facing couloir. Watch for icy snow patches. From here, it's a 6-mile descent toward the Longs Peak trailhead.

GPS: 40.256211, -105.620670 Bear right (north) to exit the Trough. Traverse the boulder-covered slopes toward the Keyhole.

GPS: 40.260485, -105.621271 Arrive at the Keyhole, a huge rock notch that rises above the Boulder Field. (**CAUTION:** Follow blazes to avoid cutting east too soon and cliffing out on the False Keyhole.) Ahead, pass a small stone building, then carefully descend the Boulder Field.

GPS: 40.263481, -105.615435 Spend the second night above treeline at the Boulder Field Campsite (nine individual sites). On day three, continue descending East Longs Peak Trail.

GPS: 40.274089, -105.605403 At wind-swept Granite Pass, turn right, heading south. Continue straight at the next three-way junction.

GPS: 40.265675, -105.592732 Turn left at the three-way junction on Mills Moraine.

GPS: 40.275007, -105.564280 Turn left at the three-way junction, heading north toward Storm Pass.

GPS: 40.286978, -105.564742 Turn left at T junction.

GPS: 40.293051, -105.573711 Crest forested Storm Pass, then turn right for a short, steep ascent of mounded, 11,006-foot Estes Cone.

GPS: 40.294306, -105.570867 ***Caution:*** Rocky trail switchbacks at odd places. Watch for random cairns.

GPS: 40.295292, -105.567398 Estes Cone (11,006 feet). The Summit serves up views of dozens of snowy peaks, including Mount Meeker and Longs Peak. Return to Storm Pass and bear right on Storm Pass Trail.

GPS: 40.311284, -105.606916 Turn right on Wind River Trail to reach the night's campsite.

GPS: 40.312336, -105.600044 Spend the third night at Upper Wind River Campsite, marked with a silver metal arrowhead. The two sites are near beaver ponds in a lodgepole pine forest. On day four, backtrack to where you turned onto the Wind River Trail, turn right, and descend Storm Pass Trail into Glacier Basin.

(continued)

GPS: 40.314936, -105.612076 Turn left at the three-way junction with Glacier Creek Trail.

GPS: 40.316791, -105.615717 Continue straight (west) at the intersection with Boulder Brook Trail. The trail climbs moderately for the next 5.1 miles to Chaos Creek.

GPS: 40.307678, -105.643402 Turn left at the three-way Glacier Gorge Junction. The trail climbs southeast toward Alberta Falls.

GPS: 40.306206, -105.638908 A few user-created trails lead to the edge of a deep ravine.

GPS: 40.299625, -105.639596 Admire the valley views at the rest stop just before the three-way junction. Turn right. The trail skirts the base of the Glacier Knobs.

LOCATION: 40.297412, -105.645948 Continue straight at the junction located between Glacier Knobs, two side-by-side granite domes. Head southwest into Loch Vale.

GPS: 40.287890, -105.664347 After crossing Andrews Creek, turn right at the Y junction.

GPS: 40.289445, -105.666976 Night four: Set up your tent at Andrews Creek (one individual site) in a spruce and fir stand. On day five, backtrack to the junction between Glacier Knobs, and turn left (north) onto the Glacier Gorge Trail.

GPS: 40.305189, -105.656707 Cross Chaos Creek, which flows out of Lake Haiyaha at the mouth of Chaos Canyon.

GPS: 40.308549, -105.658340 The trail switchbacks to the right and runs along the southern shore of skinny Dream Lake.

GPS: 40.311996, -105.646291 Pass Bear Lake trailhead, then head north toward Bear Lake for the last big climb of the route to 12,324-foot Flattop Mountain.

GPS: 40.313522, -105.646856 Turn right at three-way junction onto the Flattop Mountain Trail, and begin a steady ascent through a thick conifer forest intermixed with spruce-fir and aspen stands.

GPS: 40.317278, -105.644428 Turn left onto the Flat Top Mountain Trail at the three-way junction.

GPS: 40.316422, -105.653051 Bear left at the three-way junction and continue ascending through the trees.

GPS: 40.315211, -105.665442 As the forest thins, make sure to evaluate the weather before continuing on. During summer months, afternoon lightning storms can hit quickly.

GPS: 40.310348, -105.684187 Just below the Flattop summit, pass a large hitch rack marking the top of Tyndall Glacier, which can be seen to the east. The trail quickly ascends the last few hundred feet to the large flat summit of Flattop Mountain.

GPS: 40.308854, -105.690300 Crest Flattop Mountain (12,324 feet). The summit, largely a flat swath of alpine tundra, has no official summit marker, but hikers generally consider the junction of Flattop Mountain Trail and Tonahutu Trail the top. To continue, descend the Tonahutu Trail toward Ptarmigan Pass.

GPS: 40.309534, -105.694771 Turn left onto North Inlet Trail at this three-way junction. The trail descends south past knee-high cairns with eastern views of Longs Peak.

GPS: 40.286761, -105.702810 Cross Hallett Creek. Spend the fifth night at the July campsite (three individual and one group sites). A bear box is available directly uphill.

GPS: 40.282450, -105.715351 Descend exposed switchbacks.

GPS: 40.281300, -105.721220 Continue straight at this junction with the Lake Nanita Trail.

GPS: 40.271441, -105.766538 Arrive at Cascade Falls. A spur trail full of roots and rocks shoots off to the right and brings hikers to the base of the falls.

GPS: 40.256558, -105.814764 The route ends at the North Inlet trailhead on Rocky Mountain National Park's less-trafficked west side. Pick up your shuttle car and follow Summerland Park and West Portal Roads to the East Inlet trailhead.

A sunny day along the East Longs Peak Trail
Photo: Ben Fullerton

Saguaro cacti in Saguaro National Park, Arizona
Photo: Ian Shive / Tandem Stock

SAGUARO NATIONAL PARK

SAGUARO NATIONAL PARK

DOUGLAS SPRINGS TO MANNING CAMP LOOP

There are more than giant plants here: Arizona's premier cactus preserve conceals a cool mountain escape.

Few people know that southern Arizona has a national park. And that's the way locals like it. Saguaro pulls in 93 percent fewer visitors than the Grand Canyon, most of them day hikers. Yet its sky islands—verdant mountain ranges rising dramatically from the barren valley floor—are as much as 30 degrees cooler than the surrounding desert. Translation: easily attained solitude, a welcome break from triple-digit temps, and no elbowing for choice campsites. On this 3-day, 28.5-mile reverse-lollipop route, you'll accumulate nearly 10,000 feet of elevation gain as you rise and fall through six different ecosystems of cacti and pines rife with mountain lions and bears, and enjoy vistas so long you'll swear you can see the curvature of the earth. Mica Mountain, the highest sky island on the trek, is so close to Tucson and its 515,000 people that it might as well be considered another skyscraper. What's more startling is how easy it is to rise above it all.

Photo: Mike Cavaroc/Tandem Stock

Text: David Pidgeon

Your first day is a quad-buster as you hike 11 miles and several thousand feet into the Rincon Mountain forests. Get a mid-morning start at the Douglas Spring trailhead at the east end of Tucson's East Speedway Boulevard. The landscape bristles with prickly pear, teddy bear cholla, and giant saguaro cactus. Saguaros can live to be more than 150 years old—count their arms; it can take 75 years for just one to form. You'll climb from the sandy valley into rocky grasslands with 8,664-foot Mica Mountain rising to the south and the prominent Santa Catalina Range to the north. After 5.7 miles, fill up with water from Douglas Spring before following the trail steeply past a series of ravines as you move up Mica's northern flank, shaded by piñon and ponderosa pines. At eight miles, you'll reach Cow Head Saddle, at 6,200 feet on Mica's ridgeline. At the trail junction, go straight and descend about 700 feet to your first night's camp, Grass Shack, with three tent sites and an intermittent stream shaded by gnarly oaks and fragrant junipers.

Spend day two filling your memory card with the sweeping vistas of southern Arizona's craggy, copper-colored mountains. In the morning, continue your ascent of Mica by following the Manning Camp Trail eastward a little more than four miles, passing through oaks and piñon as you climb toward the peak. At Devils Bathtub Trail, bear left and ascend steeply one mile to Manning Camp and a reliable spring. After watering up, grab an energy bar, ditch your pack (you'll camp here), and set out to explore Mica's broad summit on a network of short trails. It's an easygoing 5-mile ramble to Spud Rock, Reef Rock, Mica Meadow, and Mica Secondary, each with unforgettable views of saguaro-filled valleys. Return to Manning Camp, the largest backcountry campground in the park, with six sites and a year-round water source.

The final day brings a 12-mile hike back to the desert flats and your car. No worries, though, it's all downhill. Set out from Manning Camp along the Cow Head Saddle Trail, dropping nearly 2,000 feet to the Douglas Spring Trail. Turn right into the canyon you ascended just two days earlier, snap some panoramas of the craggy Santa Catalinas, and arrive at the trailhead in no time. Easy access goes both ways; stop by Tucson McGraw's Cantina (tucsonmcgraws.com), a park staff favorite on Houghton Road, for margaritas and ribs. It's only 10 minutes away.

DISTANCE: 28.5 miles

TIME REQUIRED: 3 days

DIFFICULTY: Strenuous

CONTACT: Saguaro National Park, (520) 733-5153; nps.gov/sagu

THE PAYOFF: Sky islands and wild deserts a stone's throw from Tucson.

TRAILHEAD GPS: N32 14.120 W110 41.220

FINDING THE TRAILHEAD: In Tucson, take East Speedway Boulevard 17.5 miles to the Douglas Spring trailhead.

WAYPOINTS & DIRECTIONS

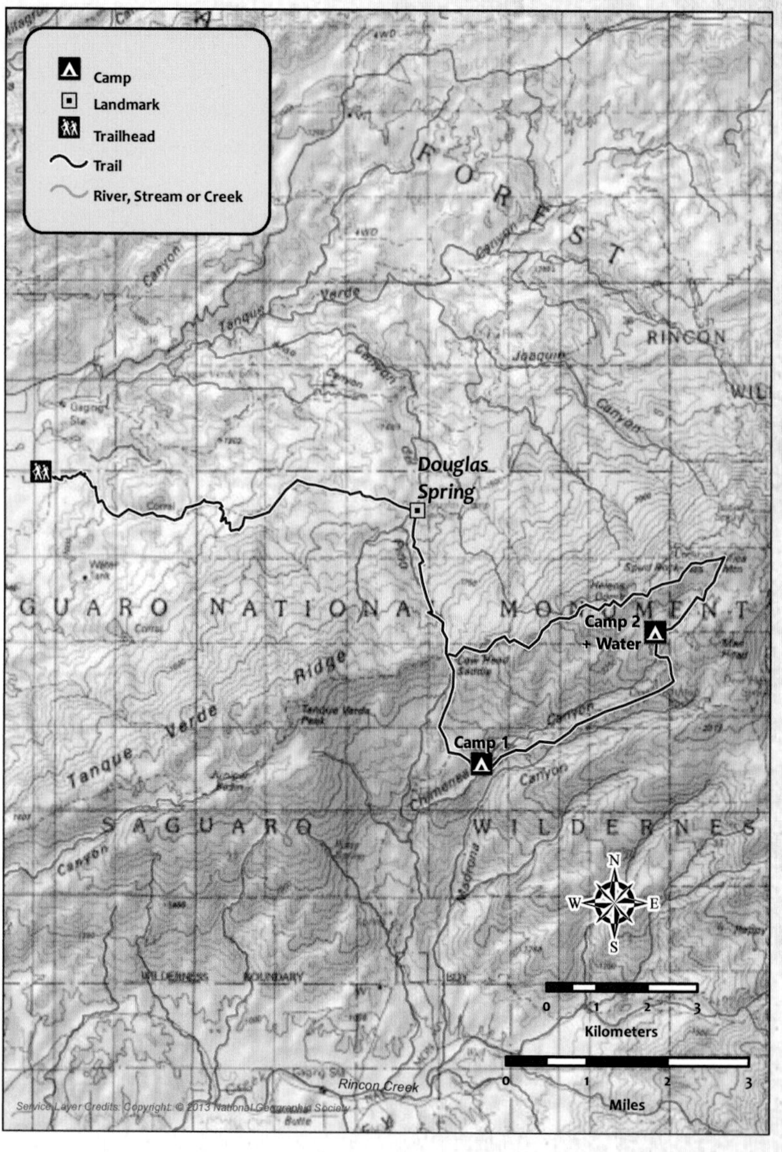

GPS: N32 14.120 W110 41.220
Head east from the Douglas Spring trailhead. You'll climb from the sandy valley into rocky grasslands with 8,664-foot Mica Mountain rising to the south and the prominent Santa Catalina Range to the north.

GPS: 32.228558, -110.606060
Fill up with water from Douglas Spring before following the trail steeply past a series of ravines as you move up Mica's northern flank. At 8 miles, you'll reach Cow Head Saddle on Mica's ridgeline. At the trail junction, go straight and descend about 700 feet to Grass Shack Campsite.

GPS: 32.185056, -110.592628
Spend the first night at the three-site Grass Shack Campsite. In the morning, continue your ascent of Mica by following the Manning Camp Trail eastward a little more than 4 miles, passing through oaks and piñon as you climb toward the peak. At Devils Bathtub Trail, bear left and ascend steeply 1 mile to Manning Camp and a reliable spring.

GPS: 32.207572, -110.555978
You will spend the night here at Manning Camp, so get hydrated and ditch your pack before heading to the summit of Mica. Set out for the summits of Spud Rock, Reef Rock, Mica Meadow, and Mica Secondary, each with unforgettable views of saguaro-filled valleys. Return to Manning Camp.

GPS: 32.213818, -110.567694 Set out from Manning Camp along the Cow Head Saddle Trail, dropping nearly 2,000 feet to the Douglas Spring Trail. Turn right into the canyon you ascended just two days earlier, and arrive at the trailhead in no time.

HOW TO UPGRADE YOUR CAMP KITCHEN

No matter how great a trail chef you are, if your kitchen is a sty, mea time will be a drag. Do it up right, though, and you can turn any patch of ground into a five-star establishment.

Don't Make These Mistakes

PUTTING A TOO-BIG POT ON A TOO-SMALL STOVE. It'll probably fall over.

GETTING UP AND DOWN to retrieve more water or ingredients, which can lead to spills and hassle.

DUMPING OUT THE CONTENTS of your bear canister or food bag—you'll lose things.

BRINGING HOME UTENSILS. Get some camping-specific ones, they're lighter.

CLEANING UP AT THE END instead of as you go. You'll lose stuff in the dark.

Upgrade Your Camp Kitchen in 6 Easy Steps

1. SELECT YOUR SITE. You want a flat, fire-safe area; avoid brush. In bear country, go at least 200 feet downwind of your tent.

2. SET IT UP. If possible, go to a large, flat rock. If needed, haul one to your kitchen area and put it back when you're done. Think of it as your backcountry countertop—this is your do-it-all space for food prep. Deadfall and bear canisters make good chairs if you didn't bring one. Arrange your kitchen equipment into a half moon around your seat so everything is within arm's reach (Including a garbage bag).

3. FETCH WATER. Using a dromedary bag or folding bucket, collect all the water you'll need for a meal at once. For one person, that's a gallon to cook dinner, clean dishes, and top up bottles. For each additional person, add a couple of liters.

4. PREP. Make sure all of your ingredients are at hand before starting. Next,chop, slice, and measure everything and set it aside on or near your countertop so it's ready to go. Erect a windbreak around your stove before lighting it. If you didn't bring one, jury-rig one out of packs, logs, boots, whatever.

5. COOK. Now the fun part. Refer to the tips above to ensure your camp kitchen continues to get good reviews.

6. CLEAN. Not the fun part. But since you cooked, make someone else do it.

Photo: Ben Fullerton

Text: Maren Horjus

Heather Lake in Sequoia-Kings Canyon National Park, California
Photo: iStockPhoto.com / David Parsons

SEQUOIA-KINGS CANYON

NATIONAL PARKS

SEQUOIA-KINGS CANYON NATIONAL PARKS

RAE LAKES VIA BAXTER AND SAWMILL PASSES

Explore a granite wonderland, cross two little-used passes, and score High Sierra solitude on this life-list point-to-point hike.

Nothing against John Muir and his beloved Yosemite Valley, but backpackers in the know hit the southern Sierra's east side for the best high-country experience in the Range of Light. The peaks are bigger, the people fewer, and there are so many lakes above the treeline that, when you gaze down from above, it's like looking into a liquid sky.

This 43.7-mile route, joining the Baxter Pass and Sawmill Pass Trails, leads through the best of it. You'll climb to granite-rimmed alpine basins, camp in secluded sites above treeline, and, yes, stroll 11 miles on the John Muir Trail. Start from the Baxter Pass trailhead; it's 1,500 feet higher than Sawmill, and the initial climb is more shaded. Camp in a site west of Summit Meadow at mile 6 to break up the 6,300-foot ascent.

The next day, finish the climb to 12,300-foot Baxter Pass—watch for rare California bighorn sheep. Then descend and detour south on the John Muir Trail to the Rae Lakes Basin, where you'll camp in a cirque beneath an arc of 12,000- and 13,000-footers. Planning tip: This spot is so exquisite, it demands a layover day and a dip in Dollar Lake (enter from the sandy beach at the north end). Hike to Sixty Lakes Basin during your layover at Rae Lakes: Turn off the John Muir Trail on the northwest shore of the upper Rae Lake onto an unmaintained use trail; it's 4 miles round-trip. The solitude and scenery ratchet up a notch in this hidden paradise, and you'll linger to count every single tarn in your Sierra kingdom.

Next, backtrack north 2 miles on the John Muir Trail to the unmarked Sawmill Trail junction (at 10,346 feet, less than 1 mile south of Twin Lakes). Here, the John Muir Trail swings north below the west face of 12,372-foot Mount Cedric Wright at mile 24. Cut south and climb 2 miles to Woods Lake. Camp near the lake. On your last day, finish the climb to 11,347-foot Sawmill Pass, then work through a 10-mile, 6,800-foot drop to the trailhead.

Photo: Ethan Welty/Tandem Stock

Text: Mike Lanza

DISTANCE: 43.7 miles

TIME REQUIRED: 4–6 days

DIFFICULTY: Strenuous

CONTACT: Sequoia-Kings Canyon National Park, (559) 565-3341; nps.gov/seki

THE PAYOFF: Arguably the best scenery in the Sierra Nevada.

TRAILHEAD GPS: 36.795815, -118.582724

FINDING THE TRAILHEAD: From US 395, 8.6 miles north of Independence, link Black Rock Springs, Tinemaha, and Division Creek Powerhouse Roads and go 3.5 miles to the Sawmill trailhead, where you leave a shuttle. Then, from US 395, 2.3 miles north of Independence, drive 5.8 miles west on Fish Hatchery Road (bearing right at a fork).

WAYPOINTS & DIRECTIONS

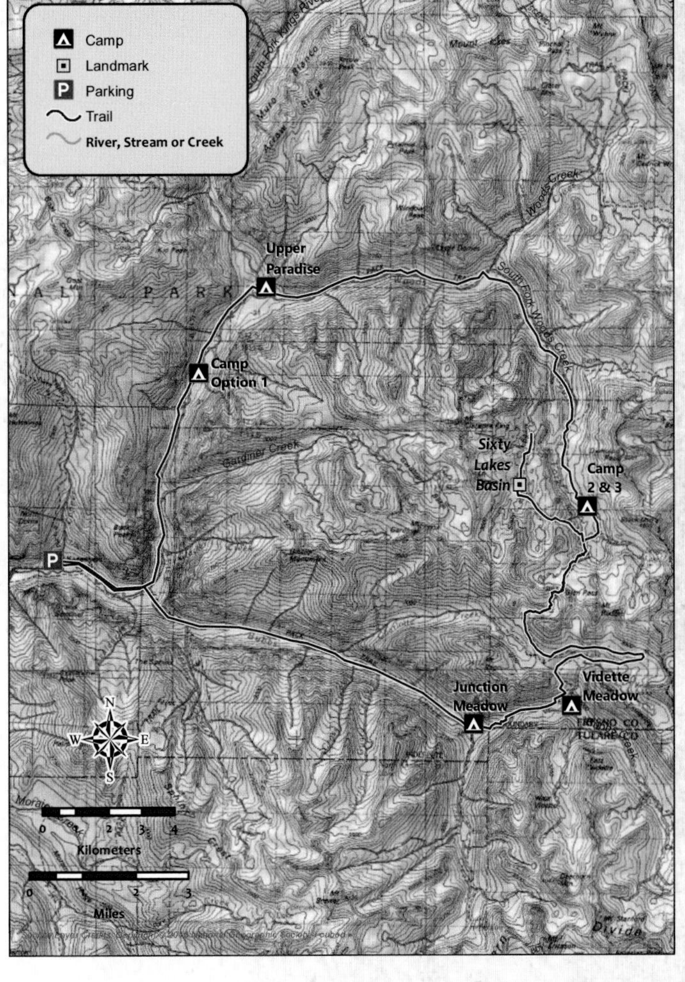

GPS: 36.795815, -118.582724 Hike west from the Baxter Pass trailhead along the north fork of Oak Creek.

GPS: 36.833745, -118.359103 Camp the first night at Summit Meadow Campsite. In the morning, continue west before turning north for the steep climb of Baxter Pass.

GPS: 36.835393, -118.376398 Baxter Pass. On the descent, contour counterclockwise around the basin of Baxter Pass and then the north shore of Baxter Lake before continuing west.

GPS: 36.812480, -118.401504 Spend nights two and three at this site in the Rae Lakes Basin. It's the perfect place to base your explorations of this beautiful area.

GPS: 36.834947, -118.407598 Go swimming from the sandy beach at the north end of Dollar Lake.

GPS: 36.818012, -118.424850 (***Side Trip:*** Hike to Sixty Lakes Basin during your layover at Rae Lakes: Take a sharp right off the John Muir Trail on the northwest shore of the upper Rae Lake onto an unmaintained use trail headed northwest. It's 4 miles round-trip.)

GPS: 36.902823, -118.400044 To continue on the route, head north from the Rae Lakes Basin Campsite and veer left at the fork north of Dollar Lake, continuing on the John Muir Trail to the Sawmill Pass Trail Junction. Turn right at the junction, diverging from the northbound John Muir Trail, to head south to Woods Lake.

GPS: 36.889335, -118.382063 Spend the night on the North Shore of Woods Lake.

GPS: 36.882779, -118.364811 On your last day, finish the climb to 11,347-foot Sawmill Pass, then trek northeast through a 10-mile, 6,800-foot drop to the Sawmill Trailhead—passing Sawmill Lake, Sawmill Meadow, and the Hogsback on your way.

GPS: 36.938985, -118.289752 Sawmill trailhead and your shuttle car.

SEQUOIA-KINGS CANYON NATIONAL PARKS
HIGH SIERRA TRAIL

Spend a week (or more) trekking from the Giant Forest's sequoias to Mount Whitney.

Summit of Mt. Whitney

Photo: Jonathan Dorn

So you crave iconic Sierra Nevada scenery? Judging from the crowds on the Pacific Crest and John Muir Trails, you're not alone. But you very well could be in Sequoia National Park's often empty backcountry on the rugged 72-mile High Sierra Trail. Starting at 6,700 feet on the southern fringe of the Giant Forest, you'll hike through heaven-kissing groves of giant sequoias. A week of climbing through scoured domes and fins reminiscent Yosemite's Cathedral Range later, you'll stand atop the hike's 14,495-foot exclamation point: Mount Whitney.

Head out from Crescent Meadow (near the park's Lodgepole visitor center) through dense stands of sequoia and sugar pine, whose football-size cones litter the path. Savor this stretch, since it's the only one on the High Sierra Trail where these massive conifers flourish. Later, you'll reach Eagle View, a lookout over a 1,000-foot gorge cradling the Middle Fork Kaweah River. After traversing seven major creeks coursing down the granite ledges of Alta Bluffs, make camp among the pines at Bearpaw Meadow. Over the next few days, you'll whack through chest-high bracken ferns, grind up the Precipice Bench to the snow-ringed rock gardens of Kaweah Gap (10,700 feet), cross the Great Western Divide, climb the Chagoopa Plateau, and drop into the deep, U-shaped trough of Kern Canyon.

Text: Andrew Matranga

Around day five, you'll join the John Muir Trail for the ascent to Guitar Lake and campsites below Whitney. Get a predawn start for the summit march. You'll rejoin the masses atop Whitney, but the vantage from the rooftop of the southern Sierra deserves an awe-struck assembly. Around Whitney, spot rosy finches and purple sky pilots dotting the gray granite tableau.

Summer, from the last week in July to early September, is idyllic. Afternoon thunderstorms aren't as likely, and temperatures stay between 40 and 70 degrees. Want to see flaming red Indian paintbrush or bright pink shooting star wildflowers? Go in early July, when blooms carpet the entire meadow in Big Arroyo.

DISTANCE: 72 miles

TIME REQUIRED: 7–10 days

DIFFICULTY: Strenuous

CONTACT: Sequoia-Kings Canyon National Park, (559) 565-3341; nps.gov/seki

THE PAYOFF: Tag the biggest trees and tallest peaks in the country.

TRAILHEAD GPS: 36.554758, -118.748925

FINDING THE TRAILHEAD: Go east on Highway 198 to the park entrance. Head to the Lodgepole visitor center for a backcountry permit, then backtrack to Crescent Meadows to begin.

WAYPOINTS & DIRECTIONS

GPS: 36.554758, -118.748925 Head east from the trailhead in Crescent Meadows.

GPS: 36.553379, -118.747959 Turn right onto the High Sierra Trail.

GPS: 36.554430, -118.742101 Veer right at three-way junction; wrap around a south-facing slope at Eagle View.

GPS: 36.570252, -118.721480 Turn right at the Y. Continue east-northeast along the steep slopes and bluffs of the south side of Alta Meadow and Alta Peak.

GPS: 36.569633, -118.679382 Keep right at Y, toward Bearpaw Meadow. Pass two forks of Nine Mile Creek and descend to Buck Canyon, well known for floods, avalanches, and rockslides. (***Note:*** The Buck Creek crossing may be hazardous early in the summer. Check on conditions when you pick up your permit.)

GPS: 36.566960, -118.623440 Go left at the Y to the Bearpaw Meadow High Sierra Camp. Camp here for the first night.

GPS: 36.565375, -118.620715 Descend on High Sierra Trail from the A-frame Ranger Station.

GPS: 36.572665, -118.598871 Cross bridge and go right at the T.

GPS: 36.565392, -118.587005 Wet crossing of Hamilton River just above lower Hamilton Falls. Climb switchbacks past Lower Hamilton Lake.

GPS: 36.564358, -118.578165 Hamilton Lake has good camping, with a pit toilet and bear lockers, but no fires are allowed. To continue to Kaweah Gap, cross the stream and head up switchbacks.

GPS: 36.552465, -118.560548 At Upper Precipice Lake, the trail enters an alpine zone of snowfields, ponds, and meadows, and might be faint or snowed over.

GPS: 36.533502, -118.541493 Knee-deep crossing of Arroyo Creek.

GPS: 36.521156, -118.533640 Head left at Y; the Big Arroyo Junction Campsites are located here.

GPS: 36.492215, -118.470554 Head right at the Y for the scenic south High Sierra Trail route along the lip of the Chagoopa Plateau; the left trail follows a more direct route across the Chagoopa Plateau, rejoining the Moraine Lake Trail at Sky Parlor Meadow.

GPS: 36.462573, -118.454676 The Moraine Lake Campsite features a bear locker and six sites with fire rings.

GPS: 36.462607, -118.437166 Turn right at the T.

GPS: 36.455531, -118.413348 Take a left at the T to head north to Kern Hot Springs through a marshy forest.

GPS: 36.480068, -118.405220 Small campsite along Kern River with bear locker.

GPS: 36.577386, -118.413348 Large campsite at Junction Meadow that includes a bear locker and multiple fire rings.

GPS: 36.578617, -118.414116 Turn right at the three-way junction and ascend Wallace Creek to Mount Whitney.

GPS: 36.591997, -118.416824 Turn right at T heading up Wallace Creek toward Mount Whitney. Leave Jeffrey pine stands and cross a steep, rocky slope, climbing out of the Kern Trench.

GPS: 36.594289, -118.371098 Head right at the T, joining the John Muir Trail, and cross Wallace Creek.

GPS: 36.559084, -118.359017 Turn left to follow the John Muir Trail east at the three-way junction.

GPS: 36.563841, -118.349533 Head right to camp at Crabtree, or continue left toward the Whitney Zone. (***Note:*** pack out human waste in WAG chemical bags, provided in the box at the trail junction.)

GPS: 36.564400, -118.348015 Bear locker near Ranger Station.

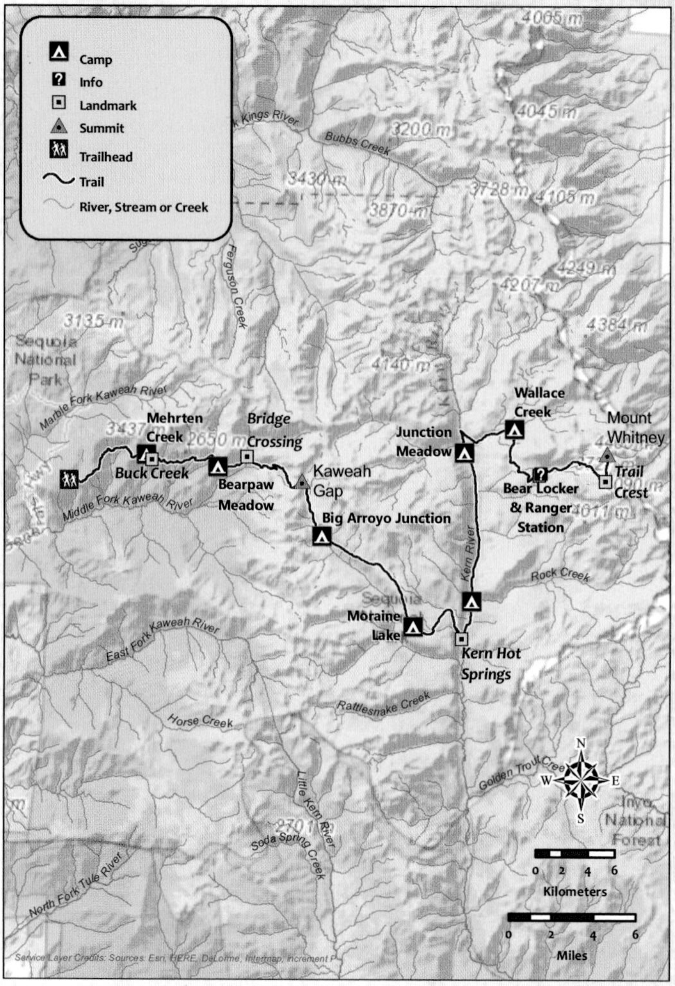

GPS: 36.571768, -118.312690 Guitar Lake Campsite nestles below Whitney. No fires allowed, and bear cans required by law. Last water source before the summit, so top off bladders for the climb.

GPS: 36.560428, -118.293078 Reach Trail Crest and drop packs for the final push to the Big Hill; pass Mount Muir and "windows" that drop for thousands of feet, giving big views east toward the Owens Valley.

GPS: 36.578489, -118.292263 Mount Whitney (14,505 feet) is the highest point in the Lower 48. Sign the summit register and either head down to Whitney Portal or retrace the route to Giant Forest.

SEQUOIA-KINGS CANYON NATIONAL PARKS

REDWOOD MEADOW

Redwood Meadow's massive trees and wild countryside have changed little since John Muir passed through 100 years ago.

Sequoia giganteum. Sierra redwoods. California big trees. Lie at the base of one of these forest giants, staring up at the massive expanse of cinnamon-red bark, and consider John Muir's introduction to the stately sequoias: "When I entered this sublime wilderness, the day was nearly done, the trees with rosy, glowing countenances seemed to be hushed and thoughtful and one naturally walked softly and awestricken among them."

To re-create Muir's emotional experience, head for Sequoia National Park in the southern Sierra Nevada. Deep in the park's backcountry, at Redwood Meadow, you can still experience the big trees as Muir did—in the wilderness, full of wonder, without the carloads of camera-wielding tourists. Established in 1890, Sequoia is the nation's second-oldest national park (managed jointly with adjacent Kings Canyon National Park) and encompasses 628 square miles of superlative Sierra scenery. The highest mountain in the Lower 48 (Whitney), one of the deepest canyons in the United States (Kings), and biggest trees in

Photo: Aidan Klimenko

Text: Dennis Lewon

Sequoias are amongst the largest trees in the world

the world (sequoias) are all within these parks' boundaries. Most backpackers zero in on the first two, which means you can walk slack-jawed among the sequoias as everyone else waits in line for permits.

The most direct route to Redwood Meadow is a 13-mile trail along the Middle Fork of the Kaweah River. It starts low (3,300 feet) and ascends gradually past oaks and chaparral, sneaks up into the shade of sugar pines and incense cedars, then pops through an invisible door at 6,000 feet into a towering grove of sequoias. On the way, it skirts the sheer-sided Kaweah River Gorge and serves up endless views of the 12,000-foot crest of the Great Western Divide. Snow-encrusted Eagle Scout Peak and Lippincott Mountain loom over the Kaweah's headwaters, a pleasant reminder of where you're heading as you toil through the initial miles of manzanita and buck brush.

The Middle Fork Trail is the least crowded of the routes, especially in spring and fall. You can continue on into the Sierra high country from Redwood Meadow: Take the High Sierra Trail east through Bearpaw Meadow to Hamilton Lakes, Precipice Lake, and 10,700-foot Kaweah Gap. Or head south along Cliff Creek and over 11,600-foot Black Rock Pass. Both destinations can be reached in a day, but the hikes to these passes are arduous.

Photo: iStockPhoto.com / Best Travel Photography

DISTANCE: 26 miles

TIME REQUIRED: 2–4 days

DIFFICULTY: Strenuous

CONTACT: Sequoia-Kings Canyon National Park, (559) 565-3341; nps.gov/seki

THE PAYOFF: See the big trees as Muir did.

TRAILHEAD GPS: 36.554758, -118.748925

FINDING THE TRAILHEAD: Exit CA 99 at Visalia and drive east on CA 198 for 40 miles to the park entrance. Stop at the Foothills visitor center to pick up a free wilderness permit, then continue for 6 miles to the signed road for Buckeye Campground. Turn right (east) and continue 0.5 mile to the signed fork. Stay left and drive 1 mile to the Middle Fork trailhead.

WAYPOINTS & DIRECTIONS

GPS: 36.521570, -118.763151 Head east from the Middle Fork trailhead.

GPS: 36.546811, -118.689852
Side Trip: Turn right to descend into the Kaweah River Gorge.

GPS: 36.538881, -118.684187 The Kaweah River is an excellent spot for trout fishing and water refills. Backtrack to rejoin main trail.

GPS: 36.539984, -118.650370
Side Trip: Turn left here to reach Bearpaw Meadow and eventually the high country of Kaweah Gap.

GPS: 36.530467, -118.636208 Camp under the towering grove of sequoia trees in Redwood Meadow. Either retrace the route back to the trailhead, or press on for a side trip to Black Rock Pass.

GPS: 36.528398, -118.635092
Side Trip: Head south along Cliff Creek for high-country access to Black Rock Pass.

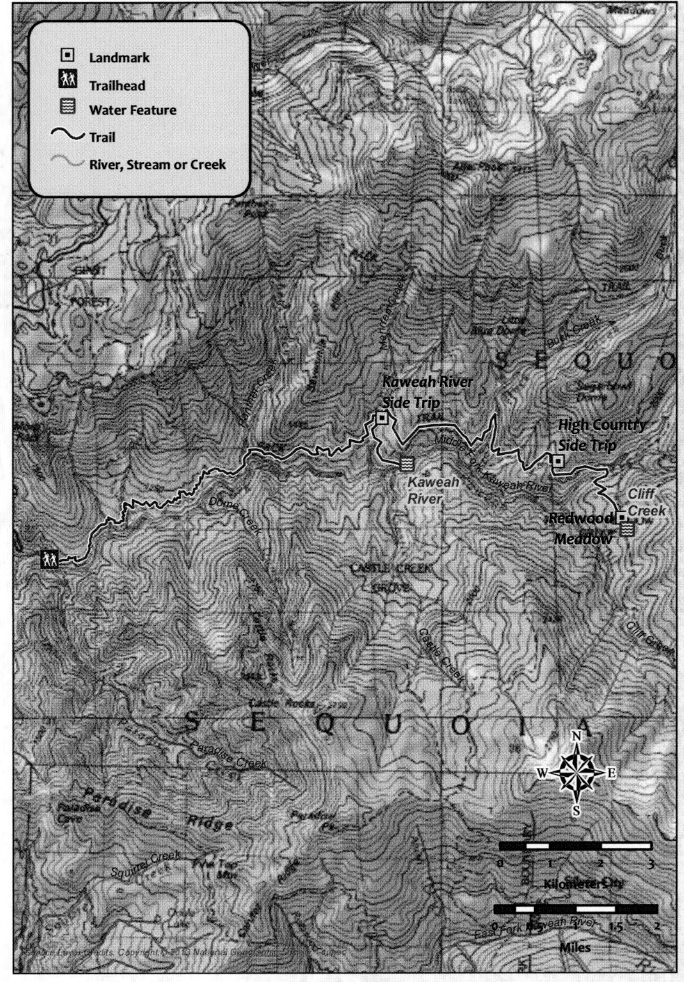

Pear Lake

SEQUOIA-KINGS CANYON NATIONAL PARKS

GIANT FOREST LOOP

This rolling, 7-mile hike travels through some of the largest trees on earth.

You'll be massaging the kinks out of your neck after gaping up at some of the world's largest sequoias. Tourists head back to the gift shop after snapping portraits at super-size General Sherman, only 0.3 mile in. All that gawking is understandable: Earth's bulkiest single organism is 275 feet tall and 100 feet around. But this is where the fun—and this 7-mile loop—begin. At mile 3.9, go right at T junction and pass a hollowed-out sequoia that was made into a seasonal shelter in 1858 by cattleman Hale Tharp. Got a day? Tour the wide meadows and enormous forests. Got two? At mile 1.1, go east on the 13-mile Alta Trail and summit 11,204-foot Alta Peak. Your first choice campsite comes at Mehrten Meadow, just 3.6 miles east down the Alta Peak Trail.

Photo: Eileen K. Seto / Tandem Stock

DISTANCE: 7 miles

TIME REQUIRED: 1–2 days

DIFFICULTY: Easy

CONTACT: Sequoia-Kings Canyon National Park, (559) 565-3341; nps.gov/seki

THE PAYOFF: General Sherman, the most massive tree on earth.

TRAILHEAD GPS: 36.584899, -118.749536

FINDING THE TRAILHEAD: Parking is off of the General's Highway; follow the signs to General Sherman.

WAYPOINTS & DIRECTIONS

GPS: 36.584899, -118.749536 From the trailhead, follow the signs to General Sherman.

GPS: 36.581246, -118.751607 General Sherman, the world's largest tree by volume. Continue 3.6 miles and go right at the T junction.

GPS: 36.561635, -118.741307 Pass Tharp's Log, a hollowed-out sequoia made into a seasonal shelter in 1858 by cattleman Hale Tharp.

GPS: 36.567012, -118.748345 Tour the wide Circle Meadow, looking for flowers in the spring, before heading back to the trailhead through enormous forests.

GPS: 36.590688, -118.663373
Side Trip: If you have an extra day, head east for magnificent views from the top of Alta Peak. Head east on the Alta Peak Trail north of the Congress Group. Continue past Panther Meadow, Panther Gap, Mehrten Meadow and Tharp's Rock on the way to the Summit. Head back to Mehrten Meadow to spend the night.

GPS: 36.582452, -118.691096 Camp here and retrace your steps back to the trailhead in the morning.

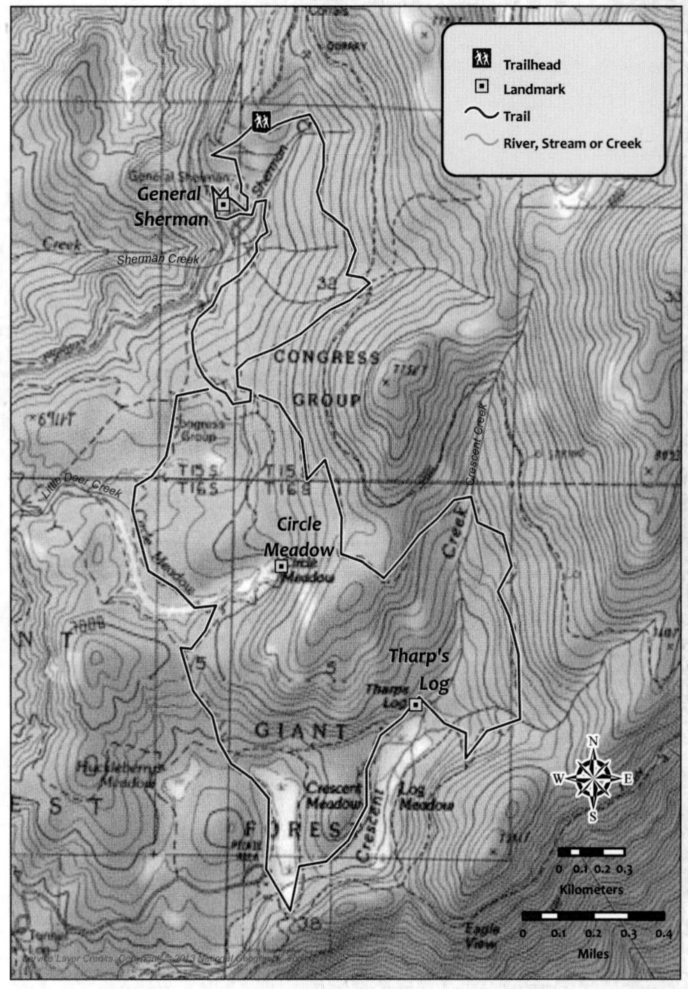

View from Mary's Rock in Shenandoah National Park, Virginia
Photo: iStockPhoto.com / P_L_Photography

SHENANDOAH

NATIONAL PARK

Fall in Shenandoah

SHENANDOAH NATIONAL PARK

RIPRAP TRAIL

Gurgling mountain streams and peaceful vistas line this 9-mile loop in the southern half of the park.

Want all that Shenandoah's lonesome ridges have to offer? Try the Riprap Trail. Located in southern Shenandoah National Park, this 9.1-mile loop—with an optional Appalachian Trail extension—highlights the park's two best features. Start at the Riprap Trail parking area off of Skyline Drive, tracking the AT south. Turn right onto Wildcat Ridge and descend 1,500 feet. Turn right onto the Riprap Trail and ahead pass the park's largest swimming holes and a temple of cliffs called Calvary and Chimney Rocks. Continue on Riprap to the AT. Turn right and close the loop back at your car. Optional: To tag a peak, take the AT south to 2,981-foot Turk Mountain, adding 6 out-and-back miles to the circuit.

DISTANCE: 9.1 mile

TIME REQUIRED: 1 day

DIFFICULTY: Easy

CONTACT: Shenandoah National Park, (540) 999-3500; nps.gov/shen

THE PAYOFF: Swimming holes, airy cliffs, quiet forests.

TRAILHEAD GPS: 38.1783066, -78.7644043

FINDING THE TRAILHEAD: Take I-66 W to I-81 S to I-64 E. Continue to Rockfish Gap, then head north on Skyline Drive. Go 15 miles to the Riprap Trail parking area.

WAYPOINTS & DIRECTIONS

GPS: 38.178307, -78.764404 From the Riprap trailhead, follow the spur trail north for 200 yards before turning left to head south on the Appalachian Trail.

GPS: 38.153050, -78.774048 Turn right at four-way onto Wildcat Ridge Trail, and begin the 1,500 foot descent.

GPS: 38.163185, -78.798614 Turn right at the T onto Riprap Trail.

GPS: 38.170399, -78.793205 At the old location of Riprap Shelter, look for swimming holes in the nearby creek. Then continue straight to Cold Spring Hollow.

GPS: 38.183765, -78.786156 The trail gently moves north-northwest to an airy ridgeline.

GPS: 38.186466, -78.776764 Chimney Rock. A big rocky outcrop looks over Shenandoah Valley.

GPS: 38.182667, -78.762032 Turn right at the T and continue 0.4 mile to parking lot.

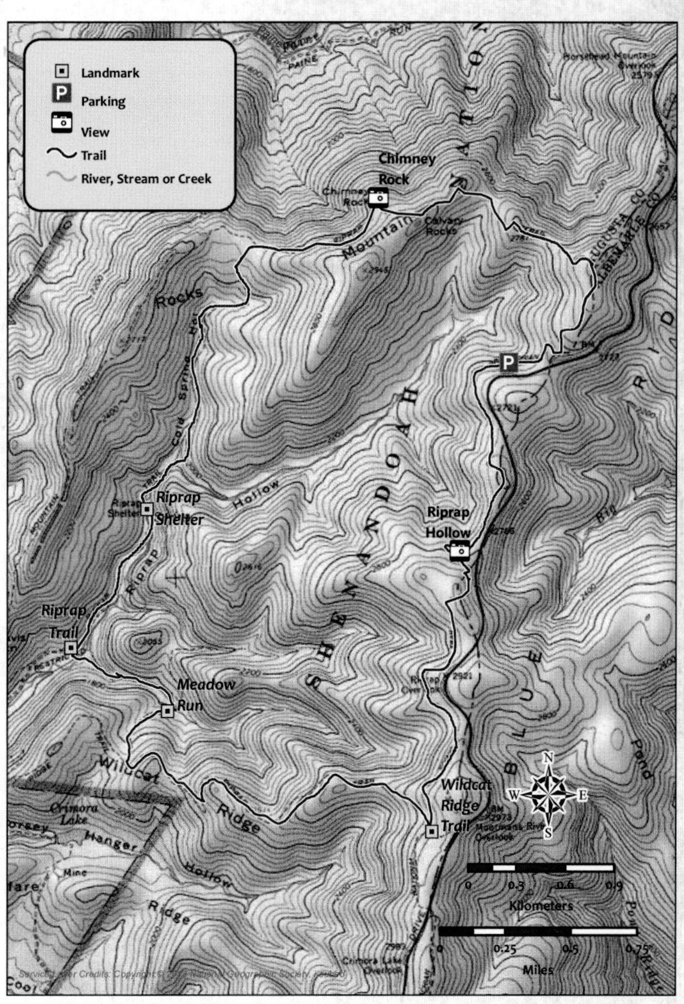

SHENANDOAH NATIONAL PARK

OLD RAG MOUNTAIN

The trail up Old Rag Mountain

Navigate switchbacks, boulder scrambles, and rock mazes on a loop that ascends Old Rag Mountain, one of Shenandoah's most famous peaks.

Weaving around car-size boulders to the summit of 3,268-foot Old Rag Mountain is the quintessential Shenandoah thrill. Its airy precipice is also the best place for 360-degree leaf-peeping; plan to go on November's first weekend. But unknown it isn't, so pack a headlamp and set out on this 8.8-mile circuit three hours before sunset to enjoy a crowd-free summit. Take the Ridge Trail up shady switchbacks to an open ridgeline and 2 miles of scrambling to the big whoa—a sweeping panorama of mountainsides ablaze in fall color. Descend via the Saddle Trail and Weakley Hollow Fire Road to close the loop.

Photo: iStockPhoto.com / carrollmt

Text: Ivan Levin

DISTANCE: 8.6 miles

TIME REQUIRED: 1 day

DIFFICULTY: Intermediate

CONTACT: Shenandoah National Park, (540) 999-3500; nps.gov/shen

THE PAYOFF: Climb Shenandoah's most famous mountain.

TRAILHEAD GPS: 38.570816, -78.286758

FINDING THE TRAILHEAD: From Sperryville, take VA 231 south for 7.3 miles. Turn right on Sharp Rock Road. Go 1.2 miles, and turn right on Nethers Road. Continue 2.2 miles to the lower parking lot and trail-fee station. The upper parking lot and trailhead is 0.5 mile up the road.

WAYPOINTS & DIRECTIONS

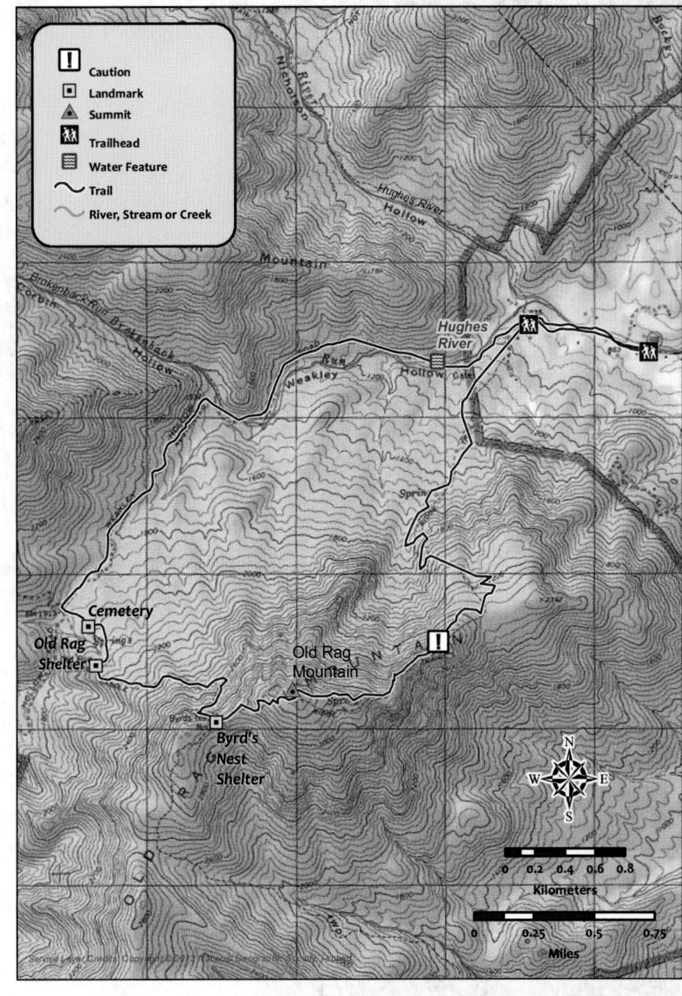

GPS: 38.572609, -78.295845 From the Weakley Hollow Trailhead, in the upper parking lot, head southwest on the blue-blazed Ridge Trail.

GPS: 38.562550, -78.304153 The first switchback cuts to the left. Eight more switchbacks remain on the ascent to the summit.

GPS: 38.554413, -78.303528 This is where the hike to Old Rag turns into a scramble over midsize boulders and through narrow, rocky passages. There are two rock mazes to navigate in this section. Blue blazes and arrows are painted on the boulders.

GPS: 38.551929, -78.314896 Old Rag Mountain (3,268 feet). Go past the cement post to get unrivaled panoramic views of Shenandoah. Pick up the blue-blazed Saddle Trail to begin your descent.

GPS: 38.550186, -78.320831 Pass Byrd's Nest Shelter (day use only). Continue downhill on the Saddle Trail.

GPS: 38.553669, -78.329887 Old Rag Shelter (day use only). Continue on the Saddle Trail as it curves to the right.

GPS: 38.555962, -78.330368 Just off the right side of the trail is a hidden cemetery dating back to the 1700s. Look closely: At first glance, the headstones look like small rocks coming out of the ground.

GPS: 38.557156, -78.332321 Turn right at T junction onto the Weakley Hollow Fire Road. The road is marked with yellow blazes as the gradual descent to the parking lot continues.

GPS: 38.568890, -78.320816 Go straight on the fire road at three-way junction.

GPS: 38.568314, -78.320007 Continue straight on the fire road at the three-way junction. Cross a bridge over the Hughes River and follow the fire road to the trailhead.

"Badland" hills in Theodore Roosevelt National Park, North Dakota
Photo: Mike Cavaroc / Tandem Stock

THEODORE ROOSEVELT
NATIONAL PARK

THEODORE ROOSEVELT NATIONAL PARK

MAAH DAAH HEY TRAIL

Beautiful solitude

You won't have a lot of company in North Dakota's colorful, twisting badlands—which is why hiking the Maah Daah Hey Trail is so good.

Teddy Roosevelt once called North Dakota's legendary badlands his hero land, and later claimed that his experiences there prepared him for the rigors of presidency. If that's so, maybe we should require all presidential candidates to hike the Maah Daah Hey Trail before inauguration.

The Maah Daah Hey dips and twists for 96 character-building miles, paralleling the Little Missouri River and snaking through the Little Missouri National Grassland, which lies between the north and south units of Theodore Roosevelt National Park. Along the way, you'll encounter fantastic badlands hiking that makes you wonder why anyone called it bad in the first place.

In the first few miles, the Maah Daah Hey bounds from stark ridges to juniper- and buffaloberry-choked coulees, from wide-open prairies to big bluestem- and wheatgrass-covered buttes. But beautiful as it is, don't expect much company. This is still rough-and-tumble territory, shaped by wind and rain and haunted by myth. Few venture here, but the rewards are great for those who do.

This 97-mile point-to-point has sprawling prairie scenes interspersed with the starkly beautiful, striped-rock outcroppings of the badlands.

Photo: Madison Perrins

Text: James Campbell

DISTANCE: 96 miles

TIME REQUIRED: 5–9 days

DIFFICULTY: Intermediate

CONTACT: Theodore Roosevelt National Park, (701) 623-4730; nps.gov/thro / Maah Daah Hey Trail Association, mdhta.com

THE PAYOFF: True solitude, northern lights, badlands.

TRAILHEAD GPS: 46.889777, -103.537817

FINDING THE TRAILHEAD: The southern terminus is in Sully Creek State Park, just off I-94 near Medora. From Bismarck, take I-94 west to US 85 north near Belfield and drive for almost 50 miles. The CCC campground and Maah Daah Hey trailhead are signed on the left, immediately before the bridge across the Little Missouri River.

WAYPOINTS & DIRECTIONS

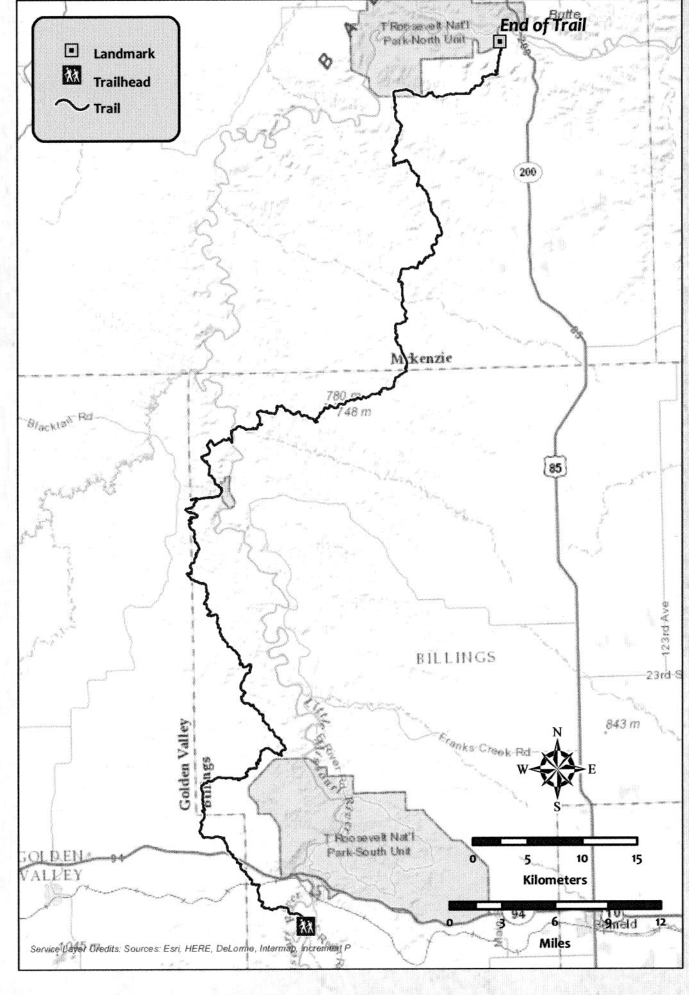

GPS: 46.889777, -103.537817 From Sully Creek State Park, just south of Medora, hike north through native mixed grass, watching for bighorn sheep on the buttes.

GPS: 46.889938, -103.538675
Sully Creek Camp.

GPS: 46.945223, -103.538761
Primitive Camp.

GPS: 46.953426, -103.674717
Buffalo Gap Campground.

GPS: 47.054949, -103.587470
Wannagan Campground.

GPS: 47.228501, -103.668816
Elkhorn Campground.

GPS: 47.281791, -103.616095 River crossing: The Missouri River is usually shallow and safe to cross here.

GPS: 47.307812, -103.473101
Magpie Camp.

GPS: 47.545220, -103.324012 Water is located near intersection of Long X and Maah Daah Hey trails.

GPS: 47.586339, -103.278705 The route ends at the trailhead at the CCC Campground west of US 85.

GPS: 47.545423, -103.323240 (***Day Hike Alternative:*** Begin at the CCC Campground trailhead, west of US 85, and hike the Long X Trail to the Maah Daah Hey Trail. Instead of continuing south, follow that trail north back to the campground. Continue west and south for the overnight variation.)

GPS: 47.377545, -103.404307 (***30-Mile Hike Alternative:*** Start at the CCC Campground trailhead as above, but rather than looping north, continue south on the Maah Daah Hey Trail for 25 miles to Forest Service Road 809.)

From Sully Creek State Park, just south of Medora, hike north through native mixed grass, watching for bighorn sheep on the buttes. Camp in four established sites (18 miles apart) with vault toilets and potable water, or plan to haul water (or cache at campsites near road crossings). More highlights: Glimpse the northern lights (in early winter), bison, and feral horses.

If you can't hike the whole 96 miles, try a 30-mile point-to-point hike in the northern section. Jump on the Long X Trail at the CCC campground. After a 5-mile tour of the Little Missouri River Valley, the trail connects with the Maah Daah Hey. Head south for 25 miles to Forest Service Road 809 (just off County Road 50). Other access points allow you to carve the trail into any number of segments.

For an 11-mile day-hike loop through the river valley, start at the CCC campground and hike the Long X Trail to the Maah Daah Hey. Instead of continuing south, follow that trail north back to the campground.

RANGER PROFILE

CELESTE DRAGO

The Cheerleader

Wind Cave National Park, South Dakota

"Celeste was full of enthusiasm and patience as she guided us through the world's most complex cave system." —Aidan and Madison, Park Visitors

There is no show of exuberance that can trump actual passion for our national parks. With rangers like Celeste Drago around, visitors will never have to wonder if their guide's heart is really in it. Nothing dampens her spirit for the place. "Passion, and the chance to engage with someone who's just as curious as I am—that's what makes me so excited to come to work every day," she says, "if you can even call it work."

FAVORITE SPOT: Rankin Ridge

Leave the cave-going crowds and climb into solitude on Rankin Ridge, the park's 4,803-foot high point. A quick 1-mile loop delivers you to views of the great bison herds that roam the grass-flecked high plains. Drago recommends setting up camp anywhere that's 0.3 mile from a road or trail to enjoy supreme prairie stargazing.

TRAILHEAD: Rankin Ridge

INFO: nps.gov/wica

A wild horse galloping through the badland meadows in Theodore Roosevelt National Park
Photo: iStockPhoto.com / golfladi

Lake Kabetogama, Voyaguers National Park, Minnesota
Photo: iStockPhoto.com / StevenSchremp

VOYAGEURS
NATIONAL
PARK

VOYAGEURS NATIONAL PARK

KABETOGAMA PENINSULA TO WILLIAMS LAKE

With a thousand islands and countless passages, this little-visited treasure is a watery maze. Here's the way in—and out.

The first visitors to what would become Voyageurs National Park were fur-trading French Canadian explorers—aka *voyageurs*—piloting 26-foot birch-bark canoes between Montreal and the uncharted West. Water is still the only way into this 220,000-acre wilderness located five hours north of Minneapolis. With more than 1,000 forested islands, interconnected waterways, and four giant lakes ringed by 600 miles of rocky shoreline, you'd need several lifetimes to pack in all the voyages here. But you can scratch the surface with this 5-day, 65-mile sampler that begins at Kabetogama Lake.

From the Ash River visitor center, steer your canoe or kayak 0.25 mile north to 75,000-acre Kabetogama Peninsula, home of the 9.5-mile Cruiser Lake Trail. Stow your boat in the dense pines and hike the full 9.5 miles to a cliffside campsite at Anderson Bay Overlook, 80 feet above Rainy Lake. In the morning, hike back and paddle to Peterson Point, an idyllic craggy site you'll reach by dinner. Day three is an easy 5-mile paddle east past squiggly inlets to tiny Hamilton Island, which features a single campsite tucked among soaring pines.

In the morning, push 14 miles to Beaver Bay, a 100-rod portage (one rod = 16.5 feet) to Fields Channel and nearly 30 campsites scattered across the park's eastern half.

Take your time rounding back to Ash River, stopping to visit the Gull Island Rookery on Namakan Lake. The island is a birthing site for thousands of gulls and great blue herons, whose nests are so ephemeral-looking they appear to hover—rather than rest—in the trees' crowns. From Gull Island, paddle 4 hours to Williams Island, dotted with two more remote campsites. Take your pick from a south- or west-facing site, and beach your boat for one more night before returning to solid ground just a morning paddle away.

Photo: Aidan Klimenko

Text: Steve Johnson

12,010-foot Mount Drum in Wrangell-St. Elias National Park, Alaska
Photo: Ryan Wright / Tandem Stock

DISTANCE: 65 miles

TIME REQUIRED: 5 days

DIFFICULTY: Strenuous

CONTACT: Voyageurs National Park, (218) 283-6600; nps.gov/voya

THE PAYOFF: Paddler's paradise.

TRAILHEAD GPS: 48.386012, -92.931290

FINDING THE TRAILHEAD: From International Falls, take Highway 53 east to Ash River Trail/County Road 129. Follow for 8 miles and turn left (north) to reach the visitor center.

WAYPOINTS & DIRECTIONS

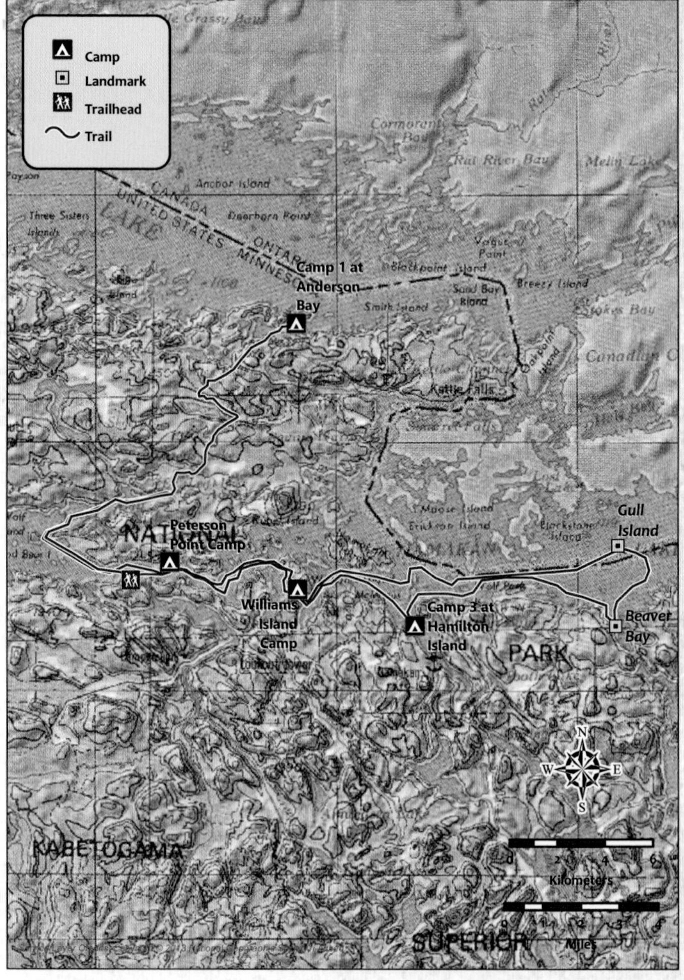

GPS: 48.434867, -92.844472 From the Ash River visitor center, steer your canoe or kayak to the Kabetogama Peninsula, first paddling northwest before rounding Round Bear Island into Lost Bay and heading northeast to the eastern end of the bay, where the 9.5-mile Cruiser Lake Trail begins. Stow your boat in the dense pines and hike north for the full length of the trail, to a cliffside campsite at Anderson Bay Overlook.

GPS: 48.527605, -92.751045 Spend the first night at Anderson Bay Overlook. In the morning, hike south on Cruiser Lake Trail back to your boat and paddle to Peterson Point, retracing the previous day's route and continuing a bit farther east-northeast to the point.

GPS: 48.441387, -92.822285 Make camp at the craggy Peterson Point Site. Day three is an easy 5-mile paddle east, past squiggly inlets to tiny Hamilton Island.

GPS: 48.417923, -92.685299 Your third camp is found tucked among soaring pines on Hamilton Island. In the morning, push 14 miles to Beaver Bay.

GPS: 48.417695, -92.572345 Head south from this point of Beaver Bay to access a 100-rod portage to Fields Channel. (***Note:*** one rod = 16.5 feet)

GPS: 48.432618, -92.547283 Spend the night at one of nearly 30 campsites scattered across the park's eastern half.

GPS: 48.446853, -92.570972 Take your time rounding back to Ash River, stopping to visit the Gull Island Rookery on Namakan Lake. The island is a birthing site for thousands of gulls and great blue herons. Paddle 4 hours west to Williams Island, dotted with two more remote campsites.

GPS: 48.431137, -92.750530 Enjoy the last night of the trip at one of the sites on Williams Island. Return to the Ash River visitor center in the morning.

WRANGELL-ST. ELIAS NATIONAL PARK & PRESERVE

Skolai Pass

WRANGELL-ST. ELIAS NATIONAL PARK & PRESERVE

GOAT TRAIL TO SKOLAI PASS

These 10 miles of pure Alaska experience are among the best 100 miles of trail in the whole national park system. The catch: It's barely a trail.

How did we zero in on just 16 miles of trail in the 13.2 million acres encompassed by the biggest, wildest park in the entire national park system? It's partly a technicality: Actual trails are hard to come by in Wrangell-St. Elias (and in truth, the aptly named Goat Trail is still only sort of a path). But mostly, it's because this chunk of tundra where the Wrangell and St. Elias Ranges meet is raw Alaska at its finest. On this high-flying variation, you'll get all the scenic highlights while avoiding the alder thickets and potentially dangerous river fords of lower Chitistone Gorge. The route passes waterfalls, skirts enormous moraines, and plunges into a deep gorge. Allow at least 5 days in case of weather delays—and for excellent detour hikes, like a circumnavigation of Wolverine Mesa, or exploring around Chitistone Pass and the Skolai Lakes.

Reaching this primo stretch requires taking a bush plane to the Wolverine Airstrip, then hiking miles of forest and canyon plus making several dicey river crossings. From Wolverine landing strip, keep an eye on your footing as you cross a massive talus slope to the northeast—it's easy to be distracted by the Twaharpies, giant peaks across Chitistone Gorge that rise 10,500 feet. After 2.5 miles, the wildlife track you've been following vanishes in the tundra around Hasen Creek. You won't see established track again until you hit the Goat Trail at mile 9.8.

Cross Hasen Creek where it splits into upper tributaries, and continue northeast up gradual tundra benches, passing two massive waterfalls that thunder just to your right.

Photo: Aidan Klimenko

Text: Steve Howe, Kris Wagner, and Elisabeth Kwak-Hefferan

Above the waterfalls, cross upper Hasen Creek, then veer right (east) through a broad, meadowy pass. Stay left (north) as needed to avoid swampy areas, but stay on tundra and don't wander too far north onto glacial moraine as you round the headwaters of the Chitistone River's western fork, aiming for the lowest, farthest toe of an obvious, massive moraine about 2 miles away.

Round the moraine toe as closely as possible to avoid cliffs in the streambed below. As you walk, look right (southeast) toward the craggy ridgeline ahead, which descends southward off of Point 7,755. You'll need to cross this ridge on the obvious grassy bench that sits roughly across from you and slightly below, at around 5,500 feet elevation. From the moraine toe, descend on a gradual traverse along the eastern margin of the stream gorge. You'll drop almost 300 feet before you can gain the tundra bench at ridgeline, which is the gateway to the Goat Trail, renowned for its narrow, exposed track that cuts across exposed talus.

Here's where the fun really begins: The route follows a path literally worn by Dall sheep and picks its way across a ketchup-and-mustard-striped cliff band of crumbly limestone for 1 mile. Scout carefully for the real trail, following one of the hoof-made spurs too far can cliff you out. Caution: Do not descend into the darker greenish rocks or you'll wander into dangerous, exposed cliff bands. On the Goat Trail, you'll traverse nearly 1 mile of steep talus, and then descend another 1,000 feet to the Chitistone River. On calm days, you can hear the roar of 400-foot Chitistone Falls, not far downcanyon from your route.

Once across, follow the Chitistone River northeast. Stay on the west side of the river, following patchy trail across several stream crossings, all the way to broad Chitistone Pass at 5,800 feet of elevation. Here you'll spill out onto the spongy tundra of Chitistone Pass, where forget-me-nots and moss campion bloom under nameless, glacier-crusted peaks and, on a clear day, the views stretch deep into the colossal University Range. As you crest the northern side of the 3-mile-long pass, the Russell Glacier comes into view like a 20-mile-long, 2-mile-wide tongue unfurling from 16,421-foot Mount Bona. From there, you'll drop another 2 miles to Skolai Pass. Here the track takes a 180-hairpin turn left (west) at the brink, then becomes very faint. Search closely for a way down through the cliffs. Once you're spit out at the base of the long ridgeline after a 1,300-foot descent down cliff bands and steep slopes, follow it left (west) for 2.5 miles to the small, grassy Lower Skolai Lake Airstrip, which is just above the southwest shore of Lower Skolai Lake. Keep your eyes peeled for grizzlies, caribou herds, and the occasional wolf before meeting your plane. Congratulations, you've just punched your Alaska hiking card in a big, big way.

DISTANCE: 16 miles

TIME REQUIRED: 5–7 days

DIFFICULTY: Expert

CONTACT: Wrangell-St. Elias National Park and Preserve, (907) 554-1105; nps.gov/wrst

THE PAYOFF: Pure Alaska.

TRAILHEAD GPS: 61.508746, -142.299173

FINDING THE TRAILHEAD: Flights to the Wolverine Airstrip start in McCarthy, reached from Chitina via a rough 60-mile dirt road. (Flights: wrangell-mountainair.com)

WAYPOINTS & DIRECTIONS

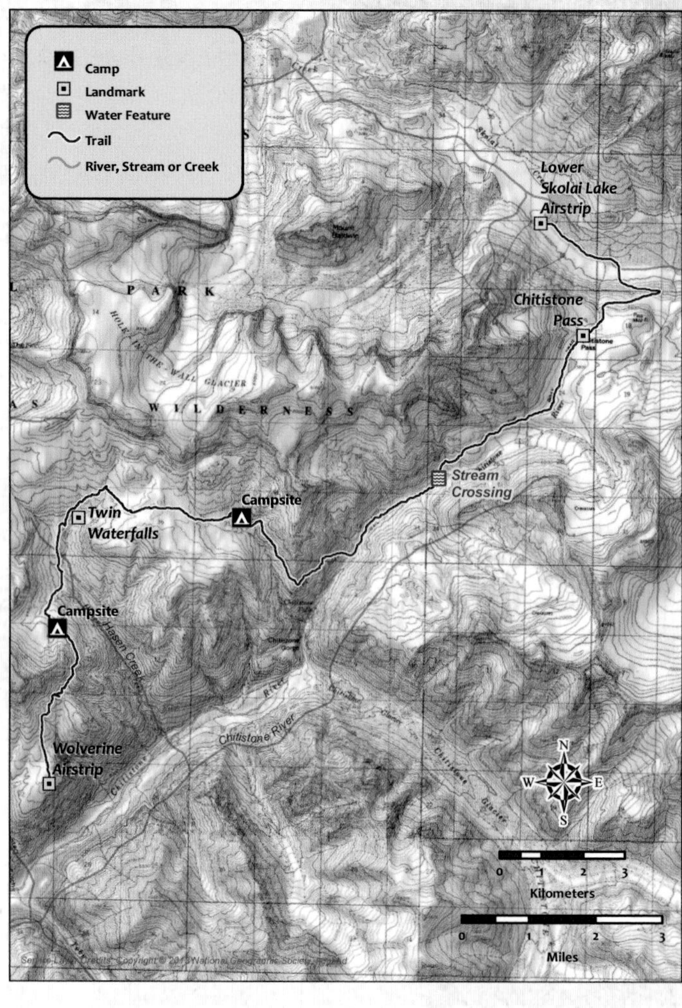

GPS: 61.509413, -142.296256 The bush plane will drop you off at the Wolverine Airstrip; from here, hike north across a talus slope.

GPS: 61.527919, -142.294149 Head northeast.

GPS: 61.529459, -142.290843 Stay above cliff bands.

GPS: 61.532520, -142.286465 Hike north.

GPS: 61.541957, -142.293959 Good campsite.

GPS: 61.542745, -142.296211 Veer right and begin to descend.

GPS: 61.553739, -142.292352 Cross the western tributary of Hasen Creek, then climb the dirt ridge between the tributaries and continue north.

GPS: 61.567632, -142.248909 Veer right (east) through pass. Stay on tundra, but track north as needed to avoid swampy areas.

GPS: 61.566168, -142.211676 Good campsite.

GPS: 61.565046, -142.205184 Round moraine toe as closely as possible.

GPS: 61.553102, -142.187417 Goat Trail. Cross the ridge as high as possible in light yellowish talus, avoiding the darker green band on a trail worn by Dall sheep. After traversing talus, descend 1,000 feet to the Chitistone River.

GPS: 61.560160, -142.159567 Stay on Goat Trail on the west side of the Chitistone River.

GPS: 61.575198, -142.122145 Trail swings up to cross stream.

GPS: 61.590311, -142.072535 Continue north; pass tarn ahead.

GPS: 61.605825, -142.057772 Chitistone Pass.

GPS: 61.615303, -142.023027 Drop down through cliff band, cutting northwest to the shore of Lake Skolai.

GPS: 61.629210, -142.077894 Lower Skolai Lake Airstrip.

GPS: 61.630721, -142.010519 (***Caution:*** This landing strip on the other side of the lake is no longer operational.)

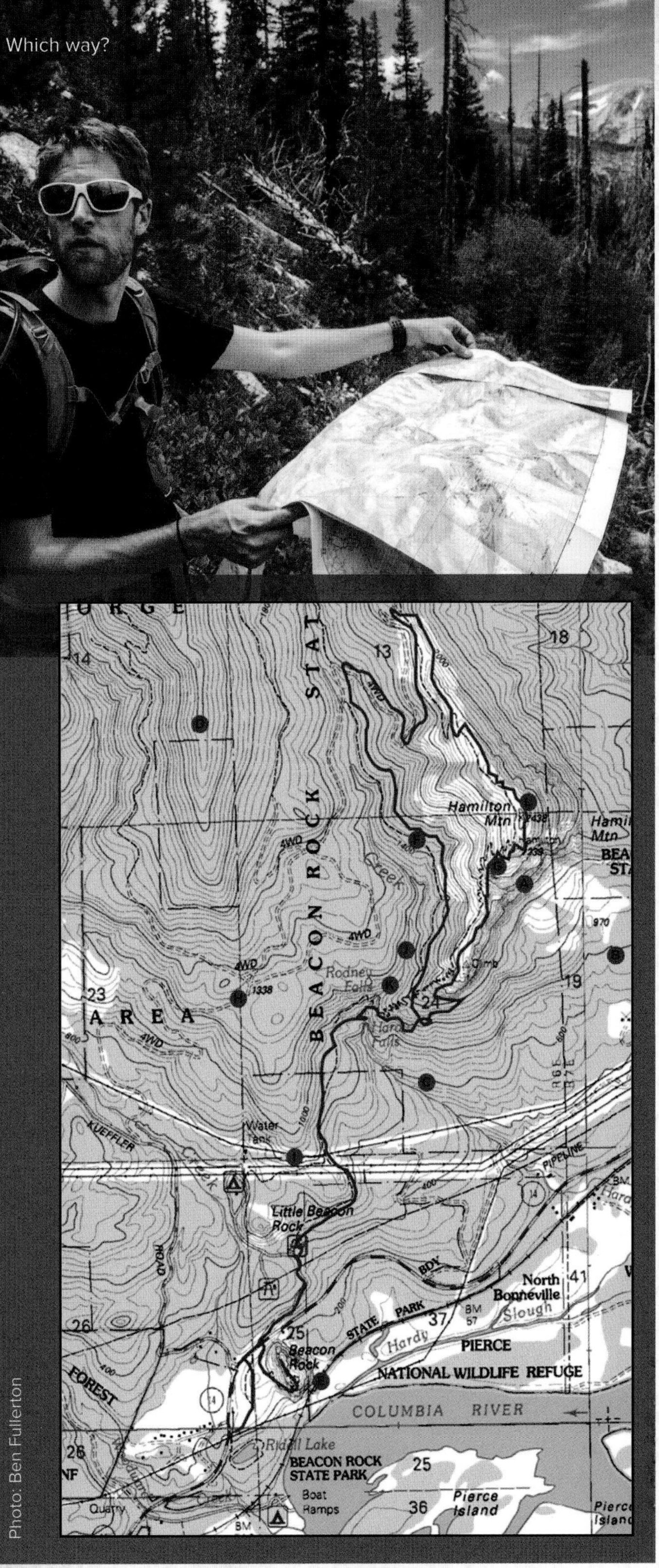

Which way?

Photo: Ben Fullerton

HOW TO READ A TOPO MAP

Learn how to discern the markings on your two-dimensional map.

CONTOUR LINES Each thin, brown line represents a single elevation. Check the bottom corner of your map for the contour interval, which tells you how many vertical feet apart they are from one another (usually 40 feet). Index lines, which are thicker, are labeled with the elevation in feet.

A. STEEP TERRAIN
Crowded sections of contour lines

B. GRADUAL TERRAIN
Spacious sections of contour lines

C. GULLY
V-shaped contour lines "point" toward higher elevations

D. RIDGE
V-shaped contour lines "point" to lower elevations

E. CLIFF
Super-concentrated lines

F. TRAIL
Black, dashed line

G. SWITCHBACKS
Zigzagging trail

H. DIRT ROAD
Black dashed double line

I. RAILROAD TRACKS
Solid black line with hatch marks

J. STREAM
Solid blue line

K. WATERFALL
Single blue hatch intersecting a stream

L. SUMMIT
Contour line forms a small circle

Know where you're going

Photo: Ben Fullerton

HOW TO NAVIGATE LIKE A PRO

Liz Thomas has backpacked more than 15,000 miles, and she holds the women's unsupported speed record on the Appalachian Trail (80 days). Here are her top ways to stay on track.

1. Keep your mind and body sharp. It's really hard to navigate if you're hungry, thirsty, or cold. "An unfueled brain is more likely to make poor decisions," Thomas says.

2. Confirm your location on your map often. Sounds obvious, but this is the single best way to prevent wandering off course. "I hike with a map in my hand, pocket, or—a little embarrassingly— stuffed in my bra," Thomas says.

3. Learn to read contour lines. GPS units are great, but you still need to be able to read a map. That means understanding how contour lines represent real-world terrain. An activity to get you started: Make a fist into "Knuckle Mountains." Draw a circle around each peak, or knuckle, keeping your pen at the same "elevation" as you draw each line. Moving down from your knuckles, draw concentric circles around your fist, about a half-inch apart. Flatten your hand: The lines represent different "elevations" on the topographic map of your fist Knuckle Mountains.

- **CONTOUR LINE.** The closer the lines, the steeper the terrain. Check your map for the contour interval (the elevation change between lines).

- **SADDLE,** indicated by opposing Us.
- **PEAK.** The bulls-eye circle in the middle of concentric rings.
- **DRAINAGE OR VALLEY,** with the Us (or Vs) pointing the same direction, uphill. Ridges look similar, with the Vs pointing the same direction, but they face downhill.
- **SEE PAGE 335** for tips on identifying other common features.

4. Learn the difference between true north and magnetic north. A compass needle points to magnetic north. That's not the same as true north (the North Pole, or the direction of the North Star). The difference between true north and magnetic north is called declination; it changes over time (as the Earth's magnetic field shifts), and it varies according to your location (see below). Learn how to account for it at backpacker.com/declination.

5. Think like a railroad builder. Traveling cross-country? Observe the landscape and imagine, "If I were a railroad engineer, where would I build the line?" You will likely choose the path of least resistance.

6. Use nature's bumper lanes. Ridges, rivers, and prominent peaks can all serve as route boundaries. Pay attention to the terrain that borders your route, and use landmarks to avoid going astray.

7. Avoid shortcuts. Not only does cutting switchbacks or taking shortcuts cause erosion, it's also an easy way to get lost.

8. Enter the right datum in your GPS. Technology is great—if you use it correctly. The most common GPS error: Failing to match datums, the systems used to match features on the ground to coordinates on the map. For example, a WGS 84 coordinate taken from Google Earth and entered into a GPS set to NAD 27 can be up to a quarter-mile off.

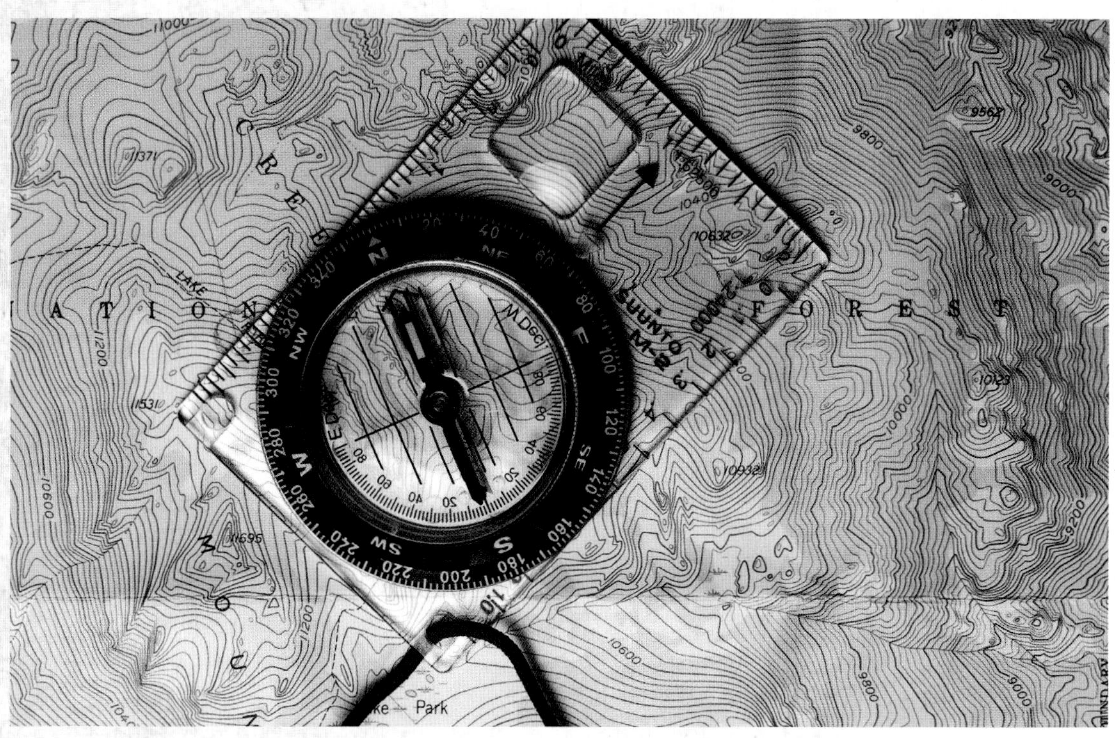

The Wrangell Mountains

WRANGELL-ST. ELIAS NATIONAL PARK & PRESERVE

HIDDEN CREEK LAKE

Explore a 10-mile-long glacial highway on the Root and Kennecott Glaciers.

Even by Alaska standards, the Wrangells are big and wild. Access can be intimidating, but this sneak route ensures that mere mortals can experience the biggest park in America on a long, spectacular glacier walk without ropes or even an ice ax. The low-elevation Root and Kennecott Glaciers (less than 3,000 feet high) are like broad ice highways with crevasses that are either squeezed shut (safe) or exposed and easy to avoid (also safe). Without icefall clutter or crevasse mazes, these bare ice glaciers are Alaska's backcountry highways.

From the remote town of McCarthy, the 25.5-mile round-trip trek leads from historic mine ruins to spectacular Hidden Creek Lake, tucked in a 3,000-foot-deep rock gorge populated by mountain goats.

From the mine ruins at Kennicott, follow the Root Glacier Trail northward past thickets of soapberry bushes (watch for bears and make noise) and overlooks with views of the Kennecott Glacier's moraine rock piles. At mile 1.85, turn left toward the Root Glacier toe and step onto the ice at mile 2.25; here you leave the trails for good and begin a 10.5-mile journey up the Root and Kennecott glaciers. Follow smooth ice northward near the medial moraine (a line of rock rubble up the glacier's center) for 0.25 mile, then turn west and traverse around the southern tip of land below obvious Donoho Peak, at the junction of the Root and Kennecott Glaciers. Hiking upglacier along the northeastern margin of the Kennecott, you'll find the Kennecott Highway, a smooth, crevasse-free tongue of ice that runs northward for 5.5 miles between lateral (glacier's side) and medial moraines.

Follow the highway until you're well north of the canyon entrance to Hidden Creek Lake, which lies west, across the Kennecott Glacier. Then turn southwest and approach Hidden Creek Lake on smoother ice from the northeast. Strong, experienced parties can make the lake in a day, but you can also camp on the ice or moraines en route. Round Hidden Lake on its northern shore and camp on the flats above. Plan a minimum of 4 days for the round-trip hike. If you've got more time, you'll find good hiking west of the lake, up Glacier Gulch. Got a week or more? Access beautiful tundra lakes overlooking the Lakina Glacier by hiking all the way up Hidden Creek and crossing southwest over the pass at its head.

Photo: iStockPhoto.com / Natalia Bratslavsky

Text: Steve Howe

DISTANCE: 25.5 miles

TIME REQUIRED: 4–5 days

DIFFICULTY: Intermediate

CONTACT: Wrangell-St. Elias National Park and Preserve, (907) 554-1105; nps.gov/wrst

THE PAYOFF: Relatively easy access to Alaska's gnarliest mountains; close up views of massive glaciers.

TRAILHEAD GPS: 61.481351, -142.885408

FINDING THE TRAILHEAD: From Anchorage, drive 252 miles east on the Glenn and Richardson Highways (AK 1 and 4) to Chitina. Continue 60 miles on the dirt McCarthy Road to the bridge and the road's end. At the parking lot, grab the shuttle ($10) to skip the 5-mile road slog to the trailhead at the mine ruins of Kennicott.

WAYPOINTS & DIRECTIONS

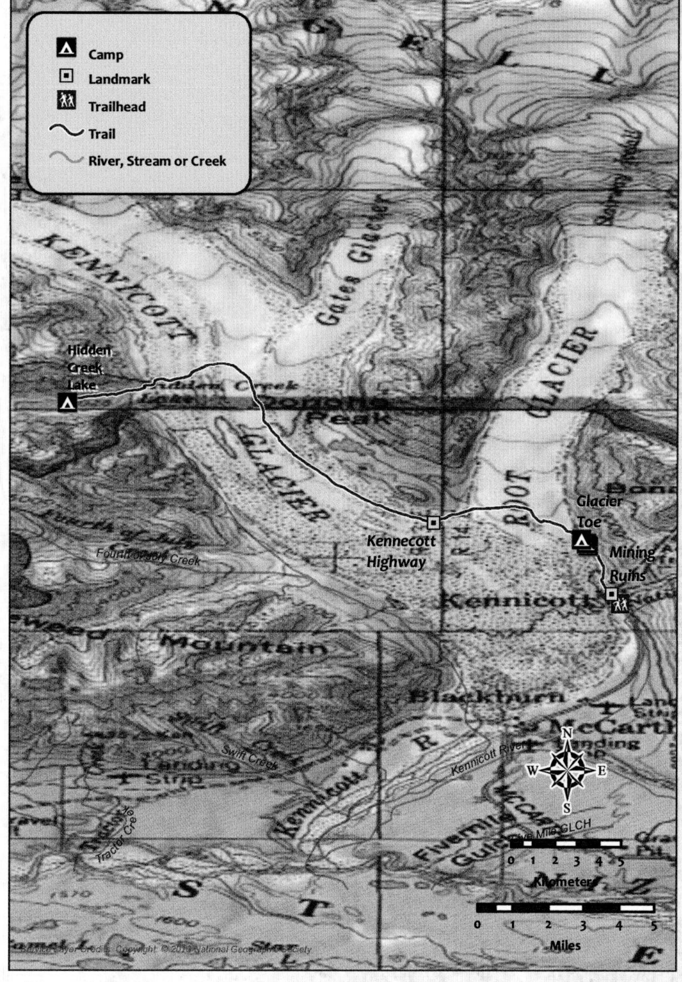

GPS: 61.481351, -142.885408 Kennicott Shuttle Bus Stop and the trailhead.

GPS: 61.485330, -142.888865 Main ruins of Kennecott mining boom. Huge ore mill and power plant buildings.

GPS: 61.491077, -142.892595 Two-track road ends; begin Root Glacier Trail.

GPS: 61.503098, -142.897043 Bridge across creek.

GPS: 61.503897, -142.898526 Bear-proof food-storage lockers for overnight campsites.

GPS: 61.504897, -142.899217 Overnight campsites.

GPS: 61.506181, -142.899899 Go left at fork and descend to glacier toe.

GPS: 61.506442, -142.901372 Upper campsites.

GPS: 61.509514, -142.906461 Beginning of exposed glacier ice; those without crampons can tread left (west) and hike along the rocky medial moraine.

GPS: 61.513118, -142.961757 Beginning of Kennecott Highway; follow smooth, bare ice along east margin of glacier.

GPS: 61.574776, -143.044953 Turn left (west) and seek path of least resistance across four rugged medial moraines, heading southwest toward the north shore of Hidden Creek Lake.

GPS: 61.564936, -143.084001 Stay right along base of bluffs, above fluctuating lake level, to avoid ice floes.

GPS: 61.560127, -143.112212 Good campsite on tundra/sand flats above the upcanyon shore of Hidden Creek Lake.

Grand Prismatic Spring, Yellowstone National Park, Wyoming
Photo: David Wells

YELLOWSTONE NATIONAL PARK

YELLOWSTONE NATIONAL PARK

SHOSHONE GEYSER BASIN

Camp in an active geyser basin teeming with wildlife.

Frontcountry geyser basins are cool. But backcountry geyser basins, where no boardwalks or crowds interrupt the steaming, bubbling, bursting landscape, are where the earth really comes alive. Getting to Shoshone's geysers and hot springs is half the fun: You'll hike deep into a wilderness filled with grizzlies and bison, crossing the Continental Divide at 8,010-foot Grants Pass before dropping to the basin on the edge of Shoshone Lake. This ain't no Old Faithful area: You'll experience Yellowstone's thermal zones like the early explorers did, so step carefully.

Start on the Lone Star Trail, hiking along the Firehole River to the Lone Star Geyser, which erupts every three hours. Turn left onto the Shoshone Lake Trail and look for bison around trailside thermal areas. Keep climbing to Grants Pass and the Continental Divide. Watch for moose after the Bechler River Trail junction as you descend along the Shoshone Creek to forested lakeshore. After taking the right fork of the Shoshone Lake Trail past a patrol cabin, you'll see spur trails to the Shoshone Geyser Basin. Careful: Signage and boardwalks are scarce. The North Shore Trail contours past the spurs to the splendid campsite 8R5, fronting Basin Point Bay; it's the closest site to the geyser basin.

Photo: Aidan Klimenko

Text: Elisabeth Kwak-Hefferan

DISTANCE: 34 miles

TIME REQUIRED: 2–3 days

DIFFICULTY: Intermediate

CONTACT: Yellowstone National Park, (307) 344-2163; nps.gov/yell

THE PAYOFF: Charismatic megafauna, private geysers.

TRAILHEAD GPS: 44.418486, -110.805745

FINDING THE TRAILHEAD: From the Old Faithful overpass, in Wyoming, go 2.5 miles south on Grand Loop Road and park in the Lone Star Trailhead lot.

WAYPOINTS & DIRECTIONS

GPS: 44.444443, -110.804565 Start on the Lone Star Trail, hiking south along the Firehole River.

GPS: 44.418946, -110.805659 Round the Lone Star Geyser, which erupts every three hours, before taking a left onto Shoshone Lake Trail.

GPS: 44.380220, -110.822825 Cross the Continental Divide at Grants Pass before descending to the Shoshone lakeshore. Take the right fork of the Shoshone Lake Trail. (***Side Trip:*** Take one of the spur trails to the Geyser Basin.) Turn left onto the North Shore Trail, which leads to campsite 8R5 on Basin Point Bay.

GPS: 44.369300, -110.748754 Spend the night at Basin Point Bay. In the morning, head back to the trailhead, forking right to cut directly up Shoshone Creek if you want to bypass the geyser basin.

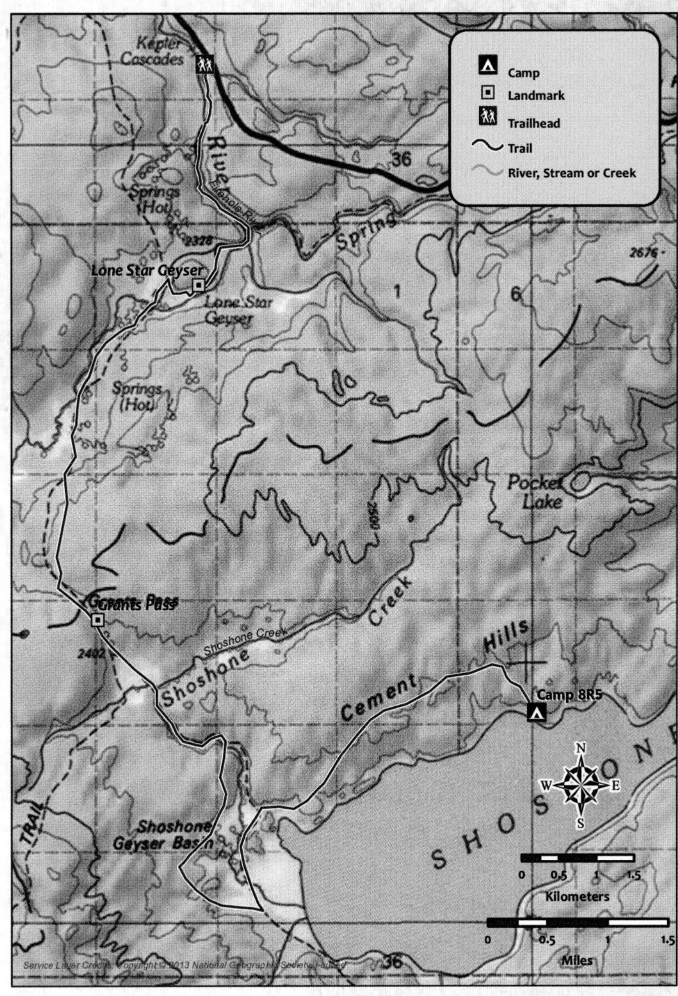

Steam rises from the Firehole River

YELLOWSTONE NATIONAL PARK

FERRIS FORK TO DUNANDA FALLS

Take a dip in the first national park's steamy rivers.

Hot springs form when molten magma heats underground water, so it makes sense that the highest concentration of geothermal spouts in North America would surface above the 300-mile-wide ocean of magma that is Yellowstone National Park. While most of Yellowstone's boiling baths are off limits to soaking (with good reason—they're hot enough to cook dinner), Dunanda Falls and Ferris Fork mix with creek water, making them fair—and Park Service–approved—game. (Make reservations at the Yellowstone backcountry information center before hitting the trail.)

You won't find much company among the belching geysers and grizzly dens of Bechler River country. Located in the southeast corner of the park, it requires a 26-mile dirt-road drive from Ashton, Idaho, just to get to the Bechler Trailhead. From there to Ferris Fork, it's a 15-mile walk along the roaring Bechler River through dense stands of lodgepole pine that give way to the steep walls of Bechler Canyon. You'll pass 12 raging drops (some slightly off-trail) that pour into the Bechler River, including funky wonders like Ragged Falls, named for its chaotic five-foot tumble, and Twister Falls, which—you guessed it—coils downward along its 55-foot flume.

Day one ends with a short detour through Bechler Meadows to 150-foot-high Dunanda Falls. Take your pick from several soaker-made pots (averaging 110 degrees) and camp in your designated site for the night. Make it a hot-springs doubleheader by trekking back to the Bechler River Trail and following it 6 miles northeast to Three Rivers Junction (where the Phillips, Gregg, and Ferris Forks converge). An obvious user trail leads to a steaming pool hidden along the banks of the river. Continue upstream to splash in cascading beauties like Gwinna Falls and Sluiceway Falls, and spend your second night just downstream of Three Forks, near sloping, 260-foot Albright Falls.

Photo: Aidan Klimenko

Text: Doug Schnitzpahn

DISTANCE: 30 miles

TIME REQUIRED: 2–3 days

DIFFICULTY: Intermediate

CONTACT: Yellowstone National Park and Preserve, (307) 344-2163; www.nps.gov/yell

THE PAYOFF: Melt your post-hike muscles in a hot pool all your own.

TRAILHEAD GPS: 44.149206, -111.046286

FINDING THE TRAILHEAD: The Bechler River trailhead is at the end of unpaved Cave Falls Road, 26 miles from Ashton, Idaho.

WAYPOINTS & DIRECTIONS

GPS: 44.144676, -110.997448 Start at the Bechler trailhead and head north for 15 miles along the roaring Bechler River and through dense stands of pine that give way to the steep walls of Bechler Canyon.

GPS: 44.245814, -111.025386 Make a short detour through Bechler Meadows to Dunanda Falls. Take your pick from several hot springs and camp in your designated site for the night. In the morning, trek back to the Bechler River Trail and following it 6 miles northeast to Three Rivers Junction. Head up the Ferris Fork (farthest right) to see Gwinna Falls and Sluiceway Falls.

GPS: 44.282140, -110.880032 Gwinna Falls.

GPS: 44.279314, -110.878916 Sluiceway Falls. Retrace route back to Three Rivers Junction and head up the center fork (Gregg Fork) to visit Twister Falls.

GPS: 44.296517, -110.859690 Twister Falls. Head just downstream of Three Rivers Junction to Albright Falls.

GPS: 44.277808, -110.907712 Make camp near the 260-foot Albright Falls. In the morning, head back south to the trailhead.

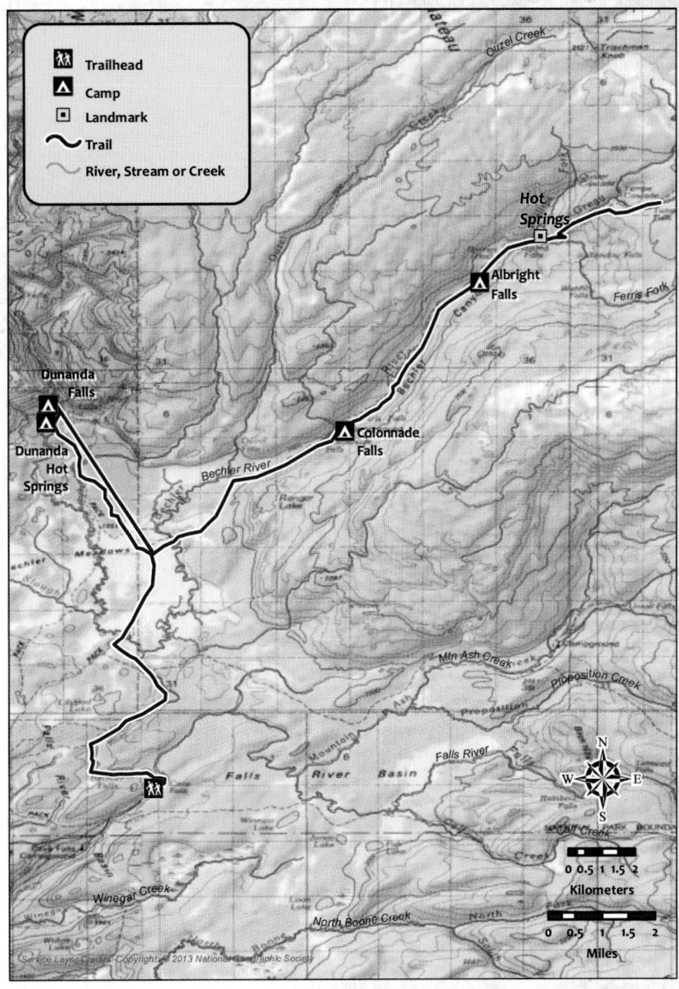

Bison grazing near Lamar River in Yellowstone

YELLOWSTONE NATIONAL PARK

SPECIMEN RIDGE

Wildlife sightings and striking views highlight this tough shuttle hike that spans the length of Specimen Ridge.

Specimen Ridge overlooks the wildlife-filled grasslands of the Lamar Valley, making this lengthy ramble a great choice for wildlife lovers visiting Yellowstone to check off the Rockies' most charismatic megafauna on their life list. Start early or stay late to spot the crowds of elk, bison, antelope, moose, wolves, and bears that roam Lamar's grassy expanse.

From the trailhead, hike southeast across the vast, rolling hills that border the eastern edge of the Grand Canyon of the Yellowstone. After 1.4 miles, the trail veers to the right below the crest of Specimen Ridge and continues to climb to the southeast. Roughly 2 miles later, take a break at the scenic vantage point overlooking Yellowstone's wildlife-rich northern range.

After 10 miles, the route tops out on 9,614-foot Amethyst Mountain, giving way to some of the best panoramic views that Yellowstone has to offer. From here, the trail drops down Amethyst's southeast ridge, then swings to the northeast into the Lamar Valley; extensive views accompany hikers into the valley. At mile 15.6, ford the Lamar River, then continue a 2-mile descent to the route's endpoint at the Lamar River trailhead.

Note: Before you hike this trail, check with park rangers to determine the levels of the Lamar River and for wildlife-related trail closures.

Photo: iStockPhoto.com / Wirepec

Text: Jason Kauffman

DISTANCE: 17.7 miles

TIME REQUIRED: 1 day

DIFFICULTY: Strenuous

CONTACT: Yellowstone National Park, (307) 344-2163; nps.gov/yell

THE PAYOFF: Ace chances for grizzly, bison, antelope, moose, and bear sightings against panoramic views.

TRAILHEAD GPS: 44.9122739, -110.3874063

FINDING THE TRAILHEAD: From Tower Junction, head northeast on NE Entrance Road/US 212. In 2 miles, turn left into the parking lot. The trail begins across the highway. End: From the Specimen Ridge Trailhead, continue east 12.8 miles to the Lamar River Trailhead.

WAYPOINTS & DIRECTIONS

GPS: 44.912274, -110.387406 Leaving the highway and trailhead behind, the Specimen Ridge Trail heads southeast over rolling hills covered in grass and sagebrush.

GPS: 44.899864, -110.378670 Continue straight along the main path as it continues climbing toward Specimen Ridge.

GPS: 44.892439, -110.361239 Keep left at the Y junction along the ridge crest.

GPS: 44.886201, -110.337020 Continue uphill as the trail fades in and out for short lengths.

GPS: 44.859246, -110.299422 Leaving the open grasslands, the trail enters a dense grove of conifer trees. Watch for occasional blazes on trees that differentiate the main path from numerous game trails.

GPS: 44.843617, -110.287025 Enjoy the first good views of wide-open Lamar Valley—known as Yellowstone's Serengeti—thousands of feet below.

GPS: 44.828330, -110.254380 Stand on the trail's high point: Amethyst Mountain. This 9,614-foot summit provides some of the best 360-degree views in Yellowstone.

GPS: 44.817278, -110.232344 The trail begins to drop off Specimen Ridge into a mostly timbered side drainage to Lamar Valley.

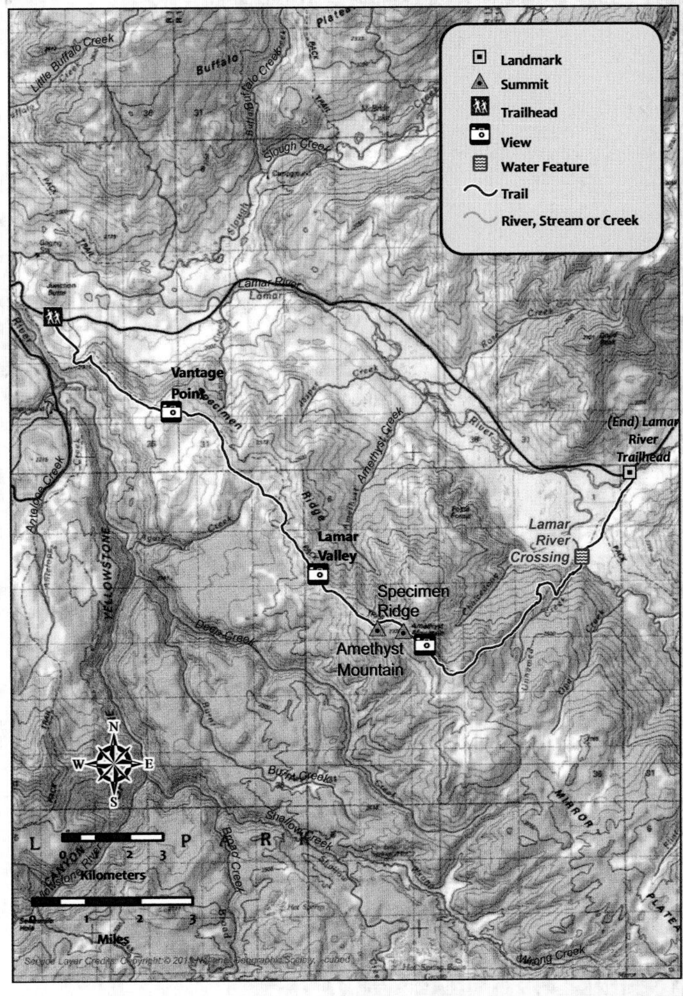

GPS: 44.835939, -110.201840 The main trail circles northwest around the ridge providing distant views down into a portion of Lamar Valley.

GPS: 44.847114, -110.185307 Ford the Lamar River. (***Caution:*** This crossing can be very dangerous and nearly impossible during the early summer melt. Before setting out on this hike, check river conditions with park rangers.)

GPS: 44.869168, -110.166389 The hike finishes at the Lamar River Trailhead. A footbridge provides easy passage over Soda Butte Creek just before the large parking lot.

YELLOWSTONE NATIONAL PARK

ELECTRIC PEAK

This 20.6-mile out-and-back in the northern reaches of Yellowstone National Park culminates with panoramic views from the rocky crown of Electric Peak.

A Yellowstone creek

Featuring a memorable mix of plains, peaks, and wildlife, this 20.6-mile trek scales the scree-laden slopes of Electric Peak for unobstructed views across Yellowstone National Park. The route begins on the south side of Kingman Pass at the Bunsen Peak/Glen Creek trailhead and travels east through the sagebrush grasslands. (Keep an eye out for grizzly and bison, which roam the area.)

Cruise past a few trail junctions and remain on the path that points directly for the pyramid-shaped Electric Peak. Past the plains, the trail continues up a small river valley and then ducks into a thick forest of Douglas fir. At mile 6, continue straight at a three-way junction to spend the night at campsite 1G3 or 1G4.

The next day, backtrack to the three-way junction and turn left to tackle the climb up Electric Peak. Near the summit, veer left at a noticeable notch to bypass a crumbling fin of rock and traverse the loose scree at its base. After 10.3 miles, the route crests Electric Peak. Gaze out across Yellowstone National Park and look south for views of the Tetons. Follow the same route back to the trailhead.

DISTANCE: 20.6 miles

TIME REQUIRED: 2–3 days

DIFFICULTY: Strenuous

CONTACT: Yellowstone National Park, (307) 344-2163; nps.gov/yell

THE PAYOFF: Top your wildlife hike with a scramble up a high Yellowstone peak.

TRAILHEAD GPS: 44.9122739, -110.3874063

FINDING THE TRAILHEAD: From the West Yellowstone entrance, in Wyoming, continue on US 20 for 11.5 miles. Turn left at Grand Loop Road/US 89 and continue for 29.5 miles to Bunsen Peak/Glen Creek trailhead.

Photo: Aidan Klimenko

Text: Jeff Chow

WAYPOINTS & DIRECTIONS

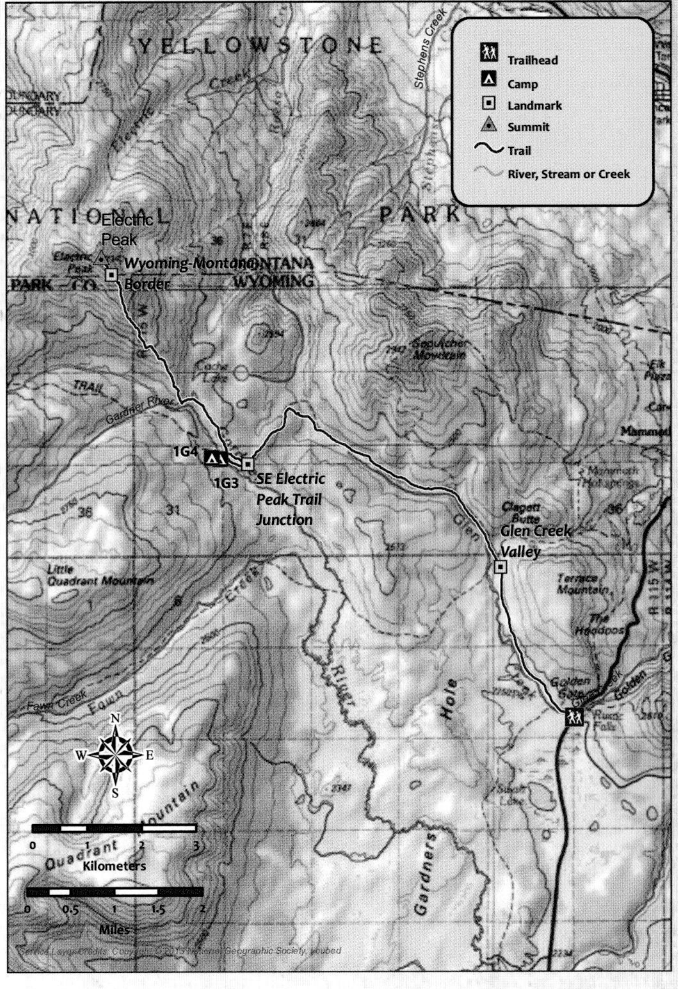

GPS: 44.932162, -110.728133 Bunsen Peak/Glen Creek trailhead. Cross the road and follow Glen Creek to the northeast.

GPS: 44.933594, -110.731829 Continue straight at the junction with Howard Eaton Trail, heading northwest. The trail travels toward the Electric Peak massif.

GPS: 44.956060, -110.744990 Stay left at fork toward Sportsman Lake, then continue straight at the next two junctions with Snowpass Trail.

GPS: 44.967116, -110.755213 Cross the small stream at the dip in the trail before reaching the junction with Sepulcher Mountain Trail. Stay left toward Sportsman Lake at the fork.

GPS: 44.978475, -110.788450 Veer away from the creek bed and enter thick Douglas fir forest.

GPS: 44.980517, -110.792895 Stay left at fork toward Sportsman Lake, avoiding Cache Lake.

GPS: 44.972472, -110.803857 At the junction with Southeast Electric Peak Trail, continue straight to the campsites.

GPS: 44.974521, -110.811474 Spend the night at the scenic Upper Gardner Campsite, returning to the previous junction in the morning and turning left to begin the summit attempt.

GPS: 44.982065, -110.819006 The warm-up is over as the trail makes an abrupt turn up the steep ridge. From here on out, it's an upward hike on the edge of grass and trees.

GPS: 44.990845, -110.825829 Cross over the soft, sandy soil to the next ridgeline. From here, it's a straight shot up the peak.

GPS: 44.994858, -110.830529 Cut left of the rock wall.

GPS: 44.997298, -110.832294 Cross the second rock wall from right to left.

GPS: 45.002566, -110.835088 Cross the Wyoming-Montana border.

GPS: 45.003310, -110.836086 Veer left at a noticeable notch and traverse the scree field at the base of the fin. (***Caution:*** Do not climb over the rock fin that towers above the route.)

GPS: 45.005282, -110.837556 Electric Peak Summit. From this Montana summit, gaze out across Yellowstone National Park; views stretch south to the Tetons. Follow the same route back to the trailhead.

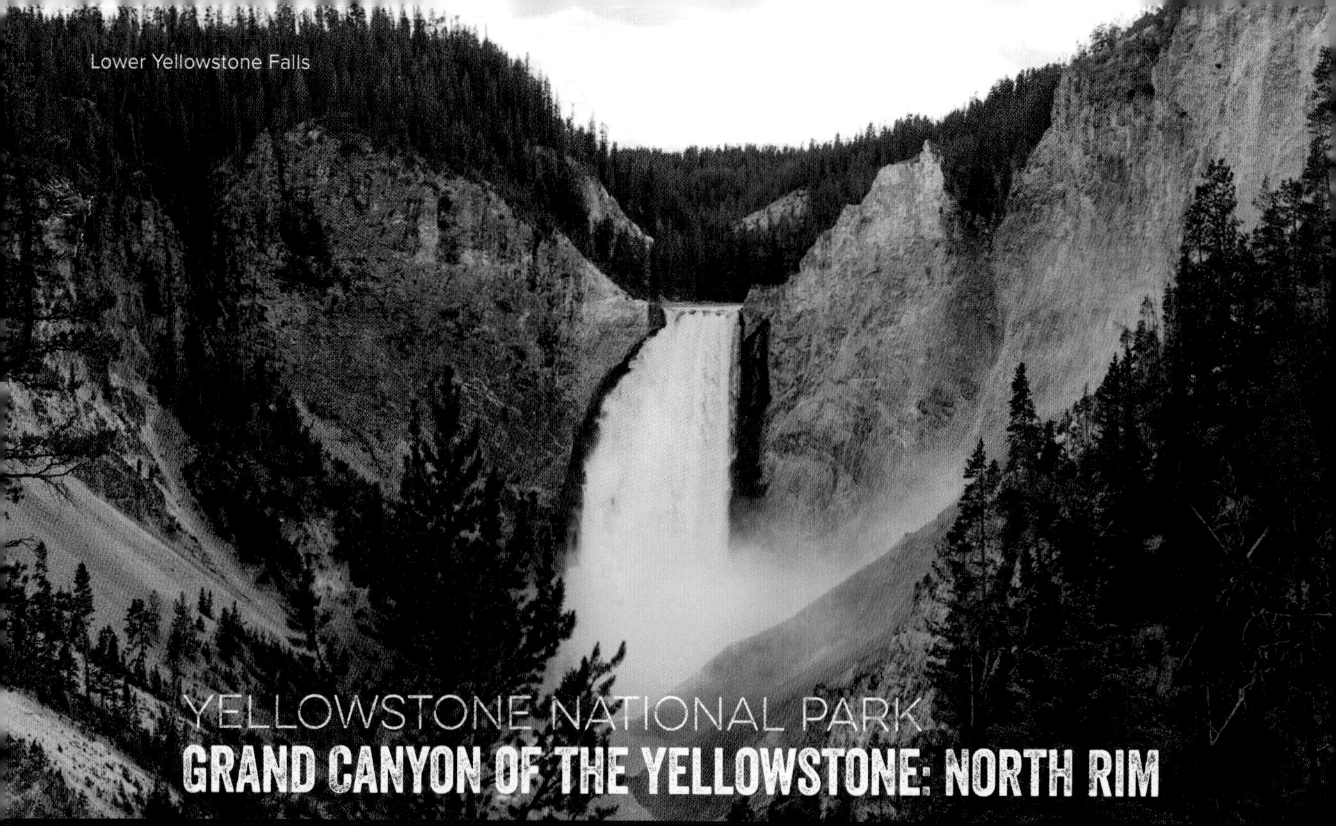

Lower Yellowstone Falls

YELLOWSTONE NATIONAL PARK

GRAND CANYON OF THE YELLOWSTONE: NORTH RIM

Walk the rim of the Grand Canyon of the Yellowstone on this 6.4-mile hike that showcases five-star views of its Lower and Upper Falls.

One of Yellowstone National Park's classic landmarks, the Grand Canyon of the Yellowstone extends roughly 20 miles from Upper Falls to the Tower Fall area and drops 1,200 feet, at its deepest point, to the Yellowstone River. Walk the north rim of this immense gorge on this spectacular 6.4-mile out-and-back that passes numerous overlooks and in-your-face views of Lower and Upper Falls.

The route starts at Inspiration Point, a natural outcrop that offers views of the canyon's inner depths. Leave the parking lot and follow the path as it briefly travels northwest and enters the woods. The trail varies from paved sidewalks to spongy, ash-like rock as it follows the contours of the canyon's edge and passes a series of popular viewpoints, including the aptly named Grandview Point and Lookout Point.

After 2.2 miles, turn left at the three-way intersection and descend a set of steep switchbacks that lead to a platform overlooking Lower Falls, the biggest waterfall in Yellowstone. From this dizzying vantage point at the brink, you'll feel the full force of the Yellowstone River as it plunges 308 feet into the depths of the canyon.

Next, climb back up the switchbacks and turn left for the 0.7-mile stretch to Upper Falls. Although this 109-foot waterfall is the baby brother to Lower Falls, it still puts on an impressive show. Soak up more views of the Yellowstone River plummeting into the canyon, then turn around and follow the same route back to the Inspiration Point parking area.

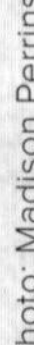
Photo: Madison Perrins

Text: Jeff Chow

DISTANCE: 6.4 miles

TIME REQUIRED: 1 day

DIFFICULTY: Intermediate

CONTACT: Yellowstone National Park, (307) 344-2163; nps.gov/yell

THE PAYOFF: See the park's jaw-dropping gorge and landmark waterfall.

TRAILHEAD GPS: 44.7250582, -110.4699272

FINDING THE TRAILHEAD: From the park's Tower-Roosevelt Area, head southeast on Grand Loop Road. In 18.3 miles, turn left onto North Rim Drive. In 0.9 mile, turn left at three-way junction. Follow 0.8 mile to the Inspiration Point parking area.

WAYPOINTS & DIRECTIONS

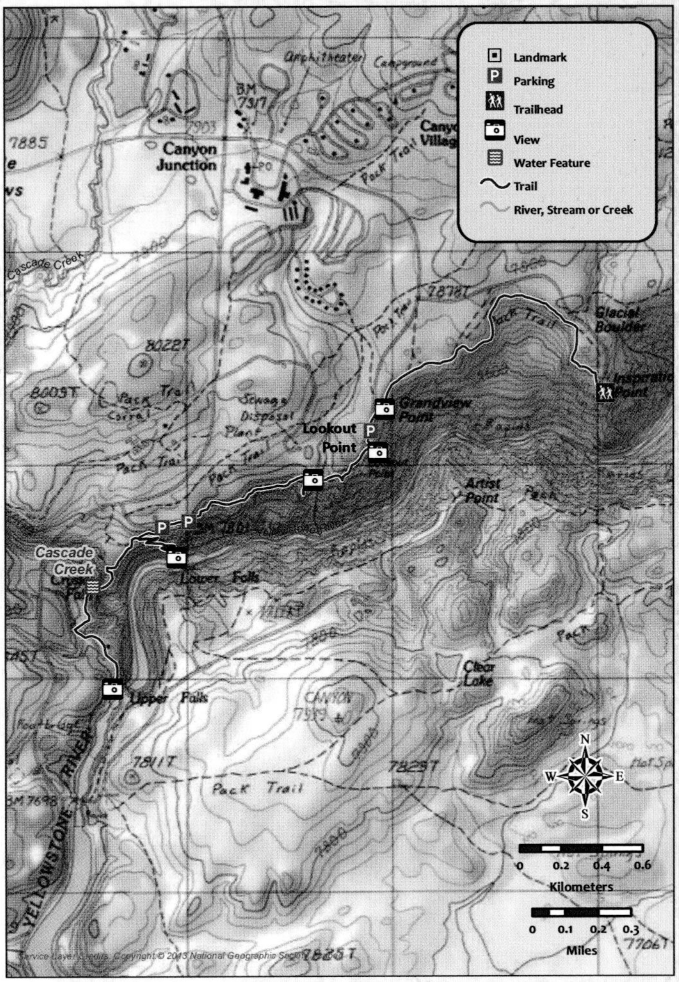

GPS: 44.725058, -110.469927 From Inspiration Point, follow the path as it briefly travels northwest and enters the woods.

GPS: 44.724441, -110.483483 Grandview Point. Stop at this aptly named perch for dramatic views of the canyon and the Yellowstone River.

GPS: 44.722615, -110.483939 Lookout Point. From this nicely shaded overlook, you can see the full spectrum of colors on the pale canyon walls. Get a sense of scale by trying to find the ant-size visitors at Artist's Point, nearly 0.5 mile away.

GPS: 44.721483, -110.487941 Turn left to find sweet views of Lower Falls, the biggest waterfall in Yellowstone. Afterward, continue west along the canyon rim.

GPS: 44.719520, -110.497275 Leave the Lower Falls parking area and head southwest.

GPS: 44.719074, -110.498766 Turn left at three-way junction and descend steep switchbacks for up-close views of Lower Falls.

GPS: 44.718247, -110.496395 From the viewing platform at the brink of Lower Falls you can see all 308 feet of waterfall.

GPS: 44.717054, -110.501497 Cross Cascade Creek just 800 feet before its confluence with the Yellowstone.

GPS: 44.715255, -110.502623 Turn left at the road and head southeast to the parking area.

GPS: 44.714370, -110.500832 Pick up the short trail to Upper Falls and follow it south to the Brink of the Upper Falls.

GPS: 44.712731, -110.500360 Brink of the Upper Falls, the 109-foot baby brother. Retrace your steps back to the Inspiration Point parking area.

YELLOWSTONE NATIONAL PARK

(MOSTLY) IN PRAISE OF OFF-TRAIL HIKING

Off-trail hiking can feel like the best idea ever—until it suddenly doesn't.

We're all grit and guts in the West Yellowstone backcountry office, playing up our preparedness for the increasingly skeptical ranger in charge of issuing our trip permit.

"You have a GPS?"

"We have maps and a compass."

"Who approved this itinerary?"

"I've been e-mailing with this office for two years."

I have no gripe with his questions. We're asking permission to spend ten days hiking border-to-border—west to east—across the park, and to do most of it off-trail, where travel happens slowly and trouble happens quickly.

"We don't usually permit trips like this. I need to make a phone call."

When my friend Travis first proposed this trek two years ago, he sold me on the idea that there's an entire undiscovered layer of wilderness to be found off-trail. Just as car-camping tourists discover a new side of Yellowstone when they leave the pavement and go for a hike, we would go one level deeper by leaving the trails. If trails are ideas imposed on the wilderness, this was our chance to think outside the box. I signed on, and a few months later, mentioned the trip to my German brother-in-law, Fabian. He said, "Pete, I go anywhere. You tell me what to bring."

We tried to go in 2013, but the government shutdown derailed our plans. But now, in August 2014, if the ranger's phone call goes well, it'll launch ten days of exploring the unknown. And here he comes now.

"The permits check out. You're good to go." Then he gives us a look that adds: But this is a bad idea.

We embark the next day, bearing east into the woods, wending through sunny green forest, tracing contour lines on the map, semidrunk on our rapid progress. We're crossing on a southerly route, slaloming between Shoshone, Heart, and Yellowstone Lakes. It's a route that avoids most of the park's major attractions (that's where the trails are) in favor of meadows far from parking turnouts and forests that haven't yet been photographed and shared online. Yellowstone gets more than 3 million visitors a year, and almost nobody goes this deep into the park.

The oft-repeated reasons to hike off-trail have to do with solitude and stillness: You see less of the big-ticket stuff and notice more of the details. And you do. But solitude never felt this electric. Every step out here grants some uncharted thrill of terra incognita. When we stop in a patch of forest clover and the map and compass reveal that we're exactly on course, it feels preordained. Where else would we be?

The feeling lasts two days.

The third morning, we run out of lush, welcoming, stroll-through-fairyland forest and enter post-wildfire, screw-you-and-your-timetable new-growth pine. Dense, springy branches thwap our faces; we curse at them just to return the insult.

Even when the pines thin out, waist-high piles of deadfall logs have us crawling up and over and down, up and over and down, like ants navigating a spilled box of spaghetti. We routinely travel 50 yards without touching the ground; tracking our progress on the map finds us on the slow side of 1 mile per hour.

The physical toll is remarkable. While on-trail effort can be grinding, a day of off-trail scrambling with a heavy pack leaves your body feeling like it's been processed by the forest's digestive system. Fabian is being German about it, but I'm hurting to the point that I can barely cook dinner.

Maybe this is a bad idea, as the ranger intimated. Well, yes. But what choice do we have now?

Six days in, we break for sandwiches on the shores of Yellowstone Lake. Our eventual camp is visible just a mile across the water but will require eight trail miles of hiking. We'd cut across if it weren't for this lake, we say, chewing slowly to keep lunch from ending.

Then someone tosses a log into the water as a joke. It floats really well. We lash a couple of 15-foot logs together. They hold our weight.

Where does it say we must go off-trail on-foot?

Soon, we're waterproofing our packs to protect from errant splashes and paddling for the horizon on a Huck Finn raft. But just as we're on the cusp of real progress, the sky begins to darken. A storm drops over the ridge and blows us straight back to shore. The four-hour effort saves us exactly 400 yards of hiking. Still, it feels like a breakthrough—the lightbulb moment following a week of failed efforts.

As we go forward, we find we're more open to new navigational ideas and better at picking our way through the landscape. We're more feral and savvy, reading the terrain to see if ridgelines curve back onto our compass bearing and massaging our course based on wind direction, hoping to see an elk or moose or black bear before it smells us. We never do, but it constantly feels like we could.

Subtle paths and game trails reveal themselves in the undergrowth where none did before. It's like we're hiking to some new off-trail rhythm we hadn't been able to hear.

Our exit from the park goes up a valley to the saddle between two peaks, where we camp and prep our last day's hike, down a ridge. But when it comes time to leave, Travis suggests that we climb one of the peaks instead. We'll lounge around all day in the sun, he says, then come back and camp in the same spot two days in a row.

Fabian and I hesitate, because now that we're able to move more easily, staying put feels truly radical. But soon we're on a grassy plain at the summit, with nothing to do but sit in the sun and look back at a hundred miles of a national park that now feels like intimately familiar terrain.

We wander around, taking in views off different sides of the peak, exchanging looks that all say the same thing: What a great idea.

—Peter Frick-Wright

Halfdome, Yosemite National Park, California
Photo: Brad Beck / Tandem Stock

YOSEMITE NATIONAL PARK

Clouds Rest Trail

YOSEMITE NATIONAL PARK
CATHEDRAL LAKES TO HAPPY ISLES VIA CLOUDS REST

Hike across perhaps America's finest miles.

With a wink and a nod to the Grand Canyon's endless curves, Glacier's spiky summits, and Yellowstone's steaming geyser basins, Yosemite is the beauty queen of the national parks. No other park can quite match the granite domes, ground-shaking waterfalls, and massive sequoia groves for sheer scenic power. And no other stretch of trail better captures it all than these miles from Tuolumne Meadows, over a classic summit, and past a pair of cascades.

The highlights start rolling after the first 3.5 miles on the John Muir Trail, when you reach Upper and Lower Cathedral Lakes in an alpine bowl under 10,940-foot Cathedral Peak. Rejoin the John Muir Trail (via a short spur) and turn south toward Cathedral Pass to Sunrise High Sierra Camp. Turn north on the Sunrise Trail to Sunrise Lakes, a clutch of tarns with white granite "beaches," then hit a trail junction and go south on the Clouds Rest Trail.

Climbing along evergreen stands, isolated alpine lakes, and the eroding curvature of Tenaya Canyon, you may begin to feel like you're the only person left in the world. The trail drops through a small forested canyon; look for sheltered campsites about 13 miles in. Once past the narrow, rocky ridge, you'll be standing on a 9,926-foot summit, looking down on Half Dome—plus Tenaya Canyon, Yosemite Falls, El Capitan, and the Clark Range. You may not technically be on top of the world, but you'll feel like it.

Descend Clouds Rest's southern side to rejoin the John Muir Trail. Take it to Little Yosemite Valley, where hordes of Half Dome hopefuls gather for a shot at peak views similar to the ones you just earned. (Join them if your backcountry permit allows.) You'll have company on the Mist Trail as you descend beside 594-foot Nevada Fall and 317-foot Vernal Fall to Happy Isles, but you won't blame anyone for wanting a look at some of America's finest miles.

Photo: Aidan Klimenko

Text: Elisabeth Kwak-Hefferan

DISTANCE: 24 miles

TIME REQUIRED: 2–3 days

DIFFICULTY: Intermediate

CONTACT: Yosemite National Park, 209-372-020; nps.gov/yose

THE PAYOFF: Highlight reel of Yosemite's airiest views, brightest pools, and smoothest granite.

TRAILHEAD GPS: 37.873323, -119.382854

FINDING THE TRAILHEAD: Take CA 120 E to Big Oak Flat Road. Follow to Tuolumne Meadows Ranger Station for parking and wilderness permits. Book a shuttle or leave a car at Happy Isles.

WAYPOINTS & DIRECTIONS

GPS: 37.873159, -119.382720 Head southwest along the John Muir Trail from the Tuolumne Meadows trailhead, passing alongside the Cathedral Lakes beneath Cathedral Peak.

GPS: 37.794423, -119.433403 Pass the first camping option, Sunrise High Sierra Camp, before rounding the base of Sunrise Mountain and cutting north to the Sunrise Lakes, before heading south again through the valley on the west side of Sunrise Mountain.

GPS: 37.785334, -119.463358 The second camping option is found in the valley to the west of Sunrise Mountain. Continue southwest, veering right at the trail junction onto Clouds Rest Trail. Take the right spur to the top of Clouds Rest to look down on Half Dome—plus Tenaya Canyon, Yosemite Falls, El Capitan, and the Clark Range. Continue southwest, turning right at the junction with the John Muir Trail.

GPS: 37.730403, -119.560046 Follow the John Muir Trail through Yosemite Valley to the trailhead at Happy Isles.

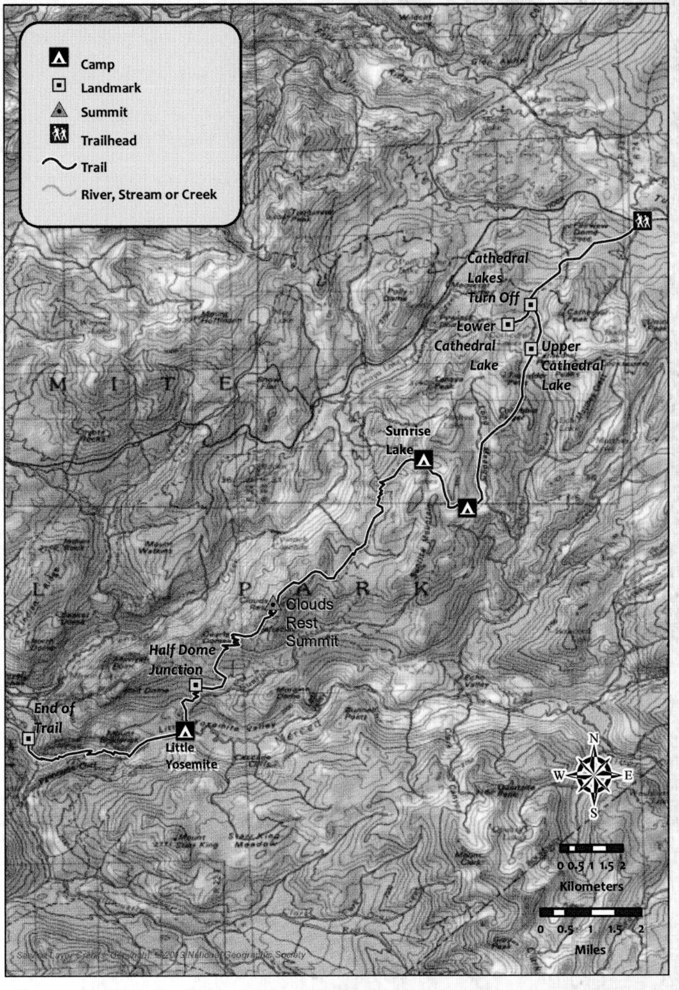

YOSEMITE NATIONAL PARK

HALF DOME

Climb 4,800 feet on this classic route to the top of the park's most iconic peak towering above the valley floor.

This is it, people: The most famous chunk of rock in the country and possibly the world. The iconic symbol of Yosemite grandeur, Half Dome just begs to be climbed. The 7-mile route to this granite landmark starts on the crowded Mist Trail, but only 300 people per day are allowed to summit Half Dome (when the cables are up; apply for a permit early). Visitors endure fatigue, altitude sickness, and dehydration in their determination to stand atop Half Dome's broad 8,836-foot-high crown. Steel cables bolted into the granite assist climbers up the final 400 vertical feet, but the combination of high, open rock and metal fixtures makes this a lousy place to get caught in a thunderstorm. And once the raindrops start falling, the rock becomes treacherously slick.

Up for the challenge? Go south from Happy Isles along the Merced River and wrap around Sierra Point. To the west, see tendrils of Illilouette Falls tumbling through a steep-walled gorge. Ahead, cross a footbridge; sheets of whitewater flow over Vernal Falls. Take a right onto the John Muir Trail and climb to Clark Point for slight views back into Yosemite Valley and Half Dome's south flank.

Stay with the John Muir Trail and cross a bridge over roaring Nevada Falls and look over to the bleached granite knob of Liberty Cap. Continue toward Little Yosemite Ranger Station and ahead, make a decision: either go left onto the John Muir Trail for Half Dome (4 hours) or go right to camp in Little Yosemite Valley (permit required) for an early start and a cherry-red sunrise tomorrow.

Continuing, take a left onto the Half Dome Trail at the 7,020-foot mark and head up tight switchbacks to the foot of the cables. When you reach the base of the cables, grab gloves and get in line for the final climb over airy slabs. Warning: If thunderheads loom, abort and go back.

Once you've crested the final cables, enjoy the summit where a nonstop, 360-degree view from Half Dome (8,836 feet) to the Sierra crest opens up. Check out El Capitan towering to the west across the Valley. Take hero shots and rest up before then backtracking for the return on the Mist Trail past Vernal Falls and Merced River. Close the loop and retrace your steps to Happy Isles.

To see Half Dome transformed—and to have it to yourself—consider tackling it while everyone else snoozes. Let the soft light of a full moon guide your way to the top on a 2 a.m. alpine start to arrive by sunrise. You'll never see Half Dome the same way again.

Half Dome's cables
Photo: iStockPhoto.com / paule858

DISTANCE: 15.7 miles

TIME REQUIRED: 1–2 days

DIFFICULTY: Strenuous

CONTACT: Yosemite National Park, (209) 372-020; nps.gov/yose

THE PAYOFF: Summit the most iconic hunk of rock in the world.

TRAILHEAD GPS: 37.73385, -119.558021

FINDING THE TRAILHEAD: From Spruce Lane and CA 140 in El Portal, head northeast on CA 140/Yosemite All-Year Highway. In 8.5 miles, turn right on CA 140. In 2.4 miles, continue straight onto Southside Drive. In 3.7 miles, turn right to stay on Southside Drive. In 0.5 mile, turn right onto Happy Isle Loop. Go 1 mile to trailhead.

WAYPOINTS & DIRECTIONS

GPS: 37.733850, -119.558021 Head south from Happy Isles along the Merced River and wrap around Sierra Point.

GPS: 37.726203, -119.548835 Turn right at Y switchbacking south on the John Muir Trail.

GPS: 37.724998, -119.544899 Keep right at Clark Point to stay on the John Muir Trail.

GPS: 37.722481, -119.535004 Stay left on John Muir Trail and then cross bridge over Nevada Falls.

GPS: 37.730691, -119.522560 Veer right toward Little Yosemite Ranger Station.

GPS: 37.732182, -119.515800 Two options here: Go left at Y to take the John Muir Trail to Half Dome (4 hours); or go right to camp at Little Yosemite Valley (permit required) for an early start.

GPS: 37.745365, -119.513016 Left at Y to Half Dome Trail (7,020 feet)

GPS: 37.746566, -119.530279 Grab gloves and get in line for the cable-aided final climb over airy slabs. (***Caution:*** If thunderheads loom, abort and go back.)

GPS: 37.745828, -119.533364 Half Dome. Pan 360 degrees for nonstop views, then backtrack to the John Muir Trail and Mist Trail divide, close to the Merced River. Turn right onto the Mist Trail.

GPS: 37.726681, -119.541603 Veer right at the Y, staying on Mist Trail past Vernal Falls. Close the loop where John Muir Trail converges with Mist Trail and retrace route to Happy Isles.

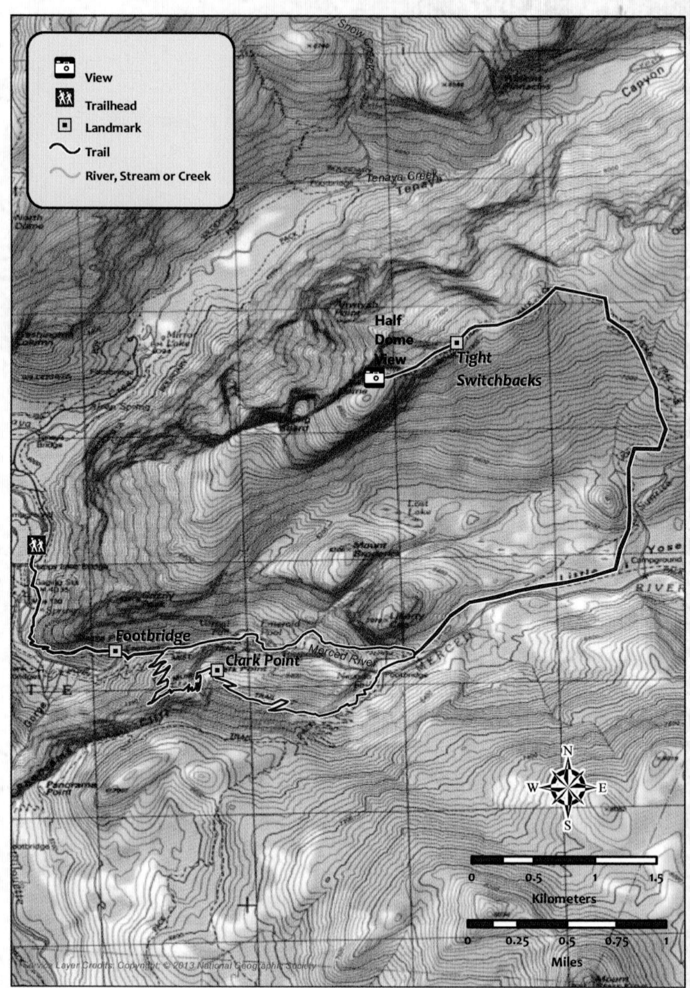

RANGER PROFILE

MIKE GAUTHIER

The Savior

Yosemite National Park, California

"He's someone who is one of us—a true end-user who just happens to be one of the country's foremost rangers." —Nancy Bouchard, *Backpacker* Contributor

Mike Gauthier has been chief of staff at Yosemite since 2010, but for more than 20 years, he worked in Rainier National Park, advancing from scrubbing toilets to managing SAR operations. Just about anyone who's swung an ice ax into the mountain's glaciers knows Gauthier's name. He built his reputation as a steady hand, the calm in the storm of climbs gone wrong, and the lives he has saved bear testament.

FAVORITE SPOT: Eagle Peak, Mount Rainier National Park, Washington

Gauthier hikes a lot in Yosemite, but still hasn't found anything to unseat Eagle Peak. Scramble a spiky saddle with views of the Tatoosh Range and a string of Cascade volcanoes (including Rainier itself) on this 7.2-mile round-trip hike. Switchback through old-growth forest, then ascend a rocky slope to the 5,700-foot saddle. The vistas are glorious from here, but the fearless can cross the exposed 0.3 mile to the 5,958-foot summit. "In the winter, I'd carry my snowboard up," Gauthier says. "It kept me in shape, and gave me a place to think."

TRAILHEAD: Longmire

INFO: nps.gov/mora

HIKE SMARTER:
4 WAYS TO HIKE RIGHT

Learn how to stay dry in a storm, navigate without a compass, and walk right.

1. Treat Your Feet

GET BOOTS THAT FIT—snug in the heel with enough room in the forefoot to allow for inevitable swelling on long days with a pack. Allow plenty of time to walk around in the store, feeling for pressure points and blister-causing heel slip. Most stores have an incline board; check for movement with your feet pointing both up- and downhill.

USE LIGHTWEIGHT, BREATHABLE SHOES (when trail conditions and weather allow). They'll reduce heat buildup, and heat accelerates blisters. Break in heavy boots on day hikes and around town. Keep your socks dry (change into a new pair if needed); air your feet at rest breaks. Treat hot spots proactively with a nonstretch sports tape like Leukotape (plain old duct tape also works).

CUT TOENAILS SHORT. Use a lubricant like Body Glide to reduce friction in problem areas. Lace boots with precision comfort: Tie an overhand loop at the ankle to create a locking twist, and repeat at each eyelet. Adjust tension where needed, or even skip an eyelet altogether.
GOT A BLISTER ANYWAY? Turn to page 189.

2. Stay Dry in a Storm

START WITH A SHELL THAT EXTENDS BELOW YOUR HIPS, so there's no gap between jacket and pants where rain can sneak in. Cinch the hem snugly. Roll up the cuffs of your baselayer so they don't wick water up your sleeves, and cinch your jacket's cuffs. Avoid raising your arms (giving water easier access to your cuffs) and shorten trekking poles, so your wrists are angled down.

KEEP YOUR HOOD SNUG, and wear a waterproof-breathable, billed cap underneath to enhance face protection in the worst weather.

WEAR GAITERS with your rain pants when you're walking through wet, leg-soaking brush.

DON'T SWEAT. Even the most breathable rain gear can be overwhelmed from the inside if your exertion is too great. Getting steamy? Open every pit zip and vent, shed layers, and if needed, simply slow down. In warm, humid conditions, skip the jacket and use an umbrella.

KEEP YOUR STUFF DRY. Use a pack liner or dry bags, and don't expose dry gear to the rain during breaks.

3. Navigate Without a Compass

STARS: Find the Big Dipper. Extend an imaginary line through the two stars at the end of the outer cup to a medium-bright star (about five times the distance between the two Big Dipper stars). This is the North Star.

PLANT: In the Eastern and Midwestern prairies, look for the bright yellow bloom of the compass plant. Its leaves generally align along the north-south axis.

WATCH: Hold an analog watch level, with the hour hand pointing to the sun. South is halfway between the hour hand and the 12. (Northern Hemisphere only.)

SHADOW STICK: Stand a three-foot stick vertically in the ground and mark the tip of its shadow with a rock. Wait at least 15 minutes, then mark the shadow again. The connecting line roughly indicates east-west; south is on the sun side of the line.

Hiking is more than just walking forward

4. Walk Right

EASY STRIDER. Taking giant steps can lead to overuse injuries like strained quads and hip bursitis. Shorter steps minimize pounding and muscle exertion, making your stride more energy efficient even though you take more steps overall.

ROCK ON. Forefoot striking is OK for running, not walking. Pounding on the forefoot, rather than gradually rocking the foot from back to front, can cause foot and leg problems, including the very painful metatarsalgia.

PUSH IT. You want to push off with your toes with each new step. Omitting this final toe-off phase by shuffling or dragging your feet jars joints from head to toe.

INSIDE JOB. Avoid lashing heavy items to the outside of your pack. They'll throw you off balance and stress pack seams.

Photo: mapraest / shutterstock

Yosemite granite

YOSEMITE NATIONAL PARK

TUOLUMNE GROVE TO HODGDON MEADOW

Attain deep-forest tranquility on this leisurely amble to Yosemite's Tuolumne Grove of giant sequoias, home to some of the largest living organisms on earth.

East of the towering crags and pointy spires of the Clarke and Cathedral Ranges, Yosemite unfolds into a peaceful landscape blanketed by sprawling forest and breeze-kissed meadows. On this predominantly downhill 5.8-miler, meander through a hallway of trees en route to the legendary Tuolumne Grove of giant sequoias before rolling to the idyllic Hodgdon Meadow. Best completed as a shuttle hike, this route connects the Tuolumne Grove Trailhead with the Big Oak Flat Entrance Station. Parking lots are available at each trailhead. To make the trip using one car, park at the Tuolumne Grove Trailhead and make the 2.2-mile out-and-back to the sequoia grove.

Begin by padding through an old-growth forest of Douglas firs, sugar pines, incense cedar, and white firs. With North Crane Creek weaving through the woods to your left, wander downhill at a gentle grade until reaching the grove's southern terminus at mile 1. Marked by an interpretive panel, the grove's southernmost sequoia soars unmistakably to the left of the trail. Follow signs to the oft-photographed Tunnel Tree, which was bored through in the early 20th century so that tourists could pass through on stagecoach.

Continue heading north to visit the grove's 20-some sequoias. After crossing North Crane Creek and Hazel Green Creek, the mildly graded trail approaches Hodgdon Meadow. Bordered by evergreens and dotted with wind-teased grasses and pockets of wildflowers, the small but open-skied Hodgdon provides a welcome respite from the cool woods. Hike along the meadow's eastern edge to reach your car at the Big Oak Flat Entrance Station. Make the 8.8-mile return trip to the Tuolumne Grove trailhead by driving south on Big Oak Flat Road.

Photo: Aidan Klimenko

DISTANCE: 5.8 miles

TIME REQUIRED: 1 day

DIFFICULTY: Easy

CONTACT: Yosemite National Park, (209) 372-020; nps.gov/yose

THE PAYOFF: Relaxing stroll among towering trees and soft meadows.

TRAILHEAD GPS: 37.758317, -119.805833

FINDING THE TRAILHEAD: From Groveland, follow CA 120 E for 33.5 miles. Turn left as CA 120 becomes Tioga Pass Road. In 0.5 mile, parking and trailhead are on the left side of the road. [Recast with first W&D point below to start with shuttle-car drop at Big Oak Flat Entrance Station?

WAYPOINTS & DIRECTIONS

GPS: 37.758317, -119.805833 Leave a car in the lot at the Tuolumne Grove Trailhead and head north to get started.

GPS: 37.767683, -119.805667 Break into Tuolumne Grove, whose southern edge is marked by the massive Tunnel Tree.

GPS: 37.768583, -119.805700 Cross through the legendary Tunnel Tree. After exploring the grove, push on to Hodgdon Meadow (4.1 miles north), or turn around to return to the Tuolumne Grove trailhead.

GPS: 37.795500, -119.856900 Go right at the Y junction, as the trail begins to trace the eastern edge of idyllic Hodgdon Meadow.

GPS: 37.798083, -119.862100 Big Oak Flat Entrance Station and Visitor Center marks this route's northern terminus. Pick up your car here and drive south on CA 120/Big Oak Flat Road to return to the trailhead.

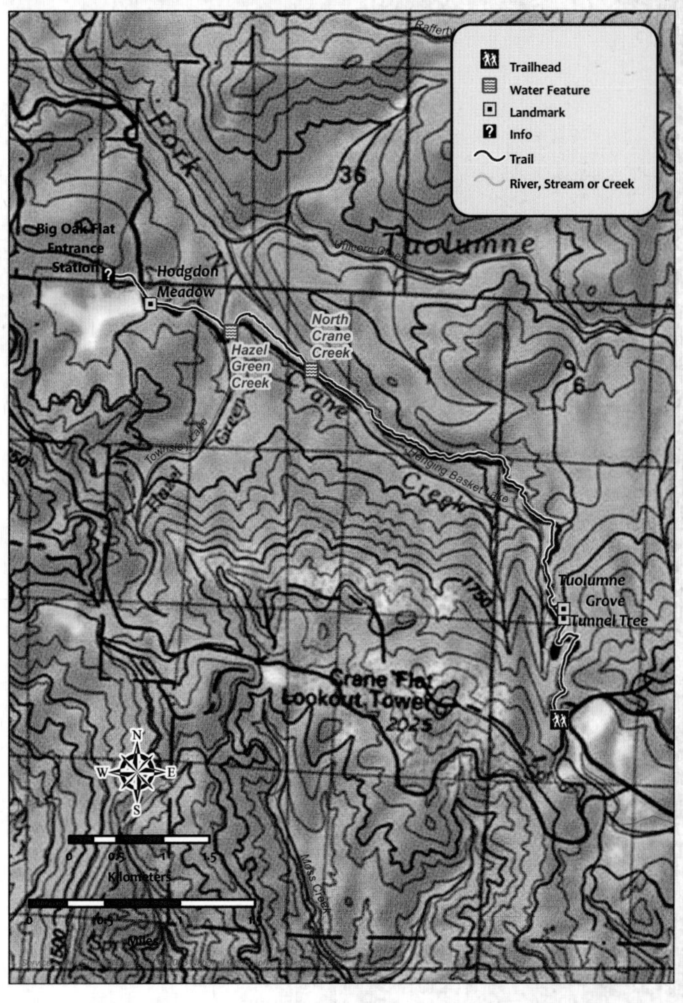

YOSEMITE NATIONAL PARK

THE MIST TRAIL

This short Yosemite classic full of rainbows, waterfalls, and sprawling mountainside views isn't called the Mist Trail for nothing.

With waterfalls come rainbows—and Yosemite's short, moderate Mist Trail allows hikers of all abilities to promenade beneath them. Start before 7 a.m. to get a jump on the 3,000 hikers that depart from the Happy Isles trailhead each summer day. Crossing the Happy Isles Bridge, head right on a paved path toward Vernal Falls Bridge and Mist Trail's only view of Illilouette Falls. The vista is located beneath Sierra Point, which is famous for being the only location in Yosemite where you can see four waterfalls—Yosemite, Illilouette, Vernal, and Nevada. Unfortunately, the trail to Sierra Point was decimated by a rockslide in the 1970s. March uphill to Sierra Point and witness the downpour of four fantastic falls: Illilouette, Vernal, Nevada, and Yosemite. After walking over the next footbridge, turn left to catch the first glance of Vernal Falls. Bear left at the three-way junction, staying on Mist Trail. Don't forget to pack rain gear, which is necessary while ascending the granite steps to Vernal Falls. After reaching the falls' summit—and turnaround point of this trip—take a moment to enjoy the lagoon-like Silver Apron and Emerald Pool. Retrace your route back to the trailhead.

Up for more? Keep going to expand the scope of the Mist Trail (and add another 5 miles to your trip). After getting doused at Vernal Fall, keep going to top out above 597-foot Nevada Falls. Hang a right on the John Muir Trail, which serves up a prize view of Half Dome and Liberty Cap towering above Nevada Falls' torrent of water. Continue on to Clark Point and more views of pounding cascades before descending to rejoin the Mist Trail.

Vernal Falls

Text: Dave Miller

DISTANCE: 3 miles

TIME REQUIRED: 1 day

DIFFICULTY: Easy

CONTACT: Yosemite National Park, (209) 372-020; nps.gov/yose

THE PAYOFF: Water, rainbows, and the awesome power of Yosemite's falls.

TRAILHEAD GPS: 37.7327271, -119.5604935

FINDING THE TRAILHEAD: From Spruce Lane and CA 140 in El Portal, head northeast on CA 140/Yosemite All-Year Highway. In 8.5 miles, turn right on CA 140. In 2.4 miles, continue straight onto Southside Drive. In 3.7 miles, turn right to stay on Southside Drive. In 0.5 mile, turn right onto Happy Isle Loop. Go 0.5 mile to trailhead.

WAYPOINTS & DIRECTIONS

GPS: 37.732727, -119.560494 From the trailhead and shuttle stop, cross the Happy Isles Bridge then turn right onto the well-paved trail. The first mile gradually ascends to the Vernal Falls Bridge.

GPS: 37.726326, -119.556816 Illilouette Falls Vista, the only point on the Mist Trail where the Illiouette Falls can be viewed.

GPS: 37.726086, -119.551681 Cross footbridge and head left up the Mist Trail. Get your first glimpse of Vernal Falls.

GPS: 37.726311, -119.548698 Keep left on the Mist Trail at the three-way junction with the John Muir Trail. Prepare yourself for granite steps and plenty of moisture. Put on your rain gear and head on up. Once you get into the mist, don't forget to look back to see rainbows and, if you're lucky, double rainbows.

GPS: 37.727364, -119.543396 At the top of Vernal Falls, take some time to dry off and gaze at the rushing waters of Vernal Falls. Before heading back, continue to the left along the Merced River. Hikers can slide down the granite at Emerald Pool and the Silver Apron when the Merced has low water levels.

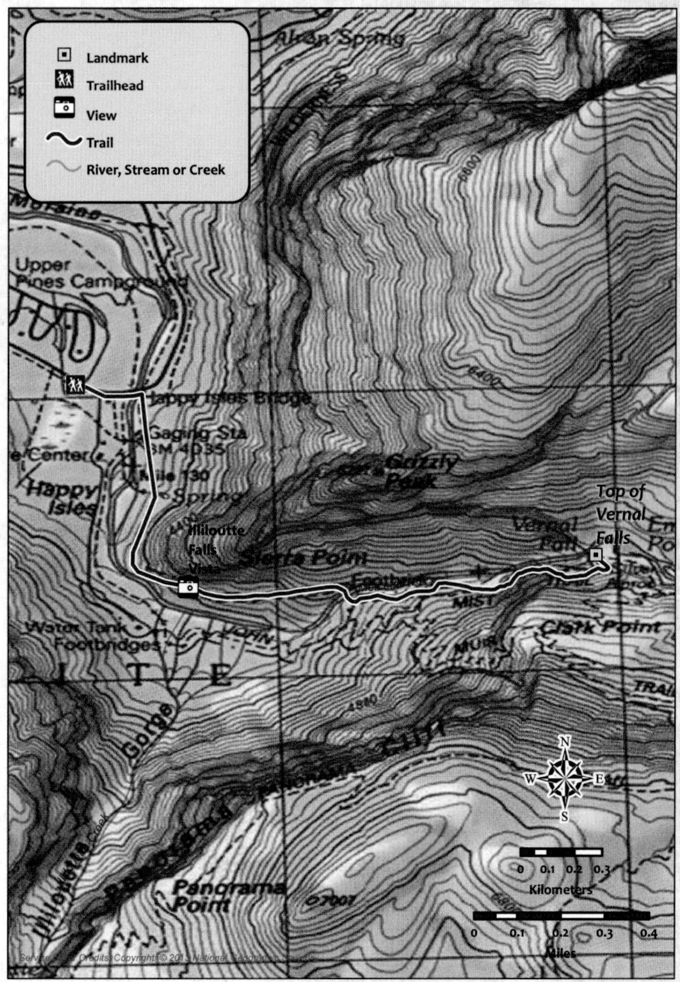

YOSEMITE NATIONAL PARK

THE NORTH RIM TRAIL

Yosemite Falls

Piece together several trails and spurs for the best views and remote campsites in and above Yosemite Valley.

Despite Yosemite's belle-of-the-ball status among national parks, backpackers willing to put in an extra mile (or 20) can still find triple-A views and surprising solitude. This 31-mile shuttle hike is one of the best ways to do just that.

From the Rockslides trailhead, follow the now defunct roadbed of Old Big Oak Flat Road Trail. In the first few minutes, you'll see the shaved granite wall of El Capitan piercing the skyline. At mile 1.7, where a massive rockslide blocks the road, follow cairns uphill to the next intact section of roadbed. The upcoming 2.5 miles pass through dense manzanita; peek out at Bridalveil Falls, and end at a campsite near Cascade Creek.

Top off water bottles and backtrack 0.6 mile the next morning to North Rim Trail. Turn left and climb through sugar pines, contour around El Cap Gully, and take the 0.3-mile spur trail to the 7,569-foot granite prow of El Capitan. Backtrack and head northeast for 1.8 miles to another spur up 7,779-foot Eagle Peak. Swing north, then east to Yosemite Falls Trail. Turn right and hike south to end this big 12-mile day at your second campsite. Catch the sunset glow at a nearby overlook of Yosemite Falls, a high-decibel whitewater ribbon falling almost 2,400 feet.

Photo: Aidan Klimenko

Text: Kelly Bastone

On day three, see the sunrise from Yosemite Point (6,936 feet), then continue east for four miles to North Dome for a front-row view of the cleaved granite face of Half Dome. Hike north for 3.5 miles, passing a side trail to Indian Rock, a rare granite arch. In 3.8 miles, turn right onto Snow Creek Trail and camp on a gravel bench with oh-my-God views of Half Dome.

The last day, descend 100-plus switchbacks over 2,500 feet into Tenaya Canyon. Follow the north side of Tenaya Creek, pass Mirror Lake, and pick up the free park shuttle back to your car.

DISTANCE: 31 miles

TIME REQUIRED: 4 days

DIFFICULTY: Strenuous

CONTACT: Yosemite National Park, (209) 372-020; nps.gov/yose

THE PAYOFF: Savor Yosemite's icons in solitude on a 4-day exploration

TRAILHEAD GPS: 37.7237756, -119.6448576

FINDING THE TRAILHEAD: To reach the unsigned Rockslides trailhead from Yosemite Village, take Valley Loop Road west to milepost 9 and park on the right, by the metal gate.

WAYPOINTS & DIRECTIONS

GPS: 37.723776, -119.644858 Hike north from the Rockslides trailhead.

GPS: 37.726055, -119.646541 Junction. Stay on Old Big Oak Flat Road Trail, heading west onto faint roadbed.

GPS: 37.722934, -119.669493 Scramble uphill and northwest, over rockslide debris, following occasional cairns.

GPS: 37.723309, -119.670843 Resume hiking on Old Big Oak Flat Road Trail.

GPS: 37.722659, -119.674171 Rainbow View. This is where photographers take pictures of Bridalveil Falls: The angle produces rainbows.

GPS: 37.734272, -119.703684 Trail junction. Veer left to continue north to the first campsite.

GPS: 37.742078, -119.702954 Camp near Cascade Creek. The next day, backtrack to the junction and turn left.

GPS: 37.741031, -119.694390 Continue east.

GPS: 37.737700, -119.636908 Trail junction. Head south on the spur trail to the top of El Capitan.

GPS: 37.734069, -119.637551 El Capitan. Head back to the main trail and turn right to continue east.

GPS: 37.752665, -119.616308 Take spur trail south to Eagle Peak.

GPS: 37.746060, -119.614806 Eagle Peak. Head back to the main trail and continue straight, trekking north on Snow Creek Trail.

GPS: 37.766474, -119.603090 Turn right (south) toward Yosemite Falls at the trail junction, staying on Snow Creek Trail.

GPS: 37.759655, -119.599013 Veer left at the Yosemite Falls Trail junction and continue just a bit farther east to the campsite.

GPS: 37.759078, -119.597597 Second campsite.

GPS: 37.757348, -119.596868 In the morning, take this spur to the Yosemite Falls Overlook. Lots of hikers miss: The descent, carved out of the cliff, is hard to see unless you're looking for it. After, continue east on Snow Creek Trail.

GPS: 37.756432, -119.593134 Yosemite Point. Catch the morning sun here on day three. Backtrack to the main trail.

GPS: 37.771970, -119.581032 Indian Canyon Creek. Continue southeast.

GPS: 37.769413, -119.574627 Trail junction. Follow the maintained Snow Creek Trail southeast.

(*continued*)

GPS: 37.761317, -119.560432 Trail junction. Take spur trail to North Dome.

GPS: 37.755617, -119.560261 Top of North Dome. Backtrack and head north.

GPS: 37.775522, -119.556527 Junction, spur trail leads to Indian Rock, a granite arch. Continue on North Dome/Snow Creek Trail.

GPS: 37.786724, -119.559027 Turn right.

GPS: 37.791337, -119.541292 Pretty little cascades. Swing south along Snow Creek.

GPS: 37.773191, -119.540091 Head right at the trail junction, to continue south along North Dome/Snow Creek Trail.

GPS: 37.770850, -119.540605 Hit Snow Creek Trail, head southeast to campsite.

GPS: 37.769731, -119.538717 Third campsite. Amazing, oh-my-God views of Half Dome and Clouds Rest. The next day, backtrack to main trail and turn left to switchback down into valley.

GPS: 37.759214, -119.539382 Turn right at junction with Tenaya Loop Trail, heading west to descend on the north side of Tenaya Creek.

GPS: 37.741569, -119.560003 Hike ends at shuttle stop.

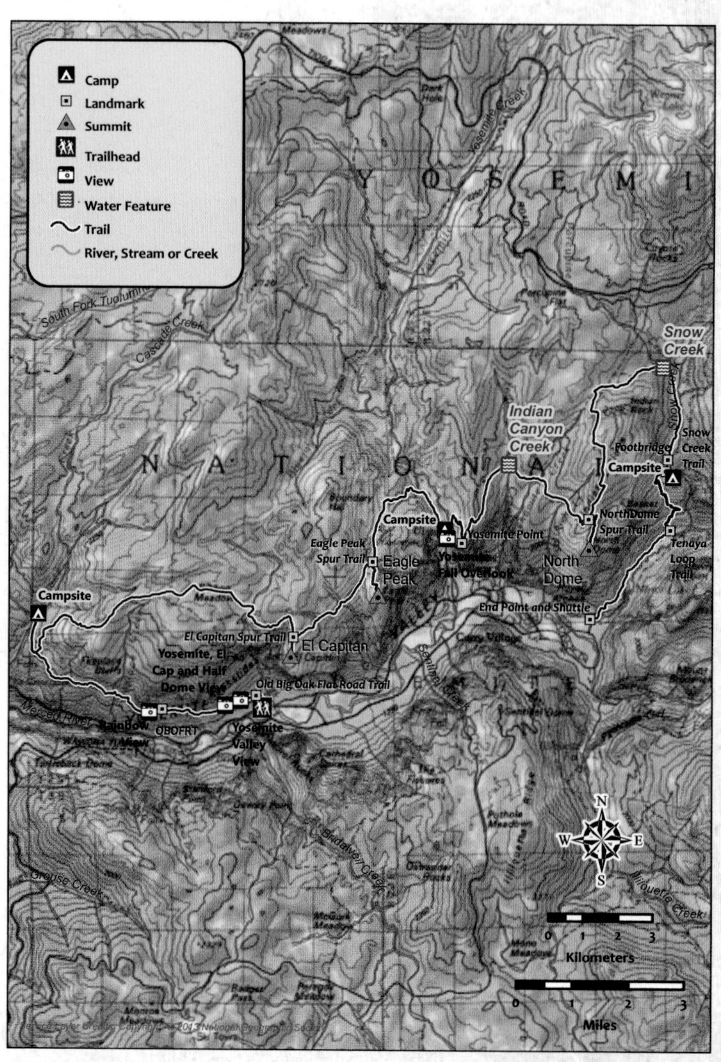

Yosemite Valley
Photo: Aidan Klimenko

Steep Valley
Photo: Thinkstock

ZION
NATIONAL
PARK

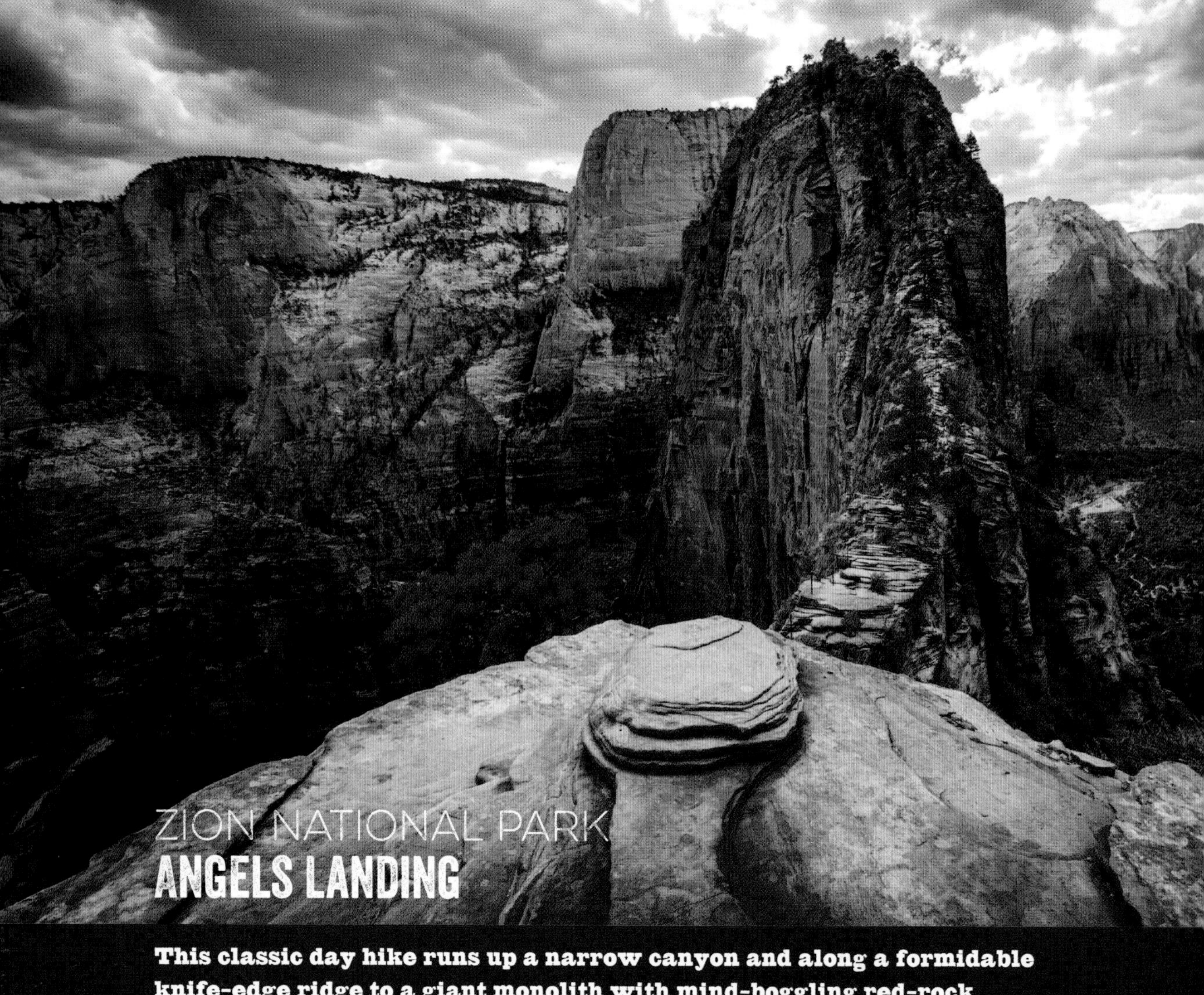

ZION NATIONAL PARK

ANGELS LANDING

This classic day hike runs up a narrow canyon and along a formidable knife-edge ridge to a giant monolith with mind-boggling red-rock views.

Few trails have as fitting a name as Angels Landing. The eagle-eye view over Zion Canyon from the crest of this 5,790-foot exposed rock fin is heavenly—and acrophobic hikers might need to summon a guardian angel for bravery. It's also the most popular day hike in Zion, and justifiably one of the top hikes in the entire national park system.

Start out along the West Rim Trail, 2 miles of mellow paved trail shaded by tall cottonwoods that follow the burbling Virgin River. These groves provide shelter for frogs, chipmunks, flowering manzanitas, and multiple bird species. Before long, the path kicks upward in a hurry, leaving the river valley via steep switchbacks that cut into canyon walls of pink Navajo sandstone. Don't forget to look up: Endangered raptors like California condors and peregrine falcons soar above the towering cliffs.

Photo: iStockPhoto.com / Martin McCarthy

Text: Rajeev Jain and Mike Trottier

View from Angels Landing

After 1.3 miles, head into the tight confines of Refrigerator Canyon, where overhanging cliffs create shade and constant cool breezes to refresh sun-blasted hikers. Then comes your first crucible: Walter's Wiggles, an infamous set of short switchbacks that zigzag 21 times to the top of the ridge. These are named after Walter Ruesch, Zion National Park's first superintendent, who in 1925 resolved to build a path to the top of Angels Landing despite having no training or experience in engineering. His resulting Wiggles, constructed mostly by hand and with natural materials, remain an aesthetic exemplar of a trail that doesn't scar the landscape. "Zion is God's country; don't make it look like hell," Ruesch said.

Catch your breath (or use the restroom) on Scout Lookout, a broad saddle with views into Zion Canyon. Those afraid of heights should consider turning back; the brave can continue south on the Angels Landing Trail to a pinched ridge. From here, it's up up up on the final dizzying 0.5 mile. The 400-foot, chain-assisted final push up this classic summit crosses an exposed ridgeline just a few feet wide with 1,000-foot drop-offs on both sides. Use the chains to steady your grip, and mind your footing as you engage in a moderate scramble up chunky sandstone to the top. Move slowly (and maybe don't look down). Then comes the payoff: Angels Landing. From the top of your deserved perch, you'll see massive, sheer-walled red canyons extending in every direction. Look down—way down—to spot the Virgin River flowing through green-carpeted Zion Canyon around the horseshoe bend of the Angels Landing promontory. Snap hero shots before retracing the exposed route back to the main trail and down to the canyon floor. The return goes much faster, but take special care: Most injuries occur on the descent of Angels Landing.

DISTANCE: 5.2 miles

TIME REQUIRED: 4–6 hours

DIFFICULTY: Strenuous

CONTACT: Zion National Park, (435) 772-3256; nps.gov/zion

THE PAYOFF: Thrill to the airiest perch in Southwest.

TRAILHEAD GPS: 37.259407, -112.9506454

FINDING THE TRAILHEAD: From Springdale, take UT 9 E/Zion Park Boulevard to Zion Canyon Road. Turn left and go 3.4 miles to the parking area, on the right. (***Note:*** From April to October, park in Springdale and take the Zion Canyon Shuttle to the trailhead.)

WAYPOINTS & DIRECTIONS

GPS: 37.259407, -112.950645 From the trailhead, walk northwest along paved trail toward the Virgin River.

GPS: 37.259899, -112.951439 Cross footbridge, then turn right onto the West Rim Trail, climbing northeast.

GPS: 37.264816, -112.950447 Trail bends left, leading uphill.

GPS: 37.268642, -112.951630 Leave river valley on steep switchbacks that cut into canyon walls.

GPS: 37.269665, -112.950378 Turn left, heading north into the tight confines of Refrigerator Canyon.

GPS: 37.275642, -112.951462 Climb Walter's Wiggles, a group of 21 short switchbacks, to the top of the ridge.

GPS: 37.274639, -112.950722 Stay straight at three-way junction, heading south on Angels Landing Trail.

GPS: 37.272499, -112.950226 Continue south on pinched ridge; watch your footing on uneven terrain (***Caution:*** There are 1,000-foot drop-offs on either side of the trail.)

GPS: 37.270843, -112.949707 Hold onto chains bolted into the rock face to ascend exposed ridgeline.

GPS: 37.269344, -112.947899 Angels Landing. Massive, sheer-walled canyons extend in every direction. Look down—way down—to spot the Virgin River flowing through Zion Canyon. Retrace route back to the trailhead.

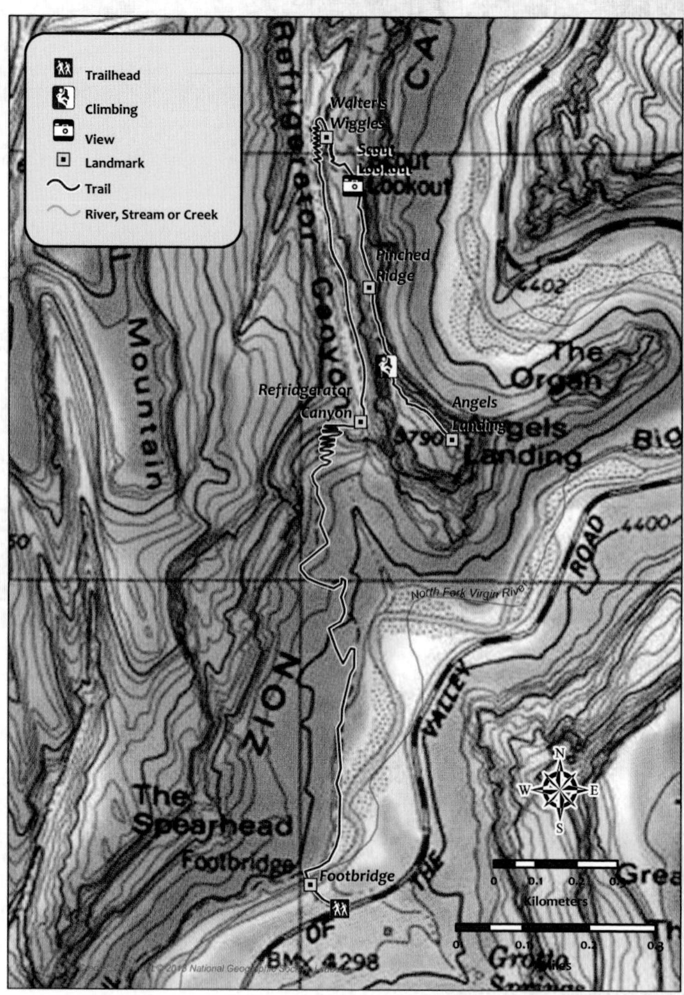

ZION NATIONAL PARK

ZION NARROWS

Sluice through towering walls of sandstone and hike-scramble-wade-swim through one of the finest river gorges on earth.

It's the sweetest mile in the best slot canyon in America—maybe the world—even if it's not a trail, per se. Rippled red rocks reaching hundreds of feet above you echo the riffled Virgin River washing around you. To hike it is to be swallowed by the canyon itself, in the best possible way. Nowhere is this feeling more apparent than when the walls pinch to 20 feet wide in the mile-long Wall Street corridor at the mouth of the Orderville Canyon (Narrows mile 2.7). Consider it the absolute zenith of a trek that's already in the upper echelon of the national-parks experience.

This justly renowned hike consists of a clear, swift stream running through a 2,000-foot-deep sandstone gorge. Quiet side canyons, striking glades of maple and ponderosa, and lush hanging gardens of monkeyflower make it a must-do for fit hikers with strong ankles and knees. From mile 3 to mile 15, you'll be wading over slick bowling-ball-size rocks most of the time. It is not a trail hike—expect to get wet to your waist often.

The Narrows can be trekked as a long day hike or an overnight (recommended). If done in a day, you'll need to start early and travel fast to mile 10. Below here, the route gets rougher, deeper, and much slower. Many overconfident hikers find themselves struggling to finish in deep water, near darkness, and chilly evening temperatures. Instead of shooting the Narrows in a day, slow down and spend a night to savor the experience.

From the Chamberlain Ranch trailhead, head southwest down the riverside road and after 3 miles, wade into the Virgin River. At 6.5 miles, the canyon narrows to just 20 feet wide. At 8.7 miles, detour 0.5 mile down Deep Creek to overnight at Campsite #5, perched above the river, or Campsite #12 if you're with a group. The next day, negotiate the Goose Creek Confluence (deep pools and boulder piles can make this 0.75-mile section a 2-hour ordeal), then continue past Big Springs (which generally requires swimming). Next up, hit the Temple of Sinawava and its 3,000-foot walls to the finish.

The best season is from May through October. Continual water makes this a fine hike even in oven-hot weather. In midsummer, the water will rarely be more than knee deep. In spring, much of it is thigh deep, and several sections may require swimming. Under normal conditions, the Narrows is a fun, safe, athletic hike, but conditions mean everything. Whitewater kayakers occasionally paddle the Narrows during spring runoff in flows between 400 and 600 cubic feet per second. Under such conditions, it's a very dangerous Class V river, with raging currents, numerous logjams, boulder piles, and a blind 20-foot waterfall.

Text: Steve Howe and Elisabeth Kwak-Hefferan

The Virgin River flows through the Zion Canyon Narrows
Photo: iStockPhoto.com / liteserv

DISTANCE: 15.6 miles

TIME REQUIRED: 1–2 days

DIFFICULTY: Strenuous

CONTACT: Zion National Park, (435) 772-3256; nps.gov/zion

THE PAYOFF: Cold water meets towering red sandstone walls hundreds of feet high.

TRAILHEAD GPS: 37.384665, -112.838934

FINDING THE TRAILHEAD: From Salt Lake City or Las Vegas, take I-15 and UT9 to the town of Springdale. From here you can take your own shuttle vehicle to Chamberlin Ranch trailhead, but it's a 1.5-hour drive each way. The preferred option is taking a commercial shuttle ($35) from one of three outfitters. If day-hiking, take an early (6:30 a.m.) shuttle. From the hike's end at Temple of Sinawava, take the free park bus to the visitor center, then transfer to the Springdale town shuttle. This will return you to your car at whichever outfitter you used.

WAYPOINTS & DIRECTIONS

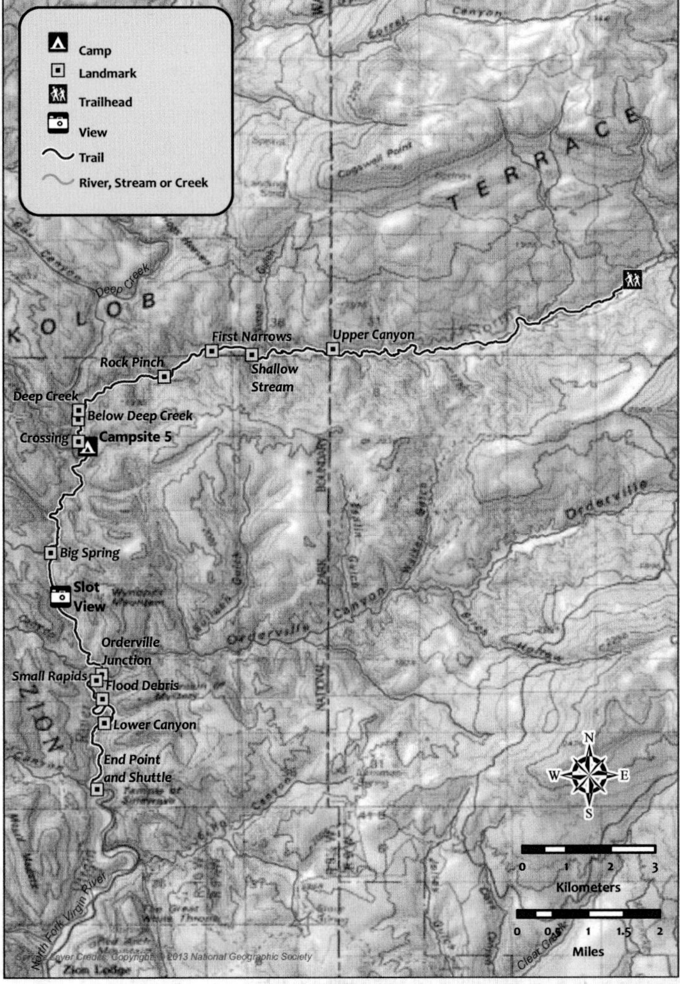

GPS: 37.384665, -112.838934 Chamberlain Ranch trailhead. Follow user trail or dirt road, your choice. (***Note:*** this trailhead is on private land. No camping.)

GPS: 37.376067, -112.858509 Meet up with the road again and follow it west downcanyon.

GPS: 37.372791, -112.864026 Leave road, descend to river and follow old ATV track.

GPS: 37.371088, -112.879084 The vehicle tracks end here as cliff-to-cliff water begins.

GPS: 37.370990, -112.923573 Deep, tight narrows begin, including sections only 20 feet wide.

GPS: 37.370636, -112.926368 Second tight narrows section.

GPS: 37.368838, -112.930093 First obvious side canyon, on river right.

GPS: 37.367744, -112.931249 National Park Service Campsite #1 is found on river left among pines on riverside bench.

GPS: 37.365960, -112.937446 20-foot-high waterfall over logjam. Detour by climbing left (south) through the crack behind a house-size boulder.

GPS: 37.365994, -112.938666 Rugged boulder pile requires extensive clambering.

GPS: 37.359376, -112.951983 Deep Creek Confluence. Park Service Campsites #2 and #3 can be found in the immediate area. Continue heading south and downstream. (*continued*)

GPS: 37.355209, -112.951701 Park Service Campsite #4. Not ideal, since the trail runs right through it.

GPS: 37.352319, -112.949713 Park Service Campsite #5. Small, with room for two. Camp on a large, flat boulder overlooking the river; limited weather shelter is provided by overhang at cliff.

GPS: 37.344027, -112.951911 Park Service Campsite #8.

GPS: 37.337998, -112.956016 Many deep pools with steep dirt detour trails and boulder scrambles in between. Slow travel to Big Spring.

GPS: 37.337259, -112.955729 Park Service Campsite #10. Overhanging wall provides rain shelter.

GPS: 37.334648, -112.955559 Park Service Campsite #11. Nice, open site that feels more alpine and less gloomy than others.

GPS: 37.332587, -112.956508 Park Service Campsite #12, hidden off-trail on the bench to the river's left. This group site sleeps maximum 12 people.

GPS: 37.329188, -112.957357 Long, straight hallway with deep water throughout. May require swimming through mid-June with average runoff or any time after significant rainfall.

GPS: 37.318008, -112.951942 Second deep water section. Boulders in sandy streambed form deep pits that you may have to swim around.

GPS: 37.309662, -112.949231 Imlay Canyon confluence is invisible on heights above river. Canyoneers finish this extremely difficult narrows with a 180-foot free rappel to river.

GPS: 37.307881, -112.946776 Mouth of Orderville Canyon. You'll encounter many hikers from here to finish.

GPS: 37.299973, -112.944552 Deepest water of the lower canyon. Waist to chest deep along the wall on the river's right.

GPS: 37.299279, -112.944303 Mystery Canyon, visible as a steep moss-covered slab with a waterfall runnel coming down. Canyoneers may be rappelling out.

GPS: 37.293947, -112.948327 Sandstone rock wall signals beginning of asphalt tourist trail to Temple of Sinawava.

GPS: 37.285201, -112.947735 Temple of Sinawava. The end of the hike, with a shuttle bus stop and parking lot.

HIKE SMARTER:

Keep your top tools going strong through seasons of use and abuse.

1. Save Your Zippers

Midnight yanking on the sleeping bag and tent door (who hasn't done that?), overstuffing a pack (ditto), and accumulated dirt and grime can all cause snags and damaged teeth.

KEEP ZIPPERS CLEAN: At home, use water and a toothbrush, or a vacuum cleaner. For problem zippers, apply Gear Aid Zip Care, a lubricant and cleaner. In a pinch, a drip of candle wax works to lubricate.

ZIPPERS USE EITHER COILS OR TEETH, AND BOTH CAN SUFFER DAMAGE. Straighten bent coils with a knife or needle. For a misaligned tooth, gently pinch it with needle-nose pliers and it should return to its place (though if it snaps, you'll need to replace the zipper).

DAMAGED—I.E. LOOSE OR WORN—SLIDERS STOP WEAVING ZIPPER SIDES TOGETHER. They can often be fixed by pinching with pliers: Squeeze evenly on both sides, and check the fit often to make sure you didn't overtighten. Depending on the type of zipper, broken sliders can be tricky to replace. Open-ended zippers, which come apart at the bottom (like those on jackets), are easier than standard zippers (like those on tents and backpacks). For an open-ended zipper: Use wire cutters to crack off the "stop" at the end of the zipper track. Pull off the old slider, replace with a new one, and use needle-nose pliers to crimp a new stop in place. (Look for zipper components at fabric stores.) Standard zipper: Pry or cut off the broken slider, then install a screw-on FixnZip slider.

2. Wash Your Sleeping Bag
Prevent dirt and body oils from diminishing loft. Before tossing the bag in a front-loading washer (it's worth the trip to a Laundromat), turn it inside out to allow the water and soap to flow freely through the insulation. Zip it up and fasten any Velcro closures. Wash in warm water on the delicate cycle using either a synthetic- or down-specific cleaning product depending on your bag's fill. Run the bag through an additional rinse cycle. At the Laundromat, dry on low heat with a couple of tennis balls for several cycles. At home, unzip the bag and let it air dry overnight.

3. Make Boots Last
No toe cap? Boost protection easily by building a cheap one out of strong, clear polyurethane. Clean the rand by wiping it down with rubbing alcohol; let dry. Apply masking tape across the front of the boot to section off the area for the cap. Sand the leather on the toe with extra-fine sandpaper. Buff the sanded area twice with a rag dipped in rubbing alcohol, air-drying in between. Paint the toe surface completely with Gear Aid Freesole. Remove the tape after 45 minutes; let dry overnight.

4. Defunk a Hydration Bladder

Fill with clean water and add a half-teaspoon of bleach per liter. After an hour, drain, rinse, and prop open to air dry. Remove any bleach taste by repeating the wash cycle with a tablespoon of baking soda per liter. Store in the freezer to prevent mildew from growing. Clean gunky hoses with a gun-barrel brush.

5. Prep Your Tent
CLEAN IT: Pitch your tent and hose it down inside and out; sponge off dirt using a bucket of water mixed with a few drops of mild dish soap. Leave set up to air dry.

ELIMINATE MILDEW SMELL: Add 1 cup of Lysol to a tub of water and soak both the fly and tent body for a few minutes. Rinse and air dry. Repeat the process with 1 cup of table salt, 1 cup of concentrated lemon juice, and a gallon of warm water.

INSPECT FOR WEAR AND TEAR: To repair holes in mesh walls, use back-to-back micromesh adhesive patches. If you spot separated seams in the floor or rain fly, adhere a Tear-Aid patch to the inside and apply a sealant to the outside of the repair and let it cure overnight.

6. Refresh Waterproofing
BOOTS: Even if your boots have a waterproof membrane, the outer material can still get saturated if not properly waterproofed, which makes feet feel heavy and cold even if no water actually penetrates. Before each season, apply a sealant: Nikwax and ReviveX make waterproofing products for both leather and fabric boots.

JACKETS: Most waterproof jackets have durable water repellent (DWR) finishes that eventually wear off. To test yours, spray it with water: If it doesn't bead off, first try machine-washing and drying (follow care-label guidelines), then ironing the outer layer (on low-temperature steam, always with a towel or cloth placed between the jacket and iron). Retest. If those techniques don't reactivate the finish, apply a spray or liquid treatment (also available from Nikwax and ReviveX).

7. Repair Your Pack's Side Pocket
Sew a tear with a large needle and #46 or #69 bonded-nylon thread (dental floss and surgical suture also work). Use the first few stitches to close the tear; if it's large, run the stitches from the outer edges of the pocket. Sew horizontally over the gap, then repeat vertically to create a grid-like patch.

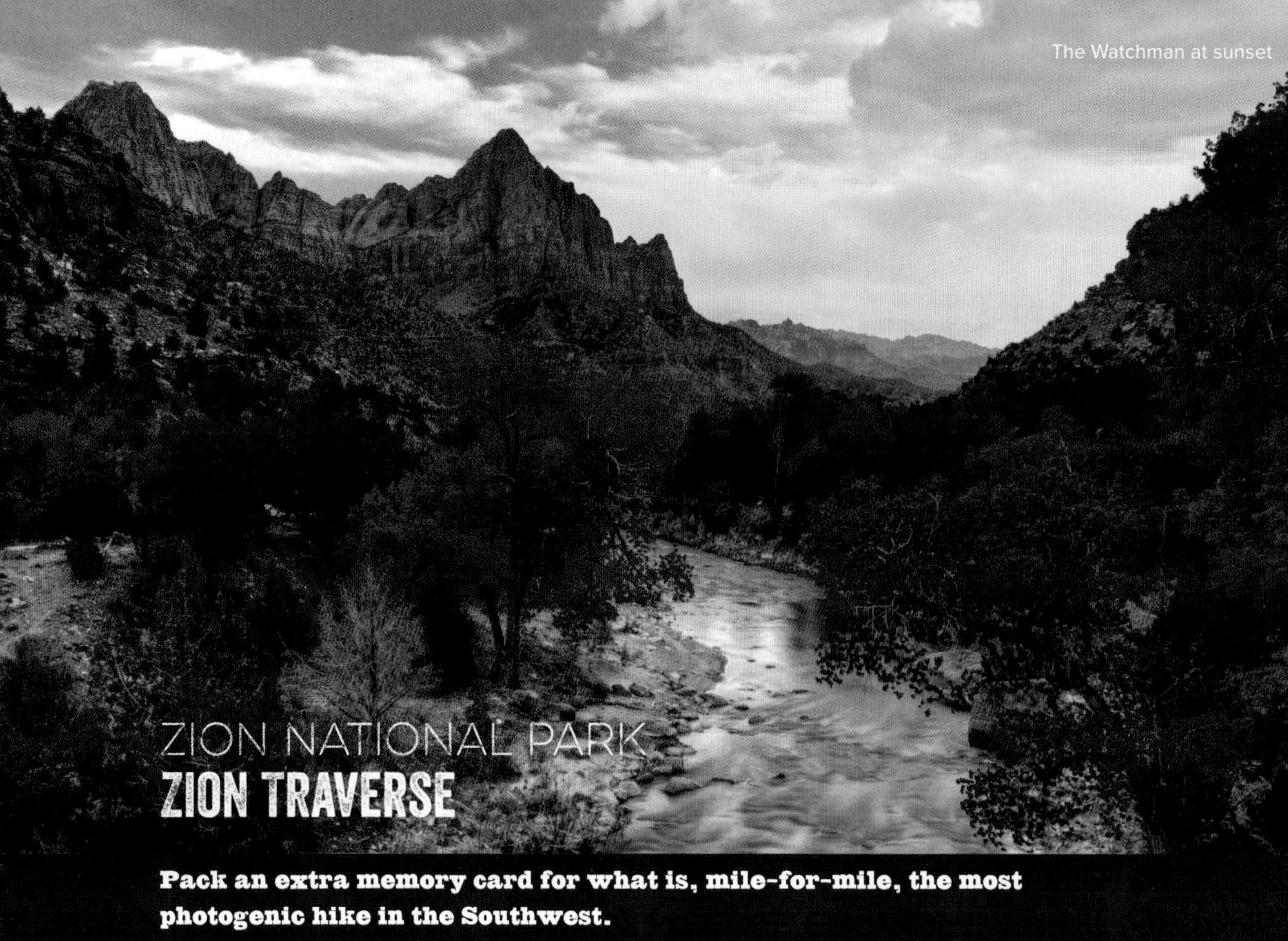
The Watchman at sunset

ZION NATIONAL PARK

ZION TRAVERSE

Pack an extra memory card for what is, mile-for-mile, the most photogenic hike in the Southwest.

One of our most veteran trail scouts, who has hiked in 24 national parks and is notoriously grudging with superlatives, calls this 47-mile traverse of Zion "one of the most spectacular multiday treks in the entire park system." The only question is why so few people know about it. The route, traversing the park north to south from Lee Pass to East Rim, includes a few popular day-hiker sections, but mostly it's simply lonely, remote, and photo-op-every-step gorgeous.

Start by crossing the orange and red Kolob Canyons and Hop Valley on the La Verkin Creek and Hop Valley Trails; camp beside burbling La Verkin Creek in Kolob. (Sites 12 or 13, at mile 6.7, have abundant flat spots above the creek.) Then use the Connector and Wildcat Canyon Trails to link to the West Rim Trail. You'll pass through the park's highest elevations (above 7,000 feet) and an area called Little Siberia that's snow-covered from November to May. Plan to linger at overlooks of labyrinthine side canyons of white and red sandstone. Overnight at Campsites #8 (mile 5, near water) or #4 (mile 6.5, good views). Wake early to watch pink and gold dawn light creep up a maze of side canyons and mesas, just a 5-minutes walk north of the Campsite #4. From here, descend giant waves of sandstone

Photo: iStockPhoto.com / lightphoto

Text: Mike Lanza

along sidewalk-wide precipices with hundred-foot drops into Zion Canyon. Detour 0.8 mile round-trip to Angels Landing—get there before 9 a.m. to beat the hundreds of day hikers who crowd the knife-edge footpath from midmorning to late afternoon. Even if you're late, it's worth jostling elbows for the view of the entire Zion Canyon dropping 1,500 feet below the 5,790-foot summit.

Continue to Echo Canyon, and finish the traverse with a climb through bizarrely sculpted red rock at the brink of a waterfall plunging into a slot canyon at Jolly Gulch, on the East Rim Trail. Drop your pack for the popular but worthwhile 1-mile side trip along crazy-exposed paths to Hidden Canyon, with sweeping panoramas from atop the vertical walls. Water beta: La Verkin Creek runs year-round, and Beatty, Sawmill, and Cabin Springs are reliable. But Stave Spring, near the East Rim's campsites, typically dries up by August.

DISTANCE: 47 miles

TIME REQUIRED: 4–6 days

DIFFICULTY: Strenuous

CONTACT: Zion National Park, (435) 772-3256; nps.gov/zion

THE PAYOFF: Arguably the best red-rock tour in the country.

TRAILHEAD GPS: 37.384665, -112.838934

FINDING THE TRAILHEAD: Begin at Lee Pass trailhead, about 8 miles up Kolob Canyon Road from I-15 Exit 40. Finish at the East Rim trailhead on UT 9. Shuttle services: zionadventures.com; zionrockguides.com.

WAYPOINTS & DIRECTIONS

GPS: 37.452342, -113.191366 Hike south from the Lee Pass trailhead.

GPS: 37.412164, -113.165274 Campsites can be found all along La Verkin Creek.

GPS: 37.416118, -113.154202 Above La Verkin, Sites #12 and #13 offer the most flat spots above the creek.

GPS: 37.421980, -113.139782 When the trail heads south into the Hop Valley, you can continue north to Campsites #12 and #13 to spend the night, retracing your route in the morning to rejoin the main trail.

GPS: 37.427570, -113.137551 Site #13.

GPS: 37.416902, -113.146520 On day two, follow the Hop Valley Trail south.

GPS: 37.360027, -113.115706 After 4.15 miles, take the faint Connector Trail as it winds through an open valley and across Kolob Terrace Road.

GPS: 37.340991, -113.076010 Join Wildcat Canyon Trail to access West Rim Trail.

GPS: 37.380558, -113.022237 Turn south on the West Rim Trail.

GPS: 37.371828, -113.017344 After gaining the West Rim Trail, your first camp option for night two is at Sawmill Springs.

GPS: 37.364222, -113.016400 Another camp option, meadows overlooking Wildcat Canyon.

GPS: 37.322974, -112.986789 Campsite #8: This site is near water and is located in a pasture east of the trail through Potato Hollow.

GPS: 37.308605, -112.986617 Campsite #4: This option for the second and third nights offers great views and is nestled below a plateau at the mouth of Sleepy Hollow.

GPS: 37.259230, -112.950997 The West Rim Trail ends in Zion Road. Head east on the park road to reach Echo Canyon Trailhead.

GPS: 37.251408, -112.954946 Campers can opt for a fancy layover and/or a burger at the Zion Lodge.

(continued)

GPS: 37.269476, -112.935805 Take steep Echo Canyon to join East Rim Trail.

GPS: 37.268998, -112.936535 Shortly after taking Echo Canyon, hikers encounter the Hidden Canyon turnoff, a challenging but incredible slot-canyon side trip.

GPS: 37.278014, -112.920570 Join the East Rim Trail and head southeast.

GPS: 37.261553, -112.904220 Stave Spring offers an option for the final night of camping.

GPS: 37.251715, -112.876196 Head south to drop into Jolly Gulch.

GPS: 37.252296, -112.867355 Enter Cave Canyon.

GPS: 37.246899, -112.866282 Head southwest along Clear Creek to reach the trailhead.

GPS: 37.232584, -112.877097 Arrive at the trailhead and your waiting shuttle.

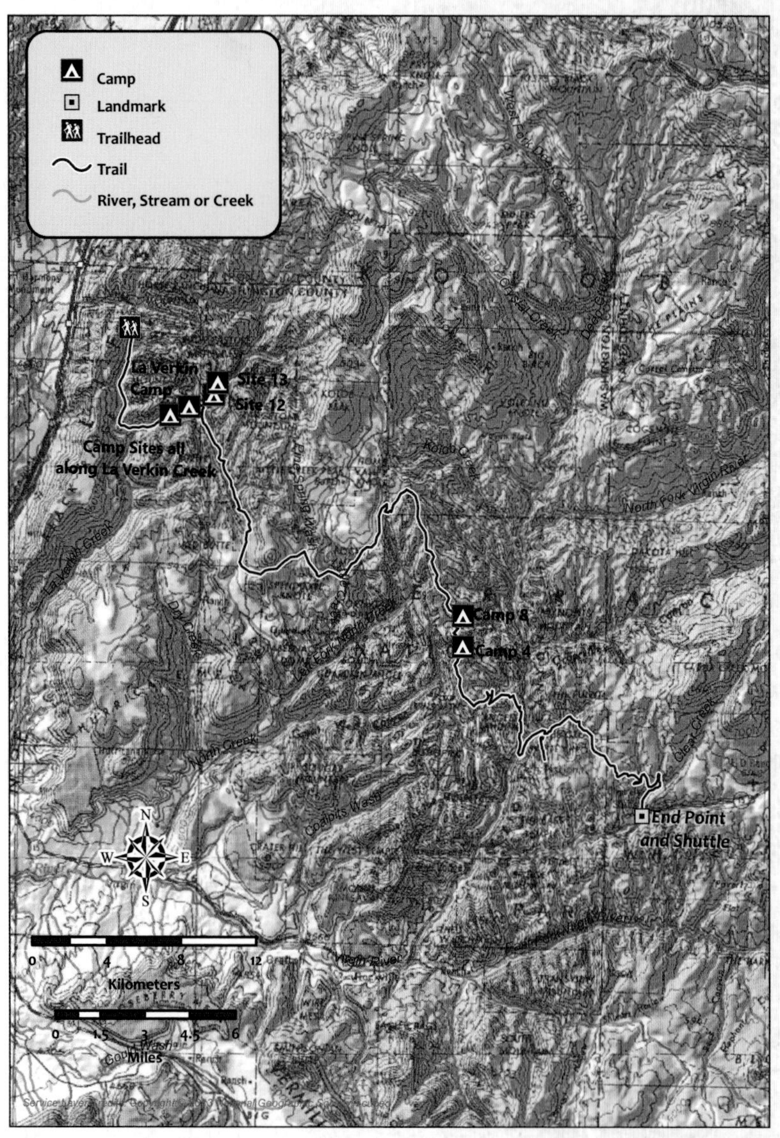

Ted Alvarez is *Backpacker* magazine's Northwest Editor and was a National Magazine Award finalist in 2014. Whether chasing grizzly bears in the North Cascades, fording an icy Alaska river, or drinking his own urine in the desert, he regularly goes to extreme lengths in pursuit of a good story—often in our national parks. He lives in Seattle, Wash., where he survives on heroic doses of strong coffee.

Photo: Daniel Penner